The Career Fitness Program

EXERCISING YOUR OPTIONS

EIGHTH EDITION

Diane Sukiennik

William Bendat

Lisa Raufman

PEARSON

Prentice Hall

Upper Saddle River, New Jersey
Columbus, Ohio

Library of Congress Cataloging-in-Publication Data

Sukiennik, Diane.
    The career fitness program: exercising your options / Diane
Sukiennik, William Bendat, Lisa Raufman.—8th ed.
        p. cm.
    Includes bibliographical references and index.
    ISBN 0-13-170294-7
    1. Vocational guidance.   2. Job hunting.   3. Personality
assessment.   I. Bendat, William.   II. Raufman, Lisa.   III. Title.

HF5381.S914 2007
650.14—dc22

                                                    2005037484

Vice President and Publisher: Jeffery W. Johnston
Executive Editor: Sande Johnson
Developmental Editor: Jennifer Gessner
Editorial Assistant: Susan Kauffman
Production Editor: Alexandrina Benedicto Wolf
Production Coordinator: Holcomb Hathaway
Design Coordinator: Diane C. Lorenzo
Cover Designer: Candace Rowley
Cover Photo: Super Stock
Production Manager: Pamela D. Bennett
Director of Marketing: David Gesell
Marketing Manager: Amy Judd

Photo Credits

p. 2, StockDisc; p. 4, Image Source; p. 14, Image Source; p. 22, StockDisc; p. 28, Rubberball; p. 32, Image Source; p. 40, Corbis; p. 50, Banana Stock; p. 52, Brand X Pictures; p. 58, Rubberball; p. 70, StockDisc; p. 73, Image Source; p. 91, Banana Stock; p. 98, Banana Stock; p. 101, Dynamic Graphics; p. 109, Image Source; p. 124, Stockbyte; p. 134, *The New York Times*; p. 141, Andrea Mohin/*The New York Times*; p. 164, Rubberball; p. 168, Thor Swift/*The New York Times*; p. 181, Pat Little; p. 190, Rubberball; p. 197, Suzanne DeChillo/*The New York Times*; p. 202, Pat Little; p. 230, StockDisc; p. 247, PhotoDisc; p. 262, Rubberball; p. 265, PhotoDisc; p. 277, PhotoDisc; p. 306, Rubberball; p. 314, PhotoDisc; p. 325, PhotoDisc; p. 330, StockDisc; p. 333, Dynamic Graphics.

This book was set in Sabon by Integra. It was printed and bound by Banta Book Group. The cover was printed by Coral Graphic Services, Inc.

Pearson Education Ltd.
Pearson Education Singapore Pte. Ltd.
Pearson Education Canada, Ltd.
Pearson Education—Japan

Pearson Education Australia Pty. Limited
Pearson Education North Asia Ltd.
Pearson Educación de Mexico, S.A. de C.V.
Pearson Education Malaysia Pte. Ltd.

PEARSON
Prentice
Hall

10 9 8 7 6 5 4 3 2
ISBN 0-13-170294-7

Contents

PREFACE   xiii

ABOUT THE AUTHORS   xvi

INTRODUCTION: ON YOUR MARK ... GET SET ...   xvii

PART I   PERSONAL ASSESSMENT   1

1   Taking Stock   3

Personal Assessment   4

   Super's Self-Concept Theory   4

Overview of Life Stages   6

Understanding the Differences Between a Job and a Career   8

   BOX: *Greatest contributors to quality of life*   9

   Striving for Career Satisfaction   9

REAL STORIES: *Meet Sandra*   10

Choosing and Changing Careers   11

   BOX: *Sample career changers*   12

   BOX: *More career changers*   13

Summary   14

EXERCISES

   1.1   First Impressions   15

   1.2   Your Lifeline   16

   1.3   Identify Your Interests   18

   1.4   Describe Yourself   18

   1.5   Consider Occupational Status   19

   1.6   WWWebwise   20

   1.7   Exercise Summary   20

2   Programming Yourself for Success   23

I Am Building Self-Esteem   24

I Maintain a Positive Outlook   25

I Am Assertive   26

I Have a Sense of Humor   27

I Am Self-Confident   27

I Am Enthusiastic   28

I Use Positive Self-Talk (Affirmations)   29

I Visualize Success   30

I Have a Positive Self-Image   31

I Have Multiple Intelligences   31

I Learn from Role Models   32

I Initiate Action   33

I Am Persistent   34

I Am Disciplined   34

REAL STORIES: *Meet Alan*   35

I Demonstrate Emotional Intelligence   36

I Identify My Goals   36

    BOX: *What makes workers succeed*   37

I Am Self-Reliant and Career Resilient   37

I Am Flexible   37

I Have Purpose   38

I Have Passion   38

I Am Responsible   39

I Have Vision   39

I Am an Innovator   40

Summary   40

EXERCISES

    2.1   Past Actions and Influences   41

    2.2   Two Perfect Days: Your Future Vision   42

    2.3   Emotional Intelligence Checklist   43

    2.4   Positive Self-Talk (Affirmations)   44

    2.5   Your Fantasy Careers   45

    2.6   Making a Fantasy Real   46

    2.7   Building Your Success Profile   46

    2.8   Think About Enthusiasm   47

    2.9   WWWebwise   48

    2.10 Exercise Summary   48

3 Values Clarification   51

Defining Values   52

Clarifying Your Values   52

REAL STORIES: *Meet Maria*   54

Needs and Motivators   55

    BOX: *Life balance*   56

Finding Balance   57

Role of Leisure   58

    BOX: *True values*   59

Summary   59

EXERCISES

    3.1   Values Grid   60

    3.2   Explore Your Values   62

    3.3   Your Values—Some Hard Choices   64

3.4 Reflective Questions   65

3.5 Top Five   66

3.6 Values Related to Careers   66

3.7 Values Related to Ethics   67

3.8 WWWebwise   67

3.9 Exercise Summary   67

4 Focusing on You: Personality and Interests   71

Exploring Personality   72

    ACTIVITY: *Identifying Your Personal Preferences*   74

    BOX: *Decisive Types*   78

    BOX: *Exploring majors*   79

REAL STORIES: *Meet Holly*   80

Identifying Fields of Interest   81

RIASEC (Holland Interest Environments)   82

    ACTIVITY: *Sample Majors Related to Holland Types*   84

    BOX: *Holland Interest Environments and hobbies, abilities, and careers*   85

    ACTIVITY: *Interest Areas and Worker Trait Groups*   87

    ACTIVITY: *Identifying occupational interest areas*   89

Career Clusters   91

Summary   91

EXERCISES

    4.1 Your Personality Type   94

    4.2 Your Holland Interest Environment   94

    4.3 Your Occupational Interests   95

    4.4 Job Clusters   95

    4.5 Interest Inventories   95

    4.6 Classified Careers   96

    4.7 College Catalogs   96

    4.8 WWWebwise   96

    4.9 Exercise Summary   96

5 Skills Assessment   99

Defining Skills   100

Identifying Your Skills   101

    Analyze Your Accomplishments   102

REAL STORIES: *Meet John*   103

    Use the DOT to Identify Skills   104

    BOX: *Sample job descriptions from the DOT*   105

    The Portfolio Employee   106

    ACTIVITY: *Assessing your skills*   107

Identifying Transferable Skills   109

Transferable Skills of a Liberal Arts Major 109

BOX: *People skills* 112

Your Most Valuable Assets: Your Personality Traits 112

BOX: *Identifying the transferable skills of a teacher* 113

BOX: *The SCANS report* 114

BOX: *Using SCANS skills* 115

BOX: *Describing skills* 116

Summary 116

EXERCISES

5.1 Experiography 117

5.2 Accomplishments 118

5.3 Description of Accomplishments 118

5.4 The Skills 118

5.5 Your Favorite Skills 118

5.6 Ideal Jobs 119

5.7 SCANS 119

5.8 Skills Review 121

5.9 WWWebwise 122

5.10 Exercise Summary 122

PART II   THE WORLD OF WORK   123

 # The World and You 125

Societal Influences on Career Choices 126

Striving for Equality in the Workforce 127

Gender Roles 127

BOX: *Equity definitions* 128

BOX: *High wages vs. life/balance issues* 130

Age and Opportunity 131

Affirmative Action 132

BOX: *Women in the workplace* 133

Other Cultural Considerations: Valuing Diversity 134

The Changing Workplace 135

The Need for Knowledge Workers 136

The Importance of New Technology 137

BOX: *The new economy vs. the old economy* 139

The Global Economy and the Changing Corporate Structure 141

BOX: *Fastest-growing small–business-dominated industries* 143

Small Businesses 143

Woman-Owned Businesses 144

BOX: *Temporary work* 144

Temporary Agencies/Leasing Companies 144

BOX: *Entrepreneurial opportunities* 145

Trends: The Twenty-First Century 145

Liberal Arts Majors Have Marketable Skills 146

REAL STORIES: *Meet Jessica* 147

Lifelong Learning 148

BOX: *Multimedia revolution ignites creative industries* 149

Job Growth Trends 149

Finding Your Place in a Changing World 150

BOX: *Job growth throughout the next decade* 151

Facts and Figures 153

BOX: *New and emerging occupations* 153

EXERCISES

6.1 First Impressions 158

6.2 Gender Roles Questionnaire 159

6.3 Pros and Cons 160

6.4 Famous People 160

6.5 Small Businesses 161

6.6 Globalization of the Work World 161

6.7 Changing Nature of Work 161

6.8 WWWebwise 162

6.9 Exercise Summary 162

7 Information Integration 165

Brainstorming Career Options 166

Understanding Career Paths and Common Organizational Divisions 168

Strategies for Researching Career Options 169

BOX: *Questions to ask when researching a job* 171

BOX: *Local government* 172

Government Employment Opportunities 172

BOX: *DOT entry for copywriter* 175

U.S. Department of Labor Publications 175

Employer Directories 176

BOX: *Research* 176

Other Written Sources of Information 177

Newspapers 177

Trade Journals 177

Magazines 177

REAL STORIES: *Meet Jackie* 178

In-House Bulletins and Announcements 180

Computerized Information Sources 180

Selected Computerized Sources 180

The Internet 181

BOX: *Job market research sites* 183

EXERCISES

7.1   A Tempting 10   185

7.2   I'd Do This Even if I Didn't Get Paid   185

7.3   The Grass Is Always Greener   186

7.4   Job Research   186

7.5   Local and Internet Resources   187

7.6   Gathering the Facts   187

7.7   WWWebwise   188

7.8   Exercise Summary   189

Making Decisions   191

Overcoming Barriers to Decision Making   192

Decision-Making Strategies (Good and Bad)   193

BOX: *Ways to make decisions (strategies)*   193

REAL STORIES: *Meet Art*   195

Conditions for Change   196

A Decision-Making Model   197

Rational/Linear Decision Making   197

BOX: *Decision styles*   199

Intuitive Decision Making   199

Goal Setting   200

BOX: *Sample goal and objectives*   200

BOX: *Time management strategies*   201

Managing Your Financial Resources   201

Setting Financial Goals   202

Saving Money   202

Establishing a Credit Rating   202

Insurance and Health Needs   203

Budgeting   203

Stress Management   204

BOX: *Stress management techniques*   205

Deciding on a Major   205

BOX: *Tomorrow*   206

Deciding on Training   206

Deciding on Change   206

Summary   207

EXERCISES

8.1   Ranking Yourself   208

8.2   Reviewing Goal Setting   208

8.3   Write a Goal Statement   209

8.4   Task Identification   210

8.5   One Year to Live   210

8.6   Meeting Your Needs   210

8.7   Your Energizers   211

8.8   Recent Decisions   211

8.9   Priorities   211

8.10   Irrevocable Decisions   211

8.11   Harmful Decisions   212

8.12   Limiting Decisions   212

8.13   Contingent Decisions   212

8.14   Values   212

8.15   Factors Adversely Affecting Decisions   213

8.16   What If   214

8.17   Specific/Nonspecific Objectives   215

8.18   Test Your Assumptions   215

8.19   Timesavers   216

8.20   Short- and Long-Term Goals   216

8.21   WWWebwise   216

8.22   Exercise Summary   216

PARTS I & II   CHAPTER SUMMARIES   219

Putting It All Together to Reach a Tentative Career Goal

CHAPTER 1   Exercise Summary   219

CHAPTER 2   Exercise Summary   220

CHAPTER 3   Exercise Summary   221

CHAPTER 4   Exercise Summary   221

CHAPTER 5   Exercise Summary   222

CHAPTER 6   Exercise Summary   223

CHAPTER 7   Exercise Summary   224

CHAPTER 8   Exercise Summary   224

Quick Impressions   225

Information Integration and Goal Setting   226

PART III   JOB SEARCH STRATEGY   229

Targeting Your Job Search   231

BOX: *Your comprehensive job search strategy*   232

Designing a Comprehensive Job Search Strategy   233

Your Job Search: Getting Started   234

Understanding and Using Classified Ads   234

Promoting Yourself Through Mail and E-Mail   234

Understanding and Using Employment Agencies   236

Volunteering   236

REAL STORIES: *Meet Xiao-Ying*   237

   BOX: *Internships*   237

   Interning   237

      BOX: *The Princeton Review Online: America's top internships*   238

REAL STORIES: *Meet Felipe*   238

   BOX: *Employers rate experience*   239

Starting Your Own Business   239

   Home Businesses   239

      BOX: *An innovative approach to the job search*   240

   Getting Help to Start Your Own Business   240

      BOX: *Women-owned firms*   241

Franchising   241

Using Career Planning Services   241

      BOX: *Franchise information*   242

      BOX: *A creative job search*   242

Interviewing for Information   242

      BOX: *Job hotlines*   243

   Information Interviewing—The Purpose   243

   Information Interviewing—The Process   244

   Information Interviewing Outline   244

   Practicing Information Interviews   247

Networking   248

      ACTIVITY: *Information interviewing outline*   249

   Moving Beyond the Fear of Networking   251

Job Search While Unemployed   251

Planning for Action   252

Implementing Your Job Search: A Lifelong Venture   253

REAL STORIES: *Meet Susan*   255

Summary   255

      BOX: *Selected online employment databases*   256

EXERCISES

   9.1   Support Network Checklist   258

   9.2   Information Interviews   259

   9.3   Personal Contact Log   259

   9.4   WWWebwise   260

   9.5   Exercise Summary   261

10 Preparing a Winning Resume   263

The Resume   264

   Portfolios   265

   Preparation for Composing Your Resume   265

   Using Action Words   267

      BOX: *Resume/portfolio review*   267

Using the Right Key Phrases 268

BOX: *Action words* 268

References 268

REAL STORIES: *Meet Eduardo* 269

The Appearance of Your Resume 269

BOX: *Resume problems* 270

Electronic Resumes 271

Types of Resumes 271

BOX: *Guidelines for preparing and submitting electronic resumes* 272

The Functional Resume 272

BOX: *Resume template* 273

BOX: *Sample functional entry under professional experience* 274

BOX: *Sample chronological entry under professional experience* 274

The Chronological Resume 276

The Combination Resume 276

Cover Letter Guidelines 277

BOX: *Resume cover letter template* 278

BOX: *Resumes for international jobs* 279

Application Forms 279

BOX: *Filling out application forms* 280

Neatness Counts 280

Summary 282

EXERCISES

10.1 Resume Review Sheet 283

10.2 Create a Card File 283

10.3 Write Your Resume 283

10.4 Save Sample Work for a Portfolio 283

10.5 Critique Your Resume 285

10.6 Ask Others to Critique Your Resume 286

10.7 Write a Cover Letter 286

10.8 WWWebwise 287

10.9 Exercise Summary 287

Sample Resumes 288

Sample Cover Letters 300

Sample Letter of Introduction 305

11 Interviewing Successfully 307

Before the Interview 308

BOX: *Job search tips* 309

BOX: *Company knowledge* 310

Interview Guidelines 311

Dressing for Success 311

Practical Preparation 312

Segments of an Interview 313

Practice Questions   314

    BOX: *Sample thank-you letters*   315

How to Handle Illegal Questions   316

The Behavioral/Situational Interview   318

REAL STORIES: *Meet Jose*   319

Body Language   319

Video Interviewing   321

Learning from the Interview   321

    BOX: *Sample questions to ask at the interview*   322

Factors Influencing Hiring   323

    BOX: *Factors that influence your success*   324

If You Are Offered the Job   325

    BOX: *Summary: Reviewing the interview process*   326

    Negotiating for Salary and Benefits   327

If You Do Not Get the Job   327

EXERCISES

    11.1   Question Review   329

    11.2   Practice Interview   329

    11.3   WWWebwise   329

    11.4   Exercise Summary   329

12   Future Focus   331

Managing Your Career   332

Developing Your Relationship Savvy   333

Developing Career Stamina   334

Embracing Career Fitness as a Way of Life   334

    BOX: *Risking*   335

REFERENCES   336

INDEX   339

Preface

Welcome to the eighth edition of *The Career Fitness Program: Exercising Your Options*. We are immensely gratified by the positive feedback from the field, which tells us that we are contributing to the quality of life for the thousands of students who use our book. We say "use our book" rather than "read our book" because the process of career planning is action oriented. We have attempted to balance the text with a variety of exercises to encourage readers to "get into the process" and allow it to unfold in the many unexpected ways that careers do take shape. We are committed to the process of career planning, which is part science and part art, part logic and part intuition, part inspiration and part perspiration. We recognize the critical role of the teacher/counselor/coach in this process as the voice of experience, reassurance, validation, and wisdom. Just as a personal trainer keeps a well-intentioned exerciser on track, the teacher keeps students moving forward in a process that tends to be circuitous rather than linear and straightforward.

Our book attempts to be a comprehensive and current compendium of the best art and science in the field of career planning. This edition more fully incorporates the electronic medium into the text and exercises without implying that the Internet is the only or even preeminent tool in the process. As in previous editions, we have updated the facts and figures and have added relevant topics, such as discussions of vision, purpose, passion, responsibility, and the role of finances in a career decision. We have also expanded the real-life stories and added critical-thinking questions to each chapter.

This book is useful to the undecided and the liberal arts-oriented students. These students have heard all too often that technology is the promise of the future, and while that may be true, they need the latitude to explore other career avenues that may be more compatible with who they are. We encourage and support them in this exploration.

Companion Website: A Virtual Learning Environment

Technology is a constantly growing and changing aspect of our field that is creating a need for content and resources. To address this need, we have updated the Companion Website for the eighth edition. Moreover, to better facilitate student learning and comprehension of chapter content, we have integrated the Companion Website into the text. In creating the Companion Website, our goal is to build on and enhance what the textbook already offers.

The Companion Website, located at **www.prenhall.com/sukiennik**, is a valuable resource for both the professor and the student. It helps students gauge their understanding of chapter content through the use of chapter objectives, reflection questions that connect chapter content to the "Real Stories" and "Facts and Figures" features in the text, and interactive self-assessments. It also provides Web links and a variety of other online resources, as well as WWWebwise Activities found in each chapter.

Acknowledgments

We would like to thank the following individuals, who reviewed this project in various stages of completion and offered suggestions as to how it might be improved. The book is better as a result of their efforts.

For the eighth edition: Sally Dingee, Monroe Community College; Nancy Elk, Anoka Ramsey Community College; and Patsy Krech; University of Memphis.

For previous editions: Howard J. Bachman, Creighton University; Dora Clarke, Whittier College; Angela Dillavou, Westwood College of Technology; Sue Eckberg, Career Focus; Theresa Green Ervin, The University of Mississippi; Sue Gannon, Vista Community College; Laura Goppold, Central Piedmont Community College; Jacqueline Hing, Rice University; Marilyn Joseph, Florida Metropolitan University; Gina Larson, Doane College; Christine Laursen, Westwood College of Technology; Jackie Lewis, Minnesota State University–Mankato; Lea Beth Lewis, California State University, Fullerton; Carole Mackewich, Clark College; Kathleen McGough, Broward Community College; Carmen McNeil, Solano College; Cynthia Moore, The University of Alabama; Victoria Sitter, Milligan College; Belen Torres-Gil, Rio Hondo College; and Laurie Williamson, Appalachian State University; Cheryl Matherly, Rice University; David White, College of San Mateo; Carla Mortensen, Simmons Graduate School of Management; Susan Ekberg, Webster University; Bruce Bloom, DeVry Institute of Technology, Chicago; Bob Stanelle, Tulane University; Patrick Schutz, Mesa State College; Joe Ritchie, Indiana University of Pennsylvania; Rita Delude, New Hampshire Community Technical College; Barbara Allen-Burke, Clackamas Community College; Michael Brooks, Texas Christian University; Beverly Brown, Southern Illinois University; Pam Conyngham, Kent State University; Mariah Daniel-Platt, Rancho Santiago College; David Davis, Delta College; Ricardo Diaz, Chaffey Community College; Robert Ehrmann, Santa Barbara City College; John Evans, Hillsboro Community College; Christina Friedman, Triton College; Sheila Goethe, Hillsborough Community College; Kathy Hanahan, Harper College; Tim Haney; Karen Hardin, Mesa Community College; Mary Harreld, McHenry County College; Kenneth Harris, College of DuPage; Sandi Krantz, Moorhead State University; Ruth McCormick, Edmonds Community College; Paul Neal, Sierra College; Judy Patrick, Community College of Aurora; Sonjia Peacock, Lewis and Clark Community College; Bob Peters, College of DuPage; Hue Pham, Orange Coast College; Susan Rhee, College of DuPage; Dennis Sadler, Rancho Santiago College; Geri Shapiro, Los Angeles Mission College; Joseph Spadafino, Arizona Department of Transportation; Peggy

Sullivan, Purdue University; Tanya Wahl, Inver Hills Community College; and David Young, Cerritos College.

We would like to thank Janis Pizer of Cerritos College for her help in developing case stories and other content, and Belen Torres-Gil of Rio Hondo Community College, who enriched our testbank questions. We also appreciate the input of many other professional contacts and colleagues throughout the country and are grateful for the stimulating opportunities to share ideas. In particular, we want to mention Cheryl Matherly of Rice University and the entire academic team who steered the development of the "Career Advantage" telecourse available through PBS. These contacts have served to influence and enhance our book. Additionally, we extend our sincere thanks to all those instructors who have used the book throughout the past seven editions. We hope you find this eighth edition even more comprehensive and helpful to your students in their career search. We are, as always, interested in hearing your feedback.

Finally, we are indebted to our friend and previous publisher, John Gorsuch, for his encouragement throughout our many years of association. Special acknowledgment is given to executive editor Sande Johnson, developmental editor Jenny Gessner, editorial assistant Susan Kauffman, and our publisher, Jeffery Johnston, for their enthusiasm and great ideas for the future of *The Career Fitness Program*.

Last but not least, on a personal note, special thanks to each of our significant supporters and partners: Masha Fleissig, Bernard Natelson, and Michael Reiss.

About the Authors

Dr. Diane Sukiennik is a career counselor; a licensed marriage and family therapist; and an internationally recognized lecturer and workshop facilitator. She holds an advanced degree from Columbia University and has extensive postgraduate training in industrial psychology, management, and organizational development. Currently Dr. Sukiennik is on the faculty of Moorpark College in California, where her areas of expertise are career development, personal and professional presentational skills, and managerial effectiveness. She is a consultant, has a private practice, has contributed to the development of a nationally distributed telecourse on career and life development called "Career Advantage" distributed by PBS, and she is an executive career coach.

Dr. William Bendat is a recognized leader and innovator in career development theory. While serving as Dean of Student Services at Moorpark College, he managed the award-winning counseling and career programs that gained both California and national eminence. His advanced degrees in counseling psychology, with emphasis in decision making and self-concept, have enriched *The Career Fitness Program*. Dr. Bendat is the Director of Careerscope, offering specialized career workshops to public and private agencies, and is currently involved in career strategies to improve high school graduation rates. He is also a licensed therapist, past President of the California Managers of Counseling, and a contributor to numerous workshops and professional journals.

Dr. Lisa Raufman has been Dean of Counseling and Career Center Coordinator at El Camino College in Torrance, California. She is a career counselor and consultant, as well as a licensed marriage and family therapist. Her master's degree is in counseling with a specialization in the community college and vocational rehabilitation. Her doctoral degree from the University of California at Los Angeles focused on higher education, work, and adult development. Previously Dr. Raufman coordinated the Career Transfer Center at Moorpark College. She is past president of the Los Padres chapter of the American Society for Training and Development (ASTD) and the California Community College Counselors Association. For the past decade, Dr. Raufman has been a member of the California Community College Chancellors Office State Advisory on Career Development.

Introduction

On Your Mark . . . Get Set . . .

The world of work is spinning at a dizzying pace. In this new millennium, the job market is more unpredictable than ever. Companies are downsizing, rightsizing, restructuring, outsourcing, and undergoing radical technological change. Bigger mega-mergers are occurring and more small businesses are being created. The globalization and outsourcing of industries and organizations present us with competitive challenges and unprecedented opportunities. You can benefit from becoming aware of the changing job market, by keeping up with trends, and by identifying how they fit your personal preferences. Nine major trends are shaping the workplace:

1. The majority of jobs are created by small businesses employing fewer than 50 employees.

2. The traditional hierarchical organization is changing into a variety of forms, with a flat (reduced middle management) organizational chart becoming more common. Flexible networking of specialists who come together for a short-term project and then re-form into a new group for the next project will be commonplace.

3. Smaller companies are able to expand and contract with the changing economy by employing temporary and contract employees.

4. Just as manufacturing used to be our mainstay, the United States is now considered a service economy that depends on knowledge workers. (See the section in Chapter 6 titled "The Need for Knowledge Workers.")

5. Lifelong learning is the rule; getting a degree to get a job may allow you entry into a company, but if you don't continually upgrade your knowledge, you will lose your competitive edge. The winners are rethinking, reinventing, and reengineering products, ideas, and services to meet continually changing needs.

6. Global competition and multinational corporations will influence more and more companies. The most valuable employee will be the one most familiar with several languages and cultural customs. The number of women and immigrants will continue to increase in the workforce.

7. The Internet will continue to influence the way we think, act, learn, do business, and manage our careers.

8. Those entering the workforce should expect to change their career path three to five times in their lifetime.

9. Workers are increasingly looking for meaning and purpose in their jobs. Seeking a new career is now about finding balance and meaning in one's life. This becomes a spiritual (not necessarily religious) component of job satisfaction.

A broad rainbow of possibilities makes this an exciting time in history. Yet many of us are overwhelmed by lack of knowledge about our choices and our place and purpose in the world. One thing that is certain is change.

It is essential to prepare ourselves to expect change, accept it, and plan for it. We can best prepare for it by learning "who we are" in terms of lifetime goals and by taking responsibility for shaping our lives. As we gain information about ourselves and begin to make our own decisions, we acquire self-confidence. In a deep, personal way, we begin to realize that no matter how drastically the world changes, we can deal with it.

The expectations and demands of today's job market require us to be physically agile, mentally alert, and psychologically able. *The Career Fitness Program* will prepare you to exercise your options whether you are planning for your first job, reentering the workforce, or rethinking your career. This program will help you build the mental stamina and psychological strength you need to be successful and satisfied today. You will also develop the mind-set and acquire the tools for continuing success despite the inevitable surprises and challenges that you will face. *The Career Fitness Program* is designed to assist you in the process of self-discovery and realization. The main goal of this book is to lead you through the process of career planning, which includes self-assessment, decision making, and job search strategy; our primary objective is to help you make satisfying career choices. By following our chapter-by-chapter program, you will learn more about yourself and how self-knowledge relates to your emerging career plan.

Let's preview the content of this book to see how it will help you achieve your career goals. The career-planning process is divided into three main parts: personal assessment (Chapters 1 to 5); the world of work (Chapters 6 to 8); and job search strategy (Chapters 9 to 12).

- In Chapter 1, you will come to understand how the process of self-assessment *begins* the process of career planning. You will explore the concept of *life stages* and examine your current life stage. Chapter 1 also discusses the difference between a job and a career.

- In Chapter 2, you will learn how building self-esteem greatly affects your actions. This chapter helps you develop a positive approach to life and career planning.

- In Chapter 3, you will identify your needs, wants, and values and explore how they influence your career choice.

- In Chapter 4, you will develop an understanding of and appreciation for your unique personality and interests—factors that will influence your career choice.

- In Chapter 5, you will learn about types of skills and you will learn to identify and describe your own skills with job requirements in mind.

- In Chapter 6, you will explore societal and cultural norms and biases that may affect your career choices. You will also read about workplace trends, promising occupations, and salary predictions.

- In Chapter 7, you will investigate published and computerized sources of information about careers and specific jobs, including government publications and Internet resources.

- In Chapter 8, you will identify how people make decisions and learn how to improve your own decision-making skills. This process includes learning to set and pursue short- and long-term goals.

- In Chapter 9, you will learn about job search strategies, including informational interviewing, networking, and electronic job search techniques.

- In Chapter 10, you will learn how to write an effective resume and cover letter.

- In Chapter 11, you will prepare for job interviews. This chapter discusses all aspects of the interview process, includes sample questions that you may encounter, and advises you about handling illegal employer queries.

- In Chapter 12, you will learn what it takes to manage your career and embrace the philosophy of career fitness as a way of life.

Even if you are not yet in the full-time job market, the job search strategy chapters (9–12) are a valuable resource. If you are in school, planning to work part-time, already employed, or seeking an internship, you can begin to prepare your resume and practice interviewing skills.

The Process

In many ways, the process of preparing to meet job and career challenges is much like the process athletes use to prepare to compete in their particular sport. It involves establishing a fitness program in which the competitor sharpens existing skills, adds needed skills, and, most important, develops a mental attitude of success.

Any good fitness program is a combination of theory and exercise, and our career fitness program maintains this balance. For each step of the planning process, we will explain the theory behind that step, how it relates to the previous and next steps, and how it moves us closer to our final goal of identifying career options.

The chapters conclude with a series of exercises designed to bring each step of the process to life. These exercises will make you more aware of your strengths, weaknesses, and attitudes, and they will also help you summarize what you think is important to remember after each chapter. You will notice that each chapter also contains a section called WWWebwise. These exercises are intended to build your skill in utilizing the Internet and broaden your exposure to the information presented. Remember that reading a chapter or a book is a passive activity. However, responding to questions makes you an active participant in the career exploration process. You may find that it helps to share your answers with at least one other person; a classroom setting in which group discussion is encouraged is even better because it adds to your own awareness and perspective.

Companion Website

It is easy for someone to sit back and read about career planning and simply agree with the text, theories, and exercises. *But until you make the commitment to actually get involved in the process, to actively participate, and to experience both progress and occasional discomfort along the way, you will not be able to reap the benefits of the process.*

The Challenge

Yes, we did mention the word *discomfort* just now. What do we mean by that? Anytime you begin a new exercise program, even if you start cautiously and sensibly in relation to your current level of activity, new muscles are stretched, and they let you know it. They feel awkward. They ache. You become aware of parts of your body that you may never have noticed before. You can also expect this to happen in the process of career planning. Along the way, confusion and some discomfort may occur. We will ask questions to help you dig deep into yourself for answers. In this process of enhancing self-awareness, you will discover much about yourself that you like, as well as some things that you would like to change.

Because of this self-discovery process, at certain points along the way in our fitness plan you may feel a bit confused, a bit anxious, a bit impatient. All of these feelings are normal. When you start out on a physical fitness program, you idealistically hope that in a week or two you will have the body that you visualize in your mind, even though you know realistically that developing a good physique is going to take a lot longer. Similarly, with your career plan you may begin to feel impatient and want things to move along more quickly or more clearly. It is important to remember that any change or growth typically includes some discomfort, uneasiness, or anxiety. Frankly, if you begin to experience some of those feelings, it is a good sign! It indicates that you are stretching, that you are growing, and that you are moving toward a newly developed awareness of who you are and how you relate to the world of work.

Committing to the Process

Whether you are taking the time at the beginning of your adult career to examine your options carefully and thoroughly or are finding at midlife that it is time to explore new directions, you will reap tremendous benefits in the future. The satisfaction you experience at "the finish line" will be directly proportional to your willingness and ability to deal with the anxiety and uncertainty you will experience at some points in the career-planning process. In essence, the more you put into any activity, the more you are likely to get out of it. Stories that we have heard and read about our cultural heroes and heroines, whether athletes, performers, scientists, or political figures, tell us that the results they achieve, which look so easy and so glamorous, are always and only the consequence of tremendous sustained effort, commitment, and perseverance. A statement attributed to famed artist Michelangelo seems to say it all: "If people knew how hard I had to work to gain my mastery, it wouldn't seem so wonderful after all."

Your career search requires a similar commitment. It requires your willingness to go with the process; to seek out specialized assistance; and to move through points of frustration, uncertainty, and confusion in the belief that you will come out with more awareness and a good sense of the next steps to take along your career path. We invite you to participate in an adventure and endeavor that are every bit as exciting and rewarding as preparing for the Olympics. You are identifying your own mountain peaks and are setting out to climb them. Among your resources is this career-planning textbook, which incorporates our insights and experience and those of other successful career planners. Most of all, the important attributes of your own spirit, vitality, and intuition, together with the desire to improve yourself, will serve you well throughout your search. This career fitness program will help you master the inevitable changes that occur within yourself and are associated with your evolving career choices and the work world around you. It will help you identify options that are consistent with who you are. It will enable you to be the champion of your own career.

I

1

Taking Stock

2

Programming Yourself for Success

3

Values Clarification

4

Focusing on You
Personality and Interests

5

Skills Assessment

PERSONAL ASSESSMENT

1

Taking Stock

Learning Objectives

At the end of the chapter you will be able to . . .

- Differentiate between a job and a career
- Identify life stages as they relate to career planning
- Discuss why personal assessment is the key factor leading to career satisfaction

Do you want to have a career that meets your needs, complements your personality, inspires you to develop your potential, and supports your vision and purpose? Are you someone who deliberately chooses the type of life you live rather than settling for what's convenient and available? If so, you need to set goals that will lead you from where you are now to where you want to be. However, to be realistic, goals must reflect your experiences, desires, needs, interests, values, and vision of the future.

Yesterday is the past, tomorrow is the future, but today is a gift. That's why they call it the present.

BIL KEANE

Personal Assessment

As the first step in self-assessment, this chapter helps you examine your personal experiences, who you are right now, your current stage of career and life development, and your ability to deal with new information. Once you begin to identify what energizes you about life, you can begin to incorporate those insights into a career. Self-awareness is the first stage of both the career choice and career change process. As we look for insights that will help us chart our careers well into the 21st century, it is useful to take a look at career development models. Renowned psychologist Donald Super (1957) is credited with developing the theory that a career makes it possible for you to actualize or express your self-concept. Your **self-concept** is essentially *how you see yourself.* Consider the following principles of Super's theory on career development and how they relate to you.

Super's Self-Concept Theory

1. We differ in abilities, interests, and personalities.

2. Every occupation requires a characteristic pattern of abilities, interests, and personality traits. Within each occupation are workers with varying degrees of these characteristics.

3. Each of us is qualified for a number of occupations.

4. Vocational preferences and skills, the situations in which we live and work, and our self-concepts change with time and experience. These factors make choice and adjustment a continual process based on our maturity and lifestyle.

5. Selecting a career involves the following stages. As we will discuss later in this chapter, many people experience these stages more than once in life. Thus, although Super discusses the stages in a more traditional sense, remember that you may return to the stages discussed below at various times in your life.

    a. **Growth.** This includes both physical and emotional growth as you form attitudes and behaviors that relate to your self-concept. What did you learn about yourself from childhood games or family roles? For example, "I am a team player," "I am

As you explore your abilities, your interests, and your personality, you will learn more about what kind of work you enjoy.

an individualist," "I am a mediator," or "I would rather read than play games." A child begins having fantasies during this period, e.g., a dream of becoming a doctor.

b. **Exploration.** This is divided into *fantasy* (e.g., a child's dream of becoming a doctor), *tentative* (e.g., high school and post–high school periods of exploration in which ideas are narrowed down), and *reality testing* (e.g., in high school or early college, working part-time or volunteering in a hospital, taking math and science classes, or raising a family). You start learning about the kind of work you enjoy and the kind of worker you are, for example, "I am good with detail," "I enjoy working with people," "I enjoy working alone," "I take criticism well."

c. **Establishment.** This includes initial work experience that may have started only as a job to earn a living but that offers experiences for growth so that it becomes part of the self-concept. For example, "I am an assistant manager, I am responsible for the bookkeeping, and I look forward to becoming the manager," rather than, "This is just a job, and I will be doing bookkeeping until I can finish my bachelor's degree and get into law school." Very often several changes in jobs will occur over a few years.

d. **Maintenance.** This is a time when we maintain or improve in our career area. Advancement can be to higher levels or laterally across fields. For example, you may start thinking: "I am extremely competent," "I can compete with others," "I can cooperate and share my knowledge," or "I can train others."

e. **Disengagement.** Super defines this as the stage just before retirement or one when we see no new challenges or chances for mobility. Traditionally, it is a period during which there is a shift in the amount of emphasis you place on your career; you may even seek a reduction of the hours you work. Disengagement may also occur some time prior to retirement. You may think: "I have many things other than this job I want to do," "I want to spend more time at home," "I want to work on my hobbies," "I want to travel more," or "I want to make a living from my leisure pursuits." Job or career changes are a form of disengagement, whether prompted by personal choice or circumstances beyond your control (a layoff, for instance).

6. The nature of any career pattern is influenced by parental socioeconomic level, mental ability, personality characteristics, and opportunities to which the individual is exposed. Both limitations and opportunities may be apparent as a result of these factors. People are affected by the realities of everyday life. A teenager living in an affluent suburb may have unlimited opportunity to focus on high school classwork because of ample financial support. On the other hand, a teenager living in the inner city with several siblings may work 20 hours or more each week to help out with the family finances. Such limitations can be overcome with effort and perseverance.

7. The process of career development is essentially that of self-concept development and implementation. All of us try to maintain a favorable picture of ourselves.

8. Work satisfaction and life satisfaction depend on the extent to which our work and our life provide adequate outlets for our abilities, interests, personality traits, and values.

What has influenced your self-concept? Do you have an accurate view of your likes and dislikes, desires, attributes, limitations, needs, wants, and values? An accurate self-assessment will enable you to make better career decisions by increasing your personal awareness and understanding. Self-awareness improves your ability to seek and select jobs that fit your unique self-concept. Super's theory applies each time you make a career change: you will reexperience the stages of growth, exploration, establishment, maintenance, and disengagement.

Our discussion of Super's theory briefly mentioned the general career stages that many people have experienced: growth, exploration, establishment, maintenance, and disengagement. Because you are probably somewhere between the stages of exploration and maintenance right now, it is useful to understand that you are also experiencing the transitional stages that relate to your age and affect your career planning.

Self-awareness = first step

Overview of Life Stages

The following life stage descriptions, derived from a variety of research on adult life stages, suggest that we emphasize different needs at different times of our lives. Planning a career involves thinking about the past, present, and future. Reviewing life stage information allows a career searcher or changer to gain and accept insight regarding certain personal and emotional issues that tend to influence values, planning, and goal setting.

Ages 16–22—late adolescence

Leaving parents' world; independence being established but not stable; uncertainty about ability to make it in the adult world; openness to new ideas.

Ages 22–28—provisional adulthood

Gaining independence in work, finances, marriage, or intimate relationships; gathering relevant work skills and setting goals; testing and choosing which to retain in adulthood. Still proving competence to peers and parents; becoming more self-reliant, building for the future; adjusting to personal or alternative lifestyle preferences.

Ages 28–32—the thirties transition

Questioning the commitments to traditional marriage and relationships, family and career; reassessments and changes may take place. A particularly vulnerable stage for continuity, although many choose to continue their earlier choices.

Ages 32–39—the time of rooting

Being involved in career and personal life decisions; helping children grow, giving priority consideration to childbearing; recognizing parental messages; modifying personality; accepting choices; giving more attention to business matters;

establishing reputation—until about age 35 when the question "Will I have time to do it all?" begins to arise; more awareness of time and renewing the important matter of "What do I really want to be?" This may be the first time a woman experiences freedom from child rearing and begins to consider career options.

Ages 39–43—the turning-point years

Experiencing a period of great upheaval and midlife crisis; may appear that earlier dreams are not attainable; wondering "Why am I here, where am I going?"; additional lifestyle changes, often not planned; feeling there is something missing in life; possible further thoughts about raising a family; starting or changing a career.

Ages 43–50—restabilization/bearing fruit

Being more at peace with questions of mortality, career and lifestyle transitions; children testing their independence; personal review of child-raising patterns; career blossoming; attention to personal growth; activity in community; reevaluating relationships as one's children become adults.

Ages 50–60—renewal

Either enjoying a time of relative calm, boredom, or acceptance and enjoyment of life or facing new challenges due to an abrupt career change; planning for retirement; physical energy and strength may decline; spouses and/or friends die; new life structure emerges; risk taking seems less likely to occur; acceptance of parents' role in one's life; spiritual questioning; potential for creative growth; disengaging from concept of "work," though some people will start a new career at this time; dealing with caretaking responsibilities for aging parents; possible tension between a wife in the prime of her career after completing child rearing and a husband eager to retire and start a new phase of life.

Ages 60 and up—transition toward retirement

As life is extended and retirement is not mandatory, this period may become the true "golden years" of continued usefulness to society and growth for oneself.

Retirement

Ending traditional work patterns for extended time; involvement with hobbies and other interests; opportunities to increase social and civic activities; enjoying travel, family, and leisure.

Remember that these life stages are based on social norms of the past and present. People are changing careers and employment at a rapid rate, and the world is changing at such a pace that social norms will surely be different in the future. For example, two-career families, single-parent households, later marriages and/or alternative lifestyles, longer life spans, fewer good entry-level jobs, and the need for lifelong learning will all influence the direction of people's lives and will lead to more fluidity and ambiguity between life stages. Decisions will vary greatly, with some people still choosing early marriages or delaying career and professional plans for more education or training. A future scenario may incorporate a flexible and adaptive work schedule both permitting and addressing leisure and longevity.

Author Gail Sheehy (1996) has explored how people change as they age and found that as longevity has increased, so have concepts and definitions of career and retirement. There is no longer a clear-cut point when we end our training or move into retirement. Finding challenging or rewarding employment may ultimately mean retraining and an early exit from a stale or boring job in order to find one's passion and pursue it. The idea is to think long-range and anticipate an active lifestyle into later years—perhaps into one's 80s or 90s. Being personally productive may now mean anticipating retiring in stages. This may mean going to an alternate plan should a primary career end by either choice or economic factors.

Because it will take longer to grow up and grow old, we need to seek meaning to our existence and be open to new experiences. These can include nonprofit ventures, volunteering, hobbies turned into businesses, or part-time hours to help others and increase earnings. Taking risks to supplement and expand our personal horizons can help us at any age to avoid becoming vulnerable, being stuck, or even being directed by unforeseen events. In essence, our later adulthood can be a time of renewal, leisure, service to society, activity, and productivity.

Understanding the Differences Between a Job and a Career

We will be using the words *job* and *career* throughout this book, so let's define them. There is an important difference between them. Basically, a job is a series of tasks or activities that are performed within the scope of what we call work. These tasks relate to a career in that a career is a series of jobs. But more than jobs, a career is a sequence of attitudes and behaviors that are associated with work and that relate to our total life experience. *A career is the integration of our personality with our job activities.* Therefore, our career becomes a primary part of our identity or our self-concept.

A career is the integration of personality with work activities

In the past, people chose a career early in life, and they tended to stay in it most of their life. Farmers worked on their farms, secretaries stayed in the office, and teachers taught until retirement. More recently the trend in America has shifted toward multiple careers. We can now expect to have four or more careers in our life. Furthermore, with the rapid changes in society as well as in economic conditions, jobs, and technologies, many traditional jobs are becoming obsolete. In fact, William Bridges in his book *Managing Transitions: Making the Most of Change* (2003) suggests that jobs as we know them will be different in the future. He means that a person hired to take a particular job can be certain the job tasks will change rapidly. Even if the job title remains the same, new and different skill sets will continually be required—the original position may become dramatically different or even disappear altogether.

Follow intuitions and not trends

This is markedly different from the world in which your family worked. Thus, the expectation that once you find a job, you are home free, secure, or set for life is no longer realistic. The traditional employee contract, although unwritten, implied an honest day's work for an honest day's wage, employee loyalty in exchange for job security, and raises and promotions in return for seniority. Today's new employee contract simply implies continued employment for individuals who possess skills that continue to meet a business need.

Be prepared to manage your career

More than ever it is important to give considerable thought to what you want to do and structure your training and education to be relevant both to your interests and to trends in the job market. You will find it beneficial to assess your skills and identify those that are transferable from a previous career to a newly emerging field with a minimum amount of retraining. Knowing yourself and developing a plan of action based on both your needs and the needs of the job market will help you embark on the career most satisfying for you rather than just following the latest trends in one field or another.

Demands in the job market rapidly come and go. Some time ago, teachers were in great demand. Then, for about a decade, there was a glut of teachers on the market. Now there seems to be a renewed need for teachers in the workforce. If you base your career decision primarily on current trends, by the time you obtain the training necessary to get into the hot field, it may well have cooled down. This strategy leaves you with slim prospects for a job that can lead to a career, and quite possibly with skills and training in a field that you weren't terribly excited about in the first place (except as a quick opportunity).

Each of us has the potential to be satisfied in any number of occupations. Getting to know yourself better through self-assessment will help you identify careers that are best suited to your personality. People who are not prepared for change allow that change to make decisions for them. They are often frustrated and unhappy because they are forced to work at jobs they don't enjoy. They may never have realized that they have choices, or perhaps they never took the time or energy to become aware of their preferences. They settle for less than what might be best for them. Dad says "get a job in business" even though his child has a special talent in art. The high school adviser recommends engineering because scholarships are available. The employment department directs a job applicant into an electronics training program because there's an opening. By knowing your own preferences, you will be ready to manage your career path instead of merely following others' suggestions.

Striving for Career Satisfaction

Survey after survey on job satisfaction among American workers indicates that well over 50 percent are dissatisfied with their jobs. In a study

---

FACTS & FIGURES

Greatest contributors to quality of life

MEN

Job/career satisfaction
32%

Relationship with family
28%

Money
18%

WOMEN

Job/career satisfaction
28%

Relationship with family
33%

Money
17%

(Data from *U.S. News & World Report.*)

THINK ABOUT IT

1. Give an example of job satisfaction. Describe the type of work, a routine day, the location and commute time, and the workplace (including your work space). List pros and cons of this job.

2. Describe your idea of a satisfying family relationship. Include the role of each participant.

3. Support or refute the statement: "Money is the root of all evil."

4. Which of the three factors would you rate most highly as contributing to your quality of life?

5. How does your current situation support the factor that you selected?

6. Have you made career decisions based on the factor that you selected?

7. Are there any other factors that you consider most important to your quality of life?

To answer these questions online, go to the *Facts and Figures* module in **Chapter 1** of the Companion Website.

Companion Website

Meet Sandra

After graduating from high school, Sandra didn't know what she wanted to do. Many of her friends were enrolling in college, but Sandra wasn't interested in continuing with her education; she was tired of going to school and wanted to experience the "real world." Since she did well in her high school business classes, she thought that clerical work might be interesting. With the help of a friend, Sandra put together a resume and went on the Internet to search for jobs. There were hundreds of clerical positions, and Sandra didn't know the type of business she might find interesting, so she decided to go back to her high school counselor for some help. The counselor said that in order to make a career or job decision, it was important for Sandra to determine her interests, values, and goals. Once she had an idea of "who" she was, she could then investigate businesses that would be right for her. The counselor suggested that she make an appointment with the career counselor at the local community college.

The counselor gave Sandra several assessments, and they revealed an interest in the legal field. Sandra went back to the Internet, but she soon discovered that the jobs that interested her required special skills. Sandra had a decision to make: return to school or look for work in a different field. Since Sandra thought she would really like the legal field, she decided to do both. She began looking for general office positions and enrolled in community college to begin a legal secretary certificate program. Sandra found a job as a receptionist with Transamerica Corporation. She learned the work quickly and found the hours allowed her to attend school and study. Although the pay did not allow her to live on her own, she took advantage of the opportunity to live at home and save money for her own apartment. After two years, Sandra was close to receiving her certificate.

One day at work she was reading her Legal Terminology text when one of the executives walked by. Sandra liked Mr. Owens; he was always interested in her opinions and she enjoyed talking to him about her studies. When she told him her career plans, he indicated that he knew several attorneys and perhaps he could be of help when she was ready. Over the next few months, Sandra worked hard, and in early April she felt ready to make a move. She called Mr. Owens and said, "I wanted you to know that I will be completing my legal secretary certificate in May, and I remember you mentioned to me that if I needed any assistance in finding employment you might be able to help. I was wondering if I could meet with you to discuss my qualifications." Mr. Owens told Sandra how proud he was of her and that he would be happy to meet with her.

WHAT DO YOU THINK?

1. Do you think Sandra made a wise choice by not attending a four-year college? List the pros and cons of her decision.

2. If Mr. Owens had not offered to help Sandra, what other resources could she have investigated?

3. While Sandra was attending college, what organizations could she have joined that would have given her networking connections?

4. What other types of jobs or careers could Sandra have selected based on her high school diploma?

5. What type of career ladder can you build for Sandra based on her legal secretary certificate?

To answer these questions online, go to the *Real Stories* module in Chapter 1 of the Companion Website.

for *U.S. News & World Report,* people were asked to name the three things that contribute most to their quality of life. The top categories for men and women were "job/career satisfaction," "relationship with family," and "money." Because people may be changing jobs and careers several times in their lives, it is more important than ever before to have accurate knowledge about yourself and the world of work.

In March 2001 the Gallup Poll organization analyzed its massive database and determined that 55 percent of employees have no enthusiasm for their work! In another Gallup survey, two-thirds of a group of adults said if they were starting all over, they would try to get more information about their career options. The Conference Board, a business research organization, recently released a survey of 5,000 people in the United States indicating that, across different ages and income levels, workers were less satisfied with their jobs in 2002 than in 1995, despite good economic times during a majority of those years. Only about half of those surveyed said they are happy in their jobs, down from 59 percent. The largest decline in overall satisfaction was from 60.9 percent in 1995 to 47.4 percent by 2002 among 35- to 44-year-olds. People in this age group were once the happiest group in the American workforce. Trust between employers and employees is at an all-time low. Similarly, Watson Wyatt Worldwide in Bethesda, Maryland, found in a study of 7,500 employees that only half trusted their senior managers (*Wall Street Journal,* "Work and Family" column, June 21, 2000).

You will face the need to reevaluate yourself and your career path continually. It is useful to know about the changing world of work and which occupations allow you to best express yourself and best use your strengths and talents. When analyzing your personal assets, it is to your advantage to think ultimately about the total job market. Search for jobs that will lead you into a career. You will benefit greatly from identifying a variety of alternatives that allow you to express your personality. Once you have looked within yourself and identified what you want and need in a job, changes will be easier to make because you'll know when you have outgrown one job and need a new one. *Be prepared to revise your career plan continually*

For most of us, career planning is not a simple, straightforward, linear process in which we follow certain prescribed steps, end up at a specific destination, and live happily ever after. It is instead a feedback loop that continues to self-correct as we add information about our changing self and the world around us. We are constantly revising our career plan as we grow and change. This means that there isn't any one "right" career. Instead, there are many careers in which we could be equally happy, equally successful, equally satisfied. *There is no single "right" career*

We are looking, then, not for the *one* right career but for the series of alternatives and career options that seem to make sense for each of us given our background, our personality, our career and life stages, and the changing world.

Choosing and Changing Careers

Each one of us, regardless of our stage in life, is in some phase of career development. You may be starting your first job or looking for a job. You may be planning for your first career, reentering the

SUCCESS STORIES

Sample Career Changers

Here are some examples of the kinds of career selections we've been discussing:

PROFESSOR NGUYEN had reached his life goal, or so he thought. He was one of the few chosen to be a professor of religion at a small college in the San Francisco area. One day he woke up with stomach pains and body aches and had little energy. He dragged himself out of bed. When the pains lasted longer than three days, he visited his family physician only to find there was no medical reason for his discomfort. He then began some soul searching. His pains and nightmares continued over a period of months and seemed to occur only during the workweek. On weekends, when he was with his family or volunteering at a hospital, he felt energetic and healthy. Soon he took a leave of absence from his job and devoted more time to his hospital avocation. The physical ailments mysteriously disappeared. He spent one year examining his needs, consulting with a career counselor, and talking things over with friends. He found that his real satisfaction came from helping people in the hospital rather than from teaching religion. Shortly thereafter, a friend told him about a job opening as an ombudsman in a hospital. He got the job and now lectures to local classes in career development on the hazards of keeping a job that is making you ill! Professor Nguyen needed to reexamine his original goals to discover why his career as a professor wasn't meeting his needs.

DAVID CHAN spent two years at a state college with a major in pre-law but a love for art. He wished to choose a career with strong financial potential that would be acceptable to his parents. During his junior year David realized he constantly daydreamed about a career in art. So he enrolled in an evening community college class and then transferred full-time to a technical art school where he specialized in drawing and sketching. David completed his degree, sought career counseling, and decided to try for his dream job. Within two years, he had a part-time job with an animation studio. He is now a full-time animator, creating characters for feature films. David was able to find a career that used his artistic talents and surpassed his financial goals.

job market after some time at home, considering your next career, planning for part-time employment, or looking for meaningful volunteer experience.

As there is no crystal ball that will predict the one right career for you, you will want to consider several options as you explore career development. The examples in the "Success Stories" box describe people who reassessed their needs and made satisfying changes. It is also possible to survey your needs, values, interests, skills, aptitudes, and sources of information about the world of work in order to create a broader career *objective*. Some careers do have established or common career paths. In teaching, one often starts out as a tutor, works up to student teacher, and then becomes an assistant teacher before becoming a full-time teacher. In the marketing profession, people often start in sales. Therefore, we need to think about career goals in the sense of their being both short term and long term. A short-term career goal is one that can be rather quickly attained. For instance, in the process of career planning, you may

SUCCESS STORIES

More Career Changers

TAYLOR JORDAN is a sophomore at a community college. For the past two years, largely on the advice of her parents, she has been preparing to transfer to the local university to complete a degree in business. Taylor now realizes that she wants to follow her true talents and interests, and pursue a career in interior design. Although she has spent much time and effort accumulating credits toward a bachelor's degree in business, she knows that many of her core courses will apply toward her associate's degree in interior design. She is determined to do what is necessary to achieve her new goal. To prepare for her discussion with her parents, Taylor has researched local job opportunities with furniture and home improvement stores, home builders, and interior design firms. She has talked to a college adviser about possible internships and volunteer work. Most important, she believes that her decision is the right one and is determined to follow through with it.

JOSE MARCADO emigrated to the United States in the 1990s. In 2000, after improving his language skills by attending adult school, he enrolled in a restaurant and hotel management program at a community college and began working as a parking attendant. Jose was very sociable and positive, often making friendly conversation with his customers. By the time he finished his schooling, he was the supervisor of parking facilities. One of his customers told him about a job possibility with a large hotel chain and recommended he apply. Jose not only got the job but within three years was managing the hotel's restaurant at an annual salary of $60,000. His ability to network, be friendly, learn on the job, and combine studies and work experience led him to a great job.

RHONDA SPEER spent five years in college completing a bachelor's degree program in teaching with an emphasis in special education. After two and a half years working in the field, she decided that she needed a change. Working with children all day was making it difficult for Rhonda to concentrate at the end of the day on her own young daughter. She found a job as a stockbroker trainee. Within six months she was a full-fledged stockbroker. Now she's a corporate financial adviser.

discover you want to be a lawyer. We would normally consider law a long-term career option because it generally takes many years of study and preparation. However, a short-term career goal related to law might be obtaining a job as a legal secretary or a paralegal. Either of these would give you the opportunity to work in an environment that excites and energizes you long before you actually achieve your final and ultimate career goal. In addition, relevant experience enhances your appeal to future employers.

Preparation = short-term and long-term goals

If you examine enough options during the career-planning process, you may be able to use career experiences to move into related areas just as Sandra did. Subsequent chapters in this book will help you identify your related options.

There is a final, very important reason that this effort at personal assessment is crucial as the first step in your career-planning process. Once you know who you are and what your preferences and talents are, you can better make sense of the information that continually bombards you regarding the

If your long-term career goal is to become a chef, your short-term goals and actions should support that goal.

world of work. It's almost impossible to read a newspaper, listen to a news broadcast, visit a Website, or watch a television show that does not have some implication for you and your career. In fact, you may feel you suffer from information overload. Surfing the Web, looking at the classified ads, and reading about employment projections and trends can cause confusion, frustration, and often discouragement about what place you might have in this elusive job market.

One of the best ways to achieve a sense of control and perspective on this constant stream of information is to know who you are, so that when you are surfing, listening, reading, watching, and experiencing, you will have a means of processing information through your consciousness, through your personality and preferences, and through your values and skills. Eventually, you will be able to recognize and reject information that does not apply to you, and to internalize and add to your career plan information that does. If a group setting such as a career class is available to you, all the better! The opportunity to discover yourself and expand your horizons is multiplied by the added benefit of group interaction.

Self-knowledge helps decision making

Summary

The best approach to the process of career planning is first to examine who you are, what you know about yourself, and what you need and want, and next to mesh that information with the world of work. You then have the distinct advantage of being able to choose training for a career about which you are truly excited and enthusiastic. These two qualities are among the most important to potential employers. Even if the job market for the field you have chosen is extremely competitive, you will have an edge because of your sense of commitment, your passion, and your joy in what you are doing. We will elaborate further on these attitudes for success in Chapter 2 and will identify and discuss the attitudinal components that will make you a success in whatever career you choose.

Attitude influences action: knowing yourself is critical in an unpredictable job market

TAKING STOCK

PURPOSE OF EXERCISES. The first set of exercises will help you explore your current feelings and attitudes and thus better understand yourself. Begin with Exercise 1.1, First Impressions. This will help you take stock of where you are currently. Exercise 1.2 is a review of where your life focus has been. You will learn more about how personality and interests relate to career planning in Chapter 4. For now, Exercise 1.3 asks you to begin thinking about your interests, and Exercise 1.4 asks you to identify your personal strengths. (Later when you are reading about the personality requirements of different careers, you can use this list as another piece to complete the "personality puzzle.") Exercise 1.5 encourages you to identify job preferences by ranking occupations according to how you perceive their status.

Companion Website

To answer these questions online, go to the *Exercise* module in Chapter 1 of the Companion Website.

First Impressions 1.1

Here is your first chance to think about yourself and record your responses. Fill in each blank carefully and honestly. Be true to yourself; don't try to please anyone else with your answers. Try to be spontaneous; the longer you think before answering, the more likely you are to censor your answers.

1. I am _____

2. I need _____

3. I want _____

4. My current life stage in selecting a career is _____

5. I would like to change _____ about myself.

6. If all goes well in the next five years, I will be doing the following things:

   _____

   _____

7. If things go poorly in the next five years, I will be doing

   _____

   _____

8. Reviewing past jobs or volunteer experiences I have had, what did I like best/least about each one? Is there a pattern?

_____

_____

1.2   *Your Lifeline*

Review the information on life stages. As we noted, these life stage descriptions suggest that we emphasize different needs at different times of our life. Can you remember the highs and lows in your personal and career life and then place them on a line? It is helpful to place symbols on a line graph of your life indicating times of major decisions such as moves or new jobs; periods when mentors or other influential people entered or affected your life; and times when you had particular problems or acquired important new skills. To assist your memory, divide your life into four time periods and write four important memories (activities, people, events) in each period.

AGES 0–12 (Try remembering friends, birthday parties, holidays, or school events to recall your earliest memories. What did you excel at?)

1. _____
2. _____
3. _____
4. _____

AGES 13–19

1. _____
2. _____
3. _____
4. _____

AGES 20–29

1. _____
2. _____
3. _____
4. _____

AGES 30–39

1. _____
2. _____
3. _____
4. _____

A sample lifeline. Space to draw your own lifeline appears on the next page. **EXHIBIT 1.1**

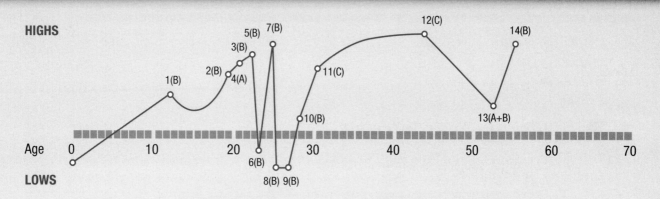

A sample lifeline. Space to draw your own lifeline appears on the next page. **EXHIBIT 1.1**

AGES 40 PLUS

1. _____
2. _____
3. _____
4. _____

Now you can transfer these memories onto the lifeline. It may help to use symbols to save space (e.g., A = people, B = events, C = jobs).

1. Leadership award in sixth grade (age 12).
2. Chosen student ambassador to France—sophomore in college (age 19).
3. Spent senior year in France (age 21).
4. Met significant person in my life (age 21).
5. Graduate school in New York (age 22).
6. Move from New York to Missouri (lost friends and career contacts) (age 23).
7. First professional job (but not my ideal job) (age 24).
8. Fired! (A bona fide case of sexual harassment!) (age 25).
9. After being unemployed for nine months, volunteered at career planning center and learned new skills (age 26).
10. Began my own serious job search, identified my ideal job (career counselor) in ideal setting for me (community college) (age 27).
11. Success! Landed perfect job for me! (age 30).
12. Was still learning on my job and began to explore further options and career enrichment opportunities (age 44).
13. Began to deal with my parents' mortality and my own aging (ages 50–54).
14. Seeking balance, giving back to the community, planning for increased leisure and continuous lifelong learning (age 55).
15. Exploring the possibilities and challenges of retirement planning and lifestyle changes (55+).

Now draw your own lifeline below:

HIGHS

| Age | 0 | 10 | 20 | 30 | 40 | 50 | 60 | 70 |

LOWS

1.3   *Identify Your Interests*

1. What subjects in school do I like?

_____

_____

2. What books or magazines do I read? What kinds of music, art, theater, and cinema do I like? What are my favorite Websites?

_____

_____

_____

3. What do I like to do for fun? How do I spend my spare time?

_____

_____

_____

4. What jobs have I had (including volunteer work) and what did I like about them?

_____

_____

1.4   *Describe Yourself*

Circle those adjectives that best describe you. Place an "X" in front of those adjectives that are least like you.

R REALISTIC		I INVESTIGATIVE		A ARTISTIC	
practical	persistent	careful	introverted	emotional	impulsive
athletic	conforming	achieving	confident	expressive	flexible
rugged	down-to-earth	curious	analytical	imaginative	idealistic
stable	self-reliant	precise	intellectual	unordered	original
frank		independent		creative	

S SOCIAL		E ENTERPRISING		C CONVENTIONAL	
helpful	understanding	energetic	adventurous	conscientious	moderate
insightful	popular	driving	powerful	persistent	orderly
kind	cooperative	ambitious	persuasive	organized	efficient
friendly	responsible	assertive	competitive	obedient	detailed
tactful	flirtatious	enthusiastic		dependable	thorough

Next, review the adjectives you circled. Note the list is divided into six clusters: Realistic, Investigative, Artistic, Social, Enterprising, and Conventional (RIASEC). Which groups of adjectives best describe you? Also note that most of the words are positive personality traits. This exercise gives you a chance to acknowledge your positive attributes.

From which three of the six groups do most of your adjectives come? Rank the groups from which most of them come as 1, second most as 2, and third most as 3.

1 _____   2 _____   3 _____

Each group of adjectives describes a certain kind of person. What kinds of people do you like to be around? Rank the top three types of people you like to be around.

1 _____   2 _____   3 _____

Consider Occupational Status   1.5

Rank the following occupations in numerical order according to the *status* you attribute to them. Number 1 should be the occupation that in your mind is most significant—how you define *significant* is, of course, up to you. For example, a police officer could appear as number 1 on your list if you place most value on societal order and safety. Number 20 should reflect the occupation you regard as least significant.

_____ administrative assistant   _____ lawyer

_____ agriculture supervisor   _____ movie director

_____ auto technician   _____ musician

_____ computer operator   _____ plumber

_____ construction worker   _____ police officer

_____ dental hygienist   _____ psychiatric nurse

_____ doctor   _____ public school teacher

_____ engineer   _____ restaurant manager

_____ hairdresser   _____ robotics technician

_____ landscape designer   _____ salesperson

Think about the aspects of these positions that impress you or seem of value to you. Next, think about how you define *status*. Is it based on probable income, amount of education required, societal standards? How individualistic do you think your rankings are? For example, was *musician* ranked in your top five because you appreciate music? There are, in actuality, no correct or incorrect answers in this exercise. However, your rankings may reflect some of your basic preferences. If most of your top-ranked occupations were higher-salaried or if your rankings were based on potential for high pay, you may be motivated by a need for security; if your highest rankings were for service-related occupations (e.g., doctor, public school teacher), your motivation might be different.

1.6   WWWebwise

For additional activities, go to the WWWebwise module in Chapter 1 of the Companion Website.

1.7   Exercise Summary

Write a brief paragraph answering these questions.

What have I learned about myself? My current life stage? How does this knowledge relate to my career/life planning? How do I feel?

_____

_____

_____

_____

_____

_____

_____

_____

_____

_____

_____

_____

_____

_____

_____

_____

Go to page 219 of the chapter summaries, and complete the Chapter 1 exercise summary.

2

Programming Yourself for Success

Learning Objectives

At the end of the chapter you will be able to . . .

- Discuss why building self-esteem is important in developing a successful career plan
- Identify specific components of the success profile
- Recognize approaches and techniques for creating opportunities for success in your career planning

Through the process of career planning, you learn how to take what you've got (values, skills, interests, aptitudes, qualities, limitations) and do what it takes (job search strategy) to reach your career goal. A satisfying career *is* attainable *if* you decide you want it. We begin the process of career planning with an assessment of your self-esteem and your attitudes because your mental

Act as if it were impossible to fail.

DOROTHEA BROUDE

outlook is the crucial variable that will move you toward (or keep you from) identifying and achieving your career goals. No book, set of exercises, system, or counselor will affect your future as much as your own belief system and your own commitment to achieving success. Your beliefs are reflected by your actions.

How many times have you told yourself, "I'm going to start on a new exercise program today" and then found a "legitimate" excuse to postpone your efforts? Are you really ready to work on your career fitness? If so, let's examine some of the beliefs and attitudes that can assist you with your plan.

Because we believe in positive attitude and imagery (both of which we'll discuss shortly), we have used positive statements to begin each section in this chapter. This is done to provide you with models of statements that reflect attitudes that lead to successful behavior.

I Am Building Self-Esteem

- I maintain a positive outlook.
- I am assertive.
- I have a sense of humor.
- I am self-confident.
- I am enthusiastic.
- I use positive self-talk (affirmations).
- I visualize success.
- I have a positive self-image.
- I have multiple intelligences.
- I learn from role models.
- I initiate action.
- I am persistent.
- I am disciplined.

Our sources of self-esteem are deeply rooted; at a very young age, we begin to formulate a concept of ourselves based on our upbringing, our schooling, our culture, and a multitude of other factors. It is an unfortunate truth that many of us reach adulthood with low self-esteem, which manifests itself in many ways. For example, we may be afraid to try new things for fear of being embarrassed. We may let others make decisions for us, or we may stay in a job that we dislike rather than risking loss in order to find one we do like.

Obviously, one book or course cannot miraculously repair low self-esteem, and we do not mean to imply that such a quick fix is possible. *However*, this book can help you identify possible problem areas, give you the incentive to make changes, and start you in the right direction. Today, many colleges offer courses on building self-esteem, learning to be assertive, and related issues. Thus, you have resources available if you discover you need help; making that discovery is an important step in the right direction.

The ultimate goal is to like yourself. The higher your appreciation of yourself, or your self-esteem, the greater are your chances of feeling and being successful in your personal and career goals. This chapter identifies several building blocks of self-esteem, listed at left and discussed next.

As you read each section, take a quick pulse. How would you rate yourself on each of these essential components? Which ones do you need to work on first? As you identify the areas in your life that need work, pay attention to the suggestions for improvement. Later, Exercises 2.1 and 2.4 will help you further your goal of building self-esteem. This should be a lifelong goal. Establish small goals that you can meet along the way, and give yourself credit for small successes.

Although the word *success* means many things to many people, success in general usually means the progressive external demonstration of internalized life goals. In other words, success refers to the step-by-step movement toward the attainment of an object, quality, or state of mind that we value and wish to possess.

- I demonstrate emotional intelligence.
- I identify my goals.
- I am self-reliant and career resilient.
- I am flexible.
- I have purpose.
- I have passion.
- I am responsible.
- I have vision.
- I am an innovator.

I Maintain a Positive Outlook

Do you have your own personal definition of success? Regardless of the particular goals you have in mind, you need to think positively to attain them. Have you ever heard the saying, "It's all in your head"? People who say this believe that our mental attitudes have control over our body and our life and can, therefore, program our success or failure. Although many of our attitudes and beliefs come from early messages we received from our parents and teachers, as adults we can choose to keep or change these messages, depending on how helpful they are to us in achieving success and satisfaction in life.

Examine your philosophy of life. How you see life in general is how you lead your life. A quick way to identify your philosophy is to examine how you visualize the future.

Read the following scenarios and select the one that best relates to your point of view (Kauffman, 1976).

The future is a great roller coaster on a moonless night. It exists, twisting ahead of us in the dark, although we can see each part only as we come to it. We can make estimates about where we are headed and sometimes see around a bend to another section of track, but it doesn't do us any real good because the future is fixed and determined. We are locked in our seats, and nothing we may know or do will change the course that is laid out for us.

The future is a mighty river. The great force of history flows inexorably along, carrying us with it. Most of our attempts to change its course are mere pebbles thrown into the river: they cause a momentary splash and a few ripples, but they make no difference. The river's course can be changed, but only by natural disasters like earthquakes and landslides or by massive, concerted human efforts on a similar scale. On the other hand, we are free as individuals to adapt to the course of history either well or poorly. By looking ahead, we can avoid sandbars and whirlpools and pick the best path through any rapids.

The future is a great ocean. There are many possible destinations, and many different paths to each destination. A good navigator takes

Remember the times you've thought the following:

"That's just the way I am."

"I can't control what I do."

"I just can't seem to finish anything I start."

"I would like to do that differently, but it's just too hard to change."

"Yes, it happened again."

"I've never been good at that."

advantage of the main currents of change, adapts the course to the capricious winds of chance, keeps a sharp lookout posted, and moves carefully in fog or uncharted waters. Doing these things will get the navigator safely to a destination (barring a typhoon or other disaster that one can neither predict nor avoid).

The future is entirely random, a colossal dice game. Every second, millions of things happen that could have happened another way and produced a different future. A bullet is deflected by a twig and kills one person instead of another. A scientist checks a spoiled culture and throws it away or looks more closely at it and discovers penicillin. A newly renovated home is destroyed by an earthquake. Since everything is chance, all we can do is play the game, pray to the gods of fortune, and enjoy what good luck comes our way.

One of these scenarios may reflect your perception of life. Is your life a roller coaster, beyond your control; a mighty river to which you must adapt; a great ocean with many directions and options; or just a game of chance? Are you a positive thinker or a negative thinker? The second and third scenarios are the more positive reflections. Your belief system will affect how you see life. Have you ever noticed how your most dominant thoughts reinforce what happens to you? This phenomenon is called the self-fulfilling prophecy.

Your mind tends to believe what you tell it. And, yes, you can if you *think* you can. Cultivating a positive, assertive outlook on life is the most crucial factor in the difference between those people who have successful, satisfying lives/careers and those who don't. Let's examine some of the aspects of this positive, assertive outlook so that we can get into a mind-set for success.

I Am Assertive

One of the basic choices we make moment to moment is whether to be assertive, aggressive, or passive in response to life situations. Being assertive means being the ultimate judge of our own behavior, feelings, and actions and being responsible for the initiation and consequence of those actions. In essence, assertive people choose for themselves and build themselves up *without* putting others down. Aggressive people choose for themselves and others; they build themselves up *by* putting others down. Passive people allow *others* to choose *for* them; they put themselves down or allow others to do so.

An assertive attitude helps to maintain control

An assertive attitude will help you maintain some control over today's competitive job market. An assertive outlook enables you to be persistent, seek more information when you run out of leads, weigh all alternatives evenly (incorporating both your logic and your intuition), revise your goals when necessary, and pursue your goals with commitment and purpose. Assertiveness specifically enables you to say what you feel, think, and want. It allows you to be expressive, open, and clear in communication. You are able to say no under pressure, recognize and deal with manipulation, and stand up for your rights in negative, confrontational situations. You gain the ability to be a better listener. Others appreciate your directness and ability to hear them. You enjoy more positive interactions with people and feel more positive about being able to handle life situations.

Assertive personal traits include body language as well as words. Studies indicate that 93 percent of the meaning of any message is communicated nonverbally. Look at your appearance, facial expressions, and typical physical movements and stance when you are feeling assertive compared to when you are feeling passive. What does your style of dress say about you? Can changing the color or style of your outfit change the mood you project to others? Have you ever noticed your gesturing? Assertiveness is often associated with expansive gestures rather than limited ones. Finally, how do you deal with touch or physical closeness? Being assertive means feeling comfortable within your own body space.

Positive, assertive behavior suggests that you truly have confidence in yourself. This behavior conveys verbally and nonverbally that you believe in your abilities and in your own worth. That positive, confident, and enthusiastic self will set you apart, make people take notice of you, and ultimately enable you to exercise control over your career and your life.

Positive, assertive behavior shows self-confidence

I Have a Sense of Humor

According to journalist Norman Cousins, laughing is internal jogging, and when you laugh, you are exercising all your internal organs. Not only does laughter feel good, it is essential to good health and a sense of well-being. Cousins has good reason to believe this. Some years ago he was diagnosed with a terminal illness and given just two months to live. Instead of spending his precious time remaining in the hospital, he checked into a hotel and watched, read, or listened to every humorous movie, book, and audiotape he could get his hands on. He virtually laughed himself well. Many years later, still in excellent health, Cousins was convinced, as were his doctors, that laughter accounted for his recovery! In fact, the medical school at U.C.L.A. invited him to join its faculty to teach interns how to lighten up.

Cousins' amazing story holds a lesson for all of us. We can all stand to lighten up a little—to find the genuine humor in an embarrassing moment, in a mistake, in a situation that is so serious that we need to laugh to keep from crying. Humor at its best means being able to laugh at yourself. Look for opportunities to see the lighter side of life and to share the experience of being human with others who can laugh with you, not at you. Cultivate the habit of walking on the "light" side of life.

I Am Self-Confident

Self-confidence, perhaps more than any other factor, is the secret to success and happiness. It is the ability to recognize that even though you are imperfect, you are a unique, worthwhile, and lovable person who deserves and can attain the best in life. You project a sense of self-confidence in your body language, your dress, your pace, your ability to take pride in your accomplishments, your ability to learn from your mistakes, and your ability to accept suggestions and praise from others. Because you believe you deserve the career of your choice, you can attain it.

Discover your own self-worth

Strive to project a sense of self-confidence and enthusiasm through your body language, your attitude, your dress.

You can begin to develop more self-confidence by recognizing and rewarding yourself for something you do *well* each day. It may feel more natural for you to review, in great detail, each and every negative event that has occurred. This is a common and understandable human reaction that can be neutralized by deliberate positive thinking. At times you may have to force yourself to think of something positive and give yourself a pat on the back. Better yet, make it a point to share the good news with a friend, a support person, someone who you know will delight in your small personal achievement. Consider starting a support group consisting of individuals who want to share their personal victories with each other. The reinforcement and support of others are powerful tools in our personal quest for success. Start small, remembering that an Olympic gold medal, just like self-confidence, is built on hours, days, weeks, months, and years of small personal victories.

I Am Enthusiastic

You can identify achievers by their consistently optimistic and enthusiastic demeanor. They know that life is a self-fulfilling prophecy, that people usually get what they actively imagine and expect. They choose to start the day on a positive note by listening to music, singing in the shower, or telling themselves this will be a good day. They view problems as opportunities to be creative. They learn to stay relaxed and calm under stress. They associate with people who share their optimism about life and who support each other through praise, encouragement, and networking. When asked about their career goals, instead of saying, "I don't know," they say, "I'm in the process of discovering my career goals."

Employers rate enthusiasm highly

When employers are asked what traits they look for in prospective employees, enthusiasm is always among those at the top of the list. What kind of people do you want as friends, associates, and colleagues? Chances are you want people who are optimistic and have a zest for life. You can become more enthusiastic about life by getting involved in something that has meaning for you. A hobby, volunteer work, mastery of a skill, a new relationship all provide opportunities to generate and express enthusiasm. On the job, displaying a professional attitude includes acting as if things are fine even when you feel upset or depressed. Although it may seem phony, you will find that acting positively pays off. Not only do you come across as mature and professional, but as you begin to act enthusiastically, you receive positive feedback from others. The smiles, nods, and positive words of others begin to make you feel enthusiastic, and you soon discover you are no longer acting: you genuinely feel better!

I Use Positive Self-Talk (Affirmations)

One of the most effective ways to improve your self-image is the deliberate use of positive self-talk. You already talk to yourself; we all do, constantly! But we usually do not consciously listen to our internal dialogue; consequently, we often hear only negative, self-defeating messages that create and reinforce a poor self-image. Once you decide to take charge of your self-talk, you can begin to repeat positive messages that will reinforce a positive self-image. These messages are commonly called affirmations.

Positive self-talk improves self-image

An *affirmation* is a statement or assertion that something is *already* so (Gawain, 2000). It is an existing seed or thought in the here and now that will grow as life unfolds. It is not intended to change what already exists but to create new, desired outcomes. Remember, all events begin with a thought. If you think you can, you can! Anything a person can conceive can be achieved. Good gardeners cultivate not only flowers but also the soil in which they grow. The thoughts you are thinking and sending out are the "soil" of your life: If you constantly project thoughts of lack of ability, you will have barren soil; if you project thoughts of ability and strength, your soil will be rich. Therefore, any career in which you can imagine yourself being happy and successful can be achieved.

However, when developing your affirmations, remember that you are planting a seed and that the seed must carry information on the exact thing you want to grow into, or produce—the result you desire. When you become specific about what you want, you are focusing the power of your mind's energy (your thoughts) on your desires. The more specific you are about your goals, the more focused you become about what must be done to reach them. You know you are being specific enough when you can visualize details about what you want. For example, if you want to become a college professor, you must be able to see yourself on a college campus in a specific classroom, standing before a room of students, lecturing, interacting with other professors, and correcting papers!

Let's put this technique into action. Think of a quality that you want to develop in yourself; we'll use enthusiasm as an example. Your first instinct might be to say or think, "I'm not very enthusiastic." As soon as this thought comes to mind, replace it with the opposite thought, "I am enthusiastic." Repeat the phrase over and over, day and night, until you feel you own it; soon it will feel comfortable. At the same time, picture yourself doing something enthusiastically, such as explaining to your boss why you deserve a day off, starting a conversation with a stranger, or confidently

SUCCESS STRATEGIES

Here are some hints to follow when stating or writing down your own affirmations:

1. Always phrase the affirmation in the present, never in the future; otherwise it may remain in the future. For example, if your goal is to be less tense or nervous in challenging and stressful situations, use an affirmation such as "I am calm; I am in control of my feelings and this situation," rather than "I will be calm."

2. Phrase your affirmation in the positive rather than the negative. In other words, avoid affirming what you don't want. Instead of writing "My present job doesn't bother me anymore," it would be much more effective to write, "My work is wonderful" or "I enjoy my job."

3. Maintain the attitude that you are creating something new and fresh. You are not trying to manipulate, redo, or change an existing condition.

disagreeing with an instructor during class. Picture yourself making your statement and being positively reinforced: Your boss says yes, you deserve it; the stranger becomes a friend; the instructor praises you for your insight.

Thus, even before you implement your affirmation by enthusiastically taking some action, you have prepared yourself mentally for a positive outcome of your action. Your chances of experiencing the positive outcome improve because you are projecting a positive self-image. Try it!

I Visualize Success

Visualization, much like affirmations, is mental practice. It is the conscious implanting of specific images in your mind. Through repetition, these images will become part of your unconscious and then conscious mind, evoking and enhancing abilities, habits, and attitudes. Visualization differs slightly from affirmations because it involves specific mental imagery as opposed to verbal expression of positive thoughts. Visualization is also referred to as *mental imagery* and *mental rehearsal*.

Use mental rehearsal for success

When we marvel at the mastery of an expert, we often assume that the person was born with superhuman talents or skills. We forget that every champion athlete, every great performer, every skilled surgeon, and every professional developed expertise through endless hours of physical and mental practice. They visualize their performance, they engage in positive self-talk ("I can," "I'll do better each time"), and through repetition they become more and more of what they desire to be.

Until you begin to understand yourself, it is difficult to contemplate success fully, in both personal matters and a career. Choose your own vision in which specific results, qualities, and abilities are evident and consistent with winning.

Visualization is one of the most powerful tools promoting personal change. It is the process of maintaining a thought long enough for the mental picture we create to evoke an emotional response. This emotion causes conviction, and conviction influences reality. Thus, a change in reality begins with visualization, which turns to emotion, and results in conviction.

Visualization can have a profound impact on your mind. Your subconscious does not distinguish between imagining something and actually experiencing it. (Try imagining you are biting into a lemon; can you taste it?) You can change your opinions, beliefs, aspirations, and levels of expectation by vividly imagining the circumstances and experiences you select. Of all the species on earth, only human beings can visualize the future and believe it can happen (Dyer, 1992).

A pessimist says, "I will believe it when I see it," whereas an optimist says, "I always see it when I believe it." What you see is what you get. The critical first step is a mental one. You must believe in and be able to see the possibilities and outcomes in your mind before you can hope to realize them in your life.

A high-jumper visualizes a successful route to clear the bar; a golfer sees in his mind the putt dropping into the cup and follows that vision. Strong visual messages are often reinforced with appropriate positive affirmations.

This process will assist you in achieving what you want to accomplish. Conscious visualization of yourself as a winner is a key step toward a self-fulfilling prophecy.

Those who use visualization successfully do so regularly over a period of time. This is the key to the success of mental rehearsal. Research indicates that a goal must be visualized a minimum of 30 minutes a day for at least a month to obtain results. This discipline distinguishes visualization from random daydreaming, an effortless activity in which we all engage from time to time!

I Have a Positive Self-Image

Successful people *like* themselves, visualize themselves at their best, and monitor their self-talk to reinforce their images of success in word and action. They know that self-image acts as a regulator, an unconscious thermostat. If you cannot picture yourself doing, being, or achieving something, you probably will not be able to do, be, or achieve it. Your self-image absorbs information, memorizes it, and guides your actions accordingly. Every time you say, "I can't," you are adding to a negative self-image. Every time you say, "I can and will," you are giving yourself permission to be your best. Successful people recognize how potent their beliefs about self are, and they take responsibility for shaping their own self-image, rather than allowing others' opinions to shape or limit it.

I Have Multiple Intelligences

Scientists used to believe that there were only two ways to demonstrate intelligence, either verbally or mathematically. The research of Dr. Howard Gardner (1993) now indicates that there are at least seven distinct areas of intelligence. Gardner proposes that each person possesses all seven intelligences to a greater or lesser degree and that we can all work on developing even more of each intelligence. As you read about each one below, ask yourself which ones you have already developed highly and which ones you would like to develop further:

1. *Verbal/linguistic intelligence* focuses on the use of language and words. Individuals with this intelligence tend to enjoy school subjects such as English, foreign languages, history, and social sciences. They participate in debate, drama, TV and radio work, newspaper and yearbook editing, and writing of newsletters and magazines. Common career choices include author, attorney, teacher, salesperson, and religious leader.

2. *Musical/rhythmic intelligence* focuses on the ability to be aware of patterns in pitch, sound, rhythm, and timbre. These individuals enjoy such school subjects as music and dance. They are involved in band, orchestra, choir, and dance productions. Some common career choices include singer, composer, dancer, conductor, disc jockey, and sound engineer.

3. *Logical/mathematical intelligence* includes the ability to think abstractly, to problem-solve, and to think critically. Favorite school subjects

If your primary intelligence is visual/spatial, your career plans should take that into account.

for these individuals include math, science, economics, and computer programming. They tend to be involved in science projects and enjoy reading maps, spreadsheets, budgets, and blueprints. Common career choices include engineer, scientist, mathematician, banker, economist, and computer programmer.

4. *Visual/spatial intelligence* includes the ability to create mental images and transform them into an art form. Individuals with this intelligence enjoy art, shop, drafting, and photography. They enjoy projects such as designing brochures, ceramics, costumes, structures, and Websites. Popular careers include visual artist, designer, architect, and Webmaster.

5. *Bodily/kinesthetic intelligence* involves the ability to connect mind and body and often relates to excelling at sports. Popular subjects include dance, drama, sports, and culinary arts. Common career choices include athlete, coach, physical therapist, dancer, trainer, and chef.

6. *Intrapersonal intelligence* involves the ability to comprehend one's feelings. Popular school subjects related to this intelligence include psychology and creative writing. These individuals enjoy reading and journal writing. Common careers include psychologist, author, and religious leader.

7. *Interpersonal intelligence* involves the ability to comprehend others' feelings. Individuals who possess this intelligence enjoy such school subjects as literature, psychology, and sociology. Typical career choices include counselor, psychologist, nurse, social worker, teacher, and politician.

Because each person possesses some of all seven intelligences, it's useful to recognize which are most highly developed, which come naturally, and which should be consciously targeted for improvement. Most research on career satisfaction suggests that in order to be satisfied, you need to identify and capitalize on areas that seem natural and take advantage of your multiple intelligences.

I Learn from Role Models

So far we have explored the components for developing a positive self-image, that is, personal behaviors and attitudes that help us identify and best use our values, skills, and interests. Now it's time to look outside ourselves at people who display the qualities of success we want to cultivate. Think about the people you admire and begin to make a list. First, think globally about prominent individuals on the national and international scene. Then, think locally about people with whom you work; individuals who are part of your community, your neighborhood, or your religious affiliation; those who attend your school; or those who share your hobbies. Finally, think of the people who are most dear to you—your family and friends. Which of their qualities do you admire? In what ways do you want to be more like them?

Spend time observing them in action. You may want to consider telling them what you admire about them and asking them to tell you how they developed those qualities. Ask them for insights and suggestions that you might use in developing your own success profile. Make these people part of your network of contacts. You will probably find that even the most successful people have struggled with moments of self-doubt or crises of self-confidence. Ask them what they do when the going gets rough.

No doubt you choose your friends and associates deliberately and carefully, knowing that you are influenced by the attitudes of the company you keep. Similarly, when you seek out individuals and acknowledge the qualities you admire in them, you are giving them the gift of recognition and appreciation, a valuable commodity in today's fast-paced, all-too-impersonal world. Also, in speaking with your role models you are practicing information interviewing (to be discussed in Chapter 9) and taking the first steps in developing networking skills.

In fact, this is a good time for doing some volunteer work, exploring internships, and getting involved in the community. It is not too soon to use the newspaper or local magazines to find leads and meet people who can give you ideas. Look for articles describing successful people or interesting jobs. Then call these people and interview them about how they chose and trained for their careers. Their strategies may also work for you. (See Exercise 2.6.) You are making connections that can later assist you in the job search process. Of course, you are also projecting the positive self-image you are cultivating.

I Initiate Action

Successful people realize that goals activate people and fears stop people. If you dwell on your fears, whether real or imagined, you will be immobilized in the pursuit of your goals. If you concentrate on your goals, you will move toward them. People who are afraid to tell the world what they want don't get it. The difference between those who are successful and those who are not is attitude. Which side of the coin do you choose to look at—fears or goals? In what direction are you going—away from or toward your goals?

Imagine yourself in your dream job, your fantasy career, the kind of job you would pay to do. Take the job of cruise ship director, for example. Now identify someone who has that occupation. If you don't know of anyone, ask your friends, relatives, neighbors, and classmates, all of whom are part of your extended network (see Exercise 9.1, page 258, for a list of people who make up your network). Ask if they know someone who actually has your dream job. Next, contact that individual in person, if possible, and arrange a brief information interview. Read the section in Chapter 9 on information interviewing, and plan to ask the sample questions.

After you have gathered some facts about your fantasy career, ask yourself if it still holds its appeal for you. If so, you may wish to talk to others in the field to further develop an accurate and detailed assessment. If not, you may want to choose another fantasy career to investigate.

I Am Persistent

Luck = opportunity, preparation, and persistence

Persistent people take responsibility for initiating desired action. They know that life is full of choices, not chances. They realize they have the personal power, both physical and psychological, to take control of their own lives. They know that blaming Mother Nature for an out-of-shape body or calling it fate when they don't get a job is simply copping out. Successful people make things happen for themselves. What appears to be luck is usually opportunity met by preparation.

Perhaps nowhere is this more evident than in the Olympics. Only the most persistent and committed athletes will be chosen to participate, and all know full well the slim chance of coming home with a medal. Nevertheless, many return time after time, and some eventually triumph. Those who compete gain public acclaim, knowing their participation places them in elite company. The successful person is the one who keeps trying after *not* reaching a goal or after experiencing rejection, the one who keeps trying until the dream is attained.

In today's unpredictable economy, many of us feel as if we, too, are preparing for the Olympics; this especially holds true for students and job seekers, who must face such hurdles as degree and training decisions, financial hardships, interviews, and rejections. Never has persistence in the face of limited opportunity been more necessary.

Through tenacity, determination, and consistent effort, you can achieve much. Talent and education are not automatic keys to success: nothing can take the place of persistence and enthusiasm.

I Am Disciplined

Discipline yourself for success

Self-discipline can also be called *self-control*. It is the ability to control or manage some aspect of your life, to have power over it. A simple example is that most of us have the self-discipline to get out of bed every morning at a particular time even though we'd probably prefer to sleep later.

Meet Alan

Alan began working for Sony's Music Division in Hollywood, California, after he received his associate's degree. He started out as an assistant to the sound cutter and then was promoted to lead sound cutter. After 12 years, his division was reorganized and Alan was laid off. Not knowing exactly what he wanted to do, Alan went to see the outplacement counselor offered to him through Sony. The counselor used a variety of career resources to uncover Alan's interests, skills, and values.

After several meetings and some serious soul-searching, Alan realized that surfing the Web and spending time in the library were two of his strongest interests. The counselor suggested that he check out his local library for volunteer opportunities while he was trying to decide what career direction he would take. With his current skills, Alan was less than confident about his ability to volunteer in the library, and he was sure that he didn't want to return to school to become a librarian.

After several months, Alan was getting discouraged and needed a place to go every day, so he decided to talk to the volunteer coordinator at the library. The coordinator was happy to have him; however, the work he was assigned was not very challenging or interesting. He was stocking shelves and erasing pencil marks from the children's books. He expressed his frustration to one of the other volunteers, who asked him what he really wanted to do in the library. Alan thought that working with the library's media collection might be interesting. Alan's volunteer friend suggested that he call the media specialist and meet with him.

After thinking about it, Alan decided he had nothing to lose so he made an appointment. The two men established an instant rapport. After checking with the volunteer coordinator, the specialist decided that Alan could work in the media department. After several months, Alan was making a significant contribution to the department. One day the media specialist and Alan started to brainstorm ideas to create a permanent job for Alan. They decided to explore writing a grant. They spoke with the grant writer associated with the library and discovered there were several grants they could apply for. After six months, the grant was submitted and the library received $250,000 to automate the media center. The library management was so impressed with Alan's initiative and abilities that they offered him a position.

1. What affirmations could Alan have used to realize his goal of working in the library? What affirmations could you use to realize your goals?

2. What skills, if any, did Alan have that made him a good candidate to volunteer in the library? (To help you answer this question, use the skills section in O*Net (http://online.onetcenter.org) to look up Alan's job title from his job at Sony.) Remember to look at soft skills as well as specific job skills.

3. How did networking help Alan pursue his goal? What networking opportunities do you have?

4. If Alan had not met the media specialist, what else could he have done to make his volunteer experience at the library more satisfying?

5. What affirmations would be effective in dealing with difficult work situations?

6. What affirmation could Alan have used when he first began working in the library?

7. Do you think Alan used visualization when he was looking for work after he left Sony?

8. Do you think Alan used visualization when he started working with the media specialist?

REAL STORIES

Companion Website

To answer these questions online, go to the *Real Stories* **module in Chapter 2 of the Companion Website.**

Self-discipline is a vital component of success. If you lack the discipline to complete a task or spend the hours needed to accomplish your immediate goal (e.g., to contact four potential employers, study for an important test), your long-term goals will not be accomplished. Each time we allow a task to go undone or a goal to go unaccomplished, we train ourselves to believe that it is okay, that there's always tomorrow. In the meantime, someone else is out there doing it. As is true of persistence and attitude, self-discipline is part of the foundation for success; it must be the basis of other strategies for success we have discussed.

I Demonstrate Emotional Intelligence

Our competitive and achievement-oriented society places great value on intellectual ability. Early in your life your parents and teachers probably tried to determine your IQ (intelligence quotient). The results of such tests are highly regarded, even though these tests are often judged to be inaccurate and incomplete. The results are often unreliable predictors of future success in life. Were you labeled an overachiever or under-achiever? Average or below average? Were you inspired by these labels— or did they cause you to lose motivation? We have all heard stories of high-IQ individuals who were not successful at chosen paths or who were unhappy in life. Conversely, many people with low to average "intelligence" have defied all predictions and become successful by any definition of the term. In fact, research on college grade point average as a predictor of success indicates the B to C student often enjoys more success in later life than the solid A performer! What explains this apparent paradox?

Research by Daniel Goleman, discussed in his books on emotional intelligence (1995, 2002), offers some answers. The common sense, wisdom, maturity, humor, and street smarts that distinguish successful individuals are the manifestation of emotional intelligence (EQ). The awareness of and ability to monitor and control our emotions, thoughts, and feelings and the ability to be aware of and sensitive to others define emotional intelligence. Complete Exercise 2.3 to test your own EQ. The better developed your EQ, the more successful you are likely to be. Although you are born with IQ, you can learn and cultivate EQ. It may be IQ that gets you the job, but it's EQ that keeps you employed and gets you promoted!

I Identify My Goals

People who succeed have clearly defined plans and objectives that they refer to regularly to keep in mind their lifetime goals, as well as to order their daily priorities. Clearly defined, written goals help move us to completion. The reason most people don't reach their goals is that they don't identify them. They don't know what they want. (See Chapter 8 for information on setting goals.)

If you don't know where you are going, you probably won't get there. Even though you're just embarking on your career fitness plan and you probably don't have a specific career in mind as yet, you can still begin the process of goal setting. Your *first goal* might be to read this book (one chapter a week) and complete all the exercises after each chapter with the intent of learning more about yourself so you can make appropriate career choices when the time comes. Ideally, you should set aside a specific time and place each week so that you will get into the habit of working on your career fitness plan in the same way that you would work on a physical fitness plan—with consistency and commitment.

I Am Self-Reliant and Career Resilient

In the face of events such as downsizing and rightsizing, successful employees must demonstrate self-reliance and resilience. These involve the ability to continually learn and develop new skills, initiate activities, demonstrate flexibility, and continuously align work with the business need. It is essential to ask constantly—and be able to answer—the question, "How does my work add value to the organization?" The question conveys a sense of commitment and a sense of loyalty to your current project. As the job tasks and business needs change, those who want to remain employed must be in a *continuous learning* mode. Simply doing a good job is no longer enough!

I Am Flexible

The world of work has never offered a greater array of choices and possibilities. A common response to this seemingly endless horn of plenty is to look desperately for the one right choice that will offer certainty and stability. Although it is an understandable response, it is unrealistic in our work life in the 21st century. Instead, we must cultivate a sense of comfort regarding the ambiguity, uncertainty, and change that challenge our every plan. We must learn to recognize and accept the fact that life happens as we're making plans.

The ability to appreciate and incorporate the unexpected twists and turns along the path is the secret to success in the new millennium. Rather than resisting change and the unexpected, learn to delight in the unpredictable.

What makes workers succeed . . .

Executives say these personality traits are most important in successful workers:

Enthusiasm 80.6%

"Can Do" Attitude 65.1%

High Energy 40.3%

Assertiveness 30.5%

Source: Data from Management Dimensions, Inc.; survey of 241 executives from all types of companies. Elys McLean-Ibrahim, *USA Today.*

THINK ABOUT IT

1. Why do you think more people ranked enthusiasm as the most important personality trait?

2. Of the four traits listed, which do you feel you express the most of and least of in a work-related environment? Are these the same traits you express most and least in your home life (not work-related)? If not, why do you think there is a difference?

3. Ask three people who have worked with you the same question. What did they say?

4. Do you see yourself as others see you? Why or why not?

5. Given this information, which of these traits should you try to express more often? How will you do this on a daily basis? (Hint: Write an affirmation.)

6. What is the difference between enthusiasm and high energy? Give examples.

7. What is the difference between a "can do" attitude and being assertive? Give examples.

Companion Website

To answer these questions online, go to the *Facts and Figures* module in Chapter 2 of the Companion Website.

Knowing what you want
is step number one

Cultivate the ability to incorporate new information quickly and adeptly into your current or emerging career plan. Challenge yourself not only to experience the unsettled feeling that comes with surprise but to think positively about the unanticipated possibilities that present themselves. Recognize that for every door that closes, a new door opens.

I Have Purpose

Successful people know that identifying their purposes and then acting "with purpose" is key to their sense of satisfaction and wellbeing. Living "on purpose" means that you are doing what you love and what you are good at and accomplishing what is important to you. A sense of purpose creates passion and enthusiasm. You attract the people, resources, and opportunities that move you toward your goals. Your ability to act in harmony with your purpose enables you to serve others easily and joyfully—which, in fact, is the ultimate aim of our lives. First Lady Laura Bush is dedicated to literacy and the love of reading. Her purpose is to instill this passion for reading in every child in the United States. She is clear and focused in her goal.

Identifying your purpose is one of the most enriching and rewarding insights that you can discover in life. To begin, you need to tap into your innermost self and gauge the amount of joy you experience from the activities that are currently part of your life. The more joy, the closer you are to your purpose. Part One of this book (Chapters 1 through 5) is designed specifically to help you become aware of your uniqueness so that you can decide on your major purpose in life and then organize your career and life goals around this purpose. The exercises in these chapters will help you clarify what you do or could do to gain the greatest sense of meaning, satisfaction, and self-worth.

I Have Passion

People who are passionate about life express an enthusiasm and zest for living that is noticeable and enviable. They are focused and committed to their purpose. Passion comes from loving what you are doing and wanting to do it whether or not you are paid. Ideally, you will find this kind of work through the purposeful career planning in which you are currently engaged. Outside of work, passionate people are doing what makes their heart and soul sing. They are in tune with their inner needs and find ways to express them. Oprah Winfrey is a prime example of an individual who has utilized her passion to reach her goals. There are people in all walks of life who exude a passion for their work and play. Can you think of three whom you know?

Passionate people understand their purpose, the "why" underneath whatever it is they are doing at the moment. They realize that some activities that might otherwise be viewed as "have to's" are simply steps along the way to their chosen passion. They view these tasks as choices, and their attitude about completing them is positive and purposeful. They have adjusted their attitudes to maximize their enjoyment and enthusiasm. Passionate people attract others who want to work with them, play with them, and support their goals. Think about the difference between a passionate teacher and a teacher who is not enthusiastic about teaching. What a difference in impact!

I Am Responsible

Responsible people assume personal accountability for their lives. They realize that they are in control of their thoughts, decisions, behaviors, and outcomes. After every important event, they analyze what went well and what could be done better next time, rather than blaming someone or something for their past or current situation. They are self-reliant and action oriented. They realize that time is their most precious resource, and they avoid procrastination, recognizing that immediate action is the most efficient way to handle most situations. Responsible individuals are always asking themselves, "What's the best use of my time right now?" and they use their purpose, passion, and goals to determine their priorities.

Responsible people know that life is a self-fulfilling prophecy, so they expect the best from every situation. They choose to respond to circumstances with a glass-half-full attitude rather than a negative, blameful, or victim-like mentality. As former U.S. President Harry S Truman said, "I studied the lives of great men and famous women, and I found that the men and women who got to the top were those who did the jobs they had in hand, with everything they had of energy and enthusiasm and hard work."

I Have Vision

Just as Martin Luther King said "I have a dream," so, too, do those who have a vision. This vision is a mental model of what currently is and what you want it to be. It is a detailed description of where you want to get to. For a balanced, successful life, your vision needs to address as many aspects of your life as possible. These include education, leisure, career, finances, health, relationships, personal and spiritual goals, and contributions to your community.

When you identify, describe, and stay focused on your vision, you will begin to encounter the people, resources, and circumstances that will bring you closer to your dream. It's important to think big, even if you are not at all certain how you will get there. Bill Gates dreams of a world where every home has a computer connected to the Internet. Lance Armstrong dreams of winning the Tour de France again and again. The world is filled with ordinary people who dream and live out extraordinary visions. Expect naysayers who will try to talk you out of your dreams. Recognize that they are coming from their own sense of limitations and move on.

Share your vision with people you trust. Even if your vision seems outrageous, you will encounter people who will offer to help make it a reality. They will make suggestions and introduce you to others who can support and nurture your vision. Most important, when you share your vision, you reinforce as well as clarify it, and you strengthen your belief that it can be achieved. At the start of his career, Jim Carrey, then a struggling actor, wrote himself a check for $10 million and promised himself that in 10 years he would be able to cash it. He framed it and looked at it daily, and sure enough, in 10 years he had sufficient funds to cash his "vision check."

Successful athletes prize and cherish their values of discipline, tenacity, and focus. Tiger Woods is just one example. President George Bush takes every opportunity to refer to his faith as a cherished and publicly affirmed value. Madonna openly refers to her study of the Kaballah, and Tom Cruise often discusses his belief in Scientology. For both Tom Cruise and Madonna, these beliefs were not part of their background but were chosen freely.

I Am an Innovator

Stephen M. Shapiro, author of *24/7 Innovation: A Blueprint for Striving and Thriving in an Age of Change*, states that if you want to separate yourself from the pack and become a valued player in our fiercely competitive 21st-century marketplace, work to develop your innovative ability. He distinguishes *invention*, which is discovering something totally new, from *innovation*, which is discovering a new way to add value. Not everyone is an inventor, but we all have the innate ability to innovate. Think about the many times when you have said to yourself, "I could do this better." That's the seed of innovation, and you must not only think about how to improve it but actually step up to the plate and do it.

Shapiro suggests that you can foster your innovative capacity by focusing on results and how your job contributes to reaching those goals, so that you begin to take responsibility not only for your job but for the larger outcomes and the best ways to achieve them. In essence, this requires adopting an entrepreneurial mind-set—the ability to act, think and feel like an owner so that you are constantly thinking about adding value, serving customers, improving operations, and exploiting new opportunities. Think of the reality TV show *The Apprentice*. The successful candidate is the individual who demonstrates this quality of innovation.

Career success is based not just on book learning but also on knowing yourself.

Summary

Career success is based on a knowledge of self. The more you understand and accept your uniqueness, the better able you will be to make appropriate life and career choices.

Programming yourself for success is the first step of your personal assessment program. As you cultivate and engage in each of the practices addressed in this chapter, you will raise and reinforce your self-esteem, the root of all success. *Your opinion of yourself will grow in proportion to the time and energy you give to developing your most valuable asset—yourself.*

PROGRAMMING YOURSELF FOR SUCCESS

PURPOSE OF EXERCISES. These exercises are designed to review your attitude and behavior. Try to answer the first set of questions as quickly and spontaneously as possible. Do not censor your answers. These are called *open-ended questions.* Open-ended questions sometimes make people think about different responses each time they see them, so it's all right to have more than one answer, as well as to change an answer whenever you review the questions. These questions will also cause you to review past actions so that you can better identify how they influence who you are today. Answer the questions in the rest of the exercises to reflect your ideal environment and how you see yourself.

Companion Website

To answer these questions online, go to the *Exercise* module in Chapter 2 of the Companion Website.

Past Actions and Influences 2.1

This review will help you apply the building blocks of self-esteem to your life and future career. Fill in each blank carefully and honestly. Be true to yourself; don't try to please anyone else with your answers.

1. I am proud that _____

2. One thing I can do now that I couldn't do a few years ago is _____

3. Name the person you most admire. This person can be living, historical, or fictional. Write down the specific characteristics that you admire in this person (using the qualities as described in the chapter).

4. Name a person who is like you, and describe this person using the qualities described in the chapter.

5. In the last two weeks, which activities gave you
   - the greatest feeling of being energized _____
   - the greatest feeling of importance _____
   - the greatest feeling of self-worth _____

6. What have you always wanted to do in your life? What's keeping you from doing it? What action could you take in the next year to get closer to this goal?

   _____
   _____
   _____

7. What negative habit have you successfully changed?

   _____
   _____

8. What three words would you like others to use in describing you?

   _____
   _____

2.2   *Two Perfect Days: Your Future Vision*

1. Written description

   In order to be clear about what you want in life, write a one-page description of two ideal days in your future. One day should be related to leisure, and one day should be related to work. Think about where you would be; what you'd be doing; who, if anyone, would be with you; and so on. Try to be as detailed as possible. Use Exercise 7.8 to help you think about the workday.

   Use this space for notes:

   _____
   _____
   _____
   _____
   _____

2. Summary in two or three words

   Write down three or more words or phrases that capture the *essence and quality* of each of these two days (e.g., peaceful, challenging, fun, harmonious, exciting, restful, productive).

Leisure day:

_____

_____

Workday:

_____

_____

Emotional Intelligence Checklist   2.3

Answer the following questions for a better idea of how your attitude is reflected in your actions. Consider asking several important people in your life to respond to these questions about you as well. Compare their answers with yours. Choose two or three areas that you think are important to work on to improve your attitude and emotional intelligence.

	I Am Satisfied	I Need to Improve
a. Do I always do my best?	○	○
b. Do I tend to look on the bright side of things?	○	○
c. Am I friendly and cooperative?	○	○
d. Am I prompt and dependable?	○	○
e. Do I do my share (or more than my share)?	○	○
f. Do I appear confident, poised?	○	○
g. Am I believable?	○	○
h. Do people ask my opinions?	○	○
i. Do I appear to be trustworthy?	○	○
j. Am I well-mannered, tactful, considerate of others?	○	○
k. Do I dress appropriately?	○	○
l. Do I put others before myself? To what extent?	○	○
m. Can I accept compliments?	○	○
n. Do I give compliments?	○	○
o. Do I make suggestions?	○	○
p. Can I say no?	○	○
q. Do I wait for others to decide for me?	○	○
r. Do I try to understand how others are feeling?	○	○
s. Do I control my negative emotions?	○	○

For an additional survey of your emotional intelligence, go to the Companion Website for Chapter 2 and click on *Weblinks*.

2.4   *Positive Self-Talk (Affirmations)*

1. Write six affirmations related to being successful in your career and life planning. Put them on 3 × 5 cards (one per card). Some examples:

   I am a confident and competent person.

   I have many transferable skills.

   I am a valuable employee.

   I am a risk taker.

   I am a skilled networker.

   I enjoy talking to people about their careers.

   a. _____

   b. _____

   c. _____

   d. _____

   e. _____

   f. _____

2. Read your affirmations to yourself two times during the day, once in the morning as you awake and once just before you go to sleep. Consider sharing your affirmations with a close friend or a classmate.

3. To accelerate their effectiveness, try the following suggestions:

   a. Write your affirmations in longhand while speaking them aloud to yourself 10, 20, or more times.

   b. Try writing in different persons, such as "I, Marilyn, am highly employable"; "You, Marilyn, are highly employable"; "She, Marilyn, is highly employable."

   c. Record your affirmations on a cassette tape recorder, and listen to them as you drive or while you do chores around the house.

   d. Before going to sleep at night or on arising in the morning, visualize yourself as the person you are becoming. For example, see yourself as more assertive, loving, social, enthusiastic.

   e. Chant or sing your affirmations aloud while driving or during any appropriate activity.

   f. Meditate on your affirmations.

   g. Tape them up around the house, on the telephone, on mirrors, on the refrigerator, on the ceiling above your bed, on the dashboard of your car, in your dresser drawers.

   h. Use affirmations as bookmarks.

4. Finally, ask yourself, "Is it what I really want?" George Bernard Shaw once commented, "The only thing worse than not getting what you want is getting what you want!" In other words, many go fishing all their lives, only to realize it wasn't the fish they wanted.

Your Fantasy Careers   **2.5**

"WOULDN'T IT BE GREAT TO BE . . . "

List your current fantasy careers below. Then think back chronologically to earlier age levels and try to recall some of your past fantasy careers; list them as well. We develop fantasy careers at a very young age. Most children see cartoons, television dramas, and movies about doctors, lawyers, police officers, firefighters, astronauts, teachers, and scientists, to name a few popular careers. Books about solving mysteries create an image of excitement about being a detective. Current movies influence many to dream of being a jet pilot or gifted performer. What have you read about, seen in the movies, or dreamed about doing?

1. For each career on your list, ask yourself this question: "What about this career is or was appealing to me?" Many of us might have the same fantasy career but for different reasons.

CURRENT FANTASY CAREER	WHAT ABOUT THIS CAREER APPEALS TO ME?
a.	
b.	
c.	
d.	

PAST FANTASY CAREERS, BY AGE	WHAT APPEALED MOST TO ME ABOUT THIS FANTASY CAREER?
1–10	
11–15	
16–20	
21–30	

31–40 _____

_____

_____

41–50 _____

_____

_____

51 PLUS _____

_____

_____

2. Now choose the one fantasy career that is most appealing. Try to locate someone who earns a living in this career. If you are part of a class, ask your instructor and classmates if they can refer you to someone. Otherwise, try to make a connection by asking people you know at school, work, and social gatherings. Read the section on information interviewing in Chapter 9. Arrange an interview, preferably in person, and ask the questions in the sample list of typical questions in Chapter 9 under Information Interviewing Outline.

2.6   *Making a Fantasy Real*

1. Find a newspaper or magazine article describing a job that seems like a fantasy job to you. Or find a story about a person you consider to be truly successful. (Remember, you have a right to your own definition of success.)

2. Summarize the features that make the job or the successful person interesting. What are the personality traits of the person holding the job? What adjectives best describe this person? (See Exercise 1.4.) How do these traits compare to your own personality traits?

_____

_____

_____

_____

_____

_____

_____

2.7   *Building Your Success Profile*

1. Review all of the affirmations in this chapter. Together, they comprise the formula for the success profile of the 21st century. Identify the six affirmations that are most true of you today (e.g., I have a sense of humor, I am persistent). Write them on the lines below. They are already part of your success profile.

MY TOP SIX SUCCESS FACTORS

(1) _____   (4) _____

(2) _____   (5) _____

(3) _____   (6) _____

2. Now, identify the three affirmations that are currently least like you. List them below. These are the three that are most likely to keep you from experiencing optimal success. Think about one action step you could take this week to develop these three areas.

THREE AREAS TO DEVELOP   **THREE ACTION STEPS TO TAKE**

(1) _____   (1) _____

(2) _____   (2) _____

(3) _____   (3) _____

Think About Enthusiasm   **2.8**

1. Give three examples of enthusiastic behavior in the workplace.

   _____

   _____

   _____

   _____

2. How can enthusiasm help a new employee? Is a "can do" attitude learned? If yes, how?

   _____

   _____

   _____

   _____

3. Give an example of an assertive behavior that can be misinterpreted.

   _____

   _____

   _____

   _____

4. Explain the difference between affirmation and visualization.

   _____

   _____

_____
_____
_____
_____
_____

2.9 *WWWebwise*

For additional activities, go to the WWWebwise module in Chapter 2 of the Companion Website.

2.10 *Exercise Summary*

1. What have I learned about myself? My purpose? My vision?

_____
_____

2. I want to improve the following:

_____
_____

3. I admire the following qualities in people:

_____
_____

4. My affirmations are as follows:

_____
_____
_____
_____

5. In the next two weeks, I can do the following to improve my self-confidence and
   build my success profile:

   _____

   _____

   _____

   _____

   _____

   _____

   _____

   _____

   _____

   _____

   _____

   _____

   *Go to page 220 of the chapter summaries and fill out the Chapter 2 exercise summary
   now.*

3

Values Clarification

Learning Objectives

At the end of the chapter you will be able to . . .

- Define and clarify your values

- Discuss how your values motivate you

- Describe how your values affect your career decisions

What is it that causes someone to study for years to enter a career such as medicine or law while others are looking for the quickest, easiest way to make money? What causes someone to switch careers midstream after spending years developing mastery and a reputation in a field? The answer to these questions is *values*. Your values are the often unidentified forces that guide and influence your decisions throughout your life. Values are *the deeply held convictions that influence your thinking when you are faced with choices.*

Destiny is not a matter of chance.

It is a matter of choice.

WILLIAM JENNINGS BRYAN

They provide you with a frame of reference for evaluating information and options. If you value fitness and good health, you make time for daily exercise, positive self-talk, and proper nutrition. If you value career satisfaction, you take time to examine your values and make choices consistent with them.

Defining Values

Values are the self-motivators that indicate what you consider most important in your life. Values are reflected in what you actually do with your time and your life. This chapter will help you identify what is needed in your work environment to make you feel satisfied with your job. You may discover that the reason you are dissatisfied with your present job is that it incorporates few of your values and interests.

From time to time it may be necessary to settle for a job just to pay the bills; in such circumstances you may feel empty, frustrated, and unfulfilled by the job. Once you learn how to identify your values, it will be natural for you to take them into account and make meaningful and satisfying decisions about jobs. In other words, your decisions can be based on what's really important to you. If you are determined to follow your chosen career path and stay committed to your values, you will find that even when times are tough, you will make every effort to stick to your long-range goal.

Clarifying Your Values

Now that you have begun to take charge of your mental attitude, identifying your values becomes the next step in your personal assessment program. By the age of 10, most of us have unconsciously adopted the values of our parents, teachers, and friends. By adolescence, we have begun to sort out which of these adopted values we want to freely choose as our own. This process of rejecting some of our family's

Your values should be reflected in your day-to-day choices as well as your long-term goals and actions.

values and developing our own is often called teenage rebellion. Parents, in particular, often take offense when we question or reject a value they believe important. In fact, however, this process of values clarification is an essential part of growing up. Mature, independent, successful individuals act on their own values rather than those of others. This frees them from unnecessary guilt ("What would my mother say if . . . ?") and indecision ("What would my boss do in this situation?"). It fosters satisfaction and self-confidence ("Regardless of the outcome, I'm in control of my life").

Adults often fail to reassess their values as life goes on. Research about life stages indicates that adults can and do make dramatic changes in their personal and career lives based on changes in values. This process of change can be less traumatic for all individuals involved if, as adults, we periodically review and reassess what is important to us.

How can you identify your values? The more intense your positive feelings are about some activity or social condition, the more you value it. Is there an issue currently in the news that excites you or makes you angry? Are there certain activities that energize you? Are there circumstances in your life that lead you to certain activities? All of these are indicators of your values.

More specifically, the following criteria will help you determine your values. Values that are alive and an active part of you have the following qualities:

Prized and cherished. When you cherish something, you exude enthusiasm and enjoyment about it. You are proud to display it and use it. Lance Armstrong is just one example of successful individuals who prize and cherish their values of discipline, tenacity, and focus.

Publicly affirmed. You are willing and perhaps even eager to state your values in public. President George Bush takes every opportunity to refer to his faith as a cherished and publicly affirmed value.

Chosen freely. No one else is pressuring you to act in a certain way. You own these values. They feel like a part of you. Madonna openly refers to her study of the Kaballah, and Tom Cruise often discusses his belief in Scientology, both of which were not a part of their backgrounds, but were chosen freely.

Chosen from alternatives. If given a choice to play a leading role in a Hollywood film or be provided with a full scholarship to study at Harvard Business School, which would you choose? Choosing to act in Hollywood highlights such values as creativity, prestige, glamour, monetary returns, and risk taking, whereas choosing to acquire a Harvard MBA suggests prestige, monetary returns, education, intellectual stimulation, and security.

Chosen after consideration of consequences. We usually consider the consequences before we make an important decision. What impressions come to mind when you consider the following scenarios?

- You have been offered a job at a firm across the country far from the place you've lived all your life.
- You are offered a well-paying job as a defense contractor in your town.
- You are presented with a dinner check that doesn't charge you for all the food ordered.

Meet Maria

Maria was the oldest of four siblings. Her parents owned a small mortgage brokerage company. Maria was an excellent student in high school, but her parents never encouraged her to or discouraged her from attending college. They felt that Maria would always be able to make a living no matter what. Before Maria graduated from high school, her counselor told her that she had a very good chance of getting a scholarship to attend college, but Maria never took advantage of the opportunity.

After graduation, she went to work in her parents' business and her life changed very little. Being a shy, quiet young woman, Maria usually let decisions happen to her, or she let others make them for her. One morning Maria awoke and she couldn't get out of bed. She felt very tired and had a bad headache. Her mother told her to see the doctor, who told her that she was probably starting to get the flu, but weeks went by and she was still feeling poorly.

One night Maria was having dinner with a friend and she started to cry. With some encouragement, Maria started to talk about how unhappy she was with her work and her life in general. Her friend suggested that she talk with a career counselor who might be able to help her look at career options. Not knowing how to find a career counselor, Maria decided to call her local community college. She discovered that she could meet with the counselor in the career center.

The counselor spent some time talking with Maria and together they felt it would be beneficial for Maria to take some assessments to examine her interests, personality preferences, values, and skills. The tests revealed a pattern of interests that were very different from the type of work Maria was doing and a value system that supported a strong moral code, creativity, and self-expression. After several appointments with the counselor, Maria began to understand why she was so unhappy.

REAL STORIES

The counselor suggested that Maria develop some goals and objectives to help her move from her current situation. She also suggested that Maria speak with her parents to help them understand her feelings. A year later, Maria had made some specific changes in her life. She enrolled in college and discovered that she was really interested in psychology. Because she was still very close to her parents, she kept her job, but with school and more social activities, she felt that she had some balance in her life.

WHAT DO YOU THINK?

1. Do you think Maria was unhappy with her job because it didn't satisfy her values or her interests or both? Why?

2. Do you think values are more important than interests when it comes to making career decisions? Why or why not?

3. Do you think Maria had problems with decision making? Why?

4. What are some of the signs that indicate you have made a poor decision?

5. What values are most critical to your career satisfaction right now?

6. To what extent does your current job or lifestyle support your most critical values?

7. Can you recall a recent decision that you've made that supported these values?

8. How easy was it to make that decision? Were you aware of the role that your values played?

Companion Website

To answer these questions online, go to the *Real Stories* module in Chapter 3 of the Companion Website.

What values come into play as you think about the decisions involved and their possible consequences?

Acted on. Again, values are reflected in what you do with your time and your life; they are more than wishful thinking or romantic ideals about how you *should* lead your life.

Acted on repeatedly and consistently, forming a definite pattern. The premise here is that you repeatedly engage in activities that relate to your highest values. To identify specific examples for yourself, complete the Values Grid in Exercise 3.1 at the end of this chapter. List five aspirations or goals you have achieved in your lifetime (e.g., finished high school, was member of debate team, planned a surprise party, found a job), and then check the values that were involved in each goal. When you're done, the values with the most checks are those most important to you.

As you begin to think about it, you will come to realize how much you rely on your values to make decisions. People facing career planning often wonder how they will ever choose a career when they have so many possibilities in mind. This is precisely the time when knowing your values is most important. Let's say you've discovered that economic return, helping others, and security are your top three values. You are thinking about becoming an artist, an actor, or a speech teacher. You might well be able to do all three, even simultaneously! However, in order to choose one direction, try deciding which career would best satisfy your top three values. You are likely to experience the most success and happiness from this kind of choice. In this case, speech teacher most closely incorporates the values mentioned.

Needs and Motivators

So far we have discussed motivation based on successful personal attitudes and values. In addition, inner drives or needs also influence how you choose a career. People experience psychological discomfort when their needs are unmet. We best satisfy our needs by identifying them and then engaging in behaviors that meet them. Once our needs are met, tension and discomfort are reduced. You may have read about five primary types of needs as identified by Abraham Maslow (1987), a famous psychologist.

These needs progress from the most basic and biologically oriented (survival needs) to more complex and socially oriented levels of needs. When people are preoccupied with finding ways to put food on the table (physiological needs), they have little time or desire to work on developing relationships or to search for a job that can utilize their talents. Rather, they tend to work at any job that will immediately bring in money. A person becomes aware of a higher-order need only when a lower-order need has been met. These basic needs are such primary and intense self-motivators that our *values* may be eclipsed when we are struggling to meet primary *needs*.

One example of changing needs often occurs among divorcing couples with children. Most newly single parents have to readjust from the shared

FACTS & FIGURES

Life balance

In a survey (PriceWaterhouseCoopers, 2000) of graduating business students from 11 countries, 57 percent said that balancing work and personal life is their top career goal.

According to *Working Mother* (2006), companies are starting to pay attention to individuals who say they intend to put family ahead of work. The most progressive corporations are striving to let men and women work flexible schedules, take time off after the birth of a child, and go home at a normal hour, without fear of job loss. When surveyed, nearly 80 percent of men and women ages 24 to 34 said that time with family was more important than earning a higher salary.

THINK ABOUT IT

1. How would you rate work versus leisure?

2. If you were continually asked to sacrifice your leisure time to ensure job promotion in the future, would you find this an acceptable arrangement? Why or why not?

3. Do you think this survey would hold up in a difficult economic period when it is hard to find a good job? What makes the concept of balance in one's life so compelling?

4. Would you be willing to earn less income and work fewer hours for the opportunity to pursue balance in your life?

To answer these questions online, go to the *Facts and Figures* module in Chapter 3 of the Companion Website.

Companion Website

responsibilities of a two-parent family and the greater financial security of a two-person income. For some, the reduction in income and addition of responsibilities may be so great that the individual returns to a focus on meeting survival needs such as securing food and shelter. If parents in this situation are out of work, they will likely be far less concerned about having the perfect job than with simply finding a job. As we discussed earlier, however, people should certainly take their values into account in career decisions whenever possible.

It is also important to assess needs from a cultural perspective and to realize that individuals may function and see things differently, depending on the cultural context. For example, recent immigrants need time to adapt or adjust to a new environment. Even if their survival needs for food, clothing, and shelter are met in the new culture, their lack of familiarity with local customs and their homesickness for familiar people and customs may diminish their sense of security, psychological well-being, and competence, as outlined by Maslow.

When your ability to meet your physiological and safety needs is stable, you may find that you demand more feedback (satisfaction of social needs) in your work environment. Renowned industrial psychologist Frederick Herzberg (1966) examined the factors that produce or contribute to job satisfaction for most workers. We have already discussed how a job that reflects your top values contributes to job satisfaction. Herzberg found that we have both external motivators and internal motivators. External motivators include salary, working conditions, company policies, and possibility for advancement, elements that fulfill physiological and safety needs. However, internal motivators involving amount of responsibility, type of work accomplished, recognition, and achievement also all contribute to job satisfaction. These motivators appear to be most important for people with values and needs related to status and self-actualization. People do not necessarily respond to each need with identical intensities of desire. For your own benefit, it would be useful to examine what brings you satisfaction on the job. Look at Exhibit 3.1 to see how Herzberg's research on job satisfaction overlaps with Maslow's identification of needs.

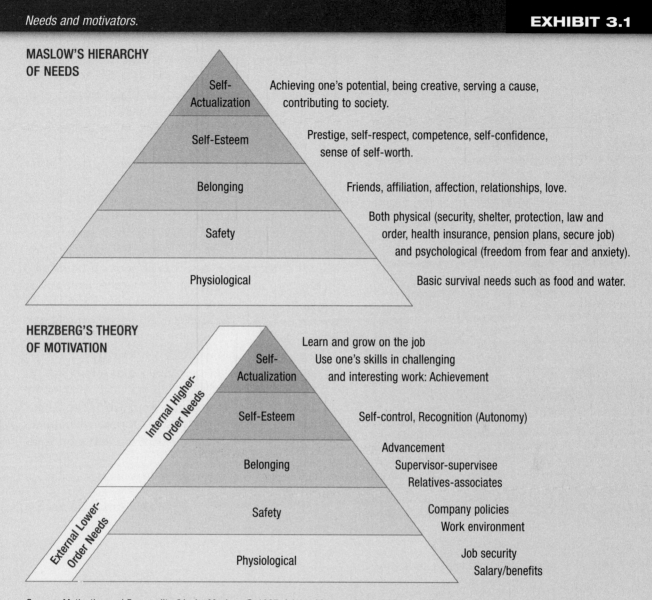

EXHIBIT 3.1

Needs and motivators.

MASLOW'S HIERARCHY OF NEEDS

Self-Actualization — Achieving one's potential, being creative, serving a cause, contributing to society.

Self-Esteem — Prestige, self-respect, competence, self-confidence, sense of self-worth.

Belonging — Friends, affiliation, affection, relationships, love.

Safety — Both physical (security, shelter, protection, law and order, health insurance, pension plans, secure job) and psychological (freedom from fear and anxiety).

Physiological — Basic survival needs such as food and water.

HERZBERG'S THEORY OF MOTIVATION

Internal Higher-Order Needs

External Lower-Order Needs

Self-Actualization — Learn and grow on the job. Use one's skills in challenging and interesting work: Achievement

Self-Esteem — Self-control, Recognition (Autonomy)

Belonging — Advancement, Supervisor-supervisee, Relatives-associates

Safety — Company policies, Work environment

Physiological — Job security, Salary/benefits

Source: *Motivation and Personality*, 3/e, by Maslow, © 1997. Adapted by permission of Pearson Education, Inc., Upper Saddle River, NJ.

Finding Balance

Balance is the ability to include all your top priorities and values in your career and life plan. Some people who live to work (*workaholics*) and claim to be happy may not experience balance.

In today's challenging economic environment, it may seem more difficult than ever to consider your values, interests, and overall happiness when making career decisions. Nevertheless, as you learn more about what makes you happy and successful, you are indeed more likely to take all factors into account when choosing schooling or training and when making job and career decisions, even in tough economic times.

Job satisfaction: internal vs. external motivators

Achieving long-term happiness involves living a balanced life in which you seek to satisfy both personal and professional concerns.

Role of Leisure

At one time, an employee who diligently honored family obligations and pursued leisure and other nonwork activities may have been considered uncommitted. The workplace now, however, acknowledges and even often encourages these pursuits. A satisfied, balanced individual is likely in the long run to be a more productive employee. Leisure activities allow individuals to let go, be spontaneous, and nurture their creativity, self-expression, and personal growth. All these qualities enhance performance on the job and counteract the negative effects of stress in many work situations. (In addition, many people have turned leisure pursuits into careers. Consider Mrs. Fields and her cookies or Tiger Woods and his golf.) The more an individual can balance the demands of family, work, and personal leisure, the better he or she can embrace the inevitable changes that challenge us daily.

Even in these challenging economic times, today's workers place a higher premium on leisure and family than in the past. Despite evidence that some employees are working longer hours to make up for corporate downsizing, employees today, when given the choice, typically place greater emphasis on finding quality time for family and outside interests than on increasing their wages by working extended hours.

Summary

In Chapters 2 and 3, we discussed several types of forces that propel you to act on your goals: attitudes, values, and needs. In Chapter 4 you will learn more about your specific interests and personality type and how these can and should affect your career decisions.

SUCCESS STRATEGIES

True Values

To help you identify your true values:

1. Think about 10 decisions you've made this week. Consider how you spent your money and your time; what you watched on TV; what you surfed on the Web; what you read; and with whom you spent time.

2. As you review your choices, observe the patterns that emerge.

3. Begin to compare what you say your values are with what you actually choose.

4. Reflect on any differences that may surface as you do your comparison.

5. Consider adjusting your decisions to reflect your values more closely, or reevaluate what you thought were your values and identify those that do reflect your decisions.

6. This process of values clarification will help you identify your true values so that you can make wise career choices that are consistent with those values. This will confirm who you are and give you a deeper sense of satisfaction when you act on your true values.

FACTS & FIGURES

Juggling Act

During the past five years, 48 percent of Americans say they have voluntarily downsized their work schedules (and salaries) to lead a more balanced life, reports the Center for a New American Dream in Takoma Park, Maryland (Self.com, Nov. 2004). Maybe less really *is* more.

PURPOSE OF EXERCISES. The following exercises will help you identify your own values. As you complete the exercises, look for the values that occur repeatedly in your answers. By the end of the exercises you will have identified the five values that come up most often. These are your primary work values. Note them in Exercise 3.5.

Exercise 3.1 is the Values Grid. It will demonstrate how activities that you consider accomplishments or aspirations reflect your values. It also shows how your highest values recur and are implemented repeatedly in a variety of activities. Exercise 3.2 seeks to clarify what is important to you in all aspects of your life, from hobbies to work environments. The job descriptions are actually general descriptions of both jobs and values. Try guessing the name of the value and job described. The answers can be found on page 68. Exercise 3.3 asks you to rank your values in the order of importance in four different situations. Often, in our careers and in life, we must give up something desirable to get something *more* desirable. Exercise 3.4 asks you to reflect on your needs and values. Exercise 3.5 asks you to examine what you say you want to do in your life. If you haven't taken any action to get what you want, your goals need to be reevaluated. The premise is that what is really valued serves as a driving force that motivates you to take action. Exercise 3.6 asks you to identify the types of careers that would utilize the values you hold dear. Exercise 3.7 explores the relationship between values and ethics.

Companion Website

To answer these questions online, go to the *Exercise* module in Chapter 3 of the Companion Website.

3.1   *Values Grid*

1. Fill out the Values Grid on the following page. After you have completed the grid, respond to the questions in parts 2 and 3 below.

2. List your top five values. (1 is the value that received the greatest number of checks.)

   (1) _____   (4) _____

   (2) _____   (5) _____

   (3) _____

3. Using the Values Grid on the following page and the list of values on page 68, identify the five jobs that best express your values, then the five that least express your values.

   BEST EXPRESS VALUES   **LEAST EXPRESS VALUES**

   (1) _____   (1) _____

   (2) _____   (2) _____

   (3) _____   (3) _____

   (4) _____   (4) _____

   (5) _____   (5) _____

Values Grid

Above the numbers 1 through 5, list five accomplishments you have achieved anytime throughout your life. Use only a key word or two to represent the accomplishment. (If you wish, use the space on the following page to describe your accomplishments in more detail.) Check the values that were involved in each accomplishment. Then add up the number of checks for each value and write this number in the last column.

Value	Definition	Accomplishments					Total checks
		1	2	3	4	5	
accomplishment	knowing you've done well						
advancement	moving up						
aesthetics	caring about beauty and harmony						
cooperation	living in harmony with others						
creativity	developing new ideas or things						
economic return	working at a job that pays well						
education	appreciating learning						
family	caring about parents, children, and relatives						
freedom	having free choice of thoughts and actions						
health	feeling emotional/physical/spiritual well-being						
helping others	being of service to people						
independence	planning your own schedule						
integrity	displaying behavior consistent with beliefs						
loyalty	showing devotion to someone or something						
management	planning and supervising work						
pleasure	seeking enjoyment or gratification						
power	having influence and the ability to act on it						
prestige	becoming well-known and respected						
recognition	gaining respect and admiration						
security	being certain of something						
teamwork	working together productively						

If you wish, describe your accomplishments 1 through 5 in more detail here:

1. _____

2. _____

3. _____

4. _____

5. _____

3.2   *Explore Your Values*

1. List five things you love to do. What values are reflected in these activities?
   (See Exercise 3.1, Values Grid, for ideas.)

   _____

   _____

   _____

   _____

2. What is one thing you would change in the world?
   In your town?
   About yourself?

   _____

   _____

3. What is something you really want to learn before you die?

   _____

4. List several values that are most important to you in your job (e.g., independence,
   creativity, working outdoors):

   _____

   _____

5. Work environments are people environments. Some people add to your energy,
   productivity, and self-esteem; others drain you. Think of three people and
   describe their influence on you:

   _____

   _____

   _____

6. If you had unlimited funds so that you would not have to work:

   a. How would you spend your time? (Try to think beyond a summer vacation;
      envision a daily lifestyle.)

   _____

   _____

   b. To what charities or causes would you contribute?

   _____

   _____

Job Descriptions

From the list of 15 job descriptions that follow, choose the three you find most interesting as career possibilities. Then list the values each of those job descriptions implies. Some possible answers appear on page 68.

1. _____

   _____

2. _____

   _____

3. _____

   _____

○ 1. An opportunity to help people in a personal way. Meet and deal with the public in a meaningful relationship. Help to make the world a better place to live. Pay and benefits in accordance with experience.

○ 2. Do your own thing! Work with abstract ideas. Develop new ideas and things. Nonroutine. A chance to work on your own or as a member of a creative team. Flexible working conditions.

○ 3. A professional position. Position of responsibility. Secretarial assistance provided. Pay dependent on experience and initiative. Position requires a high level of education and training. Job benefits are high pay and public recognition.

○ 4. A job with a guaranteed annual salary in a permanent position with a secure, stable company. Supervisory assistance is available. Minimum educational requirement is high school. Slightly better pay with one or two years of college or vocational training. Position guarantees cost-of-living pay increases annually. Retirement benefits.

○ 5. Looking for an interesting job? One that requires research, thinking, and problem solving? Do you like to deal with theoretical concepts? This job demands constant updating of information and ability to deal with new ideas. An opportunity to work with creative and intellectually stimulating people.

○ 6. This job requires an extraordinary person. The job demands risk and daring. Ability to deal with exciting tasks. Excellent physical health a necessity. You must be willing to travel.

○ 7. An ideal place to work. An opportunity to work with people you really like and—just as important—who really like you. A friendly, congenial atmosphere. Get to know your coworkers as friends. Pay and benefits dependent on training and experience.

○ 8. Work in a young, fast-growing company. Great opportunities for advancement. Starting pay is low, but rapid promotion to midmanagement. From this position, there are many opportunities and directions for further advancement. Your only limitations are your own energy and initiative. Pay and benefits related to level of responsibility.

○ 9. Set your own pace! Set your own working conditions. Flexible hours. Choose your own team or work alone. Salary based on your own initiative and time on the job.

○ 10. Start at the bottom and work your way up. You can become president of the firm. You should have the ability to learn while you work. Quality and productivity will be rewarded by rapid advancement and recognition for a job well done. Salary contingent on rate of advancement.

○ 11. Ability to direct work tasks of others in a variety of activities. Leadership qualities in controlling workforce and maintaining production schedules. Ability to maintain a stable workforce. Coordinate work of large management team. Instruct workforce. Evaluate work completed. Hiring and firing responsibilities.

○ 12. Great opportunity for money! High salary, elaborate expense accounts, stock options, extra pay for extra work. Christmas bonus. All fringe benefits paid by company. High pay for the work you do.

○ 13. Are you tired of a dull, routine job? Try your hand at many tasks, meet new people, work in different situations and settings. Be a jack-of-all-trades.

○ 14. Does the thought of a desk job turn you off? This job requires brisk and lively movement and is for the active person who enjoys using energy and physical abilities.

○ 15. Opportunity to express your personal convictions in all phases of your job. Devote your lifestyle to your work.

3.3   *Your Values—Some Hard Choices*

In this exercise you are asked to choose the best and worst among sets of options, all of which are more or less undesirable. Rank the situations and individuals, however unpleasant, that you could best and most easily accept as number 1, and the worst bad case, the situations you would find hardest to accept, as number 5, with the intervening cases ranked accordingly.

JOB SITUATIONS

_____ To work for a boss who knows less than you do about your work and over whom you have no influence.

_____ To be the key person in a job while someone else gets better pay and all the credit for what you do.

_____ To work with a group in which trust is very low.

_____ To work in an organization whose job is to serve the poor but which wastes huge amounts of its resources on red tape.

_____ To work day to day with someone who is always putting in second-rate work.

ENVIRONMENT

_____ The desert (120 degrees F) with a well-paying job.

_____ A small subsistence-level farm in Appalachia.

_____ An efficiency apartment in New York on a tight budget.

_____ A congested, smoggy urban area that is a short walk to work from your comfortable low-rent apartment.

_____ A middle-income suburban housing development, with an hour commute (one way) that is totally dependent on a freeway route.

RISKS

_____ Bet $10,000 on a gambling wager.

_____ Put $10,000 into a new and uncertain business venture.

_____ Go into business for yourself, with minimum resources.

_____ Without an assured job, move to a place where you always wanted to live.

_____ Risk arrest in a public demonstration for something about which you feel strongly.

Reflective Questions   3.4

1. Which of the needs outlined by Maslow are currently being met by your job? By your lifestyle?

   _____

   _____

2. Think of several family members. Which of Maslow's needs do you think are being met by their jobs?

   _____

   _____

3. When someone is suddenly laid off or fired from a job, what happens to this person's needs? What becomes foremost in his or her mind?

   _____

   _____

4. How do world events such as the terrorist attacks on September 11, 2001, or the tsunami of December 26, 2004, affect your values? Those of your family and friends?

   _____

   _____

3.5 Top Five

List five things you want in life. Examine each of these to see what is most important to you. What have you done to support or express these values? What actions have you taken or do you need to take to move toward what you most want in life? The difference between what you say is important and what you are actually willing to do deserves close examination.

1. _____
2. _____
3. _____
4. _____
5. _____

3.6 Values Related to Careers

List below your top five values and three job descriptions (from Exercise 3.2) that you believe would allow you to fulfill many of those values. For example, creativity, variety, money, and independence might all be associated with a career as a lawyer, writer, or sales representative. Which job description best describes your values? What job title would you give to this job description?

VALUES

1. _____
2. _____
3. _____
4. _____
5. _____

JOB DESCRIPTIONS

1. _____
2. _____
3. _____
4. _____
5. _____

Values Related to Ethics **3.7**

1. In a class or group setting, discuss how values affect ethical behavior. Consider current events and prominent figures in the worlds of

athletics	entertainment	military
business	government	science
education	law enforcement	

2. Choose one example from a newspaper or magazine article, and explain how you would act if you were in the same situation—for example, an athlete takes steroids to be competitive. What values are reflected in your actions?

_____

_____

_____

_____

_____

_____

_____

WWWebwise **3.8**

For additional activities online, go to the WWWebwise module in Chapter 3 of the Companion Website.

Exercise Summary **3.9**

1. List the values that are most frequently reflected in your answers to this chapter's exercises.

a. _____

b. _____

c. _____

d. _____

e. _____

2. Rank the values listed above, from most important to least important.

a. _____

b. _____

c. _____

d. _____

e. _____

3. List the top values that could most likely be satisfied by a future career.

_____

_____

_____

4. What I have learned from reading and answering the exercises:

_____

_____

_____

5. I feel _____ after completing this chapter (e.g., more aware, confused, satisfied).

6. I am energized by the following types of activities (use Values Grid, past jobs, or hobbies):

a. _____

b. _____

c. _____

d. _____

e. _____

JOB DESCRIPTION ANSWERS (FOR EXERCISE 3.2)

Job Number	Value	Job Title (examples)
1	Helping others	Social worker, teacher, counselor
2	Creativity	Writer, artist, graphic designer
3	Prestige	Executive, politician, doctor, police officer
4	Security	Education administrator, administrative assistant
5	Intellect	Researcher, mathematician, scientist
6	Adventure	Archaeologist, CIA investigator, firefighter
7	Association	Educator, restaurant worker, tour guide
8	Advancement	Assistant sales manager, engineer
9	Independence	Landscape artist, contract worker, marketing representative
10	Productivity	Sales representative, clerk, bookkeeper

11	Power	Manager, team leader, company president, coach
12	Money	Stockbroker, accountant, real estate developer
13	Variety	Electrician, plumber, lawyer, freelance editor
14	Physical activity	Game warden, physical trainer, physical education teacher
15	Lifestyle	Minister, guidance counselor, consultant

Go to page 221 of the chapter summaries and fill out the Chapter 3 exercise summary now.

4

Focusing on You:
Personality and Interests

Learning Objectives

At the end of the chapter you will be able to . . .

- List differences in personality types

- Explain your own personality type

- Recognize how personality type relates to career planning

- Identify college majors that interest you

- Match your interests to occupations, using the Worker
  Trait Groups and other inventories

The more you know about your natural tendencies and preferences, the easier
It will be for you to identify a career path that enables you to maximize what
comes naturally. If you take your personality and interests into account when

I am a great believer in luck, and I find
that the harder I work, the more I have of it.

THOMAS JEFFERSON

starting down your career path, you are much more likely to enjoy your work and be fulfilled by it.

Many of us dismiss the notion that we can have careers based on who we are and what we like to do. Somewhere along the line, we lose track of early dreams inspired by our true selves and begin focusing on more practical matters: What degrees are offered and what classes are needed? What occupation offers security and good pay? In many cases, we might have been able to explore careers much more closely aligned with our interests than we thought possible. For example, a young man who loves baseball might not enjoy the many hours of practice needed to become a professional ballplayer and might abandon the field altogether. Yet he might be able to pursue a career related to his interests, perhaps as an athletic trainer for a team, a facility manager at a ballpark, or a park recreation leader. These careers might be more congruous with his personality and interests than that of ballplayer or a completely unrelated position.

This chapter will help you explore some aspects of your own personality and interests. You will learn how to interpret this knowledge and apply it to your career decisions. Perhaps you will identify a career path you hadn't considered before, based on who you are and what you really like to do.

Exploring Personality

Have you ever said to a friend, "That's not like you"? Has anyone ever said to you, "You're not acting like yourself today"? These are common ways for us to talk about the complex set of tendencies, behaviors, attitudes, and characteristics that makes each of us unique. The sum total of these qualities is called your *personality*.

The more you know about yourself and your personal preferences, the better able you will be to identify work and outside activities that complement your personality type. Several different assessment instruments are available to help you learn about yourself. Like the following activity, some of these instruments are based on the work of noted Swiss psychologist Carl Jung (1923), who developed a way to help us understand and categorize our inborn tendencies. Katherine Briggs and Isabel Briggs Myers (1962) later expanded on Jung's theory to develop an assessment tool that helps identify personality preferences. This widely used survey is called the Myers–Briggs Type Indicator® instrument (MBTI).* It might be possible for you to arrange through your instructor or career center to take this or some other survey to learn more about your personality type than is possible here.

The following activity is not intended to give you an exact description of your personality, nor to indicate that a certain personality fits exactly within a certain career. In fact, there is debate about the extent to which personality relates to career choice or satisfaction. Instead, this discussion and the accompanying exercise are intended to make you aware of some characteristics of your personality and give you some insight into what types of interactions and activities might be more comfortable and satisfying for you than others.

The information you gain about your personality can help you make practical decisions about the types of classes to take and the career you pursue. Career success is based on a knowledge of self. The more you know, understand, and accept your unique self, the better able you will be to make appropriate life and career choices. Learning about personality will also make you better able to understand and accept differences in others.

Next, identify your personal preferences from the four parts in the following activity.

The more you learn about yourself, the better able you'll be to choose work that complements your personality type and that you enjoy.

*MBTI, Myers-Briggs, and Myers-Briggs Type Indicator are trademarks or registered trademarks of the Myers-Briggs Type Indicator Trust in the United States and other countries.

ACTIVITY *Identifying Your Personal Preferences*

The work of Jung, Myers, and Briggs provides us with a four-part framework in which to examine our inborn tendencies; thus, the following exercise consists of four parts. In each part, you will determine which of two characteristics or preferences better describes you. Briefly, in Parts 1 through 4 you will select items that indicate personality tendencies toward (1) extraversion or introversion; (2) sensing or intuition; (3) thinking or feeling; and (4) judging or perceiving. Each of these characteristics will be explained below.

Instructions: Read the following pairs of descriptions and check the item in each pair that is like you *most of the time.* (All of us have aspects of all of these qualities to some degree.)* To help you decide, think of your most natural self, your behavior if no one were looking.

PART 1. In describing your *flow of energy,* which pattern more closely resembles you, E or I?

E	I
○ Likes action and variety	○ Likes quiet and time to consider things
○ Likes to do mental work by talking to people	○ Likes to do mental work privately before talking
○ Acts quickly, sometimes without much reflection	○ May be slow to try something without understanding it first
○ Likes to see how other people do a job, and to see results	○ Likes to understand the idea of a job and to work alone or with just a few people
○ Wants to know what other people expect of him or her	○ Wants to set his or her own standards

E's interest turns mostly outward to the world of action, people, and things. I's interest turns more often to the inner world of ideas and personal concerns. Of course, everyone turns outward to act and inward to reflect. You too must do both, but you are more comfortable doing one or the other and rely on one more often than the other, just as right-handers are more comfortable using their right hands.

E stands for Extraversion, which means outward turning.

I stands for Introversion, which means inward turning.

---

*The checklists in this exercise are adapted from *People Types and Tiger Stripes: A Practical Guide to Learning Styles,* 3rd edition, by Dr. Gordon Lawrence, Center for Applications of Psychological Type, Gainesville, FL, 1993. This exercise is not a type indicator, nor does it replicate the Myers–Briggs Type Indicator® instrument, which is a validated instrument. MBTI, Myers-Briggs, and Myers-Briggs Type Indicator are trademarks or registered trademarks of the Myers-Briggs Type Indicator Trust in the United States and other countries. Parts of this exercise are also based on an exercise in *Building Self-Esteem: Strategies for Success in School and Beyond,* 2nd edition, 1997, by Bonnie Golden and Kay Lesh (Upper Saddle River, NJ: Prentice Hall).

SAMPLE EXTRAVERSION TYPE

Jesse is a computer consultant. He thrives on attending meetings at which several people at a company explain their computer needs, and he loves providing training for clients on their upgraded systems. His hobbies include attending conferences and serving as a Boy Scout leader for his son's troop, which he has also taken on weekend outings. Jesse gets energy from being around groups of people.

SAMPLE INTROVERSION TYPE

Jennifer is a computer consultant. She works in computer systems design. She meets individually with a company's computer networking specialist who provides her with a list of company needs; then she manipulates the company's system until it is operating as requested. She lets others train the staff. Jennifer gets her energy from working intensively with a technical system. She also gets recharged by spending time alone. Her hobbies include reading and exploring new ways of learning through the Internet and other distance-learning programs.

PART 2. In describing the ways in which you *take in information*, which pattern resembles you more closely, S or N?

S	N
○ Pays most attention to experience as it is	○ Pays most attention to the meanings of facts and how they fit together
○ Likes to use eyes, ears, and other senses to find out things	○ Likes to use imagination to come up with new ways to do things, new possibilities
○ Dislikes new problems unless there are standard ways to solve them	○ Likes solving new problems, and dislikes doing the same thing over and over
○ Enjoys using skills already learned more than learning new ones	○ Likes using new skills more than practicing old ones
○ Is patient with details but impatient when the situation gets complicated	○ Is impatient with details but doesn't mind complicated situations

S and N represent two kinds of perception, that is, two ways of finding out or giving attention to experiences. Everyone uses both sensing and intuition, but we are likely to use one more than the other. S pays most attention to the facts that come from personal experience. S can more easily see the details, while N can more easily see the big picture. N pays most attention to meanings behind the facts.

S stands for Sensing.

N stands for iNtuition.

SAMPLE SENSING TYPE

Georgette has a good memory for numbers and has been a bookkeeper at a car dealership for several years. One day, she commented to her boss that spoilers and

SAMPLE INTUITIVE TYPE

Santos is a freelance writer and teaches scriptwriting at a community college. He uses his creative and real-life experiences to assist others in creating scripts for

dash covers were selling well. Upon reviewing the sales figures, the boss confirmed Georgette's observations and promoted her to work with inventory management. The boss found it helpful that Georgette enjoyed keeping track of materials.

independent producers. He often gets ideas while daydreaming or exercising at the gym. Santos keeps a journal in his car to jot down his thoughts, and he teaches others how to keep track of their ideas for writing assignments.

PART 3. In describing your ways of *making decisions*, which pattern resembles you more closely, T or F?

T	F
○ Likes to decide things logically	○ Likes to decide things with personal feelings and human values, even if they aren't logical
○ Wants to be treated with justice and fair play	○ Likes praise, and likes to please people, even in unimportant things
○ May neglect and hurt other people's feelings without knowing it	○ Is aware of other people's feelings
○ Gives more attention to ideas or things than to human relationships	○ Can predict how others will feel
○ Doesn't need harmony	○ Gets upset by arguments and conflicts; values harmony

T makes decisions by examining data, staying less personally involved with the decision. F makes decisions by paying attention to personal values and feelings. Each of us uses both T and F judgments every day, but we tend to use one kind of judgment more than the other.

T stands for Thinking judgment.
F stands for Feeling judgment.

SAMPLE THINKING TYPE

Malcolm is a student trying to decide if he wants to major in business. He is basing his decision on the facts that he has collected: he has talked to a college counselor, researched his interests in the career center, taken classes related to business, and visited workplaces that hire people with such majors. He has even investigated graduate degrees related to the types of business specialties that employers have suggested they need.

SAMPLE FEELING TYPE

Shareen has always wanted to be a model but was influenced by her husband and adult children to get a college degree. She stays in shape and is taking modeling classes in the community while also attending college full-time. After meeting with a college counselor, she's decided that majoring in fashion merchandising will allow her to study something related to her ideal job as well as please her family.

PART 4. In describing your day-to-day lifestyle, which pattern resembles you more closely, J or P?

J	P
○ Likes to have a plan, to have things settled and decided in advance	○ Likes to stay flexible and avoid fixed plans
○ Tries to make things come out the way they "ought to be"	○ Deals easily with unplanned and unexpected happenings
○ Likes to finish one project before starting another	○ Likes to start many projects but may have trouble finishing them
○ Usually has mind made up about situations, people	○ Usually looks for additional information about situations, people
○ May decide things too quickly	○ May decide things too slowly
○ Wants to be right in forming opinions, making decisions	○ Wants to miss nothing before forming opinions, making decisions
○ Lives by standards and schedules that are not easily changed	○ Lives by making changes to deal with problems as they come along

J people show to others their thinking or feeling judgment more easily than they show their sensing and intuitive perception. The opposite is true of P people; they show their sensing or intuition rather than judgment in dealing with the world outside themselves.

J stands for Judgment.
P stands for Perception.

SAMPLE JUDGING TYPE

Chan is a film editor. He has a computerized appointment calendar programmed with alarm beeps to remind him about important dates. All of his clients know that when he makes a deadline to finish a project, the project will be delivered on time. He lets nothing interrupt his plans. Rush jobs, given to his department by higher-level management, drive him crazy; he doesn't want to start a new project before he finishes his current obligations.

SAMPLE PERCEIVING TYPE

Sarla is also a film editor. Some colleagues think that Sarla is scattered. She works on several projects at the same time. Even though her office is a mess, she seems to be able to find the tapes, telephone numbers, and accessories she needs. She often takes on new assignments before she is finished with old ones because she doesn't want to miss out. She gets irritated when her supervisor reminds her that a project should have been completed yesterday and tends to get projects done just in time.

Reviewing each of the four areas, which do you resemble most closely in each pair? (Circle the appropriate letters.)

E   or   I
S   or   N

T   or   F

J   or   P   Your 4-letter preferences are: _____ _____ _____ _____

You now have a four-letter personality preference based primarily on the work of Jung and of Myers and Briggs. This preliminary self-assessment offers one way to appreciate and value your natural individuality. Although we all represent combinations of each characteristic described, we have natural preferences, revealed in our type, that have implications for our career choices. To understand your preferences further, arrange to take the Myers–Briggs Type Indicator® instrument (MBTI) at your college counseling or career center.

FACTS & FIGURES

Decisive types

A study of college students (Hammer, 1996) has shown that developing a sense of purpose is associated with EJ preferences. Also, when career counselors ranked students on how well they made appropriate educational plans, the following order of preferences emerged: EJ, EP, IJ, and IP.

This study showed that EJ types are the most decisive about their majors and careers while IPs are the least decisive. In two other studies, the ISTPs were the most likely types to have undecided majors, and the IPs were the most likely to be attracted to special advising programs.

THINK ABOUT IT

1. Did you find yourself in the descriptions listed here?

2. Does the type that you have selected fit the way you act?

3. If you could change your type, which type listed above would you choose and why?

To answer these questions online, go to the Facts and Figures module in Chapter 1 of the Companion Website.

Companion Website

Your career choices may be based in part on your temperament or personality preferences. If you enjoy detail and structure, fields such as accounting, engineering, math, sciences, law, and health sciences might interest you. If you prefer unstructured, global thinking, then majors and fields such as the creative arts and social sciences may better suit your temperament. It is essential to note, however, that all types are found in all fields. In order to truly do well, you must stretch yourself in areas that do not come as naturally for you. This stretching takes extra effort above and beyond the demands of the occupation. Keep this in mind as you experience yourself responding to various work settings and demands.

Be aware that a major or career choice that does not mesh with your personality preferences typically takes more energy and concentration than one that more closely matches your preferences. The purpose of understanding personality type in relation to your classes and major is not to discourage you from pursuing a specific career, but to help you become more aware of why you might master certain subjects more easily than others and be attracted to certain careers over others.

SUCCESS STRATEGIES

Exploring Majors

The first and last letters of your personality type often indicate your preferred style of exploring majors. The descriptions below may help you become more aware of your preferred style, or suggest alternative strategies.

EJ TYPES (ESTJ, ESFJ, ENFJ, ENTJ)

"I want to decide and get on with my life."

EJ students often put choosing a major on their "to do" list soon after reaching college. It is not uncommon for them to seek career counseling early, hoping to declare a major before the first semester ends. Early decision making can have its drawbacks. For example, an EJ student may decide at an early age to be a doctor, lawyer, or engineer but then discover that he or she lacks the necessary ability or the continuing interest. The student may then become disappointed and want to hurry up and choose another major because "I don't want to waste any more time." Ironically, what such students often need to do is slow down and collect more information. Managers, school administrators, and organizers are found in this category.

EP TYPES (ESTP, ESFP, ENFP, ENTP)

"I want to experience it before deciding."

For **EP** types, deciding tends to be an ongoing process. They often decide by trial and error. They typically want, and try, to do it all—every course, major, or extracurricular activity that appeals to them. Changing their mind helps to reassure them that they still have options open, but they often don't know how to choose among the options. Their style, however, can be very difficult for their parents to understand, especially parents who have a Judging style. EP types can become better decision makers by accepting that the decision is part of a journey, not the final destination. Psychologists, counselors, authors, and helping types are often found in this category.

IJ TYPES (ISTJ, INFJ, ISFJ, INTJ)

"I want to be sure about my selection."

The **IJ** types will probably spend a lot of time researching and reflecting before reaching a final decision. They often consult books and other resources on majors and careers. Because they tend to stick with a decision once it's made, the information they collect must be carefully considered. Because their thinking is done alone, however, they may surprise people when they announce their plans. Accountants, computer programmers, and engineers are often found in this category.

IP TYPES (ISTP, ISFP, INFP, INTP)

"I wonder what I'll be when I grow up."

IP students often want to delay a decision about a major until they can consider all options, which they do at their own pace. Although they may resist deadlines imposed by others, they sometimes need the outside influences to help them make a decision. When they can tell themselves that no decision is ever final, they can move ahead. Even in mid-life, they often say they don't know for sure what they want to be when they grow up. Their style of decision making often reflects a struggle between the vast amount of information they are exploring from the outer world (which can be overwhelming) and their need to be true to their inner world. The world's artists and creative types are often found in this category. A career path for them is a never-ending quest for more knowledge, facts, or inspiration.

Meet Holly

"I've taken several inventories now and have gotten the results! My results for the Myers-Briggs were ENFP, which means that I am extraverted, intuitive, feeling, and perceptive. On the Interest Inventory, my results were mainly high in Social and Enterprising areas, with a medium interest in Investigative and Conventional-type activities.

"The MBTI results suggest that I like to use my creativity to help others reach goals and realize their dreams. I like to solve problems using a person-oriented approach, and I make decisions by relying on my values and the values of others. I prefer to solve problems as part of a team rather than deciding alone. Because I am social, I will benefit from working with people, especially people who are friendly and who like to socialize outside of work too. Because I am intuitive and perceptive, I like to be able to connect my daily routine to a bigger picture. I need to know why I am doing my work, and I am able to help others to see the bigger picture too. Because I am social, enterprising, and global, I enjoy leading others while helping them to see the bigger picture.

"The inventories indicate that I would enjoy teaching, counseling, social work, managing community organizations, and human resource management. I also was reminded that dietitian and athletic trainer fit my personality. It is important to me that my career will allow me to work with a cooperative, supportive group of people who are committed to helping, nurturing, and caring for others.

REAL STORIES

"The results of these inventories really fit me because I have always been a helper-type person and an organizer. In high school, I was the junior class secretary and the senior class vice president in charge of special events. I was a tutor, and I helped organize the tutorial program. I also planned recognition activities for clubs at my high school. The reminder about dietitian and athletic trainer relates to my early life as a gymnast, which I gave up when I sprained my back at age 12. I have read about and used almost every diet there is! But I also know that I do not want to take the science and math classes necessary to be a nutritionist or athletic trainer major. At this point, with the help of these assessments, I am leaning toward being a teacher or a counselor."

WHAT DO YOU THINK?

1. What are your Myers-Briggs and Interest Inventory results? Are your results as true about you as Holly's were for her?

2. Which descriptors from these results are true for you?

3. Which descriptors are not true for you?

4. Which of the occupations suggested by your results might you consider?

5. What other information do you need to consider before making an informed decision about your career?

Companion Website

To answer these questions online, go to the *Real Stories* module in Chapter 4 of the Companion Website.

Identifying Fields of Interest

The rest of this chapter explores the ways that interests can be grouped into job categories or clusters so that you can begin to select specific fields of interest to investigate.

We will be highlighting three different approaches to identify interests. The first is the *Holland Interest Environments* (or categories) (Holland, 1985), which are Realistic, Investigative, Artistic, Social, Enterprising, and Conventional. The second system is from the Department of Labor organized around *Worker Trait Groups,* which are described in the *Guide for Occupational Exploration* (GOE). Interest inventories ask if you like or dislike a variety of subjects or activities and offer you a profile of the results. The results from the GOE are clustered into interest categories based on 16 U.S. Department of Education career clusters that connect learning to careers. The third system is provided by the *American College Testing (ACT) Program*. ACT clusters, as well as the tech-prep and school to career clusters listed later in this chapter, have been used in secondary-school career centers.

Although many readers have access to career inventories, it is important to remember that the information gathered by printed or electronic assessments is not magic. Assessments simply provide a quick, efficient way of gathering and organizing the information that you know about yourself. Remember that the answers come from you. In the absence of an inventory, you are still able to collect the same information by completing the exercises and activities provided throughout this book.

Interest clusters, known as *personality types* or *environments*, are based on the following assumptions: (1) People express their personalities through their vocational choices; (2) people are attracted to occupations that they feel will provide experiences suitable to their personalities; (3) people who choose the same vocation have similar personalities and react to many situations in similar ways. Using the descriptions below, select the category that best describes you.

If you review Exercise 1.4, you will notice the adjectives are grouped by the six types described below. Most interest inventories relate your interests to these six types and provide a list of jobs related to these interests. If you are in a class that uses the Self-Directed Search® or the Strong Interest Inventory®, your instructor will explain which jobs are related to these six environments. If you don't have access to separate inventories, several online assessments can be found at www.cacareerzone.com. These inventories should give you a general idea of how your interests and values relate to potential jobs.

RIASEC (Holland Interest Environments)*

Doers

(Realistic—R) Doers like jobs such as automobile mechanic, air traffic controller, surveyor, farmer, electrician. They like to work outdoors and to work with tools. They prefer to deal with things rather than with people. They are described as:

conforming	humble	natural	shy
frank	materialistic	persistent	stable
honest	modest	practical	thrifty

Thinkers

(Investigative—I) These types like jobs such as biologist, chemist, physicist, anthropologist, geologist, medical technologist. They are task-oriented and prefer to work alone. They enjoy solving abstract problems and understanding the physical world. They are described as:

analytical	curious	introverted	precise
cautious	independent	methodical	rational
critical	intellectual	modest	reserved

Creators

(Artistic—A) These types like jobs such as composer, musician, stage director, writer, interior designer, actor/actress. They like to work in artistic settings that offer opportunities for self-expression. They are described as:

complicated	idealistic	impulsive	nonconforming
emotional	imaginative	independent	original
expressive	impractical	intuitive	unordered

Helpers

(Social—S) These types like jobs such as teacher, clergy, counselor, nurse, personnel director, speech therapist. They are sociable, responsible, and concerned with the welfare of others. They have little interest in machinery or physical skills. They are described as:

convincing	generous	insightful	sociable
cooperative	helpful	kind	tactful
friendly	idealistic	responsible	understanding

*To explore Holland's ideas more fully, ask your instructor or counselor for the Self-Directed Search, available from Psychological Assessment Resources, Inc., P. O. Box 990, Odessa, Florida 33556.

Persuaders

(Enterprising—E) These types like jobs such as salesperson, manager, business executive, television producer, sports promoter, buyer. They enjoy leading, speaking, and selling. They are impatient with precise work. They are described as:

adventurous	domineering	optimistic	risk-taking
ambitious	energetic	pleasure-seeking	self-confident
attention-getting	impulsive	popular	sociable

Organizers

(Conventional—C) These types like jobs such as bookkeeper, word processing technician, banker, cost estimator, tax expert. They prefer highly ordered activities, both verbal and numerical, that characterize office work. They have little interest in artistic or physical skills. They are described as:

careful	conservative	orderly	reserved
conforming	efficient	persistent	self-controlled
conscientious	obedient	practical	structured

Sample Majors Related to Holland Types

Now that you are familiar with Holland Interest Environments, the following chart will help you review some sample majors that may be of interest to you. Underline or circle those areas that seem to fit you. Note that this is a list of just some available majors.

REALISTIC

architectural/mechanical drafting technology
architectural construction technology

civil engineering
civil engineering technology
forestry

criminal justice technology
dietitian
medical technology

industrial engineering
mechanical engineering

INVESTIGATIVE

biological science
biology
chemical engineering
chemistry
computer sciences
dental hygiene

earth sciences
economics
electrical engineering
electrical engineering technology
electronics

environmental sciences
geography
geology
law
materials science

mathematics
paralegal
physics
psychology

ARTISTIC

advertising art
art
art history
commercial art

computer animation
computer graphics
design drafting
design technology

English
graphic technology
instructional media
multimedia technology

music
studio art
theater

SOCIAL

American studies
anthropology
child care
classical studies
communications
dental hygiene

elementary and secondary education
English
foreign languages
health
history

home economics
medical assistant
nursing
nutrition
physical education
political science

pre-law
religious studies
sociology
special education
speech

ENTERPRISING

advertising technology
business administration
business education
business management

finance
industrial and transportation management

industrial management and retail marketing
law enforcement administration

management engineering
marketing technology
public administration
real estate

CONVENTIONAL

accounting
administrative assistant
computer information systems

computer technology
court reporting
executive technology

legal/medical office management
library science

transportation management technology
word processing

84

Holland Interest Environments and Hobbies, Abilities, and Careers*

	Realistic "Doers"	Investigative "Thinkers"	Artistic "Creators"
Hobbies	Refinishing Growing Tinkering Using hands Building things	Book clubs Computers Doing puzzles Visiting museums Collecting rocks, stamps, etc.	Photography Performing Writing stories, poems Sewing Playing music
Abilities or Interests	Repair Plant Operate tools Play a sport	Think abstractly Solve math problems Do complex calculations Use a microscope Interpret formulas	Sketch, draw, paint, etc. Sing, dance, act Design fashions or 　interiors Play a musical instrument Write stories, poems, music
Sample Careers	Air conditioning mechanic (RIE) Archaeologist (IRE) Architectural drafter (RCI) Athletic trainer (SRE) Automotive engineer (RIE) Automotive mechanic (RIE) Baker/chef (RSE) Carpenter (RCI) Commercial airline pilot (RIE) Construction worker (REC) Dental assistant (RES) Electrical engineer (RIE) Fiber optics technician (RSE) Floral designer (RAE) Forester (RIS) Industrial arts teacher (IER) Optician (REI) Petroleum engineer (RIE) Police officer (SER) Radio/T.V. repair (REI) Software technician (RCI) Truck driver (RSE) Ultrasound technologist (RSI)	Actuary (ISE) Anesthesiologist (IRS) Anthropologist (IRE) Archaeologist (IRE) Biochemist (IRS) Biologist (ISR) Chemical engineer (IRE) Chemical technician (IRE) Computer analyst (IER) Computer programmer Dentist (ISR) Ecologist (IRE) Economist (IAS) Geologist (IRE) Hazardous waste technician Medical technologist (ISA) Nurse practitioner (ISA) Physician (ISE) Psychologist (IES) Statistician (IRE) Technical writer (IRS) Veterinarian (IRS) Webmaster	Actor (AES) Advertising (AES) Artist Broadcasting executive (EAS) Camera operator Clothing designer (ASR) Copywriter (ASI) Dancer (AES) Drama/music/art 　teacher (ASE) English teacher (ASE) Fashion designer (ASR) Fashion illustrator (ASR) Furniture designer (AES) Graphic designer (AES) Interior designer (AES) Journalist (ASE) Landscape architect (AIR) Librarian (SAI) Medical illustrator (AIE) Museum curator (AES) Musician Photographer (AES) Writer (ASI)

*Compiled from online career search sources.

Holland Interest Environments, continued

Social "Helpers"	Enterprising "Persuaders"	Conventional "Organizers"
Hobbies		
Volunteering	Starting own service or	Collecting memorabilia
Caring for children	business	Arranging and organizing
Religious activities	Campaigning	household
Playing team sports	Leading organizations	Playing computer or card
	Promoting ideas	games
		Studying tax laws
		Writing family history
Abilities or Interests		
Teach/train others	Initiate projects	Work within a system
Express yourself	Persuade people	Be organized
Lead a group discussion	Sell things or promote ideas	Keep accurate records
Mediate disputes	Organize activities	Use a computer
Cooperate well	Lead a group	Write effective business
		letters
Sample Careers		
Air traffic controller (SER)	Advertising executive (ESA)	Accountant (CSE)
Athletic coach (SRE)	Automobile sales worker	Administrative assistant (ESC)
Chaplain (SAI)	(ESR)	Bank teller (CSE)
College faculty (SEI)	Banker/financial planner	Budget analyst (CER)
Consumer affairs director	(ESR)	Building inspector (CSE)
(SER)	Buyer (ESA)	Business teacher (CSE)
Cosmetologist (SAE)	Claims adjuster (ESR)	Catalog librarian (CSE)
Counselor (SAE)	Computer operator (ESI)	Claims adjuster (SEC)
Dental hygienist (SAI)	Credit manager (ERS)	Clerk (CSE)
Historian (SEI)	Dental assistant (E)	Computer operator (CSR)
Homemaker (S)	Financial planner (ESR)	Congressional-district
Hospital administrator (SER)	Flight attendant (ESA)	aide (CES)
Mail carrier (SRC)	Food service manager (ESI)	Cost accountant (CES)
Medical records	Funeral director (ESR)	Court reporter (CSE)
administrator (SIE)	Hotel manager (ESR)	Customer inspector (CEI)
Nurse (SIR)	Industrial engineer (EIR)	Elementary school
Occupational therapist	Insurance agent (ECS)	teacher (SEC)
(SRE)	Journalist (EAS)	Financial analyst (CSI)
Paralegal (SCE)	Lawyer (ESA)	Insurance underwriter (CSE)
Police officer (SER)	Office manager (ESR)	Internal auditor (ICR)
Radiological technologist (SRI)	Politician (ESA)	Legal secretary (CSA)
Real estate appraiser (SCE)	Public relations	Medical records technician
Schoolteacher (SEC)	representative (EAS)	(CSE)
Social worker (SEA)	Real estate agent (ESR)	Paralegal (SCE)
Speech pathologist (SAI)	Stockbroker (ESI)	Tax consultant (CSE)
Youth services worker (SEC)	Urban planner (ESI)	Travel agent (ECS)

Worker Trait Groups are broad, general categories of interests that describe many of the occupational functions and factors related to these areas of interest, such as physical requirements, necessary academic skills, and specific vocation preparation time. These descriptions then lead to a listing of some possible occupations that fall within the interest categories and trait groups. Look at each category. Underline the types of work that initially appeal to you.

After the list of Worker Trait Groups, you will find an activity "Identifying Occupational Interest Areas." There we will show how the 16 groups relate to the Holland Interest Environments.

More complete and detailed descriptions may be found in the *New Guide for Occupational Exploration (GOE-2005)* by Michael Farr and Laurence Shatkin that can be found in college career centers and libraries.

01 AGRICULTURE AND NATURAL RESOURCES

01.01 Managerial Work in Agriculture and Natural Resources
01.02 Resource Science/Engineering for Plants, Animals, and the Environment
01.03 Resource Technologies for Plants, Animals, and the Environment
01.04 General Farming
01.05 Nursery, Groundskeeping, and Pest Control
01.06 Forestry and Logging
01.07 Hunting and Fishing
01.08 Mining and Drilling

02 ARCHITECTURE AND CONSTRUCTION

02.01 Managerial Work in Architecture and Construction
02.02 Architectural Design
02.03 Architecture/Construction Engineering Technologies
02.04 Construction Crafts
02.05 Systems and Equipment Installation, Maintenance, and Repair
02.06 Construction Support/Labor

03 ARTS AND COMMUNICATION

03.01 Managerial Work in Arts and Communication
03.02 Writing and Editing
03.03 News, Broadcasting, and Public Relations
03.04 Studio Art
03.05 Design
03.06 Drama
03.07 Music
03.08 Dance
03.09 Media Technology
03.10 Communications Technology
03.11 Musical Instrument Repair

04 BUSINESS AND ADMINISTRATION

04.01 Managerial Work in General Business
04.02 Managerial Work in Business Detail
04.03 Human Resources Support
04.04 Secretarial Support
04.05 Accounting, Auditing, and Analytical Support
04.06 Mathematical Clerical Support
04.07 Records and Materials Processing
04.08 Clerical Machine Operation

05 EDUCATION AND TRAINING

05.01 Managerial Work in Education
05.02 Preschool, Elementary, and Secondary Teaching and Instructing
05.03 Postsecondary and Adult Teaching and Instructing
05.04 Library Services
05.05 Archival and Museum Services
05.06 Counseling, Health, and Fitness Education

06 FINANCE AND INSURANCE

06.01 Managerial Work in Finance and Insurance
06.02 Finance/Insurance Investigation and Analysis
06.03 Finance/Insurance Records Processing
06.04 Finance/Insurance Customer Service
06.05 Finance/Insurance Sales and Support

Go to next page

07   GOVERNMENT AND PUBLIC ADMINISTRATION

07.01   Managerial Work in Government and Public Administration
07.02   Public Planning
07.03   Regulations Enforcement
07.04   Public Administration Clerical Support

08   HEALTH SCIENCE

08.01   Managerial Work in Medical and Health Services
08.02   Medicine and Surgery
08.03   Dentistry
08.04   Health Specialties
08.05   Animal Care
08.06   Medical Technology
08.07   Medical Therapy
08.08   Patient Care and Assistance
08.09   Health Protection and Promotion

09   HOSPITALITY, TOURISM, AND RECREATION

09.01   Managerial Work in Hospitality and Tourism
09.02   Recreational Services
09.03   Hospitality and Travel Services
09.04   Food and Beverage Preparation
09.05   Food and Beverage Service
09.06   Sports
09.07   Barber and Beauty Services

10   HUMAN SERVICE

10.01   Counseling and Social Work
10.02   Religious Work
10.03   Child/Personal Care and Services
10.04   Client Interviewing

11   INFORMATION TECHNOLOGY

11.01   Managerial Work in Information Technology
11.02   Information Technology Specialties
11.03   Digital Equipment Repair

12   LAW AND PUBLIC SAFETY

12.01   Managerial Work in Law and Public Safety
12.02   Legal Practice and Justice Administration
12.03   Legal Support
12.04   Law Enforcement and Public Safety
12.05   Safety and Security
12.06   Emergency Responding
12.07   Military

13   MANUFACTURING

13.01   Managerial Work in Manufacturing
13.02   Machine Setup and Operation
13.03   Production, Work, Assorted Materials Processing
13.04   Welding, Brazing, and Soldering
13.05   Production Machining Technology
13.06   Production Precision Work
13.07   Production Quality Control
13.08   Graphic Arts Production
13.09   Hands-On Work, Assorted Materials
13.10   Woodworking Technology
13.11   Apparel, Shoes, Leather, and Fabric Care
13.12   Electrical and Electronic Repair
13.14   Vehicle and Facility Mechanical Work
13.15   Medical and Technical Equipment Repair
13.16   Utility Operation and Energy Distribution
13.17   Loading, Moving, Hoisting, and Conveying

14   RETAIL AND WHOLESALE SALES AND SERVICE

14.01   Managerial Work in Retail/Wholesale Sales and Service
14.02   Technical Sales
14.03   General Sales
14.04   Personal Soliciting
14.05   Purchasing
14.06   Customer Service

15   SCIENTIFIC RESEARCH, ENGINEERING, AND MATHEMATICS

15.01   Managerial Work in Scientific Research, Engineering, and Mathematics
15.02   Physical Sciences
15.03   Life Sciences
15.04   Social Sciences
15.05   Physical Science Laboratory Technology
15.06   Mathematics and Data Analysis
15.07   Research and Design Engineering
15.09   Engineering Technology

16   TRANSPORTATION, DISTRIBUTION, AND LOGISTICS

16.01   Managerial Work in Transportation
16.02   Air Vehicle Operation
16.03   Truck Driving
16.04   Rail Vehicle Operation
16.05   Water Vehicle Operation
16.06   Other Services Requiring Driving
16.07   Transportation Support Work

Identifying Occupational Interest Areas

ACTIVITY

Check off (✓) the areas or words in 1, 2, and 3 that you find most interesting. If you had two hours to research careers, which area(s) would you select?

1. WHAT FIELDS INTEREST YOU?

○ Social — Do you like to work with people? Do you help others organize activities? Are you active in social events?

○ Sales–verbal — Do you like to sell, convince, persuade, influence, lead? Do you like to talk, write, read?

○ Mechanical — Do you like to fix things? Do you use and repair machines, appliances, equipment? Do you like to make or build things?

○ Scientific — Are you curious about ideas and abstract processes? Do you like to experiment and solve problems?

○ Clerical–computational — Do you like to keep things orderly? Do you like to keep records, use a keyboard, be accurate?

○ Artistic — Do you like music, dance, art, literature, photography, decorating? Do you like to express yourself creatively?

2. OCCUPATIONAL CATEGORIES ACCORDING TO THE SIX HOLLAND TYPES

○ Realistic (R) — Occupations include jobs in industry, trade, and service.

○ Investigative (I) — Occupations include jobs in the fields of science and technology.

○ Artistic (A) — Occupations include jobs in the fields of art, music, and literature.

○ Social (S) — Occupations include jobs in the fields of education and welfare.

○ Enterprising (E) — Occupations include jobs in sales and management.

○ Conventional (C) — Occupations include office and clerical jobs.

3. GOE INTEREST AREAS RELATED TO HOLLAND CATEGORIES*

The GOE Interest Areas are easily cross-referenced to Holland categories. Here is a table that shows this relationship.

GOE Interest Area	Holland Occupational Category
01 Agriculture and Natural Resources	Realistic Investigative
02 Architecture and Construction	Realistic
03 Arts and Communication	Artistic
04 Business and Administration	Conventional, Enterprising
05 Education and Training	Social, Investigative

*Based on information taken from the *New Guide for Occupational Exploration*, Fourth Edition, copyright 2006, by JIST Works, Inc., Indianapolis, IN. Permission granted by JIST Publishing, Incorporated.

GOE Interest Area	Holland Occupational Category
06 Finance and Insurance	Conventional, Enterprising
07 Government and Public Administration	Conventional, Realistic
08 Health Science	Social, Investigative
09 Hospitality, Tourism, and Recreation	Enterprising, Realistic
10 Human Service	Social
11 Information and Technology	Investigative
12 Law and Public Safety	Enterprising
13 Manufacturing	Realistic
14 Retail and Wholesale Sales and Service	Enterprising
15 Scientific Research, Engineering, and Mathematics	Investigative
16 Transportation, Distribution, and Logistics	Realistic

Career Clusters

Career centers often organize their materials by the following career clusters (created by the U.S. Office of Career Education and used in tech-prep or school to career programs):

Agriculture

Arts/Communications/Human Services

Business

Consumer and Family Services

Engineering Technology

Health Services

Industry and Technology

The American College Testing Program (ACT) has also devised a useful system of organizing jobs into career clusters (Exhibit 4.1). If you are attending school and have

Information you gain from completing assessment instruments will be a great aid to you in making educational and career choices.

chosen a major, you might research the cluster in which your major falls. Otherwise, select the area that seems to relate to your interests, values, and skills, and explore it.

Understanding your interests will be a great aid to you in making satisfying educational and career choices. Exhibit 4.2 arranges career clusters into 12 "regions" based on primary work tasks that are found in jobs: dealing with data, people, ideas, and things. Please note that this figure also uses the letters RIASEC (Realistic, Investigative, Artistic, Social, Enterprising, and Conventional) to show the relationship of each region to Holland's Interest Environments, discussed earlier in this chapter.

The more you are able to incorporate your interests into your work, the more you will enjoy your work. Once you have completed an interest inventory, plan to explore those occupations associated with your interests. Find out what people actually do, and compare these jobs to your interests.

Summary

Now that you have completed this chapter, you are aware that your satisfaction in a career is related to how much you can incorporate your unique personality and interests into your work.

In the next chapter, we will focus on skills: you will learn how to identify the skills you possess, and you will get ideas about the types of skills you may need in the future. With this information, you will be well into your career fitness program!

EXHIBIT 4.1

ACT Career Clusters and Career Areas (A–Z), illustrating how jobs can be clustered into related categories.

ADMINISTRATION AND SALES CAREER CLUSTER

A. Employment-Related Services Managers (human resources, training/education, employee benefits, etc.); recruiter; interviewer; job analyst.

B. Marketing & Sales Agents (insurance, real estate, travel, etc.); buyer; sales/manufacturers' representatives; retail salesworker; telemarketer.

C. Management Executive; executive secretary; purchaser; general managers (financial, office, property, etc.); specialty managers (retail store, hotel/motel, food service, etc.). For other managers, see specialty—e.g., Social service (Career Area Y).

D. Regulation & Protection Inspectors (customs, food/drug, etc.); police officer; detective; park ranger; security manager; guard.

BUSINESS OPERATIONS CAREER CLUSTER

E. Communications & Records Receptionist; secretary (including legal and medical); court reporter; clerks (order, billing, hotel, etc.).

F. Financial Transactions Accountant/auditor; cashier; bank teller; budget/credit analyst; tax preparer; ticket agent.

G. Distribution & Dispatching Shipping/receiving clerk; warehouse supervisor; mail carrier; dispatchers (flight, cab, etc.); air traffic controller.

TECHNICAL CAREER CLUSTER

H. Transport Operation & Related Truck/bus/cab drivers; locomotive engineer; ship captain; aircraft pilot; sailor; chauffeur.

I. Agriculture, Forestry, & Related Farmer; nursery manager; pest controller; forester; logger; groundskeeper; animal caretaker.

J. Computer & Information Specialties Programmer; systems analyst; information systems manager; computer repairer; desktop publisher; actuary.

K. Construction & Maintenance Carpenter; electrician; bricklayer; tile setter; painter; plumber; roofer; firefighter; custodian.

L. Crafts & Related Cabinetmaker; tailor; chef/cook; baker; butcher; jeweler; silversmith; hand crafter.

M. Manufacturing & Processing Tool & die maker; machinist; welder; bookbinder; printing press operator; photo process worker; dry cleaner.

N. Mechanical & Electrical Specialties Mechanics/technicians (auto, aircraft, heating & air conditioning, electronics, dental lab, etc.); repairers (office machine, appliance, electronics).

SCIENCE AND TECHNOLOGY CAREER CLUSTER

O. Engineering & Technologies Engineers (aerospace, agricultural, nuclear, civil, computer, etc.); technicians (electronics, mechanical, laser, etc.); surveyor; drafter; architect; technical illustrator.

P. Natural Science & Technologies Physicist; astronomer; biologist; statistician; soil conservationist; food technologist; crime lab analyst.

Q. Medical Technologies Pharmacist; optician; prosthetist; technologists (surgical, medical lab, EEG, etc.); dietitian.

R. Medical Diagnosis & Treatment Physician; psychiatrist; pathologist; dentist; optometrist; veterinarian; physical therapist; audiologist; physician's assistant.

S. Social Science Sociologist; experimental psychologist; political scientist; economist; criminologist; urban planner.

ARTS CAREER CLUSTER

T. Applied Arts (Visual) Artist; graphic artist; photographer; illustrator; floral/fashion/interior designers; merchandise displayer.

U. Creative & Performing Arts Writer/author; musician; singer; dancer; music composer; movie/TV director; fashion model.

V. Applied Arts (Written & Spoken) Reporter; columnist; editor; ad copywriter; P. R. specialist; TV announcer; librarian; interpreter.

SOCIAL SERVICE CAREER CLUSTER

W. Health Care Administrator; nurse; occupational therapist; psychiatric technician; dental hygienist/assistant; geriatric aide.

X. Education Administrator; teachers & aides (preschool, elementary, & secondary, special education, PE, etc.). For others, see specialty—e.g., Physics teacher (Career Area P).

Y. Community Services Social service director; social worker; lawyer; paralegal; home economist; career counselor; clergy.

Z. Personal Services Waiter/waitress; barber; cosmetologist; flight attendant; household worker; home health aide; travel guide.

The World-of-Work map.   **EXHIBIT 4.2**

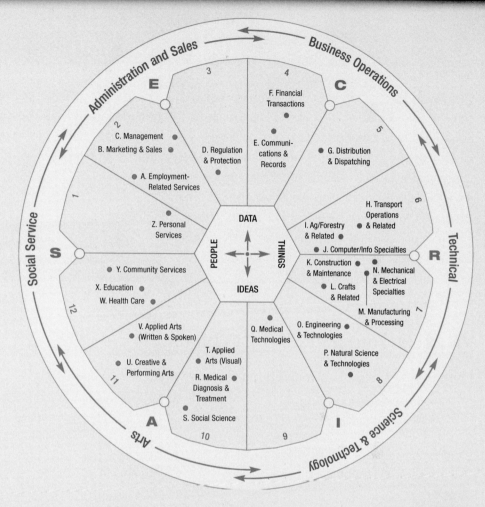

ABOUT THE MAP

- The World-of-Work Map arranges 26 career areas (groups of similar jobs) into 12 regions. Together, the career areas cover all U.S. jobs. Most jobs in a career area are located near the point shown. However, some may be in adjacent map regions.

- A career area's location is based on its primary work tasks. The four primary work tasks are working with

    Data: Facts, numbers, files, accounts, business procedures.

    Ideas: Insights, theories, new ways of saying or doing something, for example, with words, equations, or music.

    People: People you help, serve, inform, care for, or sell things to.

    Things: Machines, tools, living things, and materials such as food, wood, or metal.

- Six general types of work (Holland Interest Environments) are shown around the edge of the map. The overlapping career cluster arrows indicate overlap in the occupational content of adjacent career clusters.

- Because of their People rather than Things orientation, the following two career areas in the Science & Technology cluster are located toward the left side of the map (Region 10): Medical Diagnosis & Treatment and Social Science.

FOCUSING ON YOU

PURPOSE OF EXERCISES. The following exercises serve to help you summarize information. Exercise 4.1 asks you to record your personality type as determined earlier. Exercise 4.2 is a review of the Holland Interest Environments as they describe you. Exercises 4.3 and 4.4 ask you to list information about your interests, and Exercise 4.5 asks you to record the results of any additional assessments you have taken. Exercise 4.6 asks you to list interesting jobs found in the classifieds;

Exercise 4.7 asks for your list of interesting courses taken from a college catalog. The exercise summary encourages you to put this information together and describe an ideal job or set of activities that best reflects who you are.

Companion Website

To answer these questions online, go to the *Exercise* module in Chapter 4 of the Companion Website.

4.1   *Your Personality Type*

Check your four-letter personality preference (page 78):

○ Extraversion   ○ Introversion

○ Sensing   ○ Intuition

○ Thinking   ○ Feeling

○ Judging   ○ Perception

4.2   *Your Holland Interest Environment*

1. Check your top three Holland Environments (pages 82–83):

   ○ Realistic

   ○ Artistic

   ○ Enterprising

   ○ Investigative

   ○ Social

   ○ Conventional

2. What adjectives from these environments best describe you (pages 82–83)?

   _____

   _____

   _____

3. List three interesting majors from your top categories (page 84):

_____

_____

_____

4. List three interesting jobs/careers from your top categories (pages 85–86):

_____

_____

_____

Your Occupational Interests   **4.3**

List the occupational interest areas you have checked off in this chapter (page 89–90):

_____

_____

_____

_____

Job Clusters   **4.4**

List three ACT job clusters that are most interesting to you (page 92):

1. _____

2. _____

3. _____

Interest Inventories   **4.5**

Record below the results of any other interest or personality inventories you have taken (e.g., top three career choices):

_____

_____

_____

_____

4.6   *Classified Careers*

Locate the Sunday classifieds section from two or three weeks of newspapers in hard copy or on the Internet. These do not need to be recent or local papers. Scan the entire section of the Sunday job classifieds and identify those jobs that look interesting, *regardless of whether you consider yourself qualified*. Review the jobs that you identified and look for patterns in the announcements that caught your eye. Write the job titles and industries that interested you in the space that follows.

_____

_____

_____

_____

_____

4.7   *College Catalogs*

Locate the general catalog for the college or university you are currently attending or for a local college. The general catalog is the publication that contains the entire listings and descriptions of courses offered at that college. Read the catalog and course descriptions, marking those classes on topics about which you would like to learn more. Review the classes you have marked and notice which subjects seemed most interesting. Write the subject areas in the space below:

_____

_____

_____

_____

_____

4.8   WWWebwise

For additional activities online, go to the WWWebwise module in Chapter 4 of the Companion Website.

4.9   *Exercise Summary*

What kinds of activities or job descriptions would your ideal job reflect, based on what you have learned about your personality and interests?

_____

_____

_____

_____

_____

_____

_____

_____

_____

_____

_____

_____

_____

_____

_____

_____

_____

_____

_____

_____

_____

_____

_____

Go to page 221 of the chapter summaries and fill out the Chapter 4 exercise summary now.

5

Skills Assessment

Learning Objectives

Learning Objectives

At the end of the chapter you will be able to . . .

- Discuss the importance of skills in your career search

- Define and identify your skills

- Recognize the power of the transferability of your skills

- Use the language of skills in writing your resume and preparing for an interview

The next step in the career-planning process is to identify your skills. Skills are the building blocks of your future career just as muscles are the building blocks of your future body shape. A career fitness program helps you to identify your current skills and the skills you want to develop. A thorough skills analysis is a critical component of the career-planning process.

Ability is what you are capable of doing. Motivation determines what you do. Attitude determines how well you do it.

LOU HOLTZ

Skills are the currency used by job seekers. In the job market you receive pay in exchange for skills. Individuals who can describe themselves to a potential employer in terms of their skills are the people most likely to enjoy their careers because they are the most likely to obtain jobs that use their particular skills. People who enjoy their work tend to be more productive and healthy. After completing this chapter, you will be able to analyze a potential job on the basis of how the skills required by the job compare with both the skills you possess and enjoy using and the skills you want to develop. Furthermore, you will have a broader vocabulary to use in describing your strengths when you prepare your resume and when you are interviewed for jobs.

Defining Skills

Skills are the currency of the job market

Skills include the specific attributes, talents, and personal qualities that we bring to a job as well as the tasks we learn on the job. Every job requires skills. We also develop skills simply through the process of living, by interacting with others and going through our daily routines. Our personal preferences often affect our skills and abilities. We tend to be motivated to repeatedly use skills that are part of enjoyable activities. Our repeated use of and success with certain preferred skills identifies them as our *self-motivators*. Self-motivators are skills we enjoy and do well.

By learning the vocabulary of skills, you can recognize the hundreds of skills that may be within your grasp. Skills are generally divided into three types: functional, work-content, and adaptive. All of these can be considered transferable. *Functional skills* are those that may or may not be associated with a specific job, such as maintaining schedules, collecting data, and diagnosing and responding to problems. They are called functional skills because they are used to accomplish general tasks or functions of a job. *Work-content skills* are specific and specialized to one job (e.g., bookkeeping is done by bookkeepers, assigning grades is done by teachers, interpreting an electrocardiogram is done by specific medical practitioners). *Adaptive* or *self-management skills* are personal attributes; they might also be described as personality traits. The ability to learn quickly, the ability to pay close attention to detail, task orientation, self-direction, congeniality, and cooperativeness are some examples of adaptive skills.

Identifying Your Skills

I f you were asked right now to list your skills, what would your list look like? It might be a short list, not because you do not have skills but simply because you have never been asked to identify them and are not accustomed to thinking and talking about them. Reflecting on your skills may also be difficult because most of us have been taught to be modest and not to brag. We often feel that something we do well doesn't take any special skills, that is, we discount our own special talents. We may also feel that if we are not currently using a skill, we can no longer claim it—that somehow it has escaped us. Or, if we haven't been paid to use the skill, we may not recognize its value.

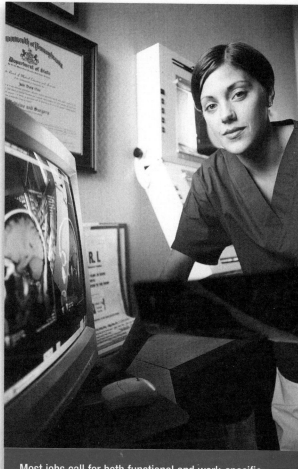

Most jobs call for both functional and work-specific skills, and self-management skills are a crucial part of any job.

All of these false assumptions make it difficult to list our skills honestly and accurately. Your goal now will be to recognize the many skills you possess that make you valuable in the job market. You have acquired hundreds of skills just by virtue of your life experiences, and, paid or not, they are part of your portfolio!

Once you begin to recognize your skills, you will become more aware of your identity as extending beyond the narrow limits you tend to apply to yourself. We all unconsciously tend to categorize ourselves too narrowly. For instance, you might typically answer the question "Who are you?" with statements such as "I am a student," "I am a history major," "I am a graphic artist," "I am a conservative," or "I am a homemaker." The problem with these labels is that they tend to stereotype you. This is especially true when you are interviewing for a job. If you say you are a student, the interviewer might stereotype you as not having enough experience. If you say you are a secretary, the interviewer may consider you only for a secretarial job or may insist that you start as a secretary. But suppose you say your experience has involved public speaking, doing organizational work, coordinating schedules, managing budgets, researching needs, problem solving, following through with details, motivating others, resolving problems caused by low morale and lack of cooperation, and establishing priorities for allocation of available time, resources, and funds. Not only does this sound impressive, but you appear eligible for many positions that require these skills.

A particular challenge may be faced by homemakers who feel that because they have been out of the job market, they have no transferable or marketable skills. To the contrary, homemaking is a full-time job requiring a wide range of skills that can translate into paid employment. (Review the creative functional resume in Chapter 10 for ideas on skills in the areas of management, office procedures, personnel, finances, and purchasing that might be included in a homemaker's list of transferable skills.)

Can you talk about your skills?

Employers look for employees who are task-oriented and who think and talk in terms of what they as employees can do to make the employer's operation easier, better, and more efficient. The best way to describe what you can do for an employer is to talk about your skills and how they apply to the job. Unfortunately, we tend to discount our accomplishments and the related skill development. Although climbing a mountain and running a four-minute mile are noteworthy accomplishments, so are the following:

Sample accomplishments

raising a child	raising funds
getting into college	giving a speech
delivering papers on a route	writing a term paper
using a software program	getting a job
repairing a car	consoling a child
designing a costume	graduating from high school
completing a computer course	planning a trip and traveling
planning a surprise party	working as a food server
surfing the Internet	mastering a sport
completing a degree	overcoming a bad habit

In reviewing this list, you may be thinking that some of these activities are simple, no big deal. Some are activities that you can do without much thought or preparation. However, just because they don't take much preparation does not mean they aren't accomplishments. Start thinking of goals that you have set and then later met as accomplishments!

Analyze Your Accomplishments

You can begin to recognize your skills by identifying and examining your most satisfying accomplishments, because your skills led you to these accomplishments. By analyzing these accomplishments, you are likely to discover a pattern of skills (your self-motivators) that you repeatedly use and enjoy using. Again, accomplishments are simply completed activities, goals, projects, or jobs held.

There are several ways to analyze accomplishments. One way is to describe something that you are proud of having completed, and then list the skills that were required to complete it. Let's look at John, whose accomplishments are described in the Real Stories box. Read it now. Then reread the list of skills that John identified in the third paragraph.

Can you think of any that he missed? We all have many more skills than we credit ourselves with having.

Meet John

John, a 16-year-old high school junior, was always someone friends went to when they needed a plan. When he was younger, John was known as a schemer, and most of the time he was in trouble for his schemes—but as he got older he learned to turn his schemes into plans. Well liked, John never thought of himself as anything special, but his friends thought he had a real talent for making things happen.

John's girlfriend, Alicia, was turning 18 and he wanted to throw a really great surprise party for her. He called all his friends and Alicia's and told them his ideas. He divided everyone into groups to cover the food, entertainment, transportation, and decorations. The party was a huge success (even though Alicia says she knew about it all along).

The following week when John had to write a paper for his career class describing an accomplishment, he used the party. He described his initial plan, how he organized and divided up the work, how he made a checklist and communicated with everyone. From a list of skills given to each student by the teacher, John identified leadership, creativity, communication, determination, organization, dependability, and attention to detail as the skills in putting together the party.

In his senior year, a friend told John of an internship opportunity with a congressman in his district. The friend felt that John's organizational skills would make him a perfect candidate. Since John did not have any real work experience, he used the party-planning activity on his resume to demonstrate his skills. His resume got him an interview and his outgoing personality and strong organizational skills got him the internship.

One of John's assignments was to organize meetings and special events. He loved the work and he was able to use the full resources of the congressman's office to put together impressive events.

After graduation, John felt more confident than he ever felt before. With an excellent reference letter from the congressman, John decided to enroll in community college. He took some marketing classes and looked for another internship. He was lucky to land a position with an ad agency that promoted Britney Spears. He learned a great deal working with the ad agency and the people associated with Ms. Spears.

When the internship ended, John began researching careers to see what education and training he needed to continue with this type of work. He discovered that event planning fit with his interests and his skills; however, the salary was not as much as he had hoped for. John met with a counselor and they agreed that in order to do the type of work he loved and make a decent salary, he would need a four-year degree. The counselor helped John create an educational plan to prepare him to transfer to the university.

WHAT DO YOU THINK?

1. What other types of jobs require the skills that John possesses?

2. Are some people born with organizational skills? If not, how can people develop those skills?

3. What gave John the confidence to attend college?

4. Which is more difficult—learning to like doing something you dislike but do well, or learning to be competent at something that you do not feel competent doing?

5. List an activity or project you have accomplished and indicate the skills that you used to complete it.

6. Write yourself a letter of reference.

To answer these questions online, go to the *Real Stories* **module in Chapter 5 of the Companion Website.**

Companion Website

Another method to identify skills is to write a story about one of your accomplishments and then list the skills used. Richard Bolles has popularized this approach in his *Quick Job Hunting Map* (1996), a booklet that lists hundreds of skills. Following is an example of one student's story and the skills involved. The student's classmates listened to her story and helped her identify 21 skills.

Completing a Team Research Report

It was necessary for me to learn new software and Web-based tools to communicate electronically and format my findings on a spreadsheet. As the team leader, I had to find a time when all members could meet in person to share findings and formulate the final report before the due date. The skills used in this team research project include:

1. learn quickly
2. display flexibility
3. meet challenges
4. direct self
5. follow through
6. face new situations
7. proof and edit
8. translate concepts
9. use technology
10. organize
11. get the job done
12. display patience
13. attend to detail
14. overcome obstacles
15. communicate clearly
16. work under stress
17. display persistence
18. ask questions
19. use new software and Web-based technology
20. exercise leadership skill
21. manage time effectively

Use the DOT to Identify Skills

You can research the skills associated with jobs by reading the job descriptions, often located in the employer's personnel office, or by researching the jobs in the *Dictionary of Occupational Titles* (referred to as the DOT). The DOT is an excellent reference source for identifying tasks required in more than 21,000 different occupations.

In addition to identifying specific tasks in each job, the DOT identifies the primary skills required for each job according to the three broad categories of *data* (instructions and information), *people* (supervisors, coworkers, or the public), and *things* (materials, equipment, or products). The nine-digit number that precedes each job title (refer to the two sample job descriptions) includes an indication of how the job is related to data (the fourth digit), people (the fifth digit), and things (the sixth digit). For example, by finding the middle three digits for *Investigator*—2, 6, 7—in their appropriate columns in Exhibit 5.1, we know that the position involves *analyzing* data, *speaking to and signaling* people, and *handling* things. For a teacher, the fifth digit would likely be 2, signifying *instruction*. For a crane operator, the sixth digit would probably be 3, representing *driving and operating*.

The DOT can be of great use to you in identifying types of skills involved in jobs. Perhaps more important, it can alert you to the existence of thousands of jobs and careers you never knew existed. In Chapter 7, the DOT will be discussed as one of many sources of career information.

Sample Job Descriptions from the DOT

www.oalj.dol.gov/libdot.htm

131.067.014 COPYWRITER (PROFESS. & KIN.)

Writes advertising copy for use by publication or broadcast media to promote sale of goods and services: consults with sales media and marketing representatives to obtain information on product or service and discuss style and length of advertising copy. Obtains additional background and current development information through research and interview. Reviews advertising trends, consumer surveys, and other data regarding marketing of specific and related goods and services to formulate presentation approach. Writes preliminary draft of copy and sends to supervisor for approval. Corrects and revises copy as necessary. May write articles, bulletins, sales letters, speeches, and other related informative and promotional material. Prepares advertising copy, using computer.

O*Net Code: 27-3034.04

241.267.030 INVESTIGATOR (CLERICAL)

Investigates persons or business establishments applying for credit, employment, insurance, loans, or settlement of claims. Contacts former employers, neighbors, trade associations, and others by telephone to verify employment record and to obtain health history and history of moral and social behavior. Examines city directories and public records to verify residence history, convictions and arrests, property ownership, bankruptcies, liens, and unpaid taxes of applicant. Obtains credit rating from banks and credit concerns. Analyzes information gathered by investigation and prepares reports of findings and recommendations. May interview applicant on telephone or in person to obtain other financial and personal data for completeness of report. When specializing in certain types of investigations, may be designated CREDIT REPORTER (bus. ser.); INSURANCE–APPLICATION INVESTIGATOR (insurance).

No description listed in O*Net

Skills relationships of jobs to data, people, and things, as identified in the Dictionary of Occupational Titles (DOT).

EXHIBIT 5.1

DATA (4TH DIGIT)	PEOPLE (5TH DIGIT)	THINGS (6TH DIGIT)
0 Synthesizing	0 Mentoring	0 Setting up
1 Coordinating	1 Negotiating	1 Precision working
2 Analyzing	2 Instructing	2 Operating–controlling
3 Compiling	3 Supervising	3 Driving–operating
4 Computing	4 Diverting	4 Manipulating
5 Copying	5 Persuading	5 Tending
6 Comparing	6 Speaking–signaling	6 Feeding–offbearing
7 No significant relationship	7 Serving	7 Handling
	8 No significant relationship	8 No significant relationship

If your local career center or One Stop Career Center has access to O*NET (http://online.onetcenter.org/), this resource can help you discover the relationship between occupations and skills. O*NET is the acronym for the Occupational Information Network developed by the U.S. Department of Labor. The program is an easy-to-use, interactive computer database that collects, analyzes, and disseminates skill and occupational information in more than 1,100 occupational areas. Simply type three skills and the computer will list various occupations that use them. O*NET has crosswalks with the DOT. Therefore, knowing a DOT code allows you to find several related occupations using O*NET. For example, if you searched for "counselor," you would find these related jobs: Supervisor; Special Services; Veterans Contact Representative; Counselor; Director of Counseling; Residence Counselor; Foreign-Student Advisor; and several others. When you click on any of these job titles, then you find the skills and job tasks describing these jobs.

Move now to the next page and complete the Activity Checklist. This list includes more than 200 skills in 13 different categories. These categories are useful because they're familiar to employers and often show up in job announcements. As you complete the checklist, carefully consider how each skill applies specifically to you.

Identify your skills

If you are currently working, think of ways to use those skills you identify in the activity checklist as your self-motivated skills as often as possible to give you job satisfaction. Talk to your supervisor and identify additional ways to use these skills now or in the future. For example, if you were hired because of your word processing skills, you might suggest that you become the company expert on formatting documents and reports to give them a consistent look. If your people skills are one of your strengths, make sure your boss keeps you in mind for office supervisor, or as a member of a committee, or as the company liaison with an important client. Don't take your skills for granted and don't let others do so!

The Portfolio Employee

As we have discussed, your skills are your most valuable asset in the job market because they are transferable. For example, the word processing and data management skills you use in your current job as administrative assistant or insurance claims processor will be equally valuable in other jobs that you seek in the future, such as journalist or lawyer. The more skills you develop, the more valuable and versatile you are in the job market. Such books as *The Future of Work* (2002) by Charles Handy and *Free Agent Nation* (2002) and *A Whole New Mind* (2005) by Daniel Pink, propose that in this decade the number of portfolio workers will grow dramatically. Such workers would not be a full-time part of one organization but instead will sell their portfolio of skills to several employers on a freelance basis. Thus, the person who has word processing and data management skills may work for more than one firm in various capacities. A greater number of workers in the future will be self-employed, and their job security will come not from the traditional employer–employee relationship, but from their ability to offer needed skills to many employers. This increased trend toward self-employed portfolio employees means that each of us will benefit from being able to identify our skills

Assessing Your Skills

For each item in this table, mark an X next to each skill you enjoy using (even if you aren't expert at it!). Then go back over the list and place a check (✓) next to each skill that you perform particularly well. Underline any skills that you have never used. Finally, place an O next to any skills that you would like to develop or acquire. Under personal qualities, check all that apply to you.

Once you have completed these steps, review those skills that are marked with both an X *and* a check. These are your *self-motivated* or preferred skills. These skills represent your areas of mastery and probably your areas of greatest satisfaction as well. If you use these skills on the job whenever possible, and look for additional ways to use them, you will increase the enjoyment and satisfaction you derive from your job.

Review your list and identify five skills that interest you and that you would like to develop. Think of ways you can develop these skills, such as taking a course or class, getting on-the-job training, joining a club, volunteering, or asking a friend, associate, colleague, or mentor for help. To further clarify your responses, complete Exercise 5.7 at the end of the chapter.

X = skills you enjoy using
✓ = skills you perform especially well

O = skills you would like to develop or acquire
underlining = skills you have never used

CLERICAL SKILLS

_____ Examining
_____ Evaluating
_____ Filing
_____ Developing
_____ Improving
_____ Recording
_____ Collating
_____ Computing
_____ Recommending
_____ Following
_____ Bookkeeping
_____ Keyboarding
_____ Transcribing
_____ Indexing
_____ Arranging
_____ Systematizing
_____ Tabulating
_____ Photocopying
_____ Collaborating
_____ Sorting
_____ Retrieving
_____ Organizing
_____ Purchasing
_____ Handling people
_____ Problem solving

TECHNICAL SKILLS

_____ Financing
_____ Evaluating
_____ Calculating
_____ Adjusting
_____ Aligning
_____ Observing
_____ Verifying
_____ Drafting
_____ Designing
_____ Cataloging
_____ Examining
_____ Adjusting
_____ Problem solving
_____ Creating
_____ Detailing
_____ Restructuring
_____ Reviewing
_____ Revising
_____ Synthesizing
_____ Structuring
_____ Solving
_____ Refining
_____ Reviewing
_____ Following specifications

PUBLIC RELATIONS SKILLS

_____ Planning
_____ Conducting
_____ Informing
_____ Consulting
_____ Writing
_____ Researching
_____ Representing
_____ Negotiating
_____ Collaborating
_____ Communicating
_____ Promoting
_____ Convincing
_____ Hosting
_____ Entertaining
_____ Mediating
_____ Performing
_____ Endorsing
_____ Recruiting
_____ Demonstrating
_____ Creating
_____ Problem solving

AGRICULTURAL SKILLS

_____ Inspecting
_____ Costing

_____ Lifting
_____ Cultivating
_____ Assembling
_____ Problem solving
_____ Devising
_____ Scheduling
_____ Demonstrating
_____ Inspecting
_____ Evaluating
_____ Estimating
_____ Diagnosing
_____ Repairing
_____ Maintaining
_____ Replacing
_____ Constructing
_____ Operating

SELLING SKILLS

_____ Contacting
_____ Persuading
_____ Reviewing
_____ Inspecting
_____ Informing
_____ Promoting

_____ Positioning
_____ Influencing
_____ Convincing
_____ Comparing
_____ Differentiating
_____ Representing
_____ Asking
_____ Closing
_____ Costing
_____ Negotiating
_____ Communicating
_____ Calculating
_____ Advising
_____ Contracting
_____ Recommending
_____ Problem solving

MAINTENANCE SKILLS
_____ Operating
_____ Repairing
_____ Maintaining
_____ Dismantling
_____ Adjusting
_____ Cleaning
_____ Purchasing
_____ Climbing
_____ Lifting
_____ Assembling
_____ Problem solving
_____ Devising
_____ Scheduling
_____ Demonstrating
_____ Inspecting
_____ Evaluating
_____ Estimating

MANAGEMENT SKILLS
_____ Planning
_____ Organizing
_____ Scheduling
_____ Assigning
_____ Delegating
_____ Directing
_____ Hiring
_____ Measuring
_____ Administering
_____ Conducting
_____ Controlling
_____ Coordinating
_____ Enabling
_____ Empowering
_____ Initiating
_____ Formulating
_____ Supervising
_____ Sponsoring
_____ Modeling

_____ Supporting
_____ Negotiating
_____ Decision making
_____ Team building
_____ Conceptualizing
_____ Problem solving

COMMUNICATION SKILLS
_____ Reasoning
_____ Organizing
_____ Defining
_____ Writing
_____ Listening
_____ Explaining
_____ Interpreting
_____ Reading
_____ Speaking
_____ Editing
_____ Instructing
_____ Interviewing
_____ Collaborating
_____ Presenting
_____ Formulating
_____ Proposing
_____ Synthesizing
_____ Integrating
_____ Connecting
_____ Summarizing
_____ Articulating
_____ Interpreting
_____ Translating
_____ Problem solving

RESEARCH SKILLS
_____ Recognizing
_____ Interviewing
_____ Questioning
_____ Synthesizing
_____ Writing
_____ Diagnosing
_____ Compiling
_____ Reviewing
_____ Designing
_____ Theorizing
_____ Testing
_____ Equating
_____ Evaluating
_____ Investigating
_____ Summarizing
_____ Communicating
_____ Collaborating
_____ Demonstrating
_____ Analyzing
_____ Refining
_____ Problem solving

FINANCIAL SKILLS
_____ Calculating
_____ Projecting
_____ Budgeting
_____ Recognizing
_____ Accounting
_____ Processing
_____ Computing
_____ Correlating
_____ Costing
_____ Forecasting
_____ Comparing
_____ Compiling
_____ Examining
_____ Leveraging
_____ Verifying
_____ Problem-solving

MANUAL SKILLS
_____ Operating
_____ Monitoring
_____ Controlling
_____ Setting up
_____ Driving
_____ Cutting
_____ Assembling
_____ Drafting
_____ Drawing
_____ Inspecting
_____ Programming
_____ Tabulating
_____ Constructing
_____ Creating
_____ Repairing
_____ Problem solving

SERVICE SKILLS
_____ Counseling
_____ Guiding
_____ Leading
_____ Listening
_____ Coordinating
_____ Teaching
_____ Responding
_____ Collaborating
_____ Facilitating
_____ Monitoring
_____ Integrating
_____ Motivating
_____ Persuading
_____ Evaluating
_____ Summarizing
_____ Planning
_____ Correcting
_____ Mediating
_____ Encouraging

_____ Contracting
_____ Demonstrating
_____ Problem solving

PERSONAL QUALITIES
_____ Adaptable
_____ Adventuresome
_____ Aggressive
_____ Alert
_____ Ambitious
_____ Assertive
_____ Calm
_____ Capable
_____ Confident
_____ Conscientious
_____ Creative
_____ Cooperative
_____ Candid
_____ Dependable
_____ Determined
_____ Diplomatic
_____ Discreet
_____ Dominant
_____ Efficient
_____ Energetic
_____ Enterprising
_____ Enthusiastic
_____ Flexible
_____ Forceful
_____ Frank
_____ Idealistic
_____ Initiating
_____ Innovative
_____ Logical
_____ Loyal
_____ Methodical
_____ Objective
_____ Optimistic
_____ Organized
_____ Patient
_____ Persistent
_____ Practical
_____ Precise
_____ Quiet
_____ Realistic
_____ Reliable
_____ Resourceful
_____ Risk taking
_____ Self-starting
_____ Sensitive
_____ Serious
_____ Sincere
_____ Tactful
_____ Tenacious
_____ Versatile

and from determining which skills we want to use, improve, and develop to stay competitive in the job market.

Identifying Transferable Skills

Whether you work as an interior designer, an engineer, or a school teacher, you will employ such transferable skills as communication, organization, and problem-solving.

As we've discussed throughout this chapter, transferable skills are those skills that you carry from one job to another and can utilize in performing many jobs. Perhaps you are concerned about a lack of paid job experience, or you may have chosen a liberal arts major and are concerned that you will not learn specific job skills or be trained for a job when you graduate.

Note how many SCANS skills you are using by reading Exhibit 5.2 and by completing exercises in this book related to resume writing, career information searching, information interviewing, and making a budget (see Using SCANS Skills, p. 115).

Let's examine the transferable skills that a liberal arts major can and should develop while in school. We will also explore the notion that your *personal, natural abilities* and *attitude* are perhaps the most important set of skills you have for selling yourself and your talents to a potential employer.

Transferable Skills of a Liberal Arts Major

A liberal arts degree is preparation for a variety of careers. In fact, the majority of those who graduate with a liberal arts degree do not find employment in fields related to their major (e.g., history majors do not necessarily become historians).

Whether you are an anthropology, English, or history major, you have (or will develop) transferable skills that are useful in the workplace as a result of being a successful college student. As you read about the following clusters of skills, think about which skills you have gained as a student. The *cluster* approach to skills will be further explained in Chapter 10 when we discuss the functional resume. Do you have research skills? Do you have organizational skills? Chances are, you do!

EXHIBIT 5.2	Tasks from diverse occupations representative of level of performance in SCANS know-how required for entry into jobs with career ladder.

POSITION AND TASK

RESOURCES	Travel Agent: Sets priorities for work tasks on a daily basis so that travel arrangements are completed in a timely manner.	Restaurant Manager: Prepares weekly sales projections; conducts inventories of food supplies; calculates the costs of purchased and on-hand food; determines sales.	Medical Assistant: Acquires, maintains, and tracks supplies on hand— inventories supplies and equipment, fills out reorder forms, and obtains extra supplies when merchandise is on sale.	Quality Control Inspector: Establishes a system for inspecting items within a given area and time frame while allowing for contingencies.	Chef: Performs a cost analysis on menu items in order to turn a profit.
INTERPERSONAL SKILLS	Childcare Aide: Works as a member of a team in the classroom.	Outside Equipment Technician: Coordinates with a peer technician to install a point-to-point data circuit in two different cities.	Carpenter: Shares experiences and knowledge with other workers, and cooperates with others on a variety of tasks to accomplish project goals.	Accounting/ Financial Analyst: Teaches a coworker the procedure for sending bimonthly memos.	Customer Service Representative: Assists customers in selecting merchandise or resolving complaints.
INFORMATION	Travel Agent: Uses online computer terminal to retrieve information relating to customer requests, plans itineraries, and books airline tickets.	Blue-Collar Worker Supervisor: Records and maintains purchase requests, purchase invoices, and cost information on raw material.	Childcare Aide: Compiles accurate written records including all facets of the child's play for the office and the parents.	Order Filler: Communicates a downtime situation to coworkers and explains the situation so that everyone can visualize and understand it.	Cosmetologist: Keeps abreast of new and emerging styles and techniques through magazines and attendance at fashion shows.
SYSTEMS	Medical Assistant: Understands the systems of the organization and the organization's ultimate goal (i.e., excellent patient care).	Accounting/ Financial Analyst: Performs analyses comparing current expenditures with projected needs and revenues.	Shipping and Receiving Clerk: Unloads and directs material throughout the plant to storage and the assembly line in accordance with company policy.	Food Service Worker: Evaluates the performance of workers and adjusts work assignments to increase staff efficiency.	Plastic Molding Machine Operator: Monitors gauges and dials to ensure that the machine operates at the proper rate.

(*Continued*)

Continued

EXHIBIT 5.2

POSITION AND TASK

TECHNOLOGY	Travel Agent: Uses the online computer terminal to retrieve information relating to the customer's request, plan the itinerary, and book the airline ticket.	Accounting/ Financial Analyst: Prepares the monthly debt schedule, including reviews of financial statements.	Expeditor/ Purchasing Agent: Accesses the computer to retrieve required forms used to request bids and to place purchase orders.	Industry Training Specialist: Uses available computer and video technology to enhance the realism of training and to conserve time.	Order Filler: Operates a forklift and ensures that it is in proper operating condition.
BASIC SKILLS	Dental Hygienist: Reads professional manuals to understand issues related to new techniques and equipment.	Sales Representative, Hotel Services: Assesses client accounts to determine adherence to company standards.	Optician: Measures a customer's facial features to calculate bifocal segment height.	Law Enforcement Officer: Prepares written reports of incidents and crimes.	Contractor: Prepares a letter to a subcontractor delineating responsibilities for completion of an earth-grading contract.
THINKING SKILLS	Expeditor/ Purchasing Agent: Decides what supplier to use during a bid evaluation based on supplier information stored in the computer.	Blue-Collar Worker Supervisor: Sets priorities for processing orders to resolve a conflict in scheduling.	Truck Delivery Salesperson/ Outside Sales: Collects money from delinquent customers and uses judgment on extending credit.	Contractor: Analyzes and corrects the problem when timber piles break before reaching specified bearing loads.	Travel Agent: Compensates a customer who is dissatisfied with a travel experience.
PERSONAL QUALITIES	Optician: Responds appropriately to customer requests, demonstrates understanding of customer needs, and exhibits friendliness and politeness to customers.	Quality Control Inspector: Performs independent research to assess compliance.	Computer Operator: Assumes responsibility for the arrangement and completion of jobs run on the mainframe.	Telemarketing Representative: Displays a sense of concern and interest in customers' business and company.	Sales Representative, Hotel Services: Asserts self and networks with people at conventions in order to obtain hotel business.

Source: *School to Career Handbook* (California Community Colleges, Chancellor's office, 1995).

FACTS & FIGURES

People skills

From the manager of the accounting department at Sony Technology Center:

> The number one thing that I look for when I am hiring someone is their people skills because it is very important that you have the skills to talk to people and find out what you need to know. I believe that everyone has the ability to learn anything in this world, but if you have the ability to find the answers to things you want, then you will succeed. . . . I spend 80 percent of my time or so dealing with other divisions within Sony . . . and my staff also deals with these people.

(http://cord.org/workplacelibrary/sony/katie5.html)

THINK ABOUT IT

1. Why is it important to have people skills if you plan to be an accountant?

2. From this description, what do you think an accountant does besides accounting?

3. What did you learn from reading this information?

To answer these questions online, go to the *Facts and Figures* module in Chapter 5 of the Companion Website.

Companion Website

Examples of the skills learned in a typical college liberal arts degree program include the following (note how these mirror the skills identified by the SCANS report):

Communication skills. Listening effectively, writing essays and reports, convincing individuals and groups of the importance of your ideas, negotiating disputes and differences.

Problem-solving or critical-thinking skills. Analytical thinking, thinking abstractly, determining broader issues, defining an issue, identifying several solutions to the same problem, creating new ways to handle an issue, persuading others to act in the best interests of the group.

Human relations skills. Speaking with colleagues, advising people, helping people resolve problems, communicating ideas effectively, cooperating with others to solve problems and to complete projects, working well with diverse groups of people, teaching or coaching others.

Organizational skills. Assessing needs, planning or arranging presentations or social events, designing programs, coordinating events, delegating responsibility, evaluating programs, managing the implementation of projects.

Research skills. Searching computerized databases and published reference materials, identifying themes, analyzing data, classifying data, handling detail work, investigating problems, recording data, writing reports and term papers.

By now, it should be apparent that you carry many skills from one job to another. Once you are able to describe a job by its skills, you can use these skills in your own letters of application, in your resumes, and during job interviews to reinforce the fact that you have what it takes to do the job, even if you have never had the exact job title.

Your Most Valuable Assets: Your Personality Traits

We've talked about transferable skills that were learned or acquired at school, work, or home, or through leisure and volunteer activities. Many of your skills may have come to you naturally, without training or education. We call these skills *natural abilities*—we're referring here to aspects of your personality such as the ability to stay calm

$\mathcal{S}$ UCCESS STRATEGIES

Identifying the Transferable Skills of a Teacher

Do you think a teacher would have the skills necessary to find employment in the business world? If you know or have read about anyone working in sales, marketing, or management, you may notice that similar skills are involved in all these jobs.

ASSESSMENT OF TEACHER SKILLS

TEACHING. Training, coordinating, communicating, arbitrating, coaching, group facilitating, accessing the Internet, using computers.

MAKING LESSON PLANS. Designing curricula, incorporating learning strategies, problem solving, creating visual aids.

ASSIGNING GRADES. Evaluating, examining, assessing performance, interpreting test results, determining potential of individuals, monitoring progress.

WRITING PROPOSALS. Assessing needs, identifying targets, setting priorities, designing evaluation models, identifying relevant information, making hypotheses about unknown phenomena, designing a process, estimating costs of a project, researching funding sources.

ADVISING THE YEARBOOK STAFF. Planning, promoting, fund-raising, group facilitating, handling detail work, meeting deadlines, assembling items of information into a coherent whole, classifying information, coordinating, creating, dealing with pressure, delegating tasks, displaying ideas in artistic form, editing, making layouts.

SUPERVISING INTERNS. Training, evaluating, mentoring, monitoring progress, diagnosing problem areas, inspiring, counseling, guiding.

INTERPRETING DIAGNOSTIC TESTS. Screening, placing, identifying needs, diagnosing.

INTERACTING WITH STUDENTS, PARENTS, AND ADMINISTRATION. Confronting, resolving conflicts, establishing rapport, conveying warmth and caring, drawing people out, offering support, motivating, negotiating, persuading, handling complaints, mediating, organizing, questioning, troubleshooting.

CHAIRING A COMMITTEE OR DEPARTMENT. Administering, anticipating needs or issues, arranging meetings, creating and implementing committee structures, coordinating, delegating tasks, guiding activities of a team, having responsibility for meeting objectives of a department, negotiating, organizing, promoting.

in a crisis, the ability to manage many things at once, a natural ability with math and numbers, a natural ability with words, and so forth. More important, we're referring to personal characteristics such as enthusiasm, a good attitude, persistence, confidence, a sense of humor, and many other qualities of success that we discussed in Chapter 2.

These abilities will help you *sell yourself and your talents*. These personal characteristics, called *adaptive skills*, may in the end separate you from other qualified applicants and enable you to get the job, top evaluations, raises, and promotions. They may even help you keep your job in tough times.

We don't mean to imply that an employer will look at your enthusiastic, smiling face and say, "It doesn't matter that you have no experience—we want you because you're cheerful!" However, once you have learned to identify your job-specific skills and summarize your experience in such a way that it relates closely to the job being discussed, you will have a greater chance of succeeding if you are aware of and express your best self with interest, enthusiasm, and friendliness. Know and use your personal skills!

SUCCESS STRATEGIES

The SCANS Report

IDENTIFYING THE BASIC SKILLS REQUIRED BY EMPLOYERS

In 1991, the U.S. Department of Labor issued the SCANS (*Secretary's Commission on Achieving Necessary Skills*) report. The goal of this report was to sum up the competencies and skills that form the basis of solid job performance. The results are based on extensive questioning of employers and educators.

Review the core competencies, qualities, and skills identified by the SCANS report below. These are considered essential skills that workers must possess to be competitive in the 21st-century job market. In how many of these areas do you currently feel you have adequate skill levels? If an employer asked you to prove your competencies, could you identify an area of accomplishment in which you demonstrated your use of these skills?

Workplace Know-How

The know-how identified by the SCANS report is made up of a three-part foundation of skills and personal qualities along with five competencies; both the foundation and the competencies are needed for solid job performance.

The Foundation

BASIC SKILLS: Reading, writing, arithmetic and mathematics, speaking, and listening. These are the *minimum* skills needed by today's workers. If you are unsure about your skills in these basic areas, now is the time to take steps to improve them. Don't shy away from basic testing and coursework or assume that, as an adult, you naturally have these abilities. Begin thinking in terms of doing all of these things *well* and taking steps to achieve this level of proficiency.

THINKING SKILLS: Thinking creatively, making decisions, solving problems, seeing things in the mind's eye, knowing how to learn, and reasoning. Thinking skills allow you to identify your strengths and weaknesses and take steps to remedy the latter. They allow you to acquire new skills, think creatively, and identify problems and solutions. Once again, if you are unsure of your abilities in these areas, talk to your career counselor or instructor about testing and coursework that can help.

PERSONAL QUALITIES: Individual responsibility, self-esteem, sociability, self-management, and integrity. Included are the personality characteristics described in Chapter 2 and the adaptive skills described in this chapter.

The Competencies

Effective workers can productively use:

RESOURCES: Allocating time, money, materials, space, and personnel.

INTERPERSONAL SKILLS: Working on teams, teaching others, serving customers, leading, negotiating, and working well with people from culturally diverse backgrounds.

INFORMATION: Acquiring and evaluating data, organizing and maintaining files, interpreting and communicating, and using computers to process information.

SYSTEMS: Understanding social, organizational, and technological systems; monitoring and correcting performance; and designing or improving systems.

TECHNOLOGY: Selecting equipment and tools, applying technology to specific tasks, and maintaining and troubleshooting technologies.

SUCCESS STRATEGIES

Using SCANS Skills

Sample skills used to complete assignments in a career planning class.

Resume Writing	Career Info Search	Informational Interview	Making a Budget	SCANS FOUNDATION	Resume Writing	Career Info Search	Informational Interview	Making a Budget	SCANS COMPETENCIES
				Basic Skills					**Resources**
X	X		X	Reading	X	X	X		Time
X				Writing		X		X	Money
			X	Arithmetic		X	X		Material and facilities
		X	X	Listening	X	X	X		Human resources
	X	X		Speaking					
									Interpersonal
				Thinking Skills		X	X		Participates as member of a team
X	X	X	X	Creative thinking		X	X		Teaches others new skills
			X	Decision making				X	Serves clients/customers
		X	X	Problem solving		X	X	X	Exercises leadership
	X	X		Seeing things in the mind's eye			X	X	Negotiates
X	X	X	X	Knowing how to learn	X	X	X		Works with diversity
	X		X	Reasoning					
									Information
				Personal Qualities		X	X	X	Acquires and evaluates information
X			X	Responsibility		X	X	X	Organizes and maintains information
X	X	X		Self-esteem		X	X		Interprets and communicates information
X		X		Sociability		X	X	X	Uses computers to process information
X	X	X	X	Self-management					
X	X	X	X	Integrity/honesty					**Systems**
						X		X	Understands systems
					X				Monitors and corrects performance
						X	X	X	Improves and designs systems
									Technology
					X	X		X	Selects technology
					X	X	X	X	Applies technology to task
						X			Maintains and troubleshoots equipment

Source: *School to Career Handbook* (VATEA funded project through the California Community Colleges, Chancellor's office, 1995).

Summary

Use past accomplishments to reveal skills

We all have our own special excellence. This excellence is most likely to be demonstrated in experiences that you consider to be achievements or life satisfactions. Your most memorable achievements usually indicate where your greatest concentration of self-motivator (motivated) skills exists. Analyzing several such achievements is likely to reveal a pattern of skills used repeatedly in making them occur. The more you know about your motivated skills, the better you will be able to choose careers that require the use of these skills. Using these skills gives you a sense of mastery and satisfaction. You will be happier, more productive, and more successful if you can incorporate your motivated skills into your chosen work. You will also find that your skills transfer to many different jobs.

If you have started reading about occupations online or in a library or college career center, you will find that occupational information sources list the skills related to the specific careers described. The new GOE, mentioned in Chapter 4, has excellent examples showing how activities in daily life and hobbies can be translated into skills. There are also computer programs such as EUREKA in California, SIGI Plus (System of Interactive Guidance and Information), and CIS (Career Information System) that include lists of skills correlated with job descriptions. Check with your local college or computer store to learn about other skills analysis software. Be certain to review Exhibit 5.2 to identify how the SCANS skills relate to a variety of entry-level jobs. Now, complete the exercises that follow.

SUCCESS STRATEGIES

Describing Skills

Remember that skills are the currency of the job market. The more you have and the better you are at describing them, the greater your opportunities will be.

- Review the list of transferable skills of a liberal arts major on page 112.

- As you read each skill under each category, think of a specific time when you developed or demonstrated that skill in school, during your leisure activities, or during a past or present job.

- Jot down some notes to remind yourself how you used any of these skills, or create a file to save on your computer for future reference.

- Review these notes the next time you are writing a resume or interviewing for a job so that you can convincingly describe the skills you possess and how you demonstrated these skills.

- Your ability to communicate this critical information to employers will set you apart from the crowd in the interview process and help put you on top of any employer's list of candidates for hire.

CHAPTER 5 EXERCISES

SKILLS ASSESSMENT

PURPOSE OF EXERCISE. The following exercises will assist you in identifying your personal constellation of skills. Exercise 5.1 asks you to write about several major experiences in your life with enough detail so that you will be able to analyze each experience for the particular skills utilized. Exercises 5.2 and 5.3 ask you to list 10 accomplishments and then to describe a few of them in detail. Exercise 5.4 allows you to identify the skills used in the accomplishments described in the two previous exercises. Exercise 5.5 identifies your cluster of favorite skills. Exercise 5.6 helps you identify the extent of your experience related to the responsibilities of your ideal jobs. Exercises 5.7 and 5.8 serve to review and summarize your preferred and most often used skills.

To answer these questions online, go to the *Exercise* module in Chapter 5 of the Companion Website.

Experiography   5.1

To explore your past experiences and relate them to your career plan, write an account of the significant experiences in your life—an *experiography*. The best way to go about this task is to think of three or four major experiences in each of the following categories and then describe each of them in writing in as much detail as you can. It is important to describe not only what happened but also your feelings (good or bad) about the experience or person and what you learned from the experience. The categories to include are:

a. work experience

b. activity experience—school, clubs, etc.

c. life events

d. leisure time

e. people in your life

f. life's frustrations

g. life's rewards

Remember, neither the chronology nor the order of significance is important. What is important is that you describe people or events that have had an impact on who you are right now. Keep in mind that the writing needs to be specific enough for you to be able to analyze these experiences for particular skills you have demonstrated.

5.2   *Accomplishments*

Make a list of up to 10 accomplishments. You may wish to look back at the ones you have already listed in the Values Grid in Chapter 3, but you do not necessarily have to include them in this list.

1. _____
2. _____
3. _____
4. _____
5. _____
6. _____
7. _____
8. _____
9. _____
10. _____

5.3   *Description of Accomplishments*

Select one or two of the accomplishments listed above, and describe each of them. Use one sheet of paper for each. To be as detailed as possible in your description of the event, try to elaborate on *who* influenced you, *what* you did, *where* it happened, *when* it occurred, *why* you did it, and *how* you did it.

5.4   *The Skills*

List the skills you used in the accomplishments described in Exercise 5.3:

_____
_____
_____

5.5   *Your Favorite Skills*

Rank the following skills categories as they reflect your favorite skills (1 = favorite; 6 = least favorite):

_____ a. Help people, be of service, be kind

_____ b. Write, read, talk, speak, teach

_____ c. Analyze, systemize, research

_____ d. Invent, create, develop, imagine

_____ e. Persuade, sell, influence, negotiate

_____ f. Build, plant crops, use hand–eye coordination, operate machinery

Ideal Jobs   **5.6**

Write five ideal job responsibilities. Next to each one, write two or more examples of your experience in each of these areas (e.g., "writing—I wrote a 10-page report that was used to justify a grant application"). In areas where you have not developed extensive experience, you may want to create additional learning experiences to make yourself eligible for your ideal jobs. You can create learning experiences or gain experience by taking classes, by volunteering for extra work in your present job, or by finding another job closely related to your ideal jobs.

_____

_____

_____

_____

_____

_____

_____

_____

_____

_____

_____

_____

_____

_____

SCANS   **5.7**

Review the SCANS skills description on page 114. Identify up to eight volunteer, job, or homework activities:

1. _____

2. _____

3. _____

4. _____

5. _____

6. _____

7. _____

8. _____

On the worksheet on the next page, check the skills you used in these activities. Use the grid on page 115 as an example.

Exercise 5.7 Worksheet

Identify up to eight volunteer, job, or homework activities and check off which skills were used in each activity.

1	2	3	4	5	6	7	8	SCANS FOUNDATION
								Basic Skills Reading Writing Arithmetic Listening Speaking
								Thinking Skills Creative thinking Decision making Problem solving Seeing things in the mind's eye Knowing how to learn Reasoning
								Personal Qualities Responsibility Self-esteem Sociability Self-management Integrity/honesty
								SCANS COMPETENCIES
								Resources Time Money Material and facilities Human resources
								Interpersonal Participates as member of a team Teaches others new skills Serves clients/customers Exercises leadership Negotiates Works with diversity
								Information Acquires and evaluates information Organizes and maintains information Interprets and communicates information Uses computers to process information
								Systems Understands systems Monitors and corrects performance Improves and designs systems
								Technology Selects technology Applies technology to task Maintains and troubleshoots equipment

Source: *School to Career Handbook* (VATEA funded project through the California Community Colleges, Chancellor's office, 1995).

Skills Review

List the skills that you have at present:

_____

_____

_____

_____

_____

_____

_____

Review your responses in the Assessing Your Skills activity on pages 107–108. What skills would you most like to use in your future career?

_____

_____

_____

_____

_____

_____

_____

Which of the above skills do you need to develop?

_____

_____

_____

_____

_____

How will you develop these skills?

_____

_____

_____

_____

_____

_____

_____

You have now identified your foundation—the areas in which you have been most effective and successful in your life. By examining these successes or achievements, you now know what you can do and what motivates you. It is especially important that you focus on skills you use and enjoy.

5.9   *WWWebwise*

For additional activities online, go to the WWWebwise module in Chapter 5 of the Companion Website.

5.10   *Exercise Summary*

Write a brief paragraph answering these questions.

What did you learn about yourself through these exercises? How does this knowledge relate to your career/life planning? How do you feel?

_____

_____

_____

_____

_____

_____

_____

_____

_____

_____

_____

_____

_____

_____

_____

_____

_____

_____

_____

_____

_____

_____

_____

_____

Go to page 222 of the chapter summaries and fill out the Chapter 5 exercise summary now.

II

6

The World and You

7

Information Integration

8

Making Decisions

THE WORLD OF WORK

123

6

The World and You

Learning Objectives

At the end of the chapter you will be able to . . .

- Identify personal beliefs and assumptions that will affect your career

- Recognize how social and cultural conditioning influences your career choice

- Identify trends that will affect your career planning through the next decade

- List changes in the workplace

- Recognize the skills employers expect in new employees

- Learn the value of a liberal arts degree

Your assumptions, limitations, aspirations, dreams, and fantasies are all influenced by the spoken and unspoken rules and norms of the society in which you live.

The illiterate of the 21st century will not only be those who cannot read or write, but those who cannot learn, unlearn, and relearn.

ALVIN TOFFLER

In every society, even one as free as that of the United States, social and cultural traditions influence career choice. For example, it may still seem a little strange to us to hear the word *nurse* applied to a male health-care worker, even though both men and women are found in this profession. Old associations and stereotypes linger because of the many years during which societal limitations and expectations played a much greater role in determining career choices for men and women.

You have completed the personal assessment portion of your career fitness program. You have reviewed and analyzed your values, your interests, your personality, and your skills. Now you need to explore the world of work and assess where you best fit. In this chapter, you will learn about some of the important and exciting changes that are occurring in the workplace. These changes will affect the kinds of occupations available to you. As you read about issues and trends in this chapter, think about your personal career profile and how it matches the opportunities that exist.

The first part of this chapter explores cultural norms, gender equity issues, cultural diversity, and ageism, as well as related factors that can constrict or expand your career options. The latter part of this chapter examines trends in the workforce as they relate to possible career choices. You will also explore careers for liberal arts and other nontechnical graduates and employer expectations of new hires, and you will complete some written exercises at the end of the chapter. The written exercises will help you to identify your own barriers, attitudes, and biases. This self-knowledge will assist you in better planning your future.

Societal Influences on Career Choices

Career planning does not happen in a vacuum. Your life situation influences the decisions you make and how you make them. The society in which you grow up, your background, your family, your peers, and the way you feel about yourself are all influences on the decisions you make. Sometimes these factors make it easier to choose and follow a career path. For instance, a friend or family member who encourages you in school and work efforts may help to build your confidence and therefore improve your chances of success in whatever field you choose. Or family support may allow you to devote full-time effort to schooling and thus more quickly complete your chosen degree.

However, social and cultural considerations, family, peers, and feelings about yourself can also act as obstacles to making and following through on decisions. For example, your time available for school may be limited by family responsibilities, or you may feel that the career you would like to pursue requires an advanced degree, or that it would not pay enough to support your family. Consider the following statements:

> "I'm too old [or perhaps too far along in school] to start thinking about changing careers now."
>
> "What I would really like to be is an engineer, but I've given up on that because I can't go to school full-time to get that kind of degree."
>
> "I don't know whether I'm going to apply for that job or not. Besides, they're not going to hire a Latino."
>
> "I'm not really qualified to do that kind of job, and my high school grades were weak. I was never good at schoolwork."
>
> "Sure, I'd like to go back to school, but how could I get all the housework done, and who would look after the kids? There's no money for day care."

Do any of the preceding statements sound like some you have heard people say, or maybe even some you yourself have said or felt? They represent some of the most common obstacles that people face when making academic and career decisions. An obstacle to a satisfactory decision is anything or anyone who prevents you from adequately considering all the possible alternatives. For example, the people who say "I'm too old to start something new" when looking for a job will miss out by not even considering some positions for which they may be well qualified. Age stereotyping prevents these people from considering all the possible alternatives.

Striving for Equality in the Workforce

Gender Roles

As recently as 40 years ago, female students seeking career advice from school counselors were frequently encouraged to choose fields such as teaching and nursing. These choices were recommended both because they were "women's jobs" and because they fit best with the traditional female family role of mothering. It wasn't until the 1970s that newspapers no longer divided the classified employment ads into the categories of "men" and "women."

We are what we do. Excellence, then, is not an act, but a habit.

ARISTOTLE

Within the past 35 years, school counselors began to recognize that female roles in society were expanding and that women could be doctors, engineers, and members of, in fact, any profession. Today, academic counselors are more aware of gender fairness issues (see the Equity Definitions box, below) and more often attempt to treat men and women similarly, without making judgments or assumptions about marriage and family roles.

As suggested above, many of our career and pay biases were based on the social norm of a "typical" four-member family in which the husband was

Equity Definitions

Affirmative action: Programs, policies, or procedures that attempt to overcome the effects of past discrimination, bias, and/or stereotyping.

Ageism: Any action or policy that discriminates on the basis of age, affecting employment, advancement, privileges, or rewards.

Americans with Disabilities Act (ADA): Legislation passed July 26, 1990, that prohibits discrimination on the basis of a disability.

Barriers: Anything that prevents a person from equal access to the use of goods, services, facilities, and so on. There are physical and architectural barriers (such as stairs) and there are attitudinal barriers (such as stereotyping).

Discrimination: Practices, policies, or procedures that are specifically prohibited by law; any action that limits or denies a person or group of persons opportunities, privileges, roles, or rewards on such prohibited bases as their sex, race, age, and so on.

Gender bias: An attitude or behavior that reflects adversely on a person or group because of gender but may not be covered under present legislation; behavior resulting from the assumption that one sex is superior to the other.

Gender fair: Practices and behaviors that treat males and females similarly; may imply separate but equal.

Gender role: Social behavior that is prescribed and defined for males and females according to tradition, as contrasted with actual biological differences.

Gender stereotyping: Attributing behaviors, abilities, interests, values, and roles to a person or group of persons on the basis of gender.

Nontraditional job: Working in a field or an occupation that typically employs 75 percent or more of the opposite gender (e.g., nursing employs only 8 percent males; construction work employs only 2.5 percent females).

Sexism: Any attitude, action, or institution that subordinates or assigns roles to a person or group of persons based on gender. Sexism may be individual, cultural, or institutional; intentional or unintentional; effected by omission or commission.

the principal wage earner and the wife was primarily responsible for raising the children. Societal changes and evolutions have moved us away from these traditional roles and toward gender equity. Because many couples find it difficult, if not impossible, to manage a home and family on one income, both partners in today's "typical" marriage work outside the home. This major change has forced us (or permitted us) to rethink traditional male and female roles. Partners in a relationship are more likely to share home and child-rearing responsibilities.

Just as women's roles have changed over the past few decades, so too have men's roles undergone change. For example, some men may choose careers that don't require extensive travel or long work hours because they want and expect to assume an equal parenting role. Many women now play the role of primary breadwinner in a family. In some families, men are choosing to work or stay at home and take care of the children. Both traditional and nontraditional types of families face new challenges with each passing year. Finding reliable, affordable child care is a struggle for many parents, and this concern may influence career decisions and directions. Today, a great many families are single-parent households, in which the adult must combine the full-time job of earning a living with the all-consuming task of raising a family.

In an ideally unbiased society composed of 50 percent men and 50 percent women, it can be expected that most occupations would employ approximately 50 percent of each gender and would pay them like salaries for like work. However, in our society such equity is being achieved gradually. Exhibit 6.1 illustrates ongoing inequities in the types of jobs held by women and men.

Nontraditional occupations for women* (numbers in thousands).   **EXHIBIT 6.1**

OCCUPATION	EMPLOYED BOTH SEXES	EMPLOYED FEMALE	PERCENT FEMALE
Sales representatives in mining, manufacturing, wholesale	121	31	25.5
Architects	207	50	24
Drafting occupations	206	48	23.7
Chief executives	1,680	391	23.3
Dentist	167	37	22
Announcers	54	11	21.6
Supervisors, police and detective	133	28	21.2
Farming, fishing, & forestry occupations	990	204	20.6
Network & computer systems administrators	190	39	20.3
Detectives and criminal investigators	121	24	20.0
Engineering technicians	416	82	19.7
Chefs and head cooks	299	56	18.9
Transportation, storage, and distribution managers	241	36	14.9
Couriers and messengers	293	43	14.8
Sheriffs and police patrol officers	664	135	13.3
Broadcast and sound engineering technicians	92	11	12.1
Groundskeepers, gardeners, and landscaping managers	227	18	8.1
Electrical and electronic engineers	343	11	7.9
Engineering managers	106	18	5.9
Airplane pilots and flight engineers	118	6	5.3
Firefighter occupations	268	13	5.0
Mechanics and repairers	5,069	233	4.6
Truck drivers	3,276	147	4.5
Tool programmers, machinists	445	19	4.4
Construction trades	8,522	213	2.5
Carpenters	1,764	32	1.8
Heating, air-conditioning, & refrigeration mechanics & installers	351	5	1.5
Automotive service technicians	936	12	1.3

*Nontraditional occupations are those for which women comprise 25 percent or less of the total employed.

Source: Bureau of Labor Statistics, *Women in Workforce Databook* (2004).

FACTS&FIGURES

High Wages vs. Life/Balance Issues

Statistics show that on average women earn 80 cents for every dollar that men make and that many high-paying occupations have less than 25 percent females in their ranks. However, it is possible that these statistics don't tell the whole story. In *Why Men Earn More: The Startling Truth Behind the Pay Gap—and What Women Can Do About It,* Warren Farrell (2005) writes that 25 differences are apparent in the nontraditional occupations for women listed in Exhibit 6.1. For example, hazardous jobs (such as garbage collector, logging, construction, firefighting) receive few applications from women. Also, men are more willing to do certain things at work that put them into higher earning categories, such as working longer hours, relocating to undesirable places, traveling extensively, and working in poor (hot, cold, cramped, isolated, outdoors, night shift, etc.) conditions. Companies that need workers to do these types of jobs often pay higher wages and benefits to make up for the demands of these jobs.

Additionally, young women often earn as much as or more than men until they have children and family responsibilities. It is typical at this point for men to take on more difficult work assignments with the hope of earning more (for the family), while women scale back in order to spend more time meeting the needs of their family and children. It may be a question of having more earnings versus having a more balanced life.

Farrell's book discusses six strategies anyone can use who is more interested in earning higher wages than in having a balanced life.

1. **Go for a job with bottom-line responsibility.** Operating (sales, finance, purchasing) jobs generate revenue, and companies are willing to pay more for people who take on the responsibility and risk of being held accountable for the bottom line.

2. **Find a field that entails financial or emotional risk-taking.** Venture capitalists and entrepreneurs are handsomely paid for taking huge risks. Where the stakes are high, the personal rewards are often high as well.

3. **Work more hours, weeks, and years.** The U.S. Bureau of Labor Statistics (BLS) reports that the average person working 45 hours per week earns 44 percent more than someone working 40 hours. (The BLS indicates that men work an average of 41 hours per week while women average 35 hours per week.)

4. **Be willing to relocate anywhere.** Tough jobs in remote locations often lead to better-paying positions, because you have more responsibility to deal with and can gain the skills necessary to rise to the top more easily. You will also show that you can stand the pressure!

5. **Pick technology or hard sciences over the arts or social sciences.** On the BLS chart of "20 Occupations That Pay the Most," nine are various types of engineering and computer science jobs. Meanwhile, less than 10 percent of engineers are women.

6. **Choose a field where you can't "check out" at the end of the day.** Farrell calls these jobs "7–11s" because they never close. Doctors, lawyers, and executives have trouble getting away from their work, even for vacations, but are paid well for their commitment. These people are working a career, not a job.

These are six strategies that many men (as well as women) have used to get ahead and to be paid better. We do not necessarily endorse these means to a higher paycheck. Ultimately, it would be best if companies could find ways to reduce the extreme hours required at work.

If the workplace doesn't change, employers may face a challenge finding young talent to take on the demanding jobs. A recent *Harvard Business Review* study (2005) indicated that women who try some of these strategies eventually may revert toward finding balance in their lives, often sacrificing their high-paying careers. The study also showed that women are more likely to leave an intense high-paying career when company policies, practices, and attitudes at work result in their feeling under utilized and unappreciated. The *Harvard Business Review* article indicated that 52 percent of women with MBAs cite the reason that they do not find their careers "either satisfying or enjoyable" as an important reason for why they leave work.

With each new generation of workers, there is hope that companies will start addressing the need for work–life balance. A Radcliffe–Harris poll (2000) reported that 70 percent of men in their twenties said they would be willing to trade more money for more time with their children. With the Bureau of Labor Statistics indicating that there will be a shortage of qualified workers for high-level positions in the next decade, what are companies likely to do?

THINK ABOUT IT

1. To what does Farrell attribute the gap in wages between men and women? Which of these strategies would work for you? Explain why or why not.

2. Do you think the demands on employees' personal time will continue to grow? Research work–life on the Internet. Then, decide where you stand on the issue. Give at least three reasons to support your point of view. *Fast Company* magazine has some good articles to begin with:

> Tischler, Linda. "Bridging The (Gender Wage) Gap." *Fast Company,* Jan. 2005, vol. 90 p. 85.
>
> Tischler, Linda. "Where Are the Women?" *Fast Company,* Mar. 2004, vol. 79 p. 52.

Companion Website

To answer these questions online, go to the *Facts and Figures* module in Chapter 6 of the Companion Website.

Although you cannot predict the exact course of your life or your career, you can begin considering possible choices and how they relate to *you*. Take time now to anticipate challenges you may encounter in the future. Now is the time to plan. By setting objectives that lead toward accomplishment of a career goal, you may later avoid having to take a job just to pay the bills. It is now more important than ever to choose a career that truly reflects your interests and abilities, your values, your personality, and your life plan. The concept of gender equity means that everyone is free to explore a career of his or her choice.

Age and Opportunity

Ten years ago, there were 20 million people over age 65 in the United States. As we move into the 21st century, the figure is over 25 million. By 2020, the over-65 population could go as high as 50 million. There will be more single people older than 65, particularly women. Approximately 45 percent of all seniors are over 75. In fact, workers 55 and older are projected to increase from 15.6 percent in 2004 to 21.2 percent in 2014, according to the Bureau of Labor Statistics.

It should be noted that the number of people retiring at age 65 continues to decrease. Many victims of corporate downsizing are let go before becoming eligible for retirement pensions. And due to no-fault divorce laws and lack of retirement plans in the traditionally female occupations, many divorced women must continue to work long after their male counterparts have retired. If present trends continue, retirement-age single women will be the poorest segment of society.

Accentuate your assets

Older workers competing in the workforce may face discrimination and the perception by employers that they are out-of-date or too old to learn. Although such ageism is illegal, it occurs. Young workers are valued for their energy, flexibility, and entry-level salaries. Some employers, however, may choose an older, more mature job candidate over a recent college graduate, in the belief that anyone, at any age, can display high energy and flexibility, but with age come maturity, reliability, problem-solving abilities, and a wealth of experience. As a prospective employee, it is your responsibility to know your assets, whether those of youth or maturity, and to highlight them at the right times with the right decision makers. The most effective way to deal with ageism (whether it's directed against your youth or lack of it) is to sell your present or prospective employer on how your age and particular experience are an asset to the job.

If you think education is expensive, try ignorance.

DEREK BOK

Many of today's retirement-age workers are finding satisfaction in the entry-level jobs once dominated by teenage workers, such as in fast-food and retail outlets. For some seniors, this work offers a social outlet, and the minimal pay is sufficient for workers whose income is supplemented by Social Security benefits.

People who live long, healthy lives may change careers frequently during their lifetimes, and their most satisfying and perhaps most financially rewarding career may come later in life. Novelist James Michener was first published after the age of 40; Colonel Sanders started Kentucky Fried Chicken after he was 50; Dr. Ruth became a celebrity talk-show sex therapist when she was 48; Sam Walton opened his first Wal-Mart at age 44; and Ted Turner started Cable News Network (CNN) at 42. Don't forget Margaret Mitchell, who won her first Pulitzer Prize, for *Gone with the Wind,* when she was 37; Senator Margaret Chase Smith, elected to the Senate for the first time when she was 49; Shirley Temple Black, named ambassador to Ghana at age 47; and Grandma Moses, who began a painting career at the age of 76!

Affirmative Action

Affirmative action has become a highly controversial and much-debated issue. Its advocates support policies and programs that increase opportunities for women, minorities, and other underrepresented groups. These policies involve special consideration or set-aside positions for candidates who would—if hired, admitted, or promoted—increase the percentage of diverse members in a professional, academic, social, or business group.

FACTS & FIGURES

Women in the Workplace

- In 1970, 43 percent of women age 16 and over were in the labor force. Today, 60 percent of women work outside the home. Approximately 80 percent of women between 25 and 44 are in the workforce.

- In 1975, 47 percent of all mothers with children under 6 years old had paid employment. That figure has now increased to over 73 percent. Since 1970, households headed by women have increased 70 percent. Women are the sole earners in more than 18 percent of families.

- Currently, a women earns, on average, 80 cents for every dollar earned by a man.

- Although percentages of women in nontraditional areas have increased, often the increase has occurred in the lower-paying jobs. About 38 percent of women work in what the U.S. Census labels "professional and technical jobs"; however, women are employed in only eight of the 50 job titles that comprise that area. Two-thirds of employed women hold clerical, service, nursing, and education jobs; these are traditionally low-paying occupations. At least nursing salaries have improved due to demand.

- Women make up over 48 percent of managers and 53 percent of professionals, including teachers and registered nurses. In the professions, women have made gains in the last 10 years and now comprise 30 percent of doctors and 22 percent of dentists. In such traditionally male jobs as pilots and navigators, women now make up 5.3 percent; among firefighters, women comprise 5 percent. Although women constitute 46 percent of the workforce, they fill only 10 percent of the top corporate positions. Only 14 percent of architects and engineers are women.

- For women, the best paying jobs include CEO, pharmacist, lawyer, electronic and electrical engineer, management analyst, computer systems analyst, and college faculty.

- Woman-owned businesses number approximately 10 million and employ more than 28 million people (35 percent more than all Fortune 500 companies employ worldwide). An estimated 40 to 50 percent of all woman-owned firms in this country are based in homes.

- 26 percent of women work part time, compared with 11 percent of men.

- Approximately 18 percent of military personnel are women.

- In 1970, only 11 percent of women (aged 25–64) had completed college; by 2004, nearly 33 percent had a four-year college degree.

THINK ABOUT IT

1. Are these statistics true for women in the community where you live?

2. Why is it important to know these facts?

3. Why is it useful to know the best paying jobs for women?

4. How does knowing this information influence how you make your decisions about your future career?

5. What challenges do women business owners face?

6. What suggestions would you give to help dual-income families handle the following: housework, meal planning and preparation, child care, and social activities?

7. Name three successful women and explain what makes or made them successful.

Source: U.S. Department of Labor, Women's Bureau and Bureau of Labor Statistics, *Women in the Labor Force: A Databook*, 2005.

To answer these questions online, go to the *Facts and Figures* module in Chapter 6 of the Companion Website.

Companion Website

Many people oppose preferences or quota selection criteria and would prefer to see impartial screening of all candidates, regardless of gender, ethnicity, or socioeconomic status. A wide range of feelings and opinions exists on this issue. Compounding the controversy is a high demand for scarce resources that is pervasive in the fields of education, health and welfare services, and employment opportunities. Immigration, both legal and illegal, also complicates affirmative action decision making.

Recent decisions by state and federal courts have narrowed the scope of affirmative action by rejecting quotas or preferential formulas in favor of open and competitive criteria. These courts, however, have reversed unjustified discrimination in hiring, firing, and admissions and have also rejected forced early retirements due to age. Affirmative action remains a challenge in the 21st century.

Other Cultural Considerations: Valuing Diversity

Today's workforce is more culturally diverse than ever, and this diversity will increase as the next wave of workers joins the workforce. To remain globally competitive, companies in the United States must improve training and advancement opportunities and use each employee's talent to the fullest. Stereotypes about and prejudices against particular ethnic or racial groups must be diminished and opportunities expanded for all workers.

Hispanics, African Americans, and Asian Americans make up approximately 32 percent of the workforce, with Caucasians declining to 68 percent. Moreover, projections for new workers entering the workplace indicate that in most urban centers, all minority group members together make up the majority of the entering workforce.

Legislation has been enacted to eliminate discrimination against persons who have a disability. The Americans with Disabilities Act (ADA) prohibits discrimination on the basis of a disability and calls for the elimination of barriers, that is, anything that prevents a person or group of persons equal access to goods, services, and facilities. Employers with 15 or more employees must make reasonable accommodations for such otherwise qualified employees, including access to rooms and buildings, use of auxiliary aids, and services such as interpreters and hearing devices. Persons with disabilities should

Learning more about our diverse world is an important part of today's global economy. Here, college students in Baghdad engage in conversation with students in Ohio on MTV's "Chat the Planet."

enjoy the same freedom of choice in making career decisions as those without disabilities, and this becomes more of a reality each year.

Companies are learning to respect diversity as an important component of the workplace. Just as many college campuses now require a course in diversity, firms are offering employee training in diversity to enable workers of differing backgrounds, educational levels, physical abilities, and cultures to accept and value one another. Whether in a social, political, academic, or economic context, we have begun to realize that our society will benefit from the fullest utilization of all its citizens and their many different talents.

The Changing Workplace

Fifteen years ago terms such as the knowledge worker, global economy, computer literacy, learning organization, virtual workplace, small entrepreneurial business, woman-owned business, meeting customer needs, and temporary/leasing agencies would have been irrelevant in a book on career planning. But these terms represent trends, and the trends affect a large percentage of new entrants to the workforce. Therefore, it is to your advantage to understand the shifting nature of the workplace.

Manufacturing used to be the mainstay of the U.S. economy, but we are increasingly becoming a service-based economy, in which the majority of workers provide services (e.g., health care, retail, food preparation) instead of producing a commodity. Manufacturing jobs are increasingly moving overseas to countries such as China and Thailand. This trend is called *offshoring* if the whole company is moved to another country and *outsourcing* if only part of the firm's work, for example, the accounting, is sent to workers in another country. One important reason that companies are hiring abroad is that is where the fastest-growing markets exist. Companies such as Procter & Gamble, IBM, Caterpillar, and Coca-Cola get more than half of their sales and income from markets outside of the United States.

Due to the globalization of the workplace, many workers will find that they need to work shifts other than 8 A.M. to 5 P.M. in order to reach and collaborate with "coworkers" in other countries at times when they are on duty. Global workplaces are made easier by the computer, which enables us to keep in touch with coworkers at all times of day and night. When someone sells an item in Detroit, the order can be transmitted and the item can be immediately made in China and available for sale. This is called supply-chaining.

The United States has remained a powerful and strong economy due to constant innovation in products, services, and companies. Now we are competing with other nations, such as China and India, that also are very good at innovating. Product innovation depends to a great extent on engineers. Both China and India are graduating more engineers than is the United States. In fact, China and India together have graduated approximately three times more engineers than the United States annually.

Many of today's jobs, such as Webmaster, diversity manager, digital librarian, and supply chain manager, did not exist 15 years ago. There are more options for ways to perform your work, such as telecommuting or starting your own business. Today's worker faces less stigma associated with changing jobs or changing careers. In fact, most workers will change their jobs up to 12 times in their career and will make three to five career changes in their lifetime.

Implications

More job opportunities will be available at all hours of the day or night, any day of the week. Employees will have the option to work out of their homes or at the company workplace and will be expected to use technology to stay in touch with coworkers. Many workers will start as temporary employees and will need to prove their skills in order to be considered for long-term positions. More job opportunities will be available in the expanding service and information systems sectors, as well as in transportation and logistics. This is an exciting time to be looking for work, but it certainly requires that you understand the key trends shaping the workplace in order to find your niche. Additionally, many options will be available for students graduating in engineering and science.

The Need for Knowledge Workers

An employee becomes more valuable as he or she accumulates new skills. The challenge is to remain an outstanding contributor on the job (e.g., as a specialist) while learning new skills. As organizations downsize or flatten, employees must possess multiple skills, such as the ability to learn, use new technology, or sell a product. These people have an edge. They may, for example, be able to transfer from the training division, if it is reduced in size, to the sales division, and therefore remain employed.

Research the fastest-growing careers

There is still opportunity to move up. For example, Courtney got a job straight out of high school as a file clerk in a firm making shoulder pads. Learning new skills on the job, she began to manage the computer system and handle most payroll and personnel duties. Courtney is an example of a knowledge worker. A generation ago, the country shifted to a service-based economy in which fewer people produced industrial goods. Instead, more people provided services such as advertising or accounting or sold retail or wholesale products. Now we are in the midst of another shift, toward a knowledge-based economy in which employees, like Courtney, will be expected to manage technology and information itself. The Bureau of Labor Statistics predicts in its occupational forecast for the year 2014 that the fastest-growing careers are mostly in high-skill, high-wage professional, managerial, and technical areas. This does not mean that service jobs will disappear. Industrial and service jobs such as auto repair and retail clerk will still be available. The fastest job growth, however, will be in those areas that involve the management and production of specialized knowledge.

Sometimes it is necessary to spend time after work taking classes and studying job-related materials at home to get a head start. LaTricia was a public relations manager at a computer firm and had to spend as many as five hours a week on her own time becoming familiar with the company's

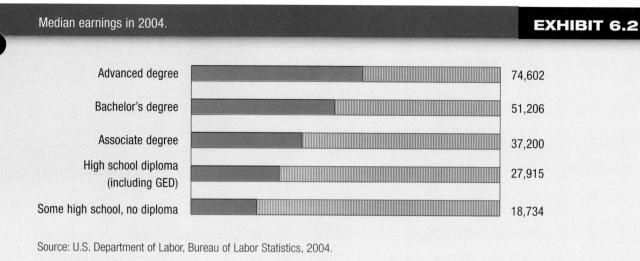

EXHIBIT 6.2

Median earnings in 2004.

Advanced degree	74,602
Bachelor's degree	51,206
Associate degree	37,200
High school diploma (including GED)	27,915
Some high school, no diploma	18,734

Source: U.S. Department of Labor, Bureau of Labor Statistics, 2004.

new products. She also took a class in teaching English as a Second Language to become more sensitive to cultural diversity at a time when her business was becoming increasingly international. Exhibits 6.2 and 6.3 illustrate the correspondence of earnings to educational attainment.

Courtney and LaTricia are examples of workers continually learning new skills so they can be available for openings within their organizations and elsewhere. Remember, *luck is preparation meeting opportunity!*

Prepare for lifelong learning

The Importance of New Technology

Technology is so much a part of everyday life that most of us don't stop to think about how much we depend on it. Think about what you did today since you woke up, and you will probably be able to name many activities that depended on technology. Just as it has affected our personal life, technology has revolutionized the kind of work we do, where we work, and how we complete our work. One in eight jobs is directly related to the field of high technology. Software engineer, CAD operator, computer programmer, and network administrator are probably familiar job titles. The real impact of technology, however, is on jobs that are indirectly related to technology. For example, today's travel agents must learn a special computer program in order to access information for their clients; ironically, these agents are becoming less crucial as clients make their own reservations directly over the Internet. Graphic designers rely on computer-aided drawing programs to produce high-quality, low-cost materials for clients. Even journalists are finding a niche online with the advent of Web-based magazines and Weblogs.

Technology has also affected where and how we do our work. Thanks to telecommuting, work does not need to be done in an office. Telecommuting means that you work from a home office, rather than at the company site, using phones, fax machines, modems, e-mail, and other communication tools to stay in touch with your coworkers and clients.

EXHIBIT 6.3   How Much is a Degree Worth?

EDUCATIONAL ATTAINMENT AND WORK–LIFE EARNINGS FOR 2004

Does going to school pay? Yes, according to the U.S. Census Bureau, which studied the relationship between workers' educational levels and work earnings over a lifetime. Men had higher average earnings than women with similar education. But the female-to-male earning ratio was better among younger workers (84 percent) than among older workers (56 percent), which would indicate that the "earnings gap" is closing.

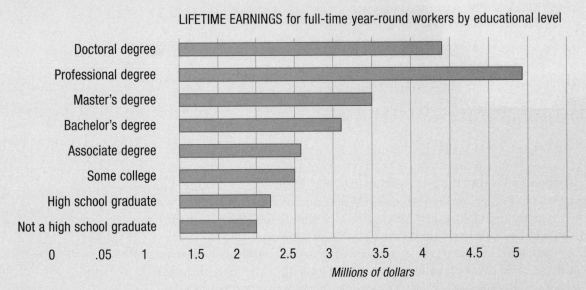

LIFETIME EARNINGS for full-time year-round workers by educational level

Millions of dollars

Community/technical college certificate: Six months to two-year course of study at a postsecondary (after high school) college/technical school in an occupation/trade area.

Associate of Arts or Associate of Science degree: (A.A./A.S.) Usually a two-year course of study that includes general education classes as well as a major: a) occupation/trade area or b) transfer studies that prepare students for transfer directly to four-year colleges.

Bachelor of Arts (B.A.), Bachelor of Science (B.S.) degrees: Usually a four-year course of study that includes general education classes as well as specialization in a subject area or major.

Master of Arts (M.A.), Master of Science (M.S.) degrees: Normally, two additional years of study beyond the bachelor's degree, specializing in a subject area or major.

Professional degree: Normally, one to three years of additional study beyond the bachelor's or master's degree depending upon the subject area. Some professionals may decide to earn the doctorate degree also. Professional degrees are earned in medicine, dentistry, law, chiropractic, pharmacy, podiatry, theology, or veterinary medicine.

Doctorate degree: Normally, two additional years of study beyond the master's degree, specializing in a subject area.

Small businesses known as SOHOs (small office/home office) are being created and operated from home with the aid of technology.

The jobs that are able to accommodate telecommuting include auto marketing consultant, reporter, investment adviser, investment research firm manager, online tutor, and virtual assistant. Cybercommuters, as some telecommuters are called, are becoming more common in all industries. Working anywhere will become even easier as cell phones, pagers, and other handheld devices become more powerful and less expensive. Additionally, all information required by a small business will be accessible over the Internet.

Think about technology and careers on a continuum. On one end are jobs that are directly related to technology, such as computer programmer. These are the jobs that produce the technology we use daily. These are the jobs of the new economy. The key industries that are expanding the fastest are those in which the main product or service is information. As you move along the continuum, jobs are less directly tied to technology. Somewhere in the middle of the continuum are administrative assistants who use various software packages for word processing, as well as those jobs that are influenced by technology. For example, teachers have vast amounts of information available for research over the Internet. The distance education teacher who teaches using technology will be in increased demand as more people try to learn at any time and any place. Such a teacher must be able to adapt to the changes in teaching that require the use of technology. Many jobs will be affected by advances in technology, and those persons who are comfortable with and knowledgeable about computers may be the best job candidates regardless of where their jobs fall on the continuum.

FACTS & FIGURES

The new economy vs. the old economy

NEW ECONOMY:

High-tech equipment/software

Computer services

Financial services consulting

Communication media

E-commerce

Distance education

Supply chain management

OLD ECONOMY:

Construction/transportation

Utilities

Manufacturing

Wholesalers/retailers

Personal services/health care

Education

At the opposite end of the continuum are the jobs that are least influenced by technology. These are the jobs of the old economy. Those in construction, transportation, general manufacturing, and retail stores are furthest from the technology end of the job continuum and must deal with real-time issues that affect the bottom line. These industries take longer to lower costs, develop new products, and increase profits. In manufacturing, new technology that reduces costs may also reduce the need for some employees, resulting in layoffs. Furthermore, wages in these industries tend to rise with cost-of-living adjustments rather than through company profits.

The contrast between the new and old economy can be seen in the salaries offered to new college graduates. According to recent data from the National Association of Colleges and Employers, starting salaries for accounting, information systems, and engineering graduates are approximately 25 percent higher than those of liberal arts graduates, as noted in Exhibit 6.4.

According to a report by the Office of Policy Development, Economics, and Statistics Administration, average wages per worker in information

EXHIBIT 6.4	Representative starting salaries for college graduates.

ASSOCIATE DEGREE	RANGE
Business Management	$21,600–69,600
Computer Maintenance Technician	$14,040–31,280
Registered Nurse	$15,600–51,960
Radiology Technician	$32,148–53,316
Respiratory Technician	$18,000–34,836
Engineering Technology	$32,000–40,000

Source: EUREKA, California Entry Salary Ranges.

BACHELOR'S DEGREE		2003	2005
Engineering	Electrical	$50,615	$52,009
	Computer (software design)	$52,722	$53,729
	Mechanical	$48,115	$51,046
	Civil	$41,541	$43,159
	Chemical	$51,301	$54,256
	Computer Science	$44,678	$51,292
	Industrial-Manufacturing	$47,861	$49,541
Business	MIS	$40,566	$43,941
	Systems Analyst	—	$50,869
	Business Administration	$36,634	$39,448
	Marketing	$35,698	$37,832
	Accounting	$42,005	$43,809
	Economics/Finance	$40,413	$42,802
Other	Liberal Arts	$29,586	$30,337

Source: NACE (National Association of Colleges and Employers), Spring 2005 press release.

technology (IT) industries are twice the national average. IT industry workers earn on average $73,800 compared with $35,000 for all workers engaged in private non-farm industries. (More than half of IT jobs are "high skilled" and require at least an associate degree.)

Information technology employment also provides self-employed and independent contractors the flexibility and mobility to work outside of a traditional organization. Although these temporary workers often earn less in wages and benefits and have less security than permanent workers, many IT workers prefer to be independent because they can command comparably high salaries and move from one employment situation to another with relative ease.

Implications

When choosing the industry that you wish to enter, the new economy provides both opportunities and challenges. For higher-skilled workers, the new economy offers strong demand and high wages. Lower-skilled workers, however, are seeing skill requirements rise. IT allows greater flexibility in working arrangements, letting employers quickly hire and release workers in response to changing market conditions and allowing workers to move more easily from job to job. Remember, such workers still need to know how to market themselves to move to new jobs.

The Global Economy and the Changing Corporate Structure

A decade ago the United States was generating most of the world's technology; today that figure has diminished. The United States is striving to develop a more global economy by establishing trade agreements with other countries, such as the North American Free Trade Agreement (NAFTA). Global competition and multinational corporations will continue to influence the business world and our economy. Today it is not just the Fortune 500 companies, such as General Electric, IBM, and AT&T, that conduct business and have offices throughout the world. Employees wishing to advance in this new international economy must have the ability to speak more than one language and understand the cultural customs of other countries.

These computer-savvy college students work summer jobs that provide valuable experience for future professional employment.

In today's global economy, NAFTA has created a need for multilingual talents. Asian investments in Latin America and Mexico are expanding. Many of the *maquiladora* (border) factories in Tijuana, for example, are run by Japanese, Chinese, and Korean corporations. Asian companies have invested billions in Mexico. Obviously, the ability to converse in several languages is an asset in the marketplace.

Success in the global economy requires innovative, high-quality, timely, customized, and efficiently produced products and flatter, leaner organizations. Successful companies need to have the following traits:

Today's organizations are flatter, leaner, more efficient

1. Maintaining a flat management structure that has shifted away from management-directed systems toward team-directed systems that require knowledgeable workers in each team, along with service providers and other self-supervising workers who are responsible for meeting the bottom line.

2. Utilizing a virtual corporation by distributing design, marketing, and customer service operations across the globe through temporary partnerships

Virtual organizations are now more practical

that can focus on completing projects. Thus, many enterprises will ultimately become tripartite virtual partnerships. One unit will handle product development and engineering, another will cover marketing needs, and the third will do the production work. Increasingly, companies avoid building expensive, time-consuming in-house capabilities.

3. Creating even greater efficiencies. The production work is speeded up with computer systems called manufacturing execution systems that coordinate production. Such systems are able to cut assembly time by 80 percent!

4. Moving manufacturing plants to locations that offer availability of good educational institutions and low labor costs, e.g., China and India.

Outsourcing is on the rise

5. Purchasing product components from outside suppliers (outsourcing).

Use of temps is on the increase

6. Maintaining low numbers of permanent employees and using specialized teams of temporary employees on short-term projects.

7. Recruiting highly skilled workers worldwide who are knowledgeable about global issues.

Businesses are growing adaptable and flexible

8. Being able to evolve and adapt as a company. George Lucas' Industrial Light & Magic (ILM), one of the largest special effects film companies, started in a converted airplane hangar building models of battleships and clay miniatures for the original *Star Wars* movie and evolved to incorporate computers in office buildings and hundreds of ILM digital artists, modeling experts, and computer programmers working for months on "Episode III." ILM once thought it would be the electronic answer to all Hollywood projects but has found that it can be most profitable by focusing on larger and flashier projects. Similarly, such companies as Hewlett Packard and IBM have evolved from being large manufacturers to becoming service providers. One other factor requiring the need to adapt will be political trends in other countries. Most companies dealing in the global economy will be noticeably affected by international recessions and military conflicts.

E-commerce is increasing

9. Pursuing e-commerce. As businesses build Websites to sell their goods and services to consumers, they are making it easier to transact business with their suppliers and distributors. Corporate information technology departments have shifted their focus to Internet-based e-commerce products that increase corporate revenue and make customers happy. A report by the U.S. Commerce Department titled "The Emerging Digital Economy" concludes that information technology industries are growing at more than double the rate of the overall economy thanks to the acceptance and use of e-commerce.

10. Pursuing customization. Built-to-order products will proliferate. Just as Dell has been able to build customized computers that are ordered over the Internet, other industries, such as the automobile industry, are able to individualize orders. Web-based technology is contributing to this transformation.

11. Managing a mega-corporation effectively. The need for managers with a master's degree in business administration will continue to expand.

Implications

The main point for you to remember is that, in a global economy, the employee who helps the company remain competitive by being informed about technology, competition, and alternative ways to complete the job requirements will be the person who is most important to the company. Such employees will have the core jobs, whereas others will be hired as temporary portfolio employees. The more skills that you can demonstrate to the employer, the more valuable you will be (as was discussed in Chapter 5). For example, a software engineer at a telecommunications company who can also market her product to customers around the world will be considered a most valuable employee and most likely will be able to evolve with the expansion or changes that occur in her industry.

Small Businesses

According to the U.S. Small Business Administration, small business is defined as any business that has fewer than 500 employees. Did you know that small firms represent 99.7 percent of all employer firms and employ half of all private sector employees? There are approximately 25 million small businesses in comparison with 17,000 large corporations. During the past decade, small business accounted for 60–80 percent of net new jobs annually. Additionally, 41 percent of high tech workers (such as scientists, engineers, and computer workers) and 97 percent of all identified exporters can be found in small businesses. If you want variety and responsibility and are results oriented, a small business might be the place for you.

It is estimated that about 35 million people have a home office. According to the Small Business Advocate website article by Jeff Zbar, about 33 percent of U.S. households support some home-working activities. These businesses include approximately 11.1 million full-time businesses, 4.1 million part-time home businesses, and 8 to 9 million more who telecommute from home. However, not all home businesses are "income-generating"—approximately half of all such businesses make a profit and it usually takes about two years to start earning anything.

Every day, small businesses are created to serve consumer needs. Did you know that the Home Shopping Network was created when a company that could not pay its bills instead gave its inventory to a TV executive? The executive needed to get rid of the inventory and announced the availability of the materials on his network. Everything sold within two hours!

Small businesses strive to meet customer needs

FACTS & FIGURES

Fastest-growing small-business-dominated industries

Computer programming

Management consulting

Residential building construction

Job training services

Credit reporting and investment firms

Providers of day care

Counseling and rehabilitation services

("U.S. Business Facts," U.S. Chamber of Commerce Statistics and Research Center, 2002.)

THINK ABOUT IT

Does knowing that these are the fastest-growing small businesses influence your education and career decision making? What other factors must be considered?

Companion Website

To answer these questions online, go to the *Facts and Figures* module in Chapter 6 of the Companion Website.

FACTS & FIGURES

Temporary work

In 1998, companies farmed out 15 percent of all manufacturing jobs. By 2000, they outsourced more than 40 percent. This means that contract employees held jobs formerly held by permanent employees. By 2005, 2.5 million people were estimated to be employed as temporary workers.

THINK ABOUT IT

1. Why were manufacturing jobs being replaced?

2. Do you agree or disagree with the following statements? Why?

   - Temporary workers are replacing permanent workers.

   - It may be useful to start as a temp in order to get your foot in the door.

   - There are more temporary job ads and fewer full-time job ads in your own community.

3. Do you know anyone who started at a job as a temp?

4. Do you think that taking technology classes will improve your chances of getting hired?

To answer these questions online, go to the *Facts and Figures* module in Chapter 6 of the Companion Website.

Companion Website

"Today, the most profound thing to me is the fact that a 14-year-old in Romania or Bangalore or the Soviet Union or Vietnam has all the information, all the tools, all the software easily available to apply knowledge however they want" (Marc Andreessen, cofounder of Netscape, in an interview with Thomas Friedman for his book *The World Is Flat*). Friedman also describes such a person in his book: Rajesh Rao, a young Indian entrepreneur who started an electronic-game company from Bangalore, which today owns the rights to Charlie Chaplin's image for mobile computer games. A *USA Today* article (2004) estimated that more than half of New York's million-plus independent workers are ages 25 to 40. More and more university business majors are considering a focus on "entrepreneurship," and creation of small businesses is improving the U.S. economy.

Woman-Owned Businesses

It is estimated that 50% or more of the more than 10 million privately held firms in the United States are owned by women, and that one in seven American workers is employed in a woman-owned business (which accounts for approximately 19.1 million workers). Between 40 and 50 percent of these companies are home-based, according to a study by the National Foundation for Women Business Owners. More than 70 percent of these businesses are concentrated in the services and retail trade. More than 60 percent of woman-owned businesses got their start as home-based operations.

Temporary Agencies/Leasing Companies

Temporary employment agencies, in addition to their traditional business of providing secretarial and clerical professionals on a contract basis, now provide employees in such areas as accounting, health care, telemarketing, the paralegal field, and management. Technical services contracting firms place a range of engineering and computer professionals as well as technicians and draftspeople in temporary positions. If this trend toward growing numbers of temporary employees continues as predicted, many people will find themselves working for an employee-leasing firm. Kelly Services, one of the largest temporary service agencies, expanded 800 percent in one five-year period.

Temporary employment is also a method of obtaining permanent employment. One multimedia graphic artist took temporary work through an agency and changed jobs four times in his first year, with a typical contract lasting about two months. Once he developed a reputation, however, potential clients began seeking him out, so he worked less through temporary agencies and agents. It has been reported that approximately 13 percent of the U.S. labor force are independent contractors, temporary workers, and self-employed individuals.

Trends: The Twenty-First Century

It helps to have a picture of tomorrow's opportunities when defining a future job target. For example, you might guess that now is not the time to prepare for a lifelong job in an automotive assembly plant. Such positions will likely be phased out in the next decade by computerized systems. In fact, 80 percent of General Motors employees now work at jobs other than assembly. By 2010, there may only be five giant automotive firms. Production and assembly will be centered in Korea, Italy, and Latin America.

Additionally, during a recession fewer college graduates secure college level jobs after graduation, and those without a degree may have to get experience as temps before they can get hired permanently. In this situation, many college graduates opt for graduate school, hoping that the recession will be over by the time they are again ready for the job market. The good news is that for the next two decades more people will be retiring than entering the job market. With 76 million "baby boomers" (people born between 1945 and 1960) predicted to retire in the next three decades and only 46 million people in "Generation X" (children of baby boomers) waiting to replace them, a shortage of 4 to 6 million workers is predicted by 2010.

These statistics take into consideration that large numbers may delay retirement for five to ten years due to cost of living expenses and not having saved enough for retirement. It is also assumed that some companies will be hiring back retired employees to fill vacancies. In fact, IBM Canada and Monsanto have pioneered the use of on-call retirees over the years. These options may slow the need for new permanent employees, but eventually, good temps will have a chance at securing these jobs.

Graduate school may be an option

However, in selected fields we are already experiencing shortages. There is more demand for nurses, pharmacists, teachers, health care technicians,

Be aware of in-demand careers

FACTS & FIGURES

Entrepreneurial opportunities

The following are the best small business opportunities for 2005 and beyond:

Business coaching (aka consulting)

Smart clothes (performance apparel, sun protection, and aging-friendly clothing)

Garage organizer services

Trash removal (now a franchise)

Medical transcription

Anti-aging spas and spa treatments

College admissions consulting

Translation services

Poker gaming (opportunities range from customized poker chip production to poker boot camps)

(*About.com, Small Business Information.*)

THINK ABOUT IT

1. Go to about.com and read about people who have started such companies.

2. Find and interview a person who has any of these kinds of jobs.

3. Given your interests and skills, what creative business opportunities might you consider for yourself?

To answer these questions online, go to the *Facts and Figures* module in Chapter 6 of the Companion Website.

Companion Website

skilled contractors, electricians, plumbers, child care workers, firefighters, and law enforcers than people being trained in these fields. The fields of accounting, auditing, and financial planning are expected to expand some 20 percent in the next decade, and a large number of workers are due to retire from all levels of government work.

Finally, skilled laborers find themselves in demand and often are enticed by higher hourly wages and even signing bonuses. Many of these trades have starting salaries around $35,000 plus overtime. The U.S. Department of Labor estimates that between 2004 and 2014, the construction industry will create nearly 1 million new jobs.

Liberal Arts Majors Have Marketable Skills

Remember what you read in Chapter 5 about the value of a liberal arts major? Liberal arts refers to majors such as art, English, history, psychology, sociology, speech, or any bachelor of arts (B.A.) degree. Such majors provide preparation for a variety of careers. Pursuing a liberal arts major enables you to develop skills such as problem solving, critical thinking, creative thinking, systems thinking, interpersonal savvy, resource management, communication, the ability to deal with ambiguity, teamwork, research, and how to learn! Employers will expect you to be able to scan information quickly and select what is relevant for your job. You will be expected to have a high level of reading comprehension and be able to prepare documents that are clear, concise, logical, and easy to understand. Such skills are necessary for this job market. You will be even better prepared for the 21st-century job market if you have also taken classes or developed skills related to business, computer software, or entrepreneurial thinking.

Although graduates with a degree in business, computer science, and engineering are often in greater demand because their curriculum has provided them with job-specific skills, there have always been employers who hire liberal arts graduates because their broad skills provide a strong foundation for job training in many fields. And such employers often find that liberal arts majors are excellent employees. One example is a political science major who graduated from a small liberal arts college. She had begun her education majoring in English, then switched to French before finally settling on political science. When she graduated she found a job with a financial services group. Vanguard provided her with six weeks of training, and she was able to continue to develop on the job. (See "Meet Jessica.")

Develop transferable skills   Getting the right skills and education today will give you an advantage tomorrow. Over 80 percent of jobs require some postsecondary education or training. Computer literacy and familiarity with several software programs are a necessity in many jobs. As discussed in Chapter 5, SCANS skills—such as reading, writing, communication, the ability to reason, problem solving, and the ability to learn on the job—will make you competitive in today's job market. If you are a college student, take advantage of the computer access that is available at school and learn as much as possible about using computers. Familiarize yourself with the Internet and learn to do your research online. When you get into the job market, you will find that many companies are relying on the Internet for their own internal communications.

Meet Jessica

Jessica was a political science major who graduated from a small liberal arts college in 2003. She had begun her education majoring in English, then switched to French before finally settling on political science. She loved learning everything and had a hard time narrowing her studies to one major. She finally settled on political science by using the College Career Planning Center, taking some career assessments, and doing some information interviews. While visiting Washington, D.C., she visited with a French diplomat to the United States, and while visiting New York, she talked to a relative who worked for a big public relations firm. Additionally, Jessica was captivated by the excitement of touring Wall Street.

By graduation time, Jessica had used the College Career Planning Center and gained multiple job offers from firms ranging from public relations to financial services and marketing. Fortunately the job market was expanding and she had choices. She had been counseled to consider graduate school and had taken the Graduate Record Exam and scored well, but she was tired of college. She took a job with the Vanguard Group, an investment company, and now helps employees of the firms' corporate clients manage their 401(k) retirement accounts. Vanguard provided her with six weeks of training, and Jessica was able to develop her job her own way (just as she had learned to do in her class assignments when she was in college). However, by 2005, the job was not as exciting as she had envisioned. Her industry was very stressful, and people actually grew upset with *her* whenever the stock market went down.

Jessica went back to her college's Career Center for Alumni and discussed her concerns. The career counselor suggested that she see if she could focus on some specialty industries at Vanguard in order to learn about other industries that might be part of her future direction. She found that she could add a specialty and selected the health care industry. When she met with clients in the

health care industry, she actually interviewed them as well as giving them assistance with their 401(k) retirement plans. She found that the issues facing hospitals interested her. Additionally, some of her clients told her that there were great needs for her expertise in the human resources department, and if she had a master's degree in health care administration she could work in industry or government or be a consultant.

Jessica is now pondering going back to college for a master's degree and has her resume out to human resources departments at several hospitals and state and county health departments. Jessica is also happy that she has already scored well on the GRE and does not have to go back and study for it while she is under so much stress. Having taken the GRE has made her more open to graduate school, and she was happy to learn that she could attend graduate school after work, on weekends and online if she decided to go back to school. Having been out of college for three years and finding that her job was getting more stressful rather than more interesting, Jessica is now ready to exercise other options.

WHAT DO YOU THINK?

1. Is your major related to any job that you have had?

2. Could you imagine yourself in a job unrelated to your field of study and experience?

3. Do you think Jessica made a good first choice out of college, or should she have done more investigation about the stresses related to her job?

4. What alternatives would you have explored that are not mentioned in this story?

5. What do you think about attending graduate school to expand your options?

To answer these questions online, go to the *Real Stories* module in Chapter 6 of the Companion Website.

Lifelong Learning

More important than knowing what jobs will be available is being *flexible*—having the ability to adapt to this changing world of work. It is estimated that 40 percent of the jobs that will be available in the year 2010 have yet to be created. Thus you cannot obtain training specifically for every career change you may encounter, but you can develop learning skills that will prepare you for training in new job skills and applications. It is also possible that, due to advancing technology and other factors, you may change careers not just once but many times during your life. Even if this is not the case and you move along one career path throughout your life, you will need to continue educating yourself just to keep up with technological change. The trend toward lifelong learning is evidenced by the fact that several million people over age 40 were in college in 2000, compared to only 477,000 in 1970. Additionally, an increasing number of people are enrolled in corporate universities. Corporate universities and colleges range from company-run classes designed primarily for that company's employees to programs run by companies that confer credible degrees such as an associate's degree or a bachelor's degree.

Explore distance learning

The days when formal education ended after college or graduate school have disappeared. Now that people work at all hours to keep in touch with colleagues all over the world, continuing education must be available at times to fit into their busy schedules. The Internet is bringing such education to people whenever they have time for it. For example, one sales manager sometimes plugs in his laptop at midnight, whether he is in a hotel room when away from home on business or at his home office (also known as the family room at other times of the day). He downloads lectures, submits papers, joins in student discussions, and gets his grades over the Net.

Corporate universities offer options

Just 23 million Americans were enrolled in continuing education programs in 1984; that figure is predicted to be over 100 million by 2007, according to the National Center for Educational Statistics. About 400 company-run universities operated in the United States in 1988, but there are now more than 2,000, according to the Corporate University Xchange, a New York research and consulting firm. Thus, many adults are getting continuing education (also known as training classes) through their company's corporate university or training department. Motorola, for example, provides courses for 100,000 of its employees every year at 100 sites around the world. It is becoming the norm for those over age 25 to go to college. According to the National Center for Educational Statistics, 41 percent of those attending colleges and universities are over age 25. In addition, professionals who must take continuing education to renew their licenses are opting for Web-based classes.

The Internet has influenced the increase by providing a way for corporations to deliver training to their employees at any time of the day or night as well as anywhere the Web can be accessed. Additionally, prestigious universities are offering reputable degrees over the Net, thus encouraging more people to get their degrees than ever before. Whereas 710,000 U.S. students were in distance education in 1998 (about 5 percent of the approximately 15 million higher-education students), about 3.20 million out of 16 million students—20 percent—were online by 2005. More and more college classes are combining class attendance and Web-based instruction to maximize use of the research that can be found on the Web.

Multimedia Revolution Ignites Creative Industries

Film, animation, entertainment, fashion, graphic design, publishing, architecture, and other media-related fields are creating a new surge of employment opportunities. The evolution of this trend is closely related to the development of computer software and hardware.

Digital Domain is an example of a company that produces special effects for movies, employs artists, digital designers, and technicians. From film special effects, this firm has expanded to commercials, music videos, CD-ROM games, and theme park attractions— with additional plans to be involved in high-resolution, interactive programming delivered over cable.

Although multimedia may best be known for the CD-ROMs and DVDs that combine text, sound, pictures, and video, the technology is advancing into new forms. One form is virtual reality, in which special glasses or headsets allow a person to perceive an experience as if it were real. Another form of multimedia technology created "smart" cameras that recognize faces and facial expressions in order to identify people for security systems. Another application of the technology is evident in incorporating animation into live-action film. The film industry labels this animation *digital effects.* It can be seen regularly in commercials (e.g., cola-drinking polar bears, flirtatious M & Ms, and an athletic Pillsbury doughboy) and in movies such as *Finding Nemo* and *The Lord of the Rings.* Employers emphasize they are looking for good technicians who have developed artistic talents and technological skills. The digital designer must understand lighting, texture, and motion. Such professionals are rewarded with salaries ranging from $40,000 to over $150,000.

Implications

To maintain your currency in your career, you must get updated training throughout your life. Be sure that the training institution you choose is considered reputable by your employer before enrolling for a program of study. Make sure that you have the time management skills and self-discipline to complete the required studying and research if you choose to take classes on the Web.

As it gets easier to study anytime and anywhere and to earn college credit for such work, more people will be getting college degrees. Already some say that as more people get degrees, jobs that did not require a degree in the past will require a degree in the future. This trend means that you will have to earn a college degree in order to remain competitive in the future job market.

Many of the best job opportunities during the next decade will demand that applicants have cross-functional training to broaden their qualifications. Dual majors, interdisciplinary programs, and foreign languages can make a difference in the competitive, increasingly global job market. Job applicants are also being informed they need both people skills and technical skills in order to be competitive. Today's college graduates are finding that, to compete for the best jobs, they must commit to lifelong continuing education to bolster their job skills and prepare for career changes.

Job Growth Trends

If you aren't interested in a career that requires a four-year degree, there will always be a need in society for people selling merchandise, running businesses, maintaining homes, caring for children, working in restaurants, attending to health and fitness needs, and working in a variety of trades that may or may not require training beyond high school. Many of these fields are experiencing greater demand due to the important sociological changes mentioned previously in this chapter and the increase in the number of two–wage earner households. Many of the jobs listed in the box titled "Job Growth Throughout the Next Decade" and in Exhibit 6.5 do not require a bachelor's degree.

The last section of this chapter includes exhibits indicating the fastest-growing jobs and the largest job markets. Again, it must be emphasized that many of these jobs require only one or two years of postsecondary education, and many are in the fields of health, computers, law (e.g., prison guards, paralegals), and education. However, the number of new jobs open to college graduates will rise twice as fast as the number of jobs requiring short-term training. And jobs requiring master's degrees are predicted to grow 30 percent over the next decade!

Among the 20 fastest growing occupations, a bachelor's or associate's degree is the most significant source of post-secondary education or training for 12 of them—network systems and data communications analysts; physician assistants; computer software engineers, applications; physical therapist assistants; dental hygienists; computer software engineers, systems software; network and computer systems administrators; database administrators; forensic science technicians, veterinary technologists and technicians; diagnostic medical sonographers; and occupational therapist assistants. In fact, healthcare occupations make up 12 of the 20 fastest growing occupations, while computer occupations account for 5 out of 20.

Please note that Exhibits 6.5 through 6.9 describe two different categories of job growth: "fastest growing" and "largest job growth." The *fastest growing occupations*, such as computer software engineer, are growing in terms of percentage of total number of current jobs, e.g., growth from 460,000 to 682,000 in 2014 is 48 percent growth for this occupation. The *largest job growth* is stated in terms of how many people are currently in this occupation and how many more will be in this occupation by 2014, e.g., retail salespersons numbered 4,256,000 in 2004 and will number 4,992,000 by 2014, so it is one of the largest job growth categories in terms of absolute numbers even though it is expanding only 17.3 percent.

> *The only place success comes before work is in the dictionary.*
>
> **DONALD KENDALL**

Although it is helpful to take growth trends into consideration as you explore your options, it is not necessary to choose a career path only in the areas most likely to have openings. In fact, as will be discussed in the job search strategy section of this book, the best direction to follow is most often *directly toward what you really want to do*. The key is *desire*. Desire plus talent and perseverance gets people jobs in even the tightest job markets.

Finding Your Place in a Changing World

How do all these social and cultural changes affect you? Your expectations about your future are influenced by your early socialization and by the culture that surrounds you. (Look back at Super's theory in Chapter 1.) Career opportunities can be discovered and pursued through family, childhood play, school experiences, volunteer

Health services: Demand will be especially great for primary-care workers such as nurse practitioners, nutrition counselors, gerontological social workers, radiology technicians, respiratory care technicians, home health-care aides, pharmacists, and health service administrators.

Hotel management and recreation: This category includes restaurants, resorts, and travel services, as well as opportunities in conference planning.

Food service: Managers and chefs will be in demand for all those restaurants and hotel kitchens, as well as for food processing plants and labs. Specialty restaurants will continue to expand.

Engineering: Specializations in high demand will include robotics, aviation, biotechnology, manufacturing technology, and civil engineering.

Environmental sciences: Specializations include hazardous waste management, environmental impact research, conservation and environmental preservation, and alternative fuels.

Basic science: Biogenetic engineering will be an important field in the next decade, as will chemistry (especially food science) and fiber optics. Biotechnology uses living cells and materials produced by cells to create pharmaceutical, diagnostic, agricultural, environmental, and other products to benefit society.

Computer science, information systems: Opportunities will continue to be strong in design, engineering, programming, networking, maintenance, and cyber-security.

Business services: Growing fields will be accounting, forensic accounting, statistical analysis, and payroll management. Many jobs will be filled by temporary workers. In management, managers of telecommunications, environmental protection, and security systems will be in demand.

Human resources and personnel: The field of employee management continues to grow as a result of legislation concerning employee rights, new payroll requirements, and new compensation options. Specialists are needed to handle such responsibilities as job evaluation, hiring and firing, benefits planning, and training.

Financial services: This field includes financial planning and portfolio management. An increased demand for temp employees and employees specializing in retirement and estate planning is expected.

Educational services and products: Demand is growing in the school system, where both teachers and administrators will be needed to meet the changing needs of immigrants and the baby boomers' children (and grandchildren!). Corporate America will be hiring educators and trainers to teach literacy skills such as English. High-demand subjects include math, science, computer software, interactive learning modalities, and foreign languages such as Spanish, Japanese, Arabic, and Chinese. The latest need for educational products is on the Internet, where new interactive products are being introduced daily.

Maintenance and repair: These are the people who will take care of all the equipment that will keep tomorrow's world running, e.g., electricians; plumbers; heating, air conditioning and refrigeration experts; and network maintenance personnel.

Artistic/multimedia: Writers, entertainers, party planners, artists, digital designers, animators, and graphic designers will have good prospects but must be entrepreneurial types.

Security systems related: The protection of society from terrorism, including biological, chemical and nuclear attacks, is creating new jobs. Jobs range from security guards to airport security to CIA and FBI analysts. Cyber-security is listed under computer science.

For specific predictions regarding growing job fields, see Exhibits 6.5 through 6.9 at the end of this chapter. Because data are presented from several sources, figures may differ from exhibit to exhibit for the same profession and are meant to be representative.

EXHIBIT 6.5   Fastest-growing occupations, projected between 2004 and 2014 by level of education and training.*

EDUCATION/TRAINING CATEGORY	FASTEST-GROWING OCCUPATIONS	
First professional degree	Veterinarians Chiropractors Physicians	Lawyers Clergy Pharmacist
Doctoral degree	Biological scientists Medical scientists	College and university faculty Physicists and astronomers
Master's degree	Hydrologists Archivists, curators, and conservators Physical therapists	Urban and regional planners Counselors Occupational therapists
Work experience plus bachelor's or higher degree	Engineering, science, and computer systems managers Medical and health services managers Advertising, marketing, and public relations managers	Artists and commercial artists Management analysts
Bachelor's degree	Computer engineers Environmental engineers Biomedical engineers Computer systems analysts	Database administrators Physicians assistants Network analysts Employment counselors
Associate degree	Computer support specialists Paralegals and legal assistants Occupational therapist assistant	Physical therapy assistants Dental hygienists Sonagraphers
Postsecondary vocational training	Occupational therapy assistants Nurses (RNs/LVNs) Surgical technologists Preschool teachers	Emergency medical technicians Automotive technicians Hairstylists
Work experience in a related occupation	Private detectives and investigators Detectives and criminal investigators Instructors, adult (nonvocational) education	Office and administrative support supervisors
Long-term on-the-job training (more than 12 months)	Desktop publishing specialists Correctional officers Sheriffs and deputy sheriffs	Police patrol officers Telephone and cable TV line installers
Moderate-term on-the-job training (1–12 months)	Medical assistants Social and human services assistants Hazardous materials removal workers	Dental assistants Models, demonstrators, and product promoters
Short-term on-the-job training (up to 1 month)	Personal care and home health aides Janitors Waiters/servers Teacher assistants	Physical therapy aides Retail salespersons Customer service representatives

*Keep in mind that the term *fast-growing* may be misleading in the sense that if the occupation employs small numbers of people to begin with, even a 100 percent growth would still mean few overall employment opportunities. See Exhibit 6.6 for occupations with largest overall job growth, in other words, the occupations that employ large numbers of people and have good job growth.

Source: U.S. Department of Labor, *Occupational Outlook Handbook,* Bureau of Labor Statistics.

work, and early work activities. *The degree of satisfaction you find in work and in life depends on your finding opportunities to develop and use your abilities, interests, values, and personality traits.*

Unfortunately, opportunity is not distributed equally throughout society. You may feel limited economically, academically, or by family responsibilities. Opportunities may be limited by gender stereotyping, by educational requirements, by discrimination, or by the changing economy. However, as perceptions change, as laws change, as the economy becomes more global and requires employers to appreciate and utilize diverse human talents, all women and men should feel free to choose and train for the type of career that best suits their interests and talents.

If you are experiencing (or worrying about) limitations of one type or another, seek help in overcoming them. Talk to a career or academic counselor, or seek help from a support group or your family. As you read this book, you are preparing for the career that best fits you. Don't let the world set unnecessary limitations on your plans and goals. Instead, reach beyond those limitations and take advantage of all possible opportunities. You will find that as you form definite plans and objectives, it becomes easier to move forward and to anticipate and avoid obstacles.

Facts and Figures

The exhibits in this chapter provide a cross-section of information about salaries, including pay equity across gender and race, and about occupations projected to experience good job growth. The exhibits are intended to provide general information of interest to you as you consider various career options. Although numerical data give the impression of being hard facts, remember that such information should be considered approximate. The future is only partially predictable, but it's a good idea to be informed!

New and Emerging Occupations

OCCUPATIONAL TITLE/JOB DESCRIPTION

- Bioinformatics specialist, analyze and collect biological data

- Videoconferencing technicians, troubleshoot, set up, and track videoconferencing equipment

- Dosimeters, operate equipment to measure bone density

- GIS technicians, manage data from a global positioning satellite

- Usability specialists, make Websites, software, and databases easier to navigate

- Security engineers and analysts, develop policies and programs to protect electronic data

- Assessment specialists, test the mental/physical functioning of assisted-living patients

- Medical aestheticians, use skin-care techniques to care for patients' skin after surgery

- Utilization review coordinators, examine patients' records to ensure adherence to standards

- Information architects, ensure distance learning courses are conducive to learning

- Course editors, modify traditional classes for Web-based distance learning

Source: Bureau of Labor Statistics, *Occupational Outlook Quarterly 2003–2005.*

EXHIBIT 6.6 Most new jobs, highest paying: Bachelor's or graduate degree.

Numeric change in employment in the top 20 large-growth, high-paying occupations that often require a bachelor's or graduate degree, projected 2004-14.

Occupation	(Thousands)	Earnings quartile
Postsecondary teachers	524	4
General and operations managers	308	4
Elementary school teachers, except special education	265	3
Accountants and auditors	264	4
Computer software engineers, applications	222	4
Computer systems analysts	153	4
Secondary school teachers, except special and vocational education	148	4
Computer software engineers, systems software	146	4
Physicians and surgeons	136	4
Network systems and data communications analysts	126	4
Management analysts	122	4
Lawyers	110	4
Network and computer systems administrators	107	4
Middle school teachers, except special and vocational education	86	4
Financial managers	78	4
Computer and information systems managers	73	4
Sales managers	66	4
Chief executives	66	4
Physical therapists	57	4
Pharmacists	57	4

Each of these occupations is projected to gain at least 50,000 new jobs over the projections decade. In many of these high-paying occupations, workers usually have experience in addition to a bachelor's degree. In some of these occupations, workers have a graduate degree.

Source: U.S.Department of Labor, *Occupational Outlook Quarterly*, Winter 2005–06.

Most new jobs, highest paying: Less than a bachelor's degree.

EXHIBIT 6.7

Numeric change in employment in the top 20 large-growth, high-paying occupations that often require less education than a bachelor's degree, projected 2004–14.

(Thousands)

Occupation	Thousands	Earnings quartile
Registered nurses	703	4
Truck drivers, heavy and tractor-trailer	223	3
Maintenance and repair workers, general	202	3
Executive secretaries and administrative assistants	192	3
Sales representatives, wholesale and manufacturing, expert technical and scientific products	187	4
Carpenters	186	3
Automotive technicians and mechanics	126	3
Licensed practical and licensed vocational nurses	124	3
First-line supervisors/managers of office and administrative support workers	120	3
Computer support specialists	119	3
Police and sheriff's patrol officers	99	4
First-line supervisors/managers of construction trades and extraction workers	82	4
Plumbers, pipefitters, and steamfitters	78	3
Electricians	77	3
Fire fighters	69	3
Dental hygienists	68	4
Paralegals and legal assistants	67	3
Self-enrichment education teachers	64	3
First-line supervisors/managers of retail sales workers	64	3
Painters, construction and maintenance	60	3

Many large-growth, high-paying occupations are projected to provide jobs for workers who have on-the-job training or some education other then a bachelor's degree.

Source: U.S. Department of Labor, *Occupational Outlook Quarterly*, Winter 2005–06.

EXHIBIT 6.8   Fastest-growing occupations, 2004–14 (numbers in thousands).

Occupations	Employment Number		Change		Quartile rank by 2004 median annual earnings[1]	Most significant source of postsecondary education or training[2]
	2004	2014	Number	Percent		
Home health aides	624	974	350	56.0	VL	Short-term on-the-job training
Network systems and data communications analysts	231	357	126	54.6	VH	Bachelor's degree
Medical assistants	387	589	202	52.1	L	Moderate-term on-the-job training
Physician assistants	62	93	31	49.6	VH	Bachelor's degree
Computer software engineers, applications	460	682	222	48.4	VH	Bachelor's degree
Physical therapist assistants	59	85	26	44.2	H	Associate degree
Dental hygienists	158	226	68	43.3	VH	Associate degree
Computer software engineers, systems software	340	486	146	43.0	VH	Bachelor's degree
Dental assistants	267	382	114	42.7	L	Moderate-term on-the-job training
Personal and home care aides	701	988	287	41.0	VL	Short-term on-the-job training
Network and computer systems administrators	278	385	107	38.4	VH	Bachelor's degree
Database administrators	104	144	40	38.2	VH	Bachelor's degree
Physical therapists	155	211	57	36.7	VH	Master's degree
Forensic science technicians	10	13	4	36.4	VH	Associate degree
Veterinary technologists and technicians	60	81	21	35.3	L	Associate degree
Diagnostic medical sonographers	42	57	15	34.8	VH	Associate degree
Physical therapist aides	43	57	15	34.4	L	Short-term on-the-job training
Occupational therapist assistants	21	29	7	34.1	H	Associate degree
Medical scientists, except epidemiologists	72	97	25	34.1	VH	Doctoral degree
Occupational therapists	92	123	31	33.6	VH	Master's degree

Footnotes:

(1) The quartile ranking of Occupational Employment Statistics Survey annual earnings data are presented in the following categories: VH=very high ($43,605 and over), H=high ($28,590 to $43,604), L=low ($20,185 to $28,589), and VL=very low (up to $20,184). The rankings were based on quartiles using one-fourth of total employment to define each quartile. Earnings are for wage and salary workers.

(2) An occupation is placed into one of 11 categories that best describes the postsecondary education or training needed by most workers to become fully qualified.

Source: *Monthly Labor Review*, November 2005, www.bls.gov/emp/emptab21.htm.

Occupations with the largest job growth, 2004–14.

EXHIBIT 6.9

Occupations	Employment Number		Change		Quartile rank by 2004 median annual earnings[1]	Most significant source of postsecondary education or training[2]
	2004	2014	Number	Percent		
Retail salespersons	4,256	4,992	736	17.3	VL	Short-term on-the-job training
Registered nurses	2,394	3,096	703	29.4	VH	Associate degree
Postsecondary teachers	1,628	2,153	524	32.2	VH	Doctoral degree
Customer service representatives	2,063	2,534	471	22.8	L	Moderate-term on-the-job training
Janitors and cleaners, except maids and housekeeping cleaners	2,374	2,813	440	18.5	VL	Short-term on-the-job training
Waiters and waitresses	2,252	2,627	376	16.7	VL	Short-term on-the-job training
Combined food preparation and serving workers, including fast food	2,150	2,516	367	17.1	VL	Short-term on-the-job training
Home health aides	624	974	350	56.0	VL	Short-term on-the-job training
Nursing aides, orderlies, and attendants	1,455	1,781	325	22.3	L	Postsecondary vocational award
General and operations managers	1,807	2,115	308	17.0	VH	Bachelor's or higher degree, plus work experience
Personal and home care aides	701	988	287	41.0	VL	Short-term on-the-job training
Elementary school teachers, except special education	1,457	1,722	265	18.2	H	Bachelor's degree
Accountants and auditors	1,176	1,440	264	22.4	VH	Bachelor's degree
Office clerks, general	3,138	3,401	263	84	L	Short-term on-the-job training
Laborers and freight, stock, and material movers, hand	2,430	2,678	248	10.2	VL	Short-term on-the-job training
Receptionists and information clerks	1,133	1,379	246	21.7	L	Short-term on-the-job training
Landscaping and groundskeeping workers	1,177	1,407	230	19.5	L	Short-term on-the-job training
Truck drivers, heavy and tractor-trailer	1,738	1,962	223	12.9	H	Moderate-term on-the-job training
Computer software engineers, applications	460	682	222	48.4	VH	Bachelor's degree
Maintenance and repair workers, general	1,332	1,533	202	15.2	H	Moderate-term on-the-job training

Footnotes:

(1) The quartile ranking of Occupational Employment Statistics Survey annual earnings data are presented in the following categories: VH=very high ($43,605 and over), H=high ($28,590 to $43,604), L=low ($20,185 to $28,589), and VL=very low (up to $20,184). The rankings were based on quartiles using one-fourth of total employment to define each quartile. Earnings are for wage and salary workers.

(2) An occupation is placed into one of 11 categories that best describes the postsecondary education or training needed by most workers to become fully qualified.

Source: *Monthly Labor Review*, November 2005, www.bls.gov/emp/emptab21.htm

PURPOSE OF EXERCISES. It is our hope that you will develop your own personal objectives, believe in yourself, acknowledge stereotypes pertaining to life and work, and develop a clear strategy for entering the career of your choice. Whether you have directly experienced bias or other barriers to employment or have had the good fortune not to, we would like you to use the following written exercises to reflect upon your personal, social, and cultural opinions and biases. Exercise 6.1 helps you become aware of how you may react to roles and events that differ from those to which you are accustomed. Exercise 6.2 asks you to explore your own stereotypes. Be spontaneous with your answers; do not censor yourself because you fear your answer is wrong. Exercise 6.3 asks you to list the advantages and disadvantages of belonging to one or more distinct groups. Exercise 6.4 helps you become aware of your knowledge of various groups of people. The more difficult it is for you to identify names for this exercise, the more likely it is that you have led a life that excludes other cultures. Stereotypes and barriers tend to develop when we stick to our own groups. Exercise 6.5 asks you to think about the small businesses you use regularly. Exercise 6.6 asks you to consider the impact of globalization. In Exercise 6.7, you are to list jobs technology has recently created.

Companion
Website

To answer these questions online, go to the *Exercise* module in Chapter 6 of the Companion Website.

6.1   *First Impressions*

Think about each of the following situations. What are your first impressions?

a. You are applying for a job. A male receptionist ushers you into an office where you are greeted by a female vice president who will conduct the interview.

b. You are flying to Chicago. A male flight attendant welcomes you aboard the plane; later a female voice says, "This is your captain speaking."

c. You go to enroll your four-year-old in a nearby nursery school and discover all three teachers at the school are male.

d. You are introduced to a new couple in the neighborhood and discover the man stays home all day with two small children while the wife works outside the home.

e. You are African American and live in a neighborhood that is all Caucasian.

f. You have a conference with your child's teacher, who grew up in Taiwan.

g. You are in a class with many students who speak a different language.

h. You move into an apartment and learn your neighbors are homosexual.

i. You are temporarily disabled, must use a wheelchair, and have found a wonderful job opening. You haven't yet told the interviewer about your disability (and the room is on the second floor, with no elevator).

j. You arrive at your new dentist's office and find she has green-and-orange spiked hair.

k. You are referred to a hospital known for excellence in surgery, and your team of doctors is all Latino.

l. You go to court and find every jury member is African American.

m. You go to a job interview and find yourself facing a panel of younger men and women.

n. You find yourself in a statistics class in which all the students are Asian American.

o. You are on an airplane, and the flight attendant is older than your grandmother.

Gender Roles Questionnaire   6.2

In order to explore your own stereotypes, complete these sentences with the first thought that comes to mind. Don't censor yourself.

1. Women are happiest in careers when ———————————

2. Men are happiest in careers when ———————————

3. The most difficult emotion for a man to display is ———————————

4. The most difficult emotion for a woman to display is ———————————

5. Women tend to be better than men at ———————————

6. Men tend to be better than women at ———————————

7. Men get depressed about ———————————

8. Women get depressed about ———————————

9. Men are most likely to compete over ———————————

10. Women are most likely to compete over ———————————

11. Men tend to get angry about ———————————

12. Women tend to get angry about ———————————

13. As a man/woman, I was always taught to ———————————

14. Men feel pressured on the job when ———————————

15. Women feel pressured on the job when ———————————

6.3   Pros and Cons

List advantages and disadvantages of being any of the following:

1. Female _____

   advantage _____

   disadvantage _____

2. Male _____

   advantage _____

   disadvantage _____

3. Caucasian _____

   advantage _____

   disadvantage _____

4. African American _____

   advantage _____

   disadvantage _____

5. Latino _____

   advantage _____

   disadvantage _____

6. Asian American _____

   advantage _____

   disadvantage _____

7. Native American _____

   advantage _____

   disadvantage _____

6.4   Famous People

For each of the groups listed above, name five famous people (may be currently living or a historical figure).

_____

_____

_____

_____

_____

_____

_____

_____

_____

_____

_____

Small Businesses   6.5

List three small businesses whose services or products you use:

1. _____

2. _____

3. _____

Name one business that is operated out of a home:

_____

Globalization of the Work World   6.6

List five impacts of globalization on the workplace:

1. _____

2. _____

3. _____

4. _____

5. _____

Changing Nature of Work   6.7

Think about jobs that you, your friends, and family have had. Name three jobs that did not exist 10 years ago:

1. _____

2. _____

3. _____

6.8   *WWWebwise*

For additional activities online, go to the WWWebwise module in Chapter 6 of the Companion Website.

6.9   *Exercise Summary*

What about you? How do you think gender, race, age, sexual orientation, or physical disability could affect your ability to get a job? While doing these exercises, did you discover anything about your stereotypes of people? Have affirmative action policies affected you or anyone you know in applying for college or a job? Summarize your feelings about what you have learned.

_____

_____

_____

_____

_____

_____

_____

_____

_____

_____

_____

_____

_____

_____

_____

_____

_____

_____

_____

_____

_____

_____

Go to page 223 of the chapter summaries and fill out the Chapter 6 exercise summary now.

Information Integration

At the end of the chapter you will be able to . . .

- Brainstorm possible career options based on information you learned about your attitudes, beliefs, interests, personality, and skills

- Adopt a strategy to approach occupational research that will enhance your efficiency and effectiveness

- List printed and computerized sources of information to use in further clarifying your career choices

- Use your skills to gather information about specific occupations and career-related opportunities by using library materials and computerized resources

- Confirm or revise your first impressions about your top career choices

By now, you probably have one or several career areas in mind. This chapter will help you get more specific. It will enable you to review, clarify, and integrate the information you've collected about your needs, desires, values, interests, skills, and personal attributes. It is important to put these pieces together to identify some specific occupational areas that you can begin to research.

Discovery is seeing what everybody else has seen, and thinking what nobody else has thought.

ALBERT SZENT-GYORDI

Sometimes the hardest part of making a career choice is knowing what kinds of jobs exist. As you learned in the last chapter, the work world is changing so rapidly that it is difficult to stay current regarding all the kinds of jobs that are available. This can be complicated if you have been out of the workplace for a period of years, are looking for your first job, or are uncertain about how your academic background has prepared you for work.

This chapter will introduce you to the written and electronic resources available in libraries, in college career centers, and on your home computer when you are connected to the Internet. By using these references, you will have the information necessary to clarify and confirm your tentative career choices. Then, in Chapter 8, you will be encouraged to make a tentative career decision.

To assist you in listing specific occupations, try using the guided fantasy (Exercise 7.8). Start by quickly reviewing all the written information that you've recorded (in the Chapter Summaries section, beginning on page 219). Then close your eyes and visualize yourself in your perfect career. Mental visualization can sometimes focus your thoughts on areas that suit you perfectly. This technique helps you tap into and integrate the wealth of information, intuition, and wisdom that you already have about yourself. It is only natural to feel hesitant and even fearful about committing yourself to a career decision. These are the feelings that block you from making a decision and getting specific. Mental visualization is a technique to help your mind "wander" into a career choice.

Brainstorming Career Options

Before you can begin researching career options, you need to know what you are looking for. Many job searchers find this very difficult because they simply do not know very much about the kinds of jobs that are available, especially if they are changing careers. Other times, job searchers will make a decision about a career without knowing very much about it. At this phase in your career decision making, you should emphasize generating many different *possibilities*. In a later section of this chapter you will learn how to research these possibilities with written and electronic resources. That process provides the information you will need in order to make decisions about your career choices.

Your personal career profile from Part I is a good place to begin. The exercises you completed at the end of each chapter may give you ideas about your skills, interests, personality, and values as they relate to the world of work. For example, think about one of your interests you identified in the exercises at the end of Chapter 4. How could you teach people about this interest? How could you sell something related to this interest? What kind of service could you perform related to this interest? Suddenly your interest has become an important occupational consideration.

Obviously, the point of this exercise is to help you identify the relationship between your personal career profile and different occupations. Each element of your profile is something that you want to try to satisfy in order to be happy in your work. You are more likely to enjoy your job if you find the work interesting and you are using your skills. Your personal preferences provide insight into your preferred work style. You want to find a job that is consistent with your values so that you are satisfied with your daily work and feel that your occupation is important. Each of these areas needs to be satisfied every day at work, not just once a month or once a year. Exploring a large number of career options is the best place to begin to find satisfying work.

At the end of this chapter, you will find a series of exercises that will help you brainstorm a large number of job titles that you will use as you begin your research using the written and electronic resources presented later in this chapter. These exercises present a variety of techniques for brainstorming career ideas, and not every technique will appeal to you. Stick with these exercises, even those that seem wacky. Each one will challenge you to think differently about all the various jobs you might do. You simply want to generate a list of many, many different career possibilities and not eliminate anything yet that seems unrealistic. The ideas you generate in these exercises will be necessary for you to complete this chapter.

As you complete these exercises, keep a few thoughts about brainstorming in mind. Brainstorming is a creative process to produce as many ideas on a particular topic as possible—career ideas, in this case. It is a very useful way to begin thinking beyond all of the obvious ideas, those career options you have considered over and over again. In order for brainstorming to work, however, you need to remember two very important rules. First, at this point you should be more concerned with quantity than quality. Your goal should be to come up with a very long list of occupational ideas and pare it down later. Second, consider even the most outrageous ideas. Maybe being a lion tamer in the circus is not a realistic occupational goal, but it might spark another idea that is realistic.

Brainstorm your way to a career choice

You might look back at the exercises in Chapter 4 that made you think about jobs (e.g., the classified ads exercise). Using some of the Websites suggested at the end of this chapter, you will be seeing some of this information in a new light. Be sure to use some of the Websites found in the Chapters 6 and 7 Web links on the Companion Website to generate ideas. For example, the University of North Carolina career majors site has a "What can I do with a major" heading that is excellent for finding jobs related to majors.

These students listen to a guidance counselor to learn more about career and education options.

Understanding Career Paths and Common Organizational Divisions

Sometimes a greater awareness of the job market can be gained by researching career paths or career ladders in a specific industry. Most career centers and libraries have books that outline career paths. Once you've assessed where you currently fit in, you can start preparing to move up the ladder. If you are presently working, your immediate supervisor and the human resources department can provide information about routes for advancement, for example, in-house workshops, institutes, on-the-job training, community college associate degrees and certificates, and bachelor's degrees.

Although the world of work includes a number of broad fields such as business, education, government (including the military), health care, and nonprofit agencies, all of these fields share certain common functional needs and have some common organizational units. As an example, many fields need the accounting functions of payroll computation and disbursement, budgeting, and servicing of accounts payable and receivable. Administration, finance, human resources, marketing, public relations, management information systems, and research and development are departmental functions common to almost all work fields. The following list explains the general functions of these and other departments in typical businesses; however, you will find identical or very similar organizational units performing very similar functions in the fields of education, government, nonprofit agencies, and health care.

If you have been concentrating on specific industries in your search for job possibilities, you can gain a fresh perspective by selecting functions that may be interesting to you and then researching jobs within those functions, but among various industries.

Be aware of common organizational elements

Administration. An organization's top executive officers and other managers, secretarial and word processing personnel, and human resources staff are included in this function.

Corporate relations. Responsible for advertising, public relations, and community relations.

Distribution. Sometimes called the transportation department; oversees warehousing and shipping of the company's products.

Engineering. Product design and modification; often oversees manufacturing of products (process engineers).

Finance. Accounting functions, including payroll, budgets, and accounts payable and receivable.

Sales. Responsible for initiating and maintaining customer accounts, selling the company's product; sometimes includes marketing function.

It is better to ask some of the questions than to know all of the answers.

JAMES THURBER

Remember that some companies are restructuring so that jobs may not be part of career paths. They may hire a coordinator with cross-functional skills: that person develops and tracks the project, motivates the team, assists the team in marketing the project/product, and also keeps track of the budget. The project may last six months or so, and then the coordinator is assigned to a different project with either similar or different duties. This type of organization is called a *web*. Another type of web is a situation in which a specialist works for *several* companies, such as an accountant who does the books for a designer, publisher, educational consultant, and marketing specialist.

Learn about web organization

Your research should reflect the location of your chosen path(s). Do you hope to work somewhere as a *generalist* and be adept in many areas in the web? Or do you prefer to be part of an organization as a *specialist,* such as an accountant? See Exhibit 7.1 for examples of career paths in business fields.

Now that you have a clearer idea of the jobs that best suit your personality, it is necessary to research the actual requirements of the jobs. There are two primary ways to obtain job information: searching through written or computerized materials in the library and contacting people who already work in your area of interest. This chapter focuses on written and computerized materials, whereas Chapter 9 focuses on people and contacts. Your local library or college career development and placement center should be able to provide you with some or all of the following resources.

Strategies for Researching Career Options

The best place to begin your research is not in the library, but with a strategy. This will help you focus your efforts, know what to look for, and not waste time on dead-end research.

1. **Decide which occupations you are going to research.** After completing the exercises at the end of this chapter, you should have a very long list of occupational possibilities. It is unrealistic to suggest that you should research every job you brainstormed. There are probably some jobs on your list that you can remove right away. Review your list and prioritize your ideas. If you still have a long list, try grouping your ideas according to industry or function. For example, if you have five occupational ideas

EXHIBIT 7.1

Sample career paths in business: typical job titles and compensation ranges of marketing, retailing, and international professionals (numbers in thousands).

SALES AND MARKETING

Vice President, Sales and Marketing
($150–750)

National Sales Manager ($150–250)	Marketing Director/VP ($80–175)
Regional Sales Manager ($125–175)	Marketing Manager ($40–100)
District Sales Manager ($80–120)	Marketing Communications Manager ($30–60)
Marketing/Sales Representative ($35–70)	Marketing Assistant ($27–35)

ADVERTISING

Executive Vice President
($180–500)

Account Supervisor
($75–120)

Senior Account Executive
($48–70)

Account Executive
($35–41)

Account Coordinator
($28–31)

Assistant Account Coordinator
($24–30)

RETAILING

Vice President, Merchandising
($225+)

Store Manager ($75–175)	General Merchandise Mgr. ($60–200)
Buyer-Planner/Buyer ($36–80)	Merchandise Manager ($50–70)
Assistant Buyer ($30–35)	Group Sales Manager ($40–60)
Management Trainee ($26–30)	Sales Manager ($30–35)

INTERNATIONAL

V.P. International Operations
($90–250)

Sales Manager International
($80–150)

Export Manager
($60–100)

Contracts Administrator
($50–100)

Export Administration
($25–60)

related to writing and journalism, you might group them for purposes of research in a category called "communication careers." You should identify a realistic number of occupations or occupational areas about which you would like to learn more.

2. **Research the industry and functional areas.** Once you have decided what you are going to research, your next step is to conduct broad research on the industry and field. It is best to start with resources that can give you enough information in a small space to decide if a particular occupational area is interesting. Some of the U.S. Department of Labor publications discussed in this chapter will be your best tools.

3. **Learn about current events affecting your areas of interest.** Magazines and newspapers, especially publications that focus on business such as *Fortune, Business Week,* or the *Wall Street Journal,* are rich resources for information about current industry trends, relevant new technology, key companies and organizations, and job growth. You can easily find the most current publications by completing a key word search on most library databases.

4. **Identify relevant professional and trade associations.** Most industries have a professional organization. These are associations that bring together professionals in a particular industry for networking and continuing education. These organizations exist to disseminate information about a particular industry. Professional and trade associations also publish journals and newsletters that can give you insight into the industry's current issues, types of employers, and common vocabulary.

The Encyclopedia of Associations and Chamber of Commerce publications are the best resources for this information. As you research occupations, develop a list of relevant professional associations to which you can write to request additional career information.

5. **Locate useful Websites on the Internet.** The Internet brings a wide range of information about different industries, professional associations, and employers literally to your fingertips. The World Wide Web has become such a valuable tool that libraries offer Internet access to their users. By using your industry as a key word in any of the different Internet search engines, you can identify many useful Websites that provide the most up-to-date information. A complete discussion of computerized job search resources, including tips for people unfamiliar with the Internet, begins on page 180.

SUCCESS STRATEGIES

Questions to ask when researching a job

- What are the job duties and responsibilities?
- What qualifications are needed in terms of college degrees, skills, or work experience?
- Are you likely to receive on-the-job training in this field?
- What is a typical career path in this field?
- What is the employment outlook for this industry?
- What is the average salary for someone entering this field? What are the top salaries in this field?
- Who are typical employers in this field?
- What are the key professional and trade associations for this field?
- What is the work environment like for this field? Is traveling required?
- Is relocation to a specific geographic location required?

FACTS & FIGURES

Local government

According to the Bureau of Labor Statistics, more than 18 million people are employed by states, counties, cities, and towns.

THINK ABOUT IT

1. What kind of local government job might interest you?

2. If you know someone working for local or state government, what is the job and how did the person get the job?

3. What are the advantages and disadvantages of working for government?

To answer these questions online, go to the *Facts and Figures* module in Chapter 7 of the Companion Website.

Companion Website

Government listings offer opportunities

6. **Identify key employers.** The last step is to compile a list of typical employers, noting all kinds of employers (e.g., nonprofit, government, or business) and actual organization names. Several of the directories listed in Exhibit 7.2 can provide you with lists of companies that hire people for a particular industry.

Government Employment Opportunities

tate and local governments hire the majority of people in public work. Local government alone hires over 50 percent of all public employees. In addition, the federal government hires hundreds of people each day across the United States. When private industry is cutting back on hiring, government often seems like it is the best place to find a job. In fact, within five years, almost half of the federal government's current employees will be eligible to retire.

Information regarding employment with local and state government offices is typically available at state or local One Stop Career Centers. Federal and state employment information is often available on the Internet through computers at colleges and One Stop Career Centers. (For more information about surfing the Web, see the Internet section of this chapter.) For those who don't have access to these locations, state personnel offices offer applications, tests, job descriptions, and occupational outlook data for that state. For example, California publishes "A Guide to the Use of Labor Market Publications" to help prospective employees research job opportunities. It is important to consider that it may take six to nine months to complete the application, test, interview, and hiring process for state government jobs. This is not a good option for someone who needs immediate employment; however, many people find it possible to complete the process while employed elsewhere. Also, many college students begin the application and testing process during their senior year in college, enabling them to interview for jobs before they graduate.

Excluding the postal service, the federal government employs almost 2 million workers. There may be 15,000 vacancies on any given day. No one in the federal government knows all the positions vacant on a particular day, week, or month, and you must contact the personnel office of each agency for a complete listing of vacancies in that agency. If you have access to the Internet, you may want to check out America's Job Bank (www.ajb.dni.us) or Federal Jobs Digest (www.fedjobs.com). These services are updated daily and have links to many other employment options. At the end of this chapter, several other career information services available on the Internet are listed. These sources also link to federal and state employment information. One other Website worth visiting is www.careersingovernment.com.

EXHIBIT 7.2

The Almanac of American Employers. Lists 500 companies with one page per firm, which includes the following information: recent financial performance, salaries and benefits, regional offices, brands, and divisions.

American Society of Association Executives. Their list of directories may be found at www.asanet.org.

California Manufacturers Directory. Lists companies by location and product, with an additional section on companies that have import/export business.

Directory of American Firms Operating in Foreign Countries. Lists about 3,000 American corporations with factories and branch offices covering more than 36 countries. Also lists key personnel, but because it is not published annually, such information may be out-of-date.

Dun and Bradstreet Million Dollar Directory. Lists 160,000 companies in five volumes. Largest directory of its kind, indexed in a variety of ways. Includes subsidiaries not mentioned in other directories and is especially useful for direct-mail campaigns (see Chapter 9).

Dun's Employment Opportunities Directory. Lists 11,000 companies throughout the United States. Includes information about educational specialties the company values, most promising areas of employment, and a brief description of the company's insurance plans. Is divided into geographic and industry sections.

Encyclopedia of Associations. Lists 15,000 associations in every field, with names of officers, telephone numbers, and brief descriptions of orientation and activities.

Encyclopedia of Business Information Services. Lists source materials on businesses.

Gale Directory of Publications and Broadcast Media. Lists every newspaper, magazine, and radio station in the United States. Information found by region or industry groups (e.g., retailing, restaurants). Excellent source of information about trade publications.

Guide to American Directories. Describes 3,300 directories subdivided into 400 topical areas.

Hoover's Handbook of American Business. Its industry master list has more than 300 industries and 4,000 detailed company profiles, including a very thorough overview of what each company owns, how it is structured, key personnel, and company performance. Shows how employment prospects compare (e.g., top 100 companies in employment opportunities). Go to www.hoovers.com.

INFOTRAC. A computer-based program providing up-to-date directory information.

Regional and community magazines. Published by most large cities and metropolitan areas and focus on business, industry, education, the arts, and politics; states and regions also have their own magazines.

Standard and Poor's Register of Corporations, Directors, and Executives. Lists about 55,000 public and private companies in three volumes. Volume one covers basic information; volume two includes summaries about key executives; volume three indexes companies according to industry classification.

Standard Periodical Directory. Describes 50,000 periodicals and directories.

Standard Rate and Data Business Publications Directory. Lists names and addresses of thousands of trade publications.

State directories. Directories of trade and industry published by each state. If one is not in your library, contact the local or state chamber of commerce, or write to U.S. Chamber of Commerce, 1615 H Street NW, Washington, DC 20006 or go to www.uschamber.com.

Thomas's Register of American Manufacturers. Lists 100,000 manufacturers by location and product.

Who's Who in Commerce and Industry. Gives names and biographical sketches of top executives.

You can also find information about federal jobs in publications such as *Federal Careers Opportunities,* a biweekly publication containing more than 4,000 job listings representing vacancies in the executive branch or congressional and judicial staff as well as in the United Nations. Also check with the Government Printing Office, your nearest branch of the Office of Personnel Management, and www.usajobs.opm.gov. Exhibit 7.3 lists some of the many federal employment opportunities.

EXHIBIT 7.3   Sample federal employment opportunities.

EXECUTIVE DEPARTMENTS

Agriculture	Health and Human Services	Labor
Commerce	Homeland Security	State
Defense	Housing and Urban	Transportation
Education	Development	Treasury
Energy	Interior	Veterans Affairs
	Justice	

SAMPLE FEDERAL EMPLOYMENT POSITIONS COVERED BY ANNOUNCEMENTS

Accountant	Forester	Occupational therapist
Architect	Geophysicist	Oceanographer
Astronomer	Hospital administrator	Patent examiner
Attorney	Hydrologist	Pest controller
Bacteriologist	Illustrator	Pharmacist
Biologist	Internal revenue agent	Prison administrator
Chemist	Librarian	Social worker
Dietitian	Mathematician	Soil conservationist
Education officer	Meteorologist	Special agent
Engineer	Nurse	Teacher

MAJOR INDEPENDENT AGENCIES

Central Intelligence Agency	Nuclear Regulatory Commission
Environmental Protection Agency	Office of Personnel Management
Equal Employment Opportunity Commission	Small Business Administration
Federal Deposit Insurance Corporation	Social Security Administration
General Services Administration	Tennessee Valley Authority
National Aeronautics and Space Administration	U.S. Information Agency
National Archives and Records Administration	U.S. Agency for International Development
	U.S. Postal Service

Federal job information centers may also have access to a national computerized job bank. This is especially useful for people who want to know about job opportunities located some distance away.

U.S. Department of Labor Publications

The Occupational Information Network (O*NET) is an interactive tool devised by the U.S. Department of Labor. The program is an easy-to-use database that collects, analyzes, and disseminates skill and job require-ment information. It is designed to replace the *Dictionary of Occupational Titles* (DOT) and *Occupational Outlook Handbook* (OOH).

O*Net provides a summary report for more than 950 occupations (including knowl-edge, skills, abilities, interests, and values, as well as examples of tasks in a job) and also identifies the physical, affective, and intellec-tual demands of a job. This information may help an individual with a disability assess his or her potential for succeeding in a job.

A newer resource from the Depart-ment of Labor is Career Voyages, www.CareerVoyages.gov. This site provides information on fast-growing, high-demand occupations, including the skills and educational requirements needed for such jobs. The site's menu targets youth (high school and older), career changers, parents, and career advisers. It also offers a link to apprenticeship training resources.

Most libraries, college career and placement centers, One Stop Career Centers, and high school career centers have copies of the DOT and OOH. You may use the online services, CD-ROM copies, or hard-copy publications.

The *Dictionary of Occupational Titles* (www.oalj.dol.gov) lists more than 35,000 job titles and more than 21,000 different occupations. This resource (as well as O*NET) has been mentioned in previous chapters and will be referred to in Chapter 10 as a tool to use in writing a resume. It is especially useful because it lists specific tasks to be done on a job, as in the entry for copywriter.

The *Occupational Outlook Handbook* (www.bls.gov/oco) includes information on job descriptions, skills, places of employment, training, educational requirements, personality traits, and values that might be important in a particular field, as well as salary ranges. It is updated every other year and represents a national survey of occupations. Salary informa-tion should be compared with local salaries and local cost-of-living factors. For example, Los Angeles employers tend to pay $1,000 to $2,000 more per year than many of the generalized estimates shown in the OOH.

DOT entry for copywriter

Writes advertising copy for use by publication or broadcast media to promote sale of goods and services. Consults with sales media and marketing representatives to obtain information on product or service and discuss style and length of advertising copy. Obtains additional background and current development information through research and inter-view. Reviews advertising trends, consumer surveys, and other data regarding marketing of specific and related goods and services to formulate presentation approach. Writes preliminary draft of copy and sends to supervisor for approval. Corrects and revises copy as necessary. May write articles, bulletins, sales letters, speeches, and other related informative and promotional material.

Between editions of the OOH, the *Occupational Outlook Quarterly* provides updates of occupational projections as well as compensation ranges and cost-of-living comparisons throughout the United States.

The *Guide for Occupational Exploration* (GOE) provides detailed information about the interests, aptitudes, skills, and job activities of various occupational groups. The data in this publication are organized into 16 interest areas, 117 Worker Trait Groups. More detailed information regarding the GOE was provided in Chapter 4.

Employer Directories

Employer directories provide information about specific companies, such as those in your field with current job openings.

Let your fingers do the researching

Information about a variety of enterprises, from foundations to corporations, can be found in directories. Directories list an employer's name and address, product, and geographic location, as well as other information including size in terms of volume of sales, number of employees, and names of top-level executives. Don't forget to use your local telephone directory. The white (or blue) pages list government agencies and departments, and the yellow pages list other places of employment.

The yellow pages are available on the Internet, at www.yellowpages.com. A benefit of this resource is that small businesses are listed. If you are thinking about starting a landscape business, for example, determine the competition in a specific geographic area by typing "landscape" under "Business Category" and the city or ZIP code in the next box. Or, if you would like to work in a certain city to get experience before opening your own business, a phone call to the businesses listed in the yellow pages may provide you with information about a job or when one might be available.

As you review the directories listed in Exhibit 7.2, look for the following types of information:

- A geographic list of companies in a specified field
- Small, growing companies
- A company with international positions
- Names and addresses of corporate officers

Note which directories give information about trade publications. These offer information about companies that are doing well, job openings in specific fields, and firms that may not be listed in any other directory. Again, a simple phone call will provide you with valuable information.

SUCCESS STRATEGIES

Research

Research helps you to accomplish the following:

- Locate high-level company information (such as names of executives)
- Obtain telephone numbers and addresses
- Locate company Web pages
- Research company financial information
- Monitor company news and periodicals
- Review public opinion about a company
- Learn about an industry
- Learn to use business and financial Websites
- Locate professional associations
- Find career-related conferences and seminars
- Research nonprofit organizations
- Identify international business resources

Other Written Sources of Information

Newspapers

Check out all the newspapers in the geographic area in which you are interested in working. Read the help-wanted section for openings as well as for local wage and fringe benefits information. There may be a separate business section that advertises professional jobs. Read everything in terms of your own job target and keep a file, but be aware that only 15 percent of job openings are listed in want ads. Therefore, note other areas of the paper, such as articles that announce business expansions, personnel changes, and new ideas. Planning commission announcements usually mention new industrial parks and the expected number of employers to be located there. Marriage announcements usually list the bride's and groom's occupations and may give you the name of an important executive of a firm that interests you. Lifestyle sections may profile leaders in the community; gossip columns may suggest where to find trendsetters.

Want ads = only 15% of job openings

Trade Journals

Almost every trade and profession has at least one regularly published journal. The business section of your library should have references. A book or pamphlet on your chosen career may list names of related associations and trade journals. Your library or career center may also have computerized retrieval systems (see "Computerized Information Sources" later in this chapter) to access trade journal information. The following resources are useful in tracking down particular trade journals: *Ulrich's International Periodical Directory,* the *Encyclopedia of Business Information Services,* the *Gale Directory of Publications and Broadcast Media,* and the *Encyclopedia of Associations.* Use these trade journals to locate job ads and to familiarize yourself with the people, products, current trends, and specific vocabulary of a field.

> *Even the lowly woodpecker owes his success to the fact that he uses his head.*
>
> **JOE MARCUCCI**

Magazines

The *Reader's Guide to Periodicals Literature,* available at any library in either printed or electronic form, can be used both to locate names of magazines and to find titles of informative and useful articles about any field you wish to research. Do you want to learn the latest in animation careers, the outlook for engineers in the western United States, opportunities for liberal arts graduates? It's been covered in some magazine recently! Business magazines also provide profiles of both businesses and their executive officers, which is information you might use in comparing companies.

Ask the librarian for the *Business Periodicals Index.* It accesses trade journal articles and has citations for hundreds of publications. The articles are arranged according to subject; broad subjects are divided into more specific categories. University business/management libraries are more likely to hold publications listed in the *Business Periodicals Index;* they are less likely to be found in local libraries.

Meet Jackie

Jackie, a single mother with two children, is working as manager of the gift shop in the Los Angeles Hilton Hotel. Her days are long and her pay is not enough to support herself and her children. Her child support helps, but she is always short at the end of the month. Her boss is not the most understanding woman in the world, and Jackie knows she has to make a change. Her mother tries to tell her that having a job, any job, is important in this economy, but she can't imagine staying at this job for much longer.

Jackie attended community college several years ago and she has completed her general education classes. She wonders how long it will take her to obtain a degree, and decides to make an appointment with a counselor. When the counselor asks Jackie what she wants to do when she receives her AA degree, Jackie can't come up with one thing. Jackie worries that the counselor might feel she is wasting his time, but instead he asks, "Why don't you take a career planning class? It will help you learn about yourself and careers that might suit you." Since the class meets on Jackie's day off, she decides to do it.

Jackie likes the class and she learns a lot about herself. From the interest inventory she takes, she learns that she likes the helping professions and that she is interested in physical fitness, science, and nutrition. She also learns that she values freedom, accomplishment, and creativity and that she prefers working with people and has an organized, logical mind.

When Jackie looks over the occupations that match her assessment results, she discovers physical therapist, personal trainer, and occupational therapist. Jackie does not know much about each occupation, so she uses the Career Center's resources to do some research. She begins with the Chronicle Guides and the Vocational Biographies, and she also uses EUREKA, a computerized information system. Her research gives her information on education, training, job outlook, salary, and job search techniques. Jackie also interviews people working in those fields to get a sense of what the daily routine of the job is like.

After all her research, Jackie decides to study physical therapy and sets about figuring out how she is going to do it. Jackie makes a plan. First she looks over the next semester's schedule and arranges all her classes in late afternoon and evening, then she goes to her employer and asks if she may work part-time. She asks

SAMPLE USEFUL MAGAZINES FOR BUSINESS INFORMATION

Black Entrepreneur	*High Technology Careers*
Business Week	*Inc.*
Entrepreneur	*National Business Employment Weekly*
Executive Female	*Success*
Fast Company	*Wall Street Journal* (newspaper)
Fortune	*Working Woman*
Business 2.0	

her ex-husband if he can increase his child support, then she applies for financial aid through the college. Finally, she asks her mother if she will watch her kids in the evening so she can save money on babysitting.

With a little luck, she can survive. The first year is a struggle but her money management is not the biggest problem. Jackie passes only 12 of the 24 units she attempts. She hadn't realized how difficult the science classes would be, and she also hadn't realized how rusty her English and math skills are. Discouraged, she makes an appointment with her adviser. He is sympathetic, but he feels that Jackie needs to be realistic about her career choice and about her chances of completing her program of study and transferring to the university in the time she has planned. After much discussion, Jackie decides to give herself two additional semesters, but after the first semester, she knows even with the extra time it will be impossible.

When Jackie sees the counselor again, he says that he might have a solution: The college is planning to add a Recreation Fitness Certificate Program to the curriculum. Students with the certificate will be able to work in recreation programs for children and adults, and with a higher degree they can become supervisors. The counselor tells Jackie that she can speak with the department head for more specific information. Jackie makes an appointment and discovers that the field holds many opportunities, some of which she can take advantage of right now. With this news, Jackie feels better. She decides to talk again with her counselor and make a new plan of action.

REAL STORIES

WHAT DO YOU THINK?

1. What strategies would you use to overcome the situation that Jackie faced?

2. Was Jackie too optimistic in the beginning? Would you have developed a different plan?

3. Was Jackie too pessimistic at the end? Would you have taken a different direction?

4. Give several reasons for quitting a job before you have another one.

5. Is college always the answer to a better life? Give examples of ways that you can improve your life or your career without attending college. Identify five jobs that pay well and don't require a college degree.

To answer these questions online, go to the *Real Stories* module in Chapter 7 of the Companion Website.

Companion Website

SPECIALIZED MAGAZINES FOR COLLEGE STUDENTS AND GRADUATES

Black Collegian

Business Week's Guide to Careers

Business World (a career magazine for college students)

College Placement Annual (check with college placement office)

Hispanic Times Magazine

Saludos Hispanos

Women's Careers

In-House Bulletins and Announcements

Human resources offices in virtually every business, agency, school, and hospital post jobs as they become available. Job posting best serves the people already employed at such places; however, some of the job listings may be open to anyone.

Large corporations such as Bank of America and General Electric publish in-house job announcement newsletters monthly or quarterly. Most of these newsletters are not intended for public use but are circulated among all employees to encourage internal job mobility. The job announcements list required skills, degrees, and relevant experience. Such in-house newsletters are an excellent way to explore current needs within large companies and to learn more about the types of job skills being sought.

Computerized Information Sources

Computerized information can often be more quickly accessed and may be more complete than that found in traditional sources. Contact your library or campus career center for assistance in locating the sources described here—and for others.

Selected Computerized Sources

Probably the largest resource on occupational information is the Career Information System (CIS; also known as EUREKA in California). This software provides occupational information, including job descriptions, locations for training such as vocational schools and colleges, and financial aid information, specific to the state in which it is located. Another component of CIS, called QUEST, helps users identify the work characteristics that are common to certain occupations. A second program, SIGI PLUS (System of Interactive Guidance and Information plus more), is designed to clarify your values and to match your values, interests, and skills with occupations. A third program, GIS (Guidance Information System), acts as a source of national occupational information. The program DISCOVER identifies career sources and includes vital information on decision making. A commercial program available on CD-ROM, Discovering Careers, contains the *Occupational Outlook Handbook, Dictionary of Occupational Titles,* current trends, projected job growth, wages and salary information, licensing rules, related publications (e.g., trade journals), associations, and potential employers. Most of this information can now be found by going to www.ajb.dni.us and O*NET.

In many colleges, computers located in counselors' offices or in the career center offer software to help students explore occupations related to their college major. For students seeking help in selecting a major, 3,000 college majors can be scanned by a computer in three to five seconds to locate the ones that match the student's interests. Often this software includes a file with information on all two- and four-year colleges in the United States, which can assist students in choosing a school, preparing for admission, and planning a course schedule.

Many college career planning and placement offices have online or CD-ROM resources that provide employment information about some of the largest companies in the United States. For example, Moody's Corporate Profiles on Dialog lists more than 5,000 publicly held companies with information such as business analysis, annual earnings, and financial data. Wetfeet.com provides company profiles in its "Career Research" section, while Fortune.com has a company profiles section including descriptive information on the "Fortune 500," "Small Business 100," and 100 fastest-growing companies. Another place to find such information is the business section of your campus library or most city libraries. Finally, if your family or a friend subscribes to an online service such as America Online, company/job information can be obtained from the business/financial sections, the career sections, or various bulletin boards, or from other Internet sources such as those listed in the next section and in Chapter 9 (see "Selected Online Employment Databases").

The Internet

The information superhighway offers immediate access to unlimited sources for both job descriptions and company information. If you don't own a computer or haven't subscribed to an Internet service provider, access is possible through libraries, colleges, universities, quick print centers, and even some coffeehouses. The local library is a great place to try out the Internet.

Library Resource Centers

Librarians, as information specialists, may be available to help you both conduct your search and use the library's information-retrieval tools to access indexes, abstracts, and (in some cases) the full text of thousands of newspapers, magazines, and journals. The library's Internet connections (called T-lines) are significantly faster than the typical family modem, allowing users to search through hundreds of thousands of references.

Libraries subscribe to powerful research index services such as Nexus, Dialog, and Infotrac and have access to databases containing hundreds of periodicals. Library Internet access can simplify the search for information and articles. You may be able to tap into the library's indexes through your home computer; however, you'll probably have to *order* copies of articles rather than download them. (It may be possible to retrieve your college library documents at home or in the office, if your school allows such an arrangement.)

With laptops and wireless access, students today have unlimited access to research tools.

Career Sites

To explore careers and the job market, online resources are available for every phase of the job search: identifying opportunities, researching specific industries and companies, posting resumes online, and making contacts with potential employers. Information on job search and resume resources is located in Chapter 9, Targeting Your Job Search, and Chapter 10, Preparing a Winning Resume.

Weblogs. "Blogs" range in scope from individual diaries to arms of political campaigns, media programs, and corporations. They range in scale from the writings of one occasional author, to the collaboration of a large community of writers. In 2004, the role of blogs became increasingly mainstream, as political consultants, news services, and candidates began using them as tools for outreach and opinion formation. The *Columbia Journalism Review* began regular coverage of blogs and blogging in 2004. Additionally, personal audioblogs are on the rise (also known as podcasting).

In January 2005 the first VloggerCon was held, catering to a new breed of bloggers, the video blogger. A vlog, or videoblog, is a weblog that uses video as its primary presentation format. Vlog posts are usually accompanied by text, image, and additional metadata to provide a context or overview for the video.

By the summer of 2005, the trend-oriented business magazine *Business 2.0* was quoting *Business Week* as claiming that weblogs are "the most explosive outbreak in the information world since the Internet itself." Meanwhile, *Business 2.0* started sponsoring a conference to teach "Business Blogging 101."

The following are two examples of "career blogs":

- *Science Magazine:* http://nextwave.sciencemag.org/. Search for the Career Blog feature.
- *Wetfeet Website:* www.wetfeet.com/advice/weblog/4–01.asp

Websites. Unique jobs are located at the following Websites (use the weblinks in Chapter 7 of the Companion Website to find more sites):

- *Librarians:* http://libraryjobpostings.org
- *Videogame jobs:* Gamasutra.com and Gamesindustry.biz
- *Museum-related jobs:* http://aam-us.org and MuseumJobs.com
- *Environmental careers:* EE-link.net and ecojobs.com
- *Affirmative action:* www.aar-eeo.com

America's Job Bank (www.ajb.dni.us) is a valuable site during a job search. If you are interested in federal government jobs, look at *Fed World* (www. fedworld.gov) and www.studentjobs.gov (beware: if you type studentjobs.com you will get Canadian job information!). You may find access to your state employment service most easily through *America's Job Bank*. At your state site, you will have access to skill requirements for many of the state's jobs.

Job Market Research Sites

To begin your online search, go to the Chapter 7 section of the Companion Website, where you can click on some of the Websites listed below.

Monster Board: www.monster.com. This is one of the largest sites on the Web, with an excellent "career center." It includes a Resources section that has information for new job seekers, career changers, and people making military transitions. Additionally, you can search for information on jobs, industries, franchises, salary statistics, resume writing, and interview techniques. Monster is also known as the largest database for job listings. More than 1.6 million job seekers use this site daily.

Monstertrak: www.monstertrak.com. This site has great career information for students, and many colleges post their job listings here. Be sure to look for the Career Guide when checking out this site.

Wetfeet: www.wetfeet.com. This popular Website offers a wide range of job listings. Subscribe to the newsletter for weekly job-finding tips and interesting and different jobs. The Resource Center offers resources including company research, stress management, personal finance, resume tips, and interview strategies. Especially useful at this stage in your exploration is the section titled "Career Research." Be sure to check out Wetfeet's blog.

Black Voices: www.blackvoices.com. This site includes job search and many other helpful features for African Americans. Another helpful site is www.blackcollegian.com, where many of the links lead to discussions of barriers to employment. This site also includes information about the best companies for African Americans.

Hire the Deaf Network: www.hiredeaf.com. This is the number one site for individuals who are hearing impaired to find jobs.

Hispanic Business: www.hispanicbusiness.com. This site offers up-to-date stories, links to business-related articles, and information about the top 500 Hispanic-owned companies in the United States.

About (www.about.com) has a section titled "Jobs & Careers" that provides helpful information on general job hunting and topics related to starting a business. It includes advice on developing effective resumes and cover letters.

Classified ads from several major newspapers can be found at www.careerbuilder.com. Or, type "resume and interview advice," "labor market information," or "career information" into a search engine to find a number of possible sites to visit. CareerBuilder also includes good career articles.

Interested in working overseas? The site www.overseasjobs.com may help you locate a position. It contains 1,500 overseas job vacancies, which can be searched by key word. It also offers hundreds of resources in more than 40 countries. In addition, it has an online bookstore with titles such as *Finding a Job in Australia.*

Industry searches. If you are interested in financial services such as investment banking and retail banking, use the following search method: in your browser's search box, type "financial services." Narrow your

Find what you like doing best and then get someone to pay you for doing it.

KATHERINE WHITEHORN

search by adding key words, such as "banks," to the search box. From the results of this search you can investigate specific companies. To learn more about the banking business, visit several banking sites on the Web and return periodically to follow developments in each business. Firms often announce new departments, services, and products first on the Web.

Trade Journals

Earlier in the chapter, we mentioned industry trade journals. Sometimes these journals have Websites. For example, *Advertising Age* is located at www.adage.com. Journals such as this provide the latest information about trends in an industry. You may be able to add your name to an e-mail list, which will allow you to receive information about current industry issues. Most magazines and trade journals print their e-mail and Website addresses in the front of the publication. One Website, www.bizjournals.com, allows you to search for articles from more than 40 local business journals across the United States. Also try www.freetrademagazinesource.com.

Sometimes a business magazine such as *Business 2.0* (www.business 2.com) or *Fortune* (www.fortune.com) provides links to many businesses. *Business 2.0*'s Website offers a "weblog". In the blog, you will find insider information, i.e., what it is really like to be at a specific company. A Website such as careerjournal.com is also a good source for insider information.

The computer resources available to you will vary from location to location. Check with your local library, college career center, college adviser, and computer store to explore how computers can help you obtain information that will aid in your career planning.

PURPOSE OF EXERCISES. The following exercises will help you digest the contents of this chapter. You can complete them by using your local library or college career center to explore some of the resources mentioned in this chapter. Exercise 7.1 asks you to list 10 tempting jobs. In Exercise 7.2, you are asked to write about a job based on your interests. Exercise 7.3 has you list five favorite jobs that people you know currently hold. Exercise 7.4 requires that you investigate resources utilizing the local library, college library, and local newspaper. Exercise 7.5 asks that you learn what kinds of information and assistance are available from your college career center, local state employment office, and other employment offices. Exercise 7.6 gives you a format for gathering facts about three jobs.

To answer these questions online, go to the *Exercise* module in Chapter 7 of the Companion Website.

A Tempting 10 7.1

Identify one industry that you find interesting, such as entertainment, business, or education. In the space below, write 10 different jobs related to that industry. When you have completed this, prioritize the job titles in order of how interesting they sound to you, and list them in the space below. Repeat this exercise with two or three different industries. Use www.yahoo.com or the webguide on www.business2.com.

1. _____   6. _____
2. _____   7. _____
3. _____   8. _____
4. _____   9. _____
5. _____   10. _____

I'd Do This Even If I Didn't Get Paid 7.2

Pretend that you do not have to work for a living but instead can do whatever you enjoy all day. Write some ideas in the space below. When you are finished, identify a likely job title for your activities and the relevant industry. For example, if you thought that you would enjoy spending your time painting, you might give portrait artist or graphic artist as your job title and art as your industry.

_____

_____

_____

7.3   *The Grass Is Always Greener*

In the space below, write the names of five friends or family members who hold jobs that interest you. Next to each name, write a key phrase to explain what interests you about the job. Prioritize the jobs and industries you find interesting.

1. _____
2. _____
3. _____
4. _____
5. _____

7.4   *Job Research*

1. Which directories could be most helpful to you now, and what do you need to know? Where are these directories found?

   _____

2. What are the names of three trade journals related to your field of interest? Where are they found?

   a. _____
   b. _____
   c. _____

3. What are some of the current trends reflected in these journals?

   _____

   _____

4. Name one professional association related to your field. List where and when local meetings are held. (What about the national conference—can you attend or join as a student?) For example:

   American Society of Women
       Accountants (ASWA)

   Local contact: Joan Smith—
       phone: 805-555-1213

   Meeting time & location:
       3rd Thursday of each
       month, 7 P.M. (dinner),
       Colonial House Restaurant, Oxnard

   Your field: _____
   Association: _____

   Contact: _____
   _____

   Meeting: _____
   _____
   _____
   _____

5. Study a local daily newspaper for three weeks, and make a scrapbook or database of articles that relate to your field. (Include want ads, feature articles, meetings, networking groups, and names of executives in your field who were mentioned anywhere in the paper.)

Local and Internet Resources   **7.5**

1. Investigate local career and placement centers. Ask if they place people in your field or if they can refer you to others who do.

2. Visit the state employment office as well as private employment or temporary agencies to find out how they place people and how long it may take to get a job.

3. Find a local job opportunity on the Internet.

4. As you collect information, create a folder on your computer titled "Research." In this "Research" folder, create subfolders entitled "Associations/Conferences," "Company Profiles," "Job Search Strategy," "Industry Specific," "Labor Market Information," and "New Articles." Keep the information you gather organized in these folders.

Gathering the Facts   **7.6**

Following the format below, research three jobs in a library or career center. You may select either three different jobs (e.g., public relations specialist, social worker, manager), three jobs that are related (e.g., lawyer, paralegal, legal secretary), or three that represent the same field but vary in the nature of the work (e.g., marketing executive, graphic artist, display assistant).

Once you identify job titles of interest to you, gather the following information for each one:

Title of career: _____

Salary: _____

Hours: _____

Benefits: _____

Outlook (whether there will be jobs in the future): _____

_____

Educational requirements—minimum training necessary: _____

_____

If college is necessary, what types of programs are available locally? _____

_____

_____

Schools or colleges offering the training: _____

_____

Personal requirements: _____

_____

Physical demands: _____

_____

Work description (attach a copy of the DOT description): _____

Working conditions: _____

_____

Location: _____

_____

Opportunities for advancement: _____

_____

Related occupations with the following educational requirements:

   No additional training needed: _____

   Some college needed: _____

   B.A. or B.S. degree needed: _____

   Other training (e.g., master's degree or special license): _____

   _____

Sources (may include resources in the career center and names of local people working in this field; include Internet addresses where you might find related information):

_____

_____

_____

After researching the specifics, are you still interested? How well does this occupation mesh with your vision of a lifestyle?

_____

_____

_____

   If, after reading about three different careers, you are still confused about how to choose one, try Exercise 7.8, a guided fantasy. Visualize yourself in each career. Which one feels most comfortable, most consistent with who you are?

   Chapter 8 will help you narrow your focus and decide among different careers.

7.7   WWWebwise

For additional activities online, go to the WWWebwise module in Chapter 7 of the Companion Website.

Exercise Summary

Here is a guided fantasy. Close your eyes, take a few deep breaths, and relax. Remove all feelings of tension from your body, and erase all previous thoughts and worries from your mind. . . .

Imagine that you are getting up on a typical workday about five years from now. You're sitting on the side of your bed trying to decide what you are going to wear. Take a moment and look over your wardrobe. . . . What type of clothing do you finally decide to wear? . . .

Imagine yourself getting ready for work. Any thoughts about the day to come while you're getting ready? . . . What kind of feelings do you have as you look forward to your workday? . . . Do you feel excited? Bored? Apprehensive? . . . What gives you these feelings? . . . It's time for breakfast now. Will you be sharing breakfast with some-one, or will you be eating alone? . . .

You've completed your breakfast now and are headed out the door. Stop for a moment and look around your neighborhood. What does it look like? . . . What does your home look like? . . . What thoughts and feelings do you experience as you look around? . . .

Fantasize now that you're heading toward work. How are you getting there? . . . How far is it? . . . What new feelings or thoughts are you experiencing? . . .

You're entering your work situation now. Pause for a bit and try to get a mental pic-ture of it. Think about where it is and what it looks like. Will you be spending most of your time indoors or outdoors? . . . How many people will you be working with? . . .

You are going to your specific job now. Who is the first person you encounter? . . . What does this person look like? . . . What is this person wearing? . . . What do you say to this person? . . .

Try to form an image of the particular tasks you perform on your job. Don't think about it as a specific job with a title, such as nurse or accountant. Instead, think about what you are actually doing, such as working with your hands, adding figures, typing, talking to people, drawing, thinking, etc.

In your job, do you work primarily by yourself or mostly with others? . . . In your work with others, what do you do with them? . . . How old are the other people? . . . What do they look like? . . . How do you feel toward them? . . .

Where will you be going for lunch? . . . Will you be going with someone else? Whom? What will you talk about? . . .

How do the afternoon's activities differ from those of the morning? . . . How are you feeling as the day progresses? Tired? Alert? Bored? Excited? . . .

Your workday is coming to an end now. Has it been a satisfying day? . . . If so, what made it satisfying? . . . Was there anything about the day that made you less happy? . . . Will you be taking some of your work home with you? . . .

Consider sharing some of your guided fantasy with a classmate and significant others in your life. How compatible is your fantasy with theirs?

_____

_____

_____

_____

_____

Go to page 224 of the chapter summaries and fill out the Chapter 7 exercise summary now.

8

Making Decisions

Learning Objectives

At the end of the chapter you will be able to . . .

- Describe and explore your own decision-making process

- Apply the principles of decision making to your career search

- Identify psychological barriers to decision making and develop alternative strategies for success

- Write a clear objective

- Summarize insights gained from past chapters and identify potential occupations

- Make tentative career/education/training choices

- Define and use stress management techniques

- Set and manage financial goals.

Career decisions are the Olympic trials of your career fitness program. They give you an opportunity to integrate and test out all the components of your career fitness program—your attitudes, values, skills, interests, and biases.

Shoot for the moon.

Even if you miss it, you will land among the stars.

LES BROWN

For most of us, it is safe to assume that whatever decisions we make are the best we can make given the information, circumstances, and feelings of the moment. However, we can all improve our decision-making performance by examining some of the assumptions and strategies that other people have used in the decision-making process.

This chapter will review decision-making strategies that are potentially limiting and those that are potentially empowering and success-oriented. The primary focus of this chapter is on explaining a decision-making model that involves setting *realistic goals.* To bring about change, you must set *specific goals with specific time frames.* They must be realistic for you, and you must maintain an attitude that you are deserving and capable of reaching these goals.

In most of the previous chapters, you completed exercises at the end of the chapter. This was done to help you solidify and integrate what you had read in the entire chapter. In this chapter on decision making, you will be asked to complete some of the chapter-end exercises as you read. This will help you begin to test your aptitude for using various aspects of the decision-making model directly after they are presented in the chapter.

Overcoming Barriers to Decision Making

Take time right now to think about recent decisions you have made. Write down at least five, large or small, below:

1. _____
2. _____
3. _____
4. _____
5. _____

Because you are reading this book, you undoubtedly want to improve your life and increase your career options. Attitude has already been identified as an important internal factor in making decisions. Essentially, your attitude controls your ability to use your skills and potential to the fullest.

Our attitudes are gut-level feelings that indicate what we expect of ourselves. If we are aware of our attitudes and habits, we can enhance our daily effectiveness. Again, if we believe we can, we can!

Much of human behavior is based on attitudes that are limiting. People often make decisions with limited conscious involvement or sense of personal responsibility, sometimes in an effort to simplify or accelerate the decision-making process. As you read the following sections, think about the process you followed in making the decisions you listed above.

Decision-Making Strategies (Good and Bad)

The box titled "Ways to Make Decisions (Strategies)" describes some of the ways people go about making decisions. Read it now, then read the story in the box titled "Meet Art." Try to determine what decision-making strategies Art used.

Choosing a career is a life development process. At different points during the process, different issues must be decided. Thus, planning (the first of the strategies listed) is the key to reaching your goals. It implies gaining

Ways to Make Decisions (Strategies)

Planning. "Weighing the facts." Consideration of values, objectives, necessary information, alternatives, and consequences. A rational approach with a balance between thinking and feeling.

Impulsive. "Don't look before you leap." Little thought or examination; taking the first alternative.

Intuitive. "It feels right." Automatic, preconscious choice based on inner harmony.

Compliant. "Anything you say." Nonassertive; let someone else decide; follow someone else's plans.

Delaying. "Cross that bridge later." Procrastination, avoidance, hoping someone or something will happen so that you won't have to make a decision. Taking a moratorium; postponing thought and action.

Fatalistic. "It's all in the cards." What will be will be. Letting the environment decide; leaving it up to fate.

Agonizing. "What if? I don't know what to do." Worrying that a decision will be the wrong one. Getting lost in all the data; overwhelmed by analyzing alternatives.

Paralytic. "Can't face up to it." One step further than "what if"—complete indecision and fear. Accepting responsibility but being unable to approach it.

WHAT ABOUT YOU?

1. Which of these approaches to decision making do you use most and least often?

2. Which would you like to use more often? Which would you like to avoid? Why?

3. Consider a current decision in progress (e.g., one you wrote at the beginning of this chapter). Think it through using several of these approaches. Which prove to be most useful?

Apply your answers here to the exercises at the end of this chapter.

control of your life. You might glance back at the lifeline you completed in Chapter 1. Analyze which strategy you used most often in making decisions. Then note the other strategies you used. Planning and intuitive strategies are the only two positive strategies listed. The others contain a hint of fear: fear of failure, fear of imperfection, fear of rejection, fear of ridicule. Such fears are based on "internal factors" related to how you feel about yourself.

When you feel stuck or unable to make a decision, try asking yourself the following questions:

Ask yourself questions to get unstuck, gain control

1. What are my assumptions (attitudes)?
2. What are my feelings?
3. Why am I clinging to this behavior? (What are the rewards or payoffs?)

What are my assumptions?

There is no "right" decision

Many of us assume that if we could only make the one right decision about the matter at hand, everything else would fall into place. In fact, most decisions do not have such power over our lives. Decisions are not typically black-and-white in terms of their consequences but simply move you in one direction rather than another. Decisions open up some options and close off others. If you assume that most decisions can be changed or altered—that most decisions do not, in fact, signify life or death—then you will not be so hesitant to make a decision, act on it, assess the implications as they occur, and make adjustments (or new decisions) as necessary.

What are my feelings?

Avoid either/or ultimatums

Some people create unnecessary stress about making decisions because they give themselves an either/or ultimatum. Neither option really feels right, but they panic and impulsively choose one just to ease the anxiety, or they become paralyzed and don't make any choice, allowing circumstances to decide for them. When you are feeling pressured or paralyzed about making a decision, stop, take several deep breaths, and begin to generate some additional alternatives. A friend, counselor, or skilled listener can often help with this process. As you gain more information about your options, you will realize which decision is best for you.

Other people cry over spilled milk; in other words, they think back over past decisions and lament not having decided differently. This psychological stance wastes time and energy and can be destructive to the self-image. When you begin to feel self-doubt or regret about past decisions, remind yourself that you made the best decision you could, given the time, circumstances, and information available.

Why am I clinging to this behavior?

Old habits can limit you

Acknowledging that you are causing this indecisiveness may generate a different point of view. For example, sometimes people cling to old, nonproductive behaviors because they are the safe ways to act; they don't have to deal with the unknown or the possibility of making mistakes (also known as taking risks). However, without risk, there is no challenge and no growth.

Visualize yourself at your best

We usually find it difficult to change habits because they have given us some form of positive payoff or reward. A person who enjoyed the status

Meet Art

Art was born and raised in California. When he was a child he and his family loved to hike in the mountains, surf, and scuba dive. After graduating from high school, Art attended state college, where he earned a degree in graphic design. After Art had spent several months job hunting, a friend of Art's from Ohio told him that he and his father were starting a new company and they felt Art would fit right in. The company was going to specialize in designing packaging for educational materials. Art's friend said that they needed someone to help with sales and develop new design concepts.

Art was very excited until he learned that they needed start-up money and wanted Art to put up $5,000. Art's friend and his father told Art that the bank was willing to loan them half of the money they needed and that from all the feedback they received from financial and business consultants, the business was a solid idea with a good chance for success. They said that the cost of living in Ohio was less than in California, so Art could find affordable housing and insurance. Art's friend also promised that Art's investment would be repaid within the first two years.

Art had a trust account from his grandmother that he was planning to use to return to school and get his master's degree. Without telling anyone, Art withdrew the money. The business did fairly well the first year, and Art began to make a life in Ohio. He met a girl and soon they were married. Joan was in her last year of nursing school, working part-time in a nursing home, and she had excellent prospects of work after she graduated.

Six months later, Art's friend declared bankruptcy. Depressed and embarrassed, Art didn't know what to do. The job market in Ohio was not strong in Art's field, so Art and Joan decided that Art would go back to California and Joan would finish nursing school and then join him.

REAL STORIES

With only phone calls and e-mails, Joan and Art found their relationship was in trouble. Art found work, but it was not what he wanted to do and the money was barely enough to support one person. Joan graduated and was offered a good job in Ohio. She encouraged Art to come back, but he knew that he could not make a good living there and he didn't want Joan to be the primary wage earner. Art tried to get Joan to come to California, but she felt comfortable in Ohio and was reluctant to make the move. After three months, Joan told Art that she didn't think the marriage was going to survive and asked for a divorce.

WHAT DO YOU THINK?

1. How would you evaluate Art's decision-making skills? What would you have done differently if you were Art?

2. What alternatives were available to Art in relation to his job search decision?

3. How would you evaluate Joan's response to Art's request?

4. What assumptions did Art and Joan make in choosing to pursue careers in different geographical areas? Were there any issues they could have discussed before making their decision?

5. If you were Art, what research would you have done before you took the job in Ohio?

6. What strategies or resources could Joan and Art have used to save their marriage?

7. How can people learn decision-making skills?

To answer these questions online, go to the *Real Stories* module in Chapter 8 of the Companion Website.

and praise gained by being an excellent and achieving student might find that superior achievement in a work environment alienates others on the job. It is important to recognize when the old, comfortable ways of doing things no longer provide the payoffs they once did.

Take calculated risks

Are you a risk taker? Whether you consider yourself a risk taker or not, it is important to remember that you have, in fact, taken many risks, just as we all have. What has been your greatest risk? What risk have you taken in the last two weeks? In its most basic sense, risk taking means moving from the safe and familiar to the unknown and scary. Most of us are fairly conservative risk takers in that we want the odds to be at least 50–50 before we jump in. Yet millions of people play the lottery, start businesses, and get married even when the odds are clearly not in their favor. Why? Because regardless of the probability of success (the odds), people sometimes take risks based on the *desirability* of the successful outcome.

In a lottery, the probabilities are a million to one against winning, yet people continue to gamble because of the high desirability of the positive outcome of winning. You are in the best position to take a calculated risk when you assess both the probability and desirability of an outcome and weigh it against other possible outcomes. Failure to consider outcomes in this fashion is the most common cause of unsuccessful risk taking. For example, most people are afraid to take the risk of changing careers or even changing jobs. They immediately think of the worst possible outcome: "I'll fail" or "I will never find another job if I quit this one." They don't ask themselves how probable or desirable the best possible outcome would be. The probability of their worries actually materializing (i.e., the likelihood of a highly negative outcome) is very low.

You should not merely try to do things. You simply must do them.

RAY BRADBURY

Generate other possible outcomes

Many people paralyze themselves with this "worst possible consequence" thinking, decide not to risk it, and consequently feel trapped. What they haven't done is generate other possible outcomes that are more probable and more desirable. What are some of these? A new job that is more energizing and financially rewarding, a new career with an opportunity to grow and develop, a chance to get retraining. The probability and desirability of these outcomes are, in fact, much higher; therefore, the decision is less risky. Yet many people miss opportunities because they fail to generate and assess all possible outcomes. This process often takes the assistance of another person who can help identify negative or limiting thinking, as well as some realistic and positive outcomes.

Conditions for Change

Decisions provide an opportunity to experience life in new ways, to learn and find out who you are and what you would like to do. Each path is filled with opportunities. Just imagine: by making good decisions, renewal and growth are within your reach. By engaging in affirming self-talk, positive change is possible.

Decisions = opportunities

It has been said that three conditions must be present to trigger change. First, there must be a real dissatisfaction with what is, and then there must be a concept of what would be better; last, there must be a belief that there is a way to get there. This whole process rests on the premise that the benefits of the change outweigh the costs of making the change. Affirmations help you believe that change is possible.

The following questions relate to obstacles that may be interfering with the achievement of your desires:

- How much determination do you really have?
- What identity would be threatened by achieving your goal? For example, would a better job make you too independent or enable you to earn more than your mate? Would it demand more time, giving you less time as mother, husband, or partner?
- Do you secretly feel you don't deserve to attain your desires?
- Are you proving to anyone else that you can't change?
- Is it (the work, concentration, time) worth it to you?
- Are you following all the steps suggested?
- Is it what you really want?

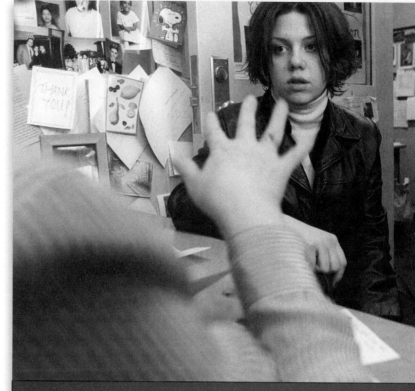

If you require help making decisions about school or work, take advantage of campus resources such as counselors and advisers.

A Decision-Making Model

Exhibit 8.1 offers a model for making informed decisions. The five steps necessary to make an informed decision are the following: *defining your goal, assessing your alternatives, gathering information, assessing the consequences (both probable and desirable),* and *establishing your plan of action or the steps needed to achieve your goal.* Read through Exhibit 8.1 now.

Rational/Linear Decision Making

Planning is also known as the rational, or linear, approach to decision making. Decisions involve prediction. Prediction involves uncertainty. And uncertainty makes most people uncomfortable. Planning is one approach that decreases the amount of uncertainty and discomfort and increases your chances of achieving your designated goals.

EXHIBIT 8.1　　Choice, not chance: Decisions are in our power.

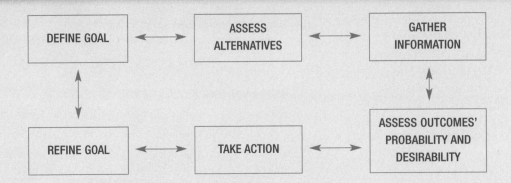

1. Define goal or objective
   - Can you change part of the problem into a definite goal?
   - What do you want to accomplish by what date?
   - Can you state your objective now?
2. Assess alternatives
   - What are your alternatives or options?
   - Are your alternative choices consistent with your important values?
   - Can you summarize your important values in writing?
   - What is a reasonable amount of time in which to accomplish your alternatives?
3. Gather information
   - What do you know about your alternatives?
   - What assumptions are you making that you should check out?
   - What more do you need to know about your alternatives?
   - What sources will help you gather more information about your alternatives?
   - What sources will help you discover further alternatives?
4. Assess outcomes or consequences
   - Probability:
     What is the probability of the success of each alternative?
     Are your highest values part of each alternative?
   - Desirability:
     Can you eliminate the least desirable alternatives first?
     When you consider the best possible alternative, how much do you want it?
     What are you willing to give up in order to get what you want?
5. Establish a plan of action
   - Weighing everything you now know about your decision, what is your plan of action?
   - What dates will you start and complete your plan of action?
   - Does your plan of action state a clear objective?
   - Does your plan of action specify the steps necessary to achieve its objective?
   - Does your plan of action specify the conditions necessary to achieve its objective?

Until you start your plan of action, you haven't really made a decision. So start now. Make systematic decision making an adventure and a habit!

Rational decision making uses the talents of the left brain, which is analytical and logical and deals with deductive thinking. It ideally follows the sequential, step-by-step procedure described in Exhibit 8.1. Please note that the arrows go in both directions to allow for new information and insights along the way.

Intuitive Decision Making

People who prefer the intuitive approach tend to be more creative and artistic. Intuitive decision makers look for the direction that feels right. They use their right brain, which thrives on imagination and creativity and adapts to change spontaneously. They feel confined when asked to write out a step-by-step process.

When faced with career planning and a job search, such individuals tend to engage in research until they have several alternatives that they believe would satisfy them equally. They like to get a feel for the overall, global picture and then decide where they fit in. Once they have researched several options, talked to people in the field, and walked around the work environment, they tend to know if it's right for them. Call it intuition or a hunch, but it is based on the cumulative insight that fits their personality. Intuitive decision makers are most apt to say they were lucky in finding the right job, the right major, or the right college. However, their luck is actually "preparation meeting opportunity." Intuitive decision makers are highly adept at finding opportunities. Thus, it is very important that such people be truly familiar with their values, interests, skills, and personalities as they explore careers.

Sometimes, the best approach for the intuitive decision maker is to fantasize and describe an ideal occupation, or to give examples of people who have an appealing career. Intuitives tend to be able to fantasize, daydream, and create verbal or written pictures of what they think is appealing. Thus a collage of images depicting a career plan may be as useful as the written action plan created by a rational decision maker. Intuitive decision making may work for some people; however, for the majority of us, a logical, step-by-step approach will yield better results.

Luck = preparation meeting opportunity

FACTS & FIGURES

Decision styles

Personality/temperament studies have estimated that up to 75 percent of the population prefer and use the rational decision-making approach. These studies also suggest, therefore, that 25 percent of the population prefer to use the strategy known as intuitive. Review your personality type results in Chapter 4 and list them here: ___ ___ ___ ___

THINK ABOUT IT

1. If you are intuitive, do you feel that many people do not understand your decision-making style?

2. If you are intuitive, what is your biggest challenge or concern when making a decision?

3. If you feel confined when asked to write a step-by-step answer to questions in this book, what would be your alternative method to show that you are understanding the information you are reading?

4. If you are a rational thinker, what is your biggest challenge in making a decision?

5. If you are a rational thinker, do you prefer to make a decision and get it done, or do you find yourself procrastinating by thinking about everything over and over again?

Companion Website

To answer these questions online, go to the *Facts and Figures* module in Chapter 8 of the Companion Website.

SUCCESS STRATEGIES

Sample goal and objectives

GOAL

To explore career alternatives to teaching by July of this year.

OBJECTIVES

1. By February, I will start reading *The Career Fitness Program.*

2. Each week, I will read one chapter & do the exercises. I will finish the book by June 1.

3. By May, I will determine the strategies I will need to identify three jobs that use my talents.

4. By May, I will attend a job search workshop at the college.

5. By June, I will research three jobs by reading about them in the career center or library and by using the Internet to identify three or more people working in those jobs locally.

6. By July, I will visit three of those people at their jobs and conduct information interviews with them.

Understand long-range career goal vs. short-term career goal

Goal Setting

Your goals and objectives are the road signs that lead you to what you want to attain in life. It is important, therefore, that a goal be distinguished from an objective.

Goals are broad statements of purpose. They are general and long-range. They refer to an ongoing process, a challenge that's meant to stretch our limits. If you have trouble defining your goals, try listing the dissatisfactions and problems in your life that are bothering you. Now ask yourself what you can do about them. You have just defined a goal. Thus, if you have been analyzing yourself while reading each chapter, you may have concluded that your problem is that you are not working in a field that utilizes your values, interests, attitudes, and skills. The goal would be to find a career that best allows you to utilize your talents. (At this point, complete Exercises 8.2 and 8.3. Exercise 8.2 will help you identify and rank some long-term goals that have importance for you. Exercise 8.3 will help you assess how ready you are to begin working on your goals.)

A career that meshes with your values, interests, attitudes, and skills but that requires five or more years of training can be considered your long-range career goal. The entry-level jobs that can prepare you for this career can be considered your short-term career goals. Thus, becoming a manager or executive would be the long-range career goal, whereas working toward a bachelor's degree in business management and/or becoming an assistant manager would be short-term goals.

Objectives are the specific and practical steps used to accomplish goals. Objectives are short-term "baby steps." They are visible and measurable signposts that indicate where you are relative to reaching a goal.

The more specific our objectives are, the higher the probability that we will accomplish them. A specific objective has some indication of the action, conditions, and amount of time it will take to achieve it. Most of us have said, "I'm going to lose weight." That's an example of a nonspecific objective. We know what the action is, but we don't know how, when, and to what extent it will be accomplished. We rarely follow through with an unclear objective. Occasionally you will hear someone say, "I'm going to lose one pound this week by cutting out all bread, butter, and sweets from my diet." That's an example of a specific objective; the action, losing weight, is made specific with information on how much, when, and how it will be accomplished.

Four points should be remembered in setting goals. First, *consider what you are willing to give up* to get what you want. When most people make career changes, life in general changes for them. You may need to give up free time to take special courses. You may need to take a cut in pay (temporarily or permanently) to obtain better fringe benefits, security, and a potential chance for growth in another field, or you may need to give up being the old-timer and become the new kid on the block (and need to prove yourself again as a competent worker).

Second, *give yourself a realistic timeline* to reach your goal. If you've incorporated "baby steps" (objectives) into your timeline, you are more likely to achieve your goals. A timeline is just a way of listing in chronological order all the objectives needed to accomplish your goal.

Develop a timeline

Once you've developed a timeline, it's a good idea to show it to a close friend or counselor and to sign and date it as if it were a contract. In actuality, this is a contract with yourself. At best, you will achieve your goals; at worst, you will need to revise them and alter the timeline. At this point, complete Exercise 8.17 to reinforce your ability to formulate specific objectives.

Third, *set your goals high*. Of course, the goal must be realistic enough to be achievable. Remind yourself that you are deserving and capable; if your initial steps are specific, clear, and small enough, you will achieve them. The example provided in the box titled "Sample Goal and Objectives" illustrates that each objective must have importance in itself and must help lead to the overall (larger) goal.

Finally, the fourth point about setting goals is quite simple indeed: *Reward yourself after completing each objective and after reaching each goal*. Some say that the mere accomplishment of the goal should be reward enough. However, most of us tend to be more motivated toward success when we have both internal and external reward systems. The internal reward is the feeling of success; the external reward is something outside of ourselves (e.g., crossing the objective off the checklist, a grade on a paper, recognition from a group of friends, dinner at a special place, or splurging on those athletic shoes you wanted). How do you reward yourself when you attain an objective or reach a goal?

> ### SUCCESS STRATEGIES
>
> #### Time management strategies
>
> 1. Plan and set priorities each day.
> 2. Prioritize specific tasks.
> 3. Eliminate unnecessary work or tasks.
> 4. Have confidence in your judgment.
> 5. Work on your concentration.
> 6. Listen actively.
> 7. Focus on the present.
> 8. Accept the help of others.
> 9. Set firm deadlines.
> 10. Schedule relaxation time.
> 11. Build on successes.
> 12. Do something; get started!
> 13. Ask: What is the best use for my time now?

One way that you can reward yourself is by learning to manage your time so that you can create the best possibilities for success. People who are successful in reaching their goals know how to manage their time. (Refer to the "Time Management Strategies" box for hints on how to be more successful.) Many recent high school graduates and reentry students face new unstructured situations in college and need to schedule their time carefully to allow for study, work, leisure, and other responsibilities.

Manage your time

Managing Your Financial Resources

As you make important career decisions, the goal of achieving financial independence is often one of the most important priorities. Learning how to budget to meet your obligations is an important step toward being the best you can be. Remember, *you* are the best investment that you will ever make as a result of your increased skills through education and career choice. It is worth your time, energy, and determination to take advantage of the opportunities that become available as you earn income and make further decisions about your future. Consider each of the following categories as you plan for financial security.

Setting Financial Goals

Having a vision is powerful as you decide what you want to achieve financially. To begin with, knowing what your financial needs are every month is essential to meet the necessities of paying for rent, food, car, cell phone, utilities, and other basic costs. Recognizing and budgeting for your short-term monthly survival goals for the present year allows you to set medium-range goals for the next one to three years. Medium-range goals would include vacations, savings, electronics, new clothes, or other items that you want to own. Finally, set longer-term objectives that savings can help you reach over a five year or longer period, such as a down payment on a home or condominium, or a very special purchase that may be part of your vision.

Consider all of your financial needs and how they are tied to achieving your future goals through a step-by-step plan. This plan should include paying off credit card debts and starting or continuing a savings program by putting aside money every month into a separate account.

Planning and budgeting are essential to future savings. Easy-to-use software is available to help you track expenses and income and fulfill savings goals.

Saving Money

Planning is essential to future savings. This means that you must have a clear vision and a positive affirmation to put money aside at the beginning of each month—well before you are tempted to spend it. Get used to saving money, and make it a habit just as you look for good deals and compare prices before making a purchase. By opening a bank savings account (if you have not done so already), you will see the dividends grow and will have money available for emergencies or special expenditures.

Establishing a Credit Rating

Since very few people use cash to fund all of their expenses, at some stage you will find yourself borrowing money. Individuals borrow money for education, a car, home furnishings, or a mortgage. Doing so carefully and responsibly builds your repayment history and a strong credit rating.

Credit cards are easily obtained, but they carry the most risk. Experts on debt management say that the best way to use a credit card is to pay the entire balance at the end of each month to avoid high interest charges. If you instead take the "easy" credit road, you will soon find yourself paying endless high interest charges. Think critically about your priorities, what you really need now, and what you can put aside until your financial assets increase. One of the best methods to ensure financial independence is to learn how to manage your credit card.

Remember to save

Insurance and Health Needs

Insurance helps individuals meet unanticipated events and obtain necessary health services. Some companies pay health benefits, including medical and dental, and may also include some retirement and insurance incentives. If you do not obtain all the insurance and health coverage you need at work, then these costs become part of your general budget. It is never too early to save money for your retirement. You may wish to consult a knowledgeable expert for advice on investments. Paying for health, life, or car insurance or making a small retirement investment will take a portion of your money and add to your yearly costs.

Budgeting

Living within your means often takes strong discipline and a willingness to establish limits to what you spend. It takes a special effort to make a careful list of your monthly income and expense activities, but this is the most essential and useful action you can take to keep track of your spending habits. Budgeting feeds directly into financial independence and allows you to take that summer vacation and avoid high interest payments. Use the monthly budget management example shown in Exhibit 8.2 to develop your own financial spreadsheet.

This preliminary budget includes typical cost-of-living categories. Some elements may be different for you based on geography, income level, or other factors. For example, if you live at home, share rent, get along without a car, or do not have personal debt, your expenses may be lower. The net salary is your disposable income—your salary after taxes.

Suppose you want to purchase property in a few years—how could you best prepare for this possibility? What would you change in your budget?

A budget is a monetary plan to control your financial resources and prepare for the future. You will soon realize that budgeting is the first step toward financial freedom.

A final caution on using credit cards. Keeping a zero monthly balance each month is the best—perhaps the only—way to avoid high-interest debt. Using "plastic" can be addictive, and every financial expert warns consumers to avoid buying on credit. A budget is the best solution to avoid getting into credit card quicksand.

Pay off debts

In the final analysis, the decisions that you make about education, career, and money all take careful attention and focus. The time you spend will pay huge dividends and lead to positive outcomes.

EXHIBIT 8.2	Monthly budget management.

EXPENSES	JAN	FEB	MAR	APR	MAY	JUN	JUL	AUG	SEP	OCT	NOV	DEC	TOTAL
Utilities/Telephone	175	175	175	175	175	175	175	175	175	175	175	175	2100
Rent	650	650	650	650	650	650	650	650	650	650	650	650	7800
Food	250	250	250	250	250	250	250	250	250	250	250	250	3000
Entertainment	200	200	200	200	200	200	200	200	200	200	200	200	2400
Clothing	125	125	125	125	125	125	125	125	125	125	125	125	1500
Medical/Insurance	120	120	120	120	120	120	120	120	120	120	120	120	1440
Car/Maintenance	300	300	300	300	300	300	300	300	300	300	300	300	3600
Laundry/Toiletries	40	40	40	40	40	40	40	40	40	40	40	40	480
Credit Card Payments	300	300	300	300	300	300	300	300	300	300	300	300	3600
TOTAL	2160	2160	2160	2160	2160	2160	2160	2160	2160	2160	2160	2160	25920

NET INCOME	JAN	FEB	MAR	APR	MAY	JUN	JUL	AUG	SEP	OCT	NOV	DEC	TOTAL
Net Salary	2400	2400	2400	2400	2400	2400	2400	2400	2400	2400	2400	2400	28800
Less Expenses	2160	2160	2160	2160	2160	2160	2160	2160	2160	2160	2160	2160	25920
SAVINGS	240	240	240	240	240	240	240	240	240	240	240	240	2880

Stress Management

Sometimes the biggest obstacles that you will encounter in your job search and decision making are those that you put in place yourself. Learn how to look out for one of those landmines that can explode and destroy your best efforts: stress.

One of the greatest sources of stress is change, even when it is positive and planned, such as the change associated with finding a new job. Two researchers studying the relationship between stress and change in the late 1960s developed the Social Readjustment Rating Scale, which listed significant life change events and corresponding stress scores. The scale includes 43 life change events that might be considered stressful, such as death of a spouse, a divorce, or a jail term. The Social Readjustment Rating Scale also included several items that are related to work and the job search, including being fired, a change to a different line of work, and a change in responsibilities at work.

Some stress can be positive, associated with high motivation, high energy, and sharp perception. Negative stress, however, can reduce your effectiveness in your job search in many ways. Stress may produce psychological results, such as anxiety, frustration, apathy, lowered self-esteem, aggression, and depression.

You will need to develop strategies to cope when you encounter these obstacles so as to maintain your self-esteem and motivation to find work. To find work does not mean, however, that you need to give up your identity, sell out, or compromise on issues important to you. It is also not your responsibility to change the work world. Employers who want to hire successfully from a diverse worker pool also have an obligation to help eliminate obstacles for recruiting and retaining quality employees. Some employers who have had little experience hiring for diversity may welcome your willingness to discuss your work needs and expectations.

The job search requires all the elements of positive affirmations and coping with stress, especially when you are seeking an interview or starting a new position. Strategies for improving your overall attitude and managing stress are essential. Some of these techniques are listed in the box titled "Stress Management Techniques."

Deciding on a Major

At this point you should be focusing your thoughts regarding your values, personality, interests, and skills toward either a college major or a few occupations that will express your career goals.

If you are thinking about a major, you will need to gather information about how jobs are related to college majors. The last chapter explained how to gather written information about careers; some resources may mention majors related to specific careers. Whenever you meet people who have interesting jobs, do your own research by asking them if they have a degree and in what major. Because many people have majored in subjects seemingly unrelated to their jobs, your big choice will be to decide whether you should choose a major closely related to an interesting area of work (for example, a business major to become a manager), or if you should select a major that seems interesting to you at this time in your life (for example, communications or psychology). The fact of the matter is that either major can lead you to a successful business career.

If all of your personal assessment does not suggest a specific major, you may need to sample some introductory courses to see if they appeal to you. For example, you might want to take a course providing an introduction to interior design, an introduction to management, or an introduction to engineering. It is better to sample several majors during one or two semesters than to choose one prematurely only to find out after several semesters that you don't really like that field.

Remember, many occupations do not have a strong relationship to a specific college major. Employers are looking primarily for candidates who are well-rounded individuals and who have done well in college no matter what their major. Therefore, identify a major that interests you and in which you can excel and enjoy the learning experience.

SUCCESS STRATEGIES

Stress management techniques

- **Take time for yourself.** Treat yourself well and pay attention to your personal needs and enjoyment.

- **Maintain or start a realistic exercise schedule.** Participate in activities you enjoy that will also get you moving. Exercise is one of the best remedies for stress.

- **Socialize with friends and family.** Your support network can help you keep your stressors in perspective.

- **Remind yourself about the things you are good at.** Some people find it reassuring to have a list of things they do well to give themselves a motivational boost when life becomes overwhelming.

- **Encourage a sense of humor.** A good healthy laugh is a great way to keep perspective on all the changes in your life.

- **Keep your eye on the goal!** Remember why you are working so hard and how good it will feel when you finally reach your goals. All the hard work pays off in the end.

Recognize priorities

Tomorrow

She was going to be all she wanted to be . . .
    tomorrow.
None would be smarter or more successful than
    she . . . tomorrow.
There were friends who could help her—she knew,
Who'd be only too happy to see what they could do.
On them she would call and pay a visit or two . . .
    tomorrow.
Each morning she stacked up the letters she'd
    write . . . tomorrow,
And thought of the things that would give her
    delight . . . tomorrow.

But she hadn't one minute to stop on her way,
"More thought I must give to my future," she'd say . . .
    tomorrow.
The greatest of workers this woman would have
    been . . . tomorrow.
The world would have hailed her—had ever she
    seen . . . tomorrow.
But, in fact, she passed on, and she faded from view,
And all that was left here when living was through
Was a mountain of things she intended to do . . .
    tomorrow!

                                                —*Unknown*

Deciding on Training

If you are not interested in attending or completing four years of college but want to select a job that can best fulfill your career goals as soon as possible, then you have at least two issues to address: (1) job information and (2) training requirements. If the job information you have collected indicates that you are ready to enter the field, then you are ready to read the chapters on job search strategy. If the job you want requires that you obtain further training, you will need to find out where to obtain it. Possible resources to use in obtaining this information were discussed in Chapter 7. Using personal contacts or the yellow pages, you can call people working in the field of your interest, or the professional or trade association for that field, to obtain information on training centers. Usually people who work in a field know which schools have the best reputation. Public community colleges, technical junior colleges, and adult and proprietary schools also offer a variety of training programs. Be sure to compare the courses that you will be required to take with the preparation and skills necessary to perform the job. Making informed decisions depends on accurate information.

Define your goals and know how to reach them

Deciding on Change

If you are exploring career opportunities as a result of company downsizing or family changes, it is even more important that you make careful decisions. All that you have learned about yourself thus far should give you the incentive and confidence to apply the decision-making skills discussed in this chapter. The exercises that follow will give you additional decision-making practice.

Summary

Successful career planning involves two processes related to goals: (1) defining your goals and (2) knowing how to reach them. The more completely you plan out your objectives, the more likely you will be to achieve your goals. The key to the process is overcoming the hurdle of negative thinking. Block out the tendency to be self-critical. Put aside your anticipation of failure, your fears and excuses, and your past habits. Allow yourself the right to create goals that energize you and take you beyond your past efforts.

The following exercises are designed to help you become aware of steps in the decision-making process and to encourage you to set some career and life goals. For example, you will be asked to decide what you want to do by the end of the current year and then one year from now. This can mean acquiring new skills or improving current skills, moving toward career advancement or career change, or staying where you are. Remember to try to picture in your mind what you want in your work life (e.g., type of work, responsibility, surroundings, salary, management relationship), and then focus on the exact steps necessary to reach your goals. If you can't picture the necessary steps, you need to gather more information (e.g., from people who have been in similar positions or from written materials about the field) so you can make attainable career decisions.

Following the outline in the decision-making model (see Exhibit 8.1), choose from alternatives, select the one that has the best possibility of success for you, create a plan of action, set specific objectives, and take action. As you attain objectives that move you toward your goal, reassess your decisions based on how you feel in moving toward this goal. Be flexible, have alternatives, and understand that change may provide you with options (and challenges) that you never expected. Be honest with yourself. If you feel uncomfortable with your goal or your plan of action, enlist the help of a career guidance professional to assist you in formulating a goal that you can successfully attain.

PURPOSE OF EXERCISES. The exercises that follow help increase your awareness about how you make decisions. Exercise 8.1 asks that you rank yourself on two dimensions of decision-making style. There are no right or wrong answers. This is a chance to become aware of your personal style of decision making. Exercises 8.2 and 8.3 review goal setting. Exercises 8.4 to 8.7 assess whether you actually do what you say is important to you. Exercises 8.8 to 8.15 should clarify other factors that can affect your decisions. Exercise 8.16 asks you to think about some alternatives to your current life choices. Exercise 8.17 indicates your ability to recognize and state clear objectives (there are right and wrong answers). Exercise 8.18 encourages you to look for creative solutions. Exercise 8.19 asks you to list your timesavers. Exercise 8.20 asks you to choose a long-term goal along with clear short-term activities that will start you toward the long-term goal now.

To answer these questions online, go to the *Exercise* module in Chapter 8 of the Companion Website.

8.1 Ranking Yourself

Place a check (✔) on each of the scales below to indicate your style of decision making:

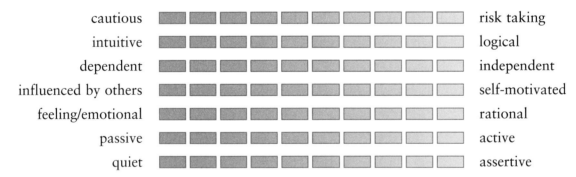

cautious	risk taking
intuitive	logical
dependent	independent
influenced by others	self-motivated
feeling/emotional	rational
passive	active
quiet	assertive

8.2 Reviewing Goal Setting

In Chapter 2, we discussed long-term goals. Now let's try to become much more specific. List three specific long-term goals. Use additional paper if you have more than three.

1. _____

2. _____

3. _____

Let's assume you knew that you would not survive a natural disaster six months from now. Would your short-term goals be any different? List at least three goals that relate to how you would live the next six months:

1. _____

2. _____

3. _____

Now you have a list of long-term and short-term goals. Deciding which ones are most important to you is the next step. This is called *setting priorities*. To do this, mark with the letter A those goals that are of most importance or value to you. Those of medium importance, mark with a B, and those of low importance, with a C. Let's look at the A goals first. With more than one A goal, you will want to rank them, for example, A1, A2, and A3, with the A1 goal being the most important to you at this time. Do the same for your B and C goals. Now rank your long- and short-term A, B, and C goals.

Activities are those actions we take to accomplish our objectives, which in turn get us closer to accomplishing our long-term goals. Take a separate sheet of paper for each of your three long-term goals, and list as many activities as you can think of to get you close to the goal. Don't question or judge the activities that come to mind; just list whatever they are. After you've listed these activities, ask yourself this question: Am I willing to commit five minutes in the next week to working on this activity? If your answer is no, then draw a line through the activity. It's okay if you don't want to spend the time on the activity; you don't have to make excuses. Your choice of the activities you're willing to commit five minutes to will enable you to choose the high-priority tasks. Now rank those activities you will do in the next week (A1, A2, A3, etc.). Your activities are now organized. You're on your way toward meeting your goals. Make it an adventure and enjoy your accomplishments along the way.

Write a Goal Statement   8.3

1. Write a goal statement, describing either a short-term or a long-term goal (see Success Strategy on p. 200 as an example):

   _____

   _____

   _____

2. Can you answer yes to the following questions about this goal?

   Did I choose it personally?

   Am I ready to make a written commitment to this goal?

   Am I setting a deadline?

Is it within my control?

Have I thought through the consequences?

Is the goal based on my values?

Can I visualize it in considerable detail? (Is this goal specific?)

Will I work toward it?

Am I taking responsibility for this goal?

Is this goal measurable?

8.4   Task Identification

Spending a maximum of five minutes, write down all the tasks you need to do in the next week.

_____

_____

_____

_____

_____

_____

_____

_____

8.5   One Year to Live

If you had only one year to live, which of the tasks listed in Exercise 8.4 would still be important to you?

_____

_____

_____

8.6   Meeting Your Needs

How much of a week's work is spent reaching your own personal goals versus meeting others' needs?

_____

_____

Your Energizers   8.7

What percentage of your daily activities gives you energy? List your energizing activities.

_____

_____

_____

_____

_____

Recent Decisions   8.8

What are some decisions you have made recently?

_____

_____

_____

_____

_____

_____

_____

Priorities   8.9

Were some of the decisions you listed in Exercise 8.8 more important than others? Why?

_____

_____

_____

_____

Irrevocable Decisions   8.10

Give an example of a decision you made or might have to make that could be extremely difficult to change.

_____

_____

_____

8.11 *Harmful Decisions*

Give an example of a decision that might be harmful to you or someone you care about in some way.

_____

_____

_____

8.12 *Limiting Decisions*

Give an example of a decision you could make that might keep you from doing something you want to do.

_____

_____

_____

8.13 *Contingent Decisions*

Give an example of a decision that would have an effect on other decisions.

_____

_____

_____

8.14 *Values*

What value or values were important to you in making the decisions you listed in Exercises 8.10 to 8.13?

_____

_____

_____

_____

_____

_____
_____
_____
_____
_____

Factors Adversely Affecting Decisions   **8.15**

The purposes of this exercise are to investigate factors that may unfavorably influence decision making and to determine whether any patterns are evident. First, write down three decisions you have made. Then, using the chart that follows, indicate which of the factors influenced you in making each decision, and to what extent they were present. To do this, use a ✓ to represent decision 1, an X for decision 2, and an O for decision 3. (Some sections of the chart may contain two or three symbols when you are done.)

Decision 1 (✓) _____

Decision 2 (X) _____

Decision 3 (O) _____

EXTERNAL FACTORS	SLIGHTLY PRESENT	MODERATELY PRESENT	STRONGLY PRESENT
1. Family expectations			
2. Family responsibilities			
3. Cultural stereotypes			
4. Male/female stereotypes			
5. Survival needs			
6. Other (specify)			
INTERNAL FACTORS	SLIGHTLY PRESENT	MODERATELY PRESENT	STRONGLY PRESENT
1. Lack of self-confidence			
2. Fear of change			
3. Fear of making a wrong decision			
4. Fear of failure			
5. Fear of ridicule			
6. Other (specify)			

After filling in the chart, look for patterns:

1. Do you experience more feelings related to internal or external factors as obstacles to making satisfying decisions?

_____

_____

_____

_____

2. If a particular factor is strongly present only once, but another factor is moderately present in two or possibly all three of your decisions, which of the two factors do you think is more significant in affecting your decision making?

_____

_____

_____

_____

_____

_____

_____

8.16 *What If . . .*

1. Suppose you have lost all sources of support (e.g., you have been laid off or your family has withdrawn support of your schooling). List three things you could do:

   a. _____

   b. _____

   c. _____

2. How satisfying would these alternatives be to you?

   _____

   _____

3. Suppose you have one year before losing the support. With one year to prepare, what would you do?

   a. What alternatives might you choose?

   b. What information would you need about your chosen alternatives?

   c. What action would you take?

   d. How satisfying would your one-year plan be?

Specific/Nonspecific Objectives　　　　　　　　8.17

The following statements are objectives. Read each objective and decide whether the objective is specific or nonspecific. These are statements anyone might make; they don't necessarily apply to you. Imagine that someone is standing in front of you making each of these statements. With that in mind, mark each objective as "S" (specific) or "N" (nonspecific) to the left of the statement.

_____ 1. I want to explore my interests.

_____ 2. I want to get a good job.

_____ 3. I'd like to get an idea of the job I'm best suited for.

_____ 4. I'd like to take Spanish next semester and for at least two years more, so I'll have another skill to use as a teacher.

_____ 5. When I leave school, I want to get a job that pays at least $10 an hour.

_____ 6. Tomorrow I'm going to make a one-hour appointment to see Ms. Rogers in her office.

_____ 7. I want to get at least a B on every history exam and earn a B as my final grade this semester.

_____ 8. I'm going to ask Teresa to help me find some information about health careers in the Career Development and Placement Center right after class.

_____ 9. I plan to move to an area where there are lots of jobs.

_____ 10. I want to be accepted by the state university when I graduate.

_____ 11. I want to find out more about myself.

_____ 12. I want to get along better with other people at work.

_____ 13. Next week I'm going to see my friends more.

_____ 14. I'm going to read one good book about social service careers tonight.

_____ 15. I want to get a good education.

(See page 217 for answers.)

Test Your Assumptions　　　　　　　　　　8.18

1. Try to connect the dots below with only four straight lines and without lifting your pen.

● ● ●

● ● ●

● ● ●

2. Make a 6 out of IX by adding one line.

IX

(See page 218 for answers.)

8.19 *Timesavers*

List three things you do to save time:

_____

_____

_____

_____

8.20 *Short- and Long-Term Goals*

Write down a long-term goal, and list two activities you can do in the next two weeks that will contribute to it.

_____

_____

_____

8.21 *WWWebwise*

For additional activities online, go to the WWWebwise module in Chapter 8 of the Companion Website.

8.22 *Exercise Summary*

Write a brief paragraph answering these questions.

What did you learn about yourself from these exercises? How does this knowledge relate to your career/life planning? How do you feel? Go back to the decisions you listed in Exercises 8.8–8.13. Has your thinking changed regarding these decisions?

_____

_____

_____

_____

_____

_____

_____

_____

_____

_____

_____

_____

_____

_____

_____

_____

_____

_____

_____

_____

_____

_____

_____

_____

_____

_____

_____

Go to page 224 of the chapter summaries and fill out the Chapter 8 exercise summary now.

Answers to Exercise 8.17:

1. N	4. S	7. N	10. N	13. N
2. N	5. N	8. S	11. N	14. S
3. N	6. S	9. N	12. N	15. N

Answers to Exercise 8.18:

1.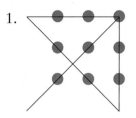

   (The directions did not indicate that you must keep the lines *within* the pattern of dots.)

2. # SIX

   (The directions did not mandate a *straight* line.)

**PUTTING IT ALL TOGETHER TO REACH
A TENTATIVE CAREER GOAL**

The summary section on the following pages will be helpful to you as you progress through *The Career Fitness Program* and as you prepare to begin Part III of the text.

First, as you complete each chapter, we encourage you to fill in the appropriate chapter summary here. Be as thorough as you can.

Second, when you reach this part of the text after completing Chapters 1 through 8, review all your responses carefully. If your responses today are different from those you recorded when you initially read the chapter, record your current responses now.

Third, complete the exercises on pages 225–228, which will help you integrate all of this information and set a career goal.

Exercise Summary   CHAPTER 1

Refer back to original Chapter 1 answers.

1. I am _____
   _____
   _____

2. I need _____
   _____
   _____

3. I want _____
   _____
   _____

4. My current life stage in selecting a career could be summarized as
   _____
   _____
   _____
   _____

5. The Holland Type most like me is:

   ○ Realistic   ○ Investigative

   ○ Artistic   ○ Social

   ○ Enterprising   ○ Conventional

6. Five adjectives that best describe me are _____

_____

_____

_____

7. My favorite school subjects include _____

_____

_____

_____

8. Five high-status occupations are _____

_____

_____

_____

_____

CHAPTER 2 *Exercise Summary*

Refer back to original Chapter 2 answers.

1. I am proud that _____

_____

_____

2. Five positive attitudes I bring to the job are _____

_____

_____

_____

3. I admire the following characteristics in people: _____

_____

_____

_____

4. I am working on developing the following qualities: _____

_____

_____

5. My affirmations are _____

_____

_____

_____

Exercise Summary

Refer back to original Chapter 3 answers.

1. I highly value _____

   _____

   _____

   _____

2. A problem in society that really concerns me is _____

   _____

   _____

   _____

3. My most important considerations in a job are _____

   _____

   _____

   _____

4. I am energized by the following types of activities (from my past jobs, volunteer experiences, or hobbies):

   _____

   _____

   _____

   _____

5. My ideal job would be (if you don't have a title, list the job tasks or activities)

   _____

   _____

   _____

   _____

Exercise Summary

Refer back to original Chapter 4 answers.

1. Circle the term in each of the following pairs that best describes your personality type:

   extravert / introvert   sensing / intuitive   thinking / feeling   judging / perceiving

2. Circle your top three Holland Interest Environments from Chapter 4:

   realistic   enterprising   investigative
   conventional   artistic   social

3. List the results of any assessments or inventories you have taken during the past year. For example:

a. Strong Interest Inventory: Code letters ___ ___ ___

General Occupational Themes:

_____

Three highest Basic Interest Scales:

_____

_____

Very similar/somewhat similar occupational scales (job titles). List five:

_____

_____

_____

b. Career Occupational Preference Survey (COPS), U.S. Interest Survey, or other interest inventory:

_____

List your three highest occupational groups from this survey or from any other interest inventory used:

_____

_____

List five related job titles that sound interesting:

_____

_____

_____

4. After reviewing your interests, list your three career choices:

_____

_____

_____

CHAPTER 5 *Exercise Summary*

Refer back to original Chapter 5 answers.

1. Fill in the percentage of time during the day you would like to work with data, people, and things.

_____ data   _____ people   _____ things

2. Three of my accomplishments are _____

_____

_____

_____

3. A summary of the skills I most enjoy using: _____

_____

_____

_____

4. The skills I want to use in my future career are _____

_____

_____

_____

5. The skills I hope to develop in the next few years are _____

_____

_____

_____

Exercise Summary

Refer back to original Chapter 6 answers.

1. The advantages of my age, sex, and background in looking for a job or working toward my career goal are _____

_____

_____

_____

2. The disadvantages of my age, sex, race, or physical limitations in looking for a job or working toward my career goal are _____

_____

_____

_____

3. Occupations that interest me (based on the trends described in Chapter 6):

_____

_____

_____

CHAPTER 7 *Exercise Summary*

Refer back to original Chapter 7 answers.

1. List one job from Exercise 7.6: _____

2. Choose a job you researched and list the titles or names of sources used in each category: _____

    a. Newspapers, bulletin boards, magazines _____

    _____

    b. Trade journals (name one) _____

    c. Directories (name one) _____

    d. Internet addresses _____

    _____

    e. Career and placement centers _____

    _____

CHAPTER 8 *Exercise Summary*

Refer back to original Chapter 8 answers.

1. I use the following decision-making strategies: _____

    _____

2. My limiting beliefs include _____

    _____

3. My belief about the future is _____

    _____

4. The best use of my time right now (according to time management strategies) is

    _____

5. A long-range goal related to my career is _____

    _____

6. A short-term goal related to my career is _____

    _____

    _____

7. External factors that can affect these career decisions include _____

_____

8. Internal factors that can influence these career decisions include _____

_____

Now complete the following exercises to integrate this information and set a tentative career goal.

Quick Impressions

Read each category and respond quickly by recording the first three thoughts that come to mind in each one. Then list short- and long-term career goals.

Career Values _____

_____

_____

Career Interests _____

_____

_____

Career Skills/Abilities _____

_____

_____

Possible Careers _____

_____

_____

Career-Related Leisure-Time Pursuits _____

_____

SHORT-TERM CAREER GOALS AND OBJECTIVES	LONG-TERM CAREER GOALS AND OBJECTIVES	SUPPORTIVE PEOPLE TO HELP ME IMPLEMENT MY CAREER GOALS
1. _____	1. _____	_____
2. _____	2. _____	_____
3. _____	3. _____	_____
4. _____	4. _____	_____
5. _____	5. _____	_____

Review your Quick Impressions with three supportive people in your life. Ask for their input and help in working toward your goals. As a final step in confirming your career goal, complete the next exercise, "Information Integration and Goal Setting." Refer to the sample on page 227 if you need a sample to help you.

EXERCISE *Information Integration and Goal Setting*

Complete the form below using the sample on the following page as a guideline.

Long-range career goal: _____

Present short-range career goal (one- to five-year goal):

I look forward to *majoring* or *getting training* in _____

so that I can become _____

because I *value* _____

_____

and my *interests* include _____

_____

and this career would allow me to _____

_____

Summary of strengths and weaknesses related to goal:

Personal strengths ("your type")	Personal weaknesses (need to improve)
_____	_____
_____	_____
_____	_____
_____	_____
Favorable external conditions related to career choice	**Unfavorable external conditions related to career choice**
_____	_____
_____	_____
_____	_____
Strategies to reach goal	**Resources available to help reach goal**
_____	_____
_____	_____
_____	_____
_____	_____

Alternative short-range career goals that would be equally satisfying: _____

_____

_____

Training needed to enter this career alternative: _____

_____

Information Integration and Goal Setting   **SAMPLE**

Long-range career goal: To enable people to use their resources.

Present short-range career goal (one- to five-year goal):

I look forward to *majoring* or *getting training* in Psychology

so that I can become a social worker or counselor

because I *value* helping others, serving people, being resourceful, variety, creativity, and continually learning.

and my *interests* include communication, holistic health, adult development, higher education, and career counseling.

and this career would allow me to share, keep informed, serve people, be an expert

Summary of strengths and weaknesses related to goal:

Personal strengths ("your type")	Personal weaknesses (need to improve)
Have a B.A., willing to study, quick learner, self-confident, able to present before groups, eligible for credential programs, have already volunteered	Impatient, lack money for further education, fear taking the Graduate Record Examination, need time management instruction

Favorable external conditions related to career choice	Unfavorable external conditions related to career choice
Many education programs available, many counselors retiring in next 3 years, already working, volunteer experiences are available, graduate programs exist	Not many openings now, not many paid positions available now, many people with this degree out of work

Strategies to reach goal	Resources available to help reach goal
Talk to graduate adviser, obtain application to graduate school, discuss alternatives with adviser, identify volunteer opportunities, volunteer, seek part-time job related to counseling (e.g., teacher's aide)	Faculty, counselors, college career and placement centers

Alternative short-range career goals that would be equally satisfying: Work in the Student Activities Club as a Club Organizer or be a Student Affairs Assistant in the Career Center helping students find resources, leading orientations, and organizing outings to industry.

Training needed to enter this career alternative: Working in Student Affairs or the Career Center while in college.

If you are still confused about which career to focus on, start with the one that is most easily attainable. Work through your job search strategy in Part III of this book using that career as your focal point. Once you understand the job search process, you can use it to explore additional career goals.

Now that you have selected a career goal and identified your strengths and weaknesses, answer the following questions:

1. What can you do now (or in the next six months) to address one or two of your weaknesses? List one weak area here (e.g., test anxiety), and list one method to help you improve (e.g., see a counselor to learn how to reduce anxiety).

   Weakness: _____

   _____

   _____

   _____

   How to improve: _____

   _____

   _____

   _____

2. What can you do now (or in the next six months) to start working toward your career goal? List three activities you can do to move you closer to your goal (e.g., see a counselor to find out requirements for the major; sign up for major-related classes).

   To do:

   a. _____

   b. _____

   c. _____

III

9

Targeting Your Job Search

10

Preparing a Winning Resume

11

Interviewing Successfully

12

Future Focus

JOB SEARCH STRATEGY

9

Targeting Your Job Search

Learning Objectives

At the end of the chapter you will be able to . . .

- Identify the components of a successful job search

- Begin the process of searching for a job

- Explain how to find the hidden job market

- Develop your network

Congratulations! You have finished the personal assessment and world of work portions of your career fitness program. You have reviewed and analyzed your skills, your interests, your personality, and your values, and you have tentatively selected some career options. They are tentative because you may find reason to alter your decisions as you continue to gather information. Just as adjustments occur in a physical fitness program based on your body's responses, so must adjustments occur in your career fitness program based on your gut-level responses.

The next step is to begin to design your job search strategy, which represents the third part of the career-planning process. Job search strategy

Experience is not what happens to you. It is what you do with what happens to you.

ALDOUS HUXLEY

involves the long-term process of acquiring the training, background, and experience needed to be competitive in the job market associated with your anticipated career goal. Simultaneously, you need to begin to identify potential employers for your skills and to develop a resume that reflects your background and your particular career goal. Finally, you need to learn how to present yourself in the best light in job interviews.

SUCCESS STRATEGIES

Your comprehensive job search strategy

1. Commit 100 percent to your job objective.

2. Compare the tasks and responsibilities required in your chosen job at different companies and organizations.

3. Get involved in voluntary and entry-level jobs related to your ultimate goal.

4. Identify the hidden job market through personal contacts and professional associations.

5. Use the Internet.

6. Utilize professional assistance, if necessary.

7. Conduct information interviews with people who are in a position to hire you. Approach all contacts with enthusiasm and sincerity and send thank-you letters to all contacts.

8. Network: let everyone know you are looking for a job (friends, neighbors, dentist, etc.).

9. Identify the needs of the organization. If the exact position you would like is not available, your task is to define a problem within the organization that you can help to solve with your unique skills.

10. Convince an employer that you have the skills he or she needs.

Your job search must be conducted consistently over a period of time. Studies indicate that it can take as long as four months or more of searching to obtain the job you are seeking. Regardless of how certain or tentative you are currently feeling about your career alternatives, you must have a specific occupation in mind in order to benefit from the remainder of this book. The goal of this chapter is for you to choose one of the occupations you have been considering. Then keep it in mind as you read and work through the following chapters.

The rest of this chapter will provide you with the information and skills to enable you to gain control in a competitive job market. In other words, you will learn many techniques to put yourself in the right place at the right time and to present yourself as the best candidate for your desired job. The underlying and most important concept, however, is focusing on what you want. Without this concentration, you run the risk of being swayed by random opportunities and jobs that don't live up to your expectations. *Focusing* means evaluating and comparing all new information with your needs, values, interests, and skills. Remember, the first job you seek should not be considered an end in itself. It is one job on the way to several more that will compose your total career. As the dictionary defines *career*, it is a "pursuit of consecutive progressive achievement in public, professional, or business life." Additionally, career experts predict that the average worker can expect to make three to five career changes in a lifetime.

This approach assumes that you have identified a job objective for which you feel *100 percent enthusiasm,* that you will go after with *100 percent determination,* and that you will interview for with *100 percent of your heart.* This approach charges you with the responsibility to make things happen!

Designing a Comprehensive Job Search Strategy

A comprehensive job search strategy involves much more than just researching to decide what your ideal job is, or simply identifying areas of employment in which you expect to find such jobs. It encourages you, once having made these basic decisions, to be assertive in locating and actually becoming employed in your ideal job. A comprehensive job search strategy stimulates you to consider a variety of aspects related to attaining your ideal job goal, such as whether you are likely to find your job in the geographical area where you live or want to live, and what sorts of activities and experiences will better qualify you for your career objectives. Equally important, job search strategy helps you to select and become involved in volunteer and entry-level activities that are the vital first steps toward your ultimate career goal. You can't always start right out in your ideal job, but guided by job search strategy, you can almost always start out in jobs and activities that will lead to your goals. Assuming that you have adequate skills and background and that you have identified a job for which you are 100 percent enthusiastic, the following approach will work for you.

Go for the job you really want!

First, you must make a contract with yourself to complete all the tasks necessary to get the job. Next, you must become totally informed about the tasks and responsibilities of the job you are seeking. Much of this information can be gained from the written and electronic materials previously cited. Additionally, you will need to amplify the written information by making personal contacts with insiders.

Once you have identified your ideal job situation, an important part of your job search strategy is to investigate activities that may be indispensable first steps toward your goal. Such activities may be temporary, volunteer, or entry-level jobs in your chosen field. They can be very important in adding to your experience and making you a better candidate for your preferred job. For example, a student who wanted to move into the advertising business took a job as a receptionist in the executive suite of an advertising agency in New York. Of course, he had brushed up on his office skills to get this entry-level job, but he didn't plan to remain at that level for long. He kept his eyes and ears open for ways that he could contribute to the efficiency of the business. Within six months he had learned enough about the advertising business to interview at a competing firm and become assistant to an executive account manager.

Identify your ideal job situation

One final suggestion before you conduct further research: You may find that your ideal job is years of education and experience away from you, or that you don't have the dedication or talent to make it in your ideal field. If so, you may be just as satisfied if you work in some job *related* to the career of your dreams. For example, behind every president of the United States there are advisers, speech writers, guards, secretaries, chefs, press representatives,

Begin with an entry level job related to your ideal.

and chauffeurs. Behind every rock musician there are disc jockeys, public relations representatives, recording technicians, piano tuners, album cover designers, sound editors, cutting designers, concert coordinators, costume and makeup artists, and background musicians.

If you stay around the field, constantly adding to your experience, you may be at the right place at the right time and get the job of your dreams. Every understudy in a play or musical has the chance to become a star some day!

Your Job Search: Getting Started

To improve the chances of getting your dream job, use a variety of strategies. Typical resources include reading newspaper want ads and trade journals, using the Internet, sending resumes to potential employers through the mail and by e-mail, using permanent or temporary employment agencies, and volunteering or interning while in school. In addition, many hidden resources exist. The first section of this chapter focuses on common employment resources; the latter part suggests ways to tap into those that are less apparent.

Understanding and Using Classified Ads

Employment or classified ads are found in local newspapers, newspapers from your desired geographical area, trade journals, a supplement from *The Wall Street Journal,* and association magazines, as well as on the Internet. Most newspapers have classified advertising sections with separate employment sections. Other job listings are found in the state employment department, county and city personnel offices, college placement centers, private employment offices, and the personnel offices of individual organizations.

Regularly reviewing the want ads, especially in larger cities, over several months can lead to meaningful employment leads. Although it has been estimated that only 15 percent of jobs are found through ads, thousands of ads are published in large newspapers. You can increase your chances of obtaining a job by applying for a variety of job titles. People with accounting degrees may be eligible for junior accountant, management trainee, accounts payable, auditor, and securities broker, in addition to accountant.

Another way to increase your chances of finding a good job involves combining a newsprint want ads search with your active accumulation of Internet information about companies. When you see a job opening at a firm that you've already visited, you should have a contact in that company to call and ask for more information about the opening. You may find that the ad is written with absolute qualifications but that the specific department will accept alternative experiences in lieu of some of the specific qualifications. Only people who have personal contacts would know such information.

Only 15–20% of all available jobs appear in employment ads

Promoting Yourself Through Mail and E-Mail

If you fail to find your ideal job in employment ads, you might try promoting yourself via mail. You may use the more traditional form of mail, or you may choose to communicate by e-mail.

Postal mailings are quickly becoming outdated; they are expensive and usually result in low response. Some career fields lend themselves to this type of self-promotion better than others. For example, if you are a graphic artist or a freelance editor or writer, your potential employers may be more likely to peruse mailed-in resumes and sample work than employers in fields such as accounting and education. If creative promotion would be a plus in your field, then a direct-mail campaign may be an important part of your job search.

In the case of postal mailings, you should limit your campaign to those companies and organizations most likely to employ people in your career field, due to the expense of blanket mailings. No matter what your field, devote time and energy to coming up with your list of target employers. (Use the sources of information we discussed in Chapter 7, and also rely heavily on local business directories and even telephone directories.) To encourage responses, include a stamped, self-addressed postcard for employers to use. Your postcard might include check-off statements such as "Sorry, no openings" and "Opening available; please contact_____," as well as blanks for the name, address, and telephone number of the organization.

In the case of e-mail, you will be able to cover much more ground for less money. Using the online programs available today, you can send your resume or other promotional material to specific groups and organizations, as in postal mailings. You can gain access to e-mail lists, lists of interest groups and discussion forums, and other means of targeting your promotion. Many resources explaining how to make good use of the electronic resume are available; refer to Chapter 10 for more information. Additionally, refer to the box titled "Selected Online Employment Databases" at the end of this chapter.

Accentuate your assets

Some unwritten rules for job-search e-mail. Getting your e-mails read requires careful strategy. Remember to customize your cover-letter message and resume for the unique requirements for each job opportunity. A mass-mailed flier is ignored among hundreds of others, as recruiters do not have time to figure out which job you are seeking. Cookie-cutter messages are not effective as they do not address an employee's unique situation; they also look like spam and may be eliminated by an organization's e-mail system. Be sure your e-mail address appears professional rather than informal or humorous.

Following precise directions also enhances your prospects. It is a common and surprising error to forget to place a job requisition number in the subject line of an e-mail. This will immediately eliminate your chances. You will also get more immediate attention by keeping your e-mails brief, yet informative. Most of the words in the subject line should be visible when the recipient sees it in the in-box list. Use about four to six words, a maximum of 25 to 35 characters. This is a positive attention getter, similar to a headline for a news story.

Finally, it is very important to keep people in the information loop and maintain your credibility by using the "cc" function appropriately. Sending a copy of the message to relevant people is a courtesy, especially to the person who may have referred you, the recruiter, or the appropriate human-resources manager.

Following these suggestions will make your e-mailing more effective and will strongly increase your chances of getting the interview and position.

Understanding and Using Employment Agencies

Before you register with an agency or Website, check carefully on its fees, the types of positions it handles, and its reputation. Some agencies simply place you on a job with limited concern for your satisfaction. However, there are good agencies that are very concerned about matching people with jobs that suit them.

Temporary employment agencies provide excellent ways to get back into the workforce or to test the climate in a variety of companies. The jobs available are no longer just clerical or entry-level. Many temporary employment agencies specialize in specific fields such as accounting or nursing. Some agencies place people part-time; some place people for short-term assignments. Agencies are placing even chief executive officers and college presidents in temporary, as well as full-time, employment.

For energetic, industrious workers, part-time and temporary assignments may lead to full-time employment and the opportunity to move up to better positions. Any job you hold may be the first step in a career. Exhibit a positive attitude, and do your best no matter what the position. However, you will probably be under contract to the temporary agency for a specified period of time, and thus cannot be hired by the employer until the contract expires.

Volunteering

The importance of getting job-related experience cannot be overestimated. As can be seen in Xiao-ying's story, her volunteer experience supplemented her previous training. Many people have negative images of volunteering. They think volunteering means doing paperwork or "go-fer" work. However, you can create meaningful volunteer positions for yourself rather than taking whatever is available. To optimize your chances for obtaining such useful experience, go through a community voluntary action center, a college volunteer services office (sometimes part of the college placement office), a college cooperative education office, or a college service learning office.

One who asks is a fool for five minutes, but one who does not ask is a fool forever.

CHINESE PROVERB

An even more intense volunteer experience for those who have the time and resources may be through the U.S. Peace Corps, VISTA, or the UN Volunteers. Such volunteer work requires a commitment of one to three years and provides room, board, benefits (including government service experience), and a living allowance.

The Peace Corps recruits individuals with varied academic backgrounds; for example, recruits may teach math and English in developing countries. Engineering graduates are especially valuable in the Peace Corps, with their math and science expertise, and civil engineers are needed to build water purification plants and roads.

Meet Xiao-Ying

Xiao-ying is tired of going to college. As she is beginning work in a master's degree program in anthropology, she realizes that studying native tribes in the wilds of Africa will not enable her to make the personal contribution to other people's lives that she feels necessary for her own job satisfaction. With the help of a career counselor at the local YWCA and by talking with people working in her ideal setting, she becomes aware that working in a family-planning clinic will best suit her personal needs. Xiao-ying volunteers for one year in a clinic and, in addition, conducts some studies on pregnancy and childbirth. Within a year she has a full-time job in the education department of Planned Parenthood.

Once she has committed to a full-time job at Planned Parenthood, Xiao-ying realizes that she is no longer interested in pursuing a master's degree in anthropology. She finds that, instead, she can be accepted to an evening graduate program in counseling at the same university. This allows her to work full-time and complete a master's degree in counseling within three years. At that time, Xiao-ying becomes a counselor for Planned Parenthood and begins a private practice on the side.

REAL STORIES

WHAT DO YOU THINK?

1. How did Xiao-ying decide that her master's degree studies were not leading to her ultimate job satisfaction?

2. How did her volunteer experience help her?

3. What kind of volunteer experience, internship, or service learning assignment could help you choose or confirm your career goals?

To answer these questions online, go to the *Real Stories* module in Chapter 9 of the Companion Website.

Companion Website

Volunteering adds visibility and experience to your job search. However, volunteering does not relate only to jobs. Think about becoming a student member of a professional association. Student membership usually offers all the same benefits of regular membership but costs much less. Once in an organization, *volunteer* for committees and leadership positions, and gain visibility and recognition. The people in these organizations will soon be your peers. This is also an excellent method of making contacts for both jobs and letters of recommendation.

Interning

Your college or university may help to arrange *internships* in some fields of study. Internships may be paid or unpaid and are usually restricted to students who have studied in the subject area of the internship. For example, a history major or a political science major may be given the highest priority among applicants

FACTS & FIGURES

Internships

The book *Internships 2005*, published by Peterson's (Princeton, NJ, 2005), includes detailed information on more than 2,000 organizations offering 50,000 internships in the business, nonprofit, and government sectors. Arranged by career field, it includes short-term positions with businesses such as *The Wall Street Journal,* Procter & Gamble, 3M, Aetna Life and Casualty, Sierra Club, and the U.S. Department of Energy.

Meet Felipe

As a business student, Felipe wanted to focus on human resources development and training in industry. So he joined the American Society for Training and Development (ASTD). He volunteered to chair the student recruitment subcommittee and joined the Career Development Special Interest Group. Two years later, when interviewing for a job as assistant to a director of training, he found he knew people who had worked with the director, was able to learn about the firm from former employees who were ASTD members, and made an excellent impression in his interview.

for an internship in local or state government; a graphic arts, English, or communications major may be given priority for an internship in an advertising agency.

Some colleges have internship offices or experiential education offices that arrange internships of different types, including *fieldwork*, which involves work required as part of a major. (Prospective teachers usually must student teach, for example, to earn their degree or certificate.)

Internships can be used to build extremely valuable experience and contacts. At Keuka College in New York, one political science major had *three* government internships before graduation. At that campus, each political science major takes a four-week field period either in January or during the summer. Students have worked for state assemblypersons, the lieutenant governor, and the Democratic Senatorial Campaign Committee in Washington, for example.

At Concordia College in Minnesota, students alternate semesters of work and study or work part-time while continuing classes in the school's cooperative education program. This gives them longer-term connections with an organization and allows them to learn more about the workplace and professional environments. Ramapo College in New Jersey provided one of its students with overseas experience at a marketing firm in England. When she graduated, she got a job as an assistant account executive at the New York office of Lloyds Bank PLC, the British bank chain.

FACTS & FIGURES

The Princeton Review Online: America's top internships

Want to intern with the Academy of Television Arts & Sciences? How about the White House? The *Princeton Review* carries descriptions and application information for some of the best internship programs in the country. Its Website describes the positions, requirements, compensation (they're not all unpaid), duration, deadlines, and other important information.

The *Princeton Review Online* can be found at www.review.com. Search for "career center" or "college and careers," and then click on **Career Internships.**

Interns are generally closely supervised by college professors to help ensure they gain educational experience and benefit from the internship personally, while they provide services for the employer. Ideally, interns working as part of a college program enjoy a meaningful learning experience that provides them with skills that could not be learned from a book.

Another way for college students to get experience that may lead to a full-time position is through cooperative education programs. (At some schools, the terms *internship* and *cooperative education* are used synonymously, but others make distinctions between the two programs.) The Cooperative Education Association publishes a list of participating colleges and universities that have official co-op programs.

The *Princeton Review Online* site (www.review.com) is typical of many Websites related to published materials, providing free registration in order to add you to their advertising database. Such sites are essentially advertisements for books and materials, but they also contain a variety of free career resources. Another way to get similar information is to go to Websites of associations where information about paid and unpaid positions can be found. For example, the Association for Multimedia Communications has job listings at www.amcomm.org. To find sites like this, use a search engine with the term "internship" and additional key words to narrow the search, such as "multimedia internship."

FACTS & FIGURES

Employers rate experience

(5 = extremely important / 1 = not important)

Relevant work experience	4.00
Internship experience	3.82
Any work experience	3.69
Cooperative education work experience	3.32

Source: Annual employer survey by NACE, 2002.

THINK ABOUT IT

1. Do you have work or volunteer experience?

2. How can you get an internship or volunteer experience related to your identified goals?

3. Who are the people or what are the resources you can use to find experience related to your goals?

4. If you are a student, have you investigated cooperative education at your college? What is preventing you from enrolling in this program?

To answer these questions online, go to the *Facts* and *Figures* module in Chapter 9 of the Companion Website

Starting Your Own Business

One more way to get a job, of course, is to start your own business. In recent years, college students faced with limited job prospects have been starting businesses in record numbers. A reduction in corporate recruiters pitching jobs for graduates has led to new entrepreneurial pursuits and the rise of students *inventing* their own careers. Some examples include a myriad of Internet-related companies, organized walking tours in major cities with bilingual materials for foreign visitors, specialized photography to enhance pictorial magazines, and networks for improved services for persons with disabilities.

Become your own boss

Home Businesses

The U.S. Bureau of Labor Statistics estimates that two-thirds of the more than 14 million full-time self-employed work at home in a wide variety of

Explore freelance opportunities

FACTS & FIGURES

An innovative approach to the job search

Tommy Cates, director of online studies at the University of Tennessee—Martin, tells this story about one of UT's graduating seniors. "One of our alumni had a unique way of searching for a job. He wrote an ad stating: If you have always wanted to leave your business to a son, but you do not have a son, I am the person you want to hire to run your business." He then gave his address and phone number. He picked 10 newspapers that would circulate nationwide. He had 40 responses in a few days. Instead of searching for a job like most grads, he had people calling him offering him a job. One offer was to "come and join our organization . . . anyone who is this creative can find a spot with us."

THINK ABOUT IT

1. How might you separate yourself from the competition by creating a unique approach to your job search?

2. What are the advantages and disadvantages of an innovative approach?

To answer these questions online, go to the *Facts* and *Figures* module in Chapter 9 of the Companion Website.

Companion Website

careers. These numbers are growing each year as computer and Internet sites continue to expand. Approximately 25 percent of these home businesses are in the field of marketing and sales, with contracted services, professional jobs, and technical jobs accounting for another 25 percent. A potential consumer population with huge and diverse needs encourages this trend in home businesses. Among home business owners, 45 percent are college graduates and 85 percent are married, with half having dependent children. The average household income is approximately $55,000 annually.

According to the Associated Press, freelancing, long associated with artists, writers, and performers, is a career option for people in all fields these days. Freelance opportunities are growing for specialists in accounting, marketing, management, and other traditional business functions. These growing opportunities are largely due to technological advances of the last decade or two. The proliferation and increased affordability of fax machines, cell phones, personal computers, and desktop/multimedia publishing capacities enable small businesses to compete for and service clients in a manner previously possible only for large businesses.

Getting Help to Start Your Own Business

Career centers, libraries, and the Internet have useful information on starting a business. The Small Business Administration (www.sbaonline. sba.gov) provides seminars and low-cost materials within local communities. A group called SCORE (Service Corps of Retired Executives) is composed of local retired businesspeople who lead low-cost workshops and offer free technical advice. Contact your local chamber of commerce for information about these resources. Also, a local community college or the extension/continuing education division of a local university may offer courses in small business administration or marketing. If colleges offer such courses, they may also have students available who get college credit by giving free technical assistance to newly formed small businesses.

If you would like to explore the possibility of beginning your own business, either home-based or traditional, do thorough market research about the need for your service. You will benefit greatly from consulting SCORE, statewide Small Business Development Centers, your local chamber of commerce, and Internet sites (which you can find by typing "small business" and "careers," or "entrepreneurs" and "careers," into a search engine). Finally, a healthy savings account will be needed to get you through many months until you can count on regular income from your enterprise. Better yet, try to begin building your new business while you are still employed (at least part-time) to ensure some income.

Related Websites are www.inc.com and www.ideacafe.com. The first is the site of *Inc.*, a magazine dealing with starting small businesses, and the second specializes in helping small business owners with marketing, market research, starting businesses, legal information, operations, accounting, and more. A useful government site can be found at SBA Online: www.sbaonline.sba.gov/gils/. A site that specializes in youth development and entrepreneurial leadership programs can be found at www.entreworld.org.

Franchising

ranchising offers another means of owning and operating your own business. Franchising may appeal to individuals who have worked for large companies and those not quite ready to be full-fledged entrepreneurs. When you buy a franchise, you become part of a larger structure; thus, you must do extensive research to ensure that your personality fits well with the goals and operations of this larger company.

Women-owned firms

According to the Center for Women's Business Research, over the past decade, women-owned firms increased by 20 percent nationwide—this was twice the rate for all firms.

THINK ABOUT IT

1. Why do you think women-owned firms are increasing at twice the rate for all firms?

2. If you find this fact encouraging, explain why.

3. Do you know any women who have opened businesses in your community? If so, what do they own?

4. In general, what types of businesses do women own?

5. Does this information help you to make your career choices?

To answer these questions online, go to the *Facts and Figures* module in Chapter 9 of the Companion Website.

Using Career Planning Services

No matter what year you are in, there is much you can do to advance your career while still in college. First-year college students and sophomores should be taking courses in career exploration, exploring academic alternatives, setting goals, and making choices. Students further along in school should be pursuing internships, doing volunteer work, networking, and doing informational interviewing. Finally, you should be working with your school's career planning and placement office at all stages of your career exploration!

Companies are recruiting on college campuses these days, and many new college graduates will find jobs via this method. If you have researched your career, done related volunteer work, completed an internship, held a part-time position, or done well in your field academically, your appeal to these recruiters and other employers will be enhanced.

SUCCESS STRATEGIES

A creative job search

A business student from New York launched a Website promising a four-day cruise or $500 to anyone providing him a successful lead for an upstate New York job not posted on a major job bank. He wanted a marketing or PR position following his graduation.

Although the contest drew widespread media coverage, 6,000 e-mails, and about 200 promising leads, he received only two face-to-face job interviews and one offer, which he declined partly due to the fact that the job required very long hours. Incidentally, he did not have to pay anyone because he did not accept a job.

As it turned out, the 22-year-old instead pursued an opening he discovered on the Website of his alma mater. In applying to be an admissions counselor, he cited his contest as evidence of his creativity and sales and marketing skills.

FACTS & FIGURES

Franchise information

Here are a few sources of preliminary information about franchises:

- *The Worldwide Franchise Directory*, published by Gale Research, is available at most libraries.
- A "Franchise Opportunities Guide" is available from the International Franchise Association (www.franchise.org).
- www.frannet.com
- www.sbaonline.sba.gov

Cultivate contacts

If the career planning office offers job search workshops covering resume writing and interviewing techniques, or the opportunity to videotape practice interviews, sign up for these services. Explore alumni contacts in the field you hope to pursue. While it is still easily accessible to you, use your college library to research career opportunities.

Be prepared to be flexible when considering job offers. Especially during tight economic times, college graduates may find it difficult to find their ideal first job and may have to lower their expectations regarding starting salary. Read and inform yourself about today's opportunities and current salaries in your geographical area.

Remember, a job that seems less than ideal may lead to one at which you can truly excel. For example, one university fine arts student became a recruiter at Prudential Life Insurance Company. Later, that art graduate's job involved purchasing art for Prudential Regional Headquarters!

One lesson to learn from the Success Strategies story in this section is the value of using your college career services office. But there is always a possibility that a creative/novel approach will help you to stand out in a competitive job market.

During tight economic times, college graduates may decide that graduate school is the best bet and enter medical or law school or graduate degree programs in science, education, or business. If, when the time comes, you are genuinely interested in an advanced degree and the knowledge it will give you, this may be a good option for you. However, if you find you are considering graduate school simply to avoid the "real world" and put off job hunting, consult a career counselor. The job market may or may not be better in two or three years. It would be wiser to devote your energies to finding out more about what you want to do and how you can accomplish your goals than to invest additional years in school.

Interviewing for Information

Survey after survey on job hunting confirms a basic fact about job search strategy—namely, that the one best way to find out about a job and to get a job is through *people.* Now that you have reviewed the written sources of information on jobs, you are ready to begin conducting *information interviews.* These interviews help you develop contacts, sources of knowledge, and guides to meeting other people in a particular field. This network of people will keep you informed and connected to possible job openings. Once you gain some experience through information interviewing and networking, you will be ready to master the techniques involved in interviewing for a job.

Information Interviewing— The Purpose

Information interviewing involves identifying people who are doing what you want to be doing and asking them questions related to their current jobs. Information interviewing serves several purposes. It helps you further refine your knowledge and understanding of the field you are exploring. It enables you to develop social skills related to feeling comfortable and knowledgeable while you are being interviewed. Information interviewing creates the setting to develop contacts. These contacts are often helpful to your specific job search. The people you interview may themselves be in a position to hire someone like you for a job, or they may simply hear about a job opening and pass the information on to you. Remember that your specific purpose in information interviewing is *not* to look for a job but to confirm your information about the field and to develop contacts that may be helpful in the future. When involved in an information interview, *you are asking* the questions. When on a job interview, *you are being asked* the questions.

Information interviewing is based on the premise that you have already read much of the written information related to a specific type of job and now need confirmation from people who are already doing that job. You want them to tell you basically what the field is really like before you commit your time, effort, and finances to the pursuit of a new field. Or, if you are already in the field, you want to know if one employer's environment would be more appealing to you than another's.

Other information you can gain from such an interview involves much more than simply confirming the skills needed and the salary range. On one hand, you can find out if you like the people, if the atmosphere feels comfortable, or if the people are friendly and helpful. On the other hand, you may find that no one has time to talk to you, they keep you waiting, they let the telephone constantly interrupt your interview, or they work in noisy cubicles. This information is available only through an on-site visit. Thus, the overt goal of information interviewing is to collect information, but an additional goal is to make contacts and determine whether you have made an appropriate match between your personal needs and your career goal.

FACTS & FIGURES

Job hotlines

- Many companies and government agencies have job openings hotlines. A book titled *Job Hotlines USA* identifies more than 1,000 telephone numbers. Numbers and organizations are listed both alphabetically and by geographic location.

- Try America's Job Bank: www.ajb.dni.us. Their helpline is 1-877-348-0502.

- In California, use www.jobstar.org/socal/index.cfm.

An error does not become a mistake until you refuse to correct it.

ORLANDO A. BATTISTA.

Information Interviewing—The Process

Identify people who are doing what you would like to do

The first step in the process of information interviewing is to identify people who are working in the fields that you've decided are interesting to you. It's especially helpful if you know a relative, friend, or neighbor involved in the field or at least someone who can refer you to a potential contact; it's always easier to talk to someone whose name is familiar. The hardest step is making the first phone call to a stranger or, even worse, a strange firm and asking for the name of a person doing that interesting job! Strangers will be more receptive to talking to you if you do the following:

1. Indicate that you are seeking personalized information about their field before you decide to enter it.
2. Confirm the person's job title by asking.
3. Sound enthusiastic and delighted to have reached this person.
4. Refer to the research you've already reviewed about this field or company.
5. Ask if you can have a specific amount of time to interview this person (e.g., 15 to 20 minutes).
6. Try to arrange the interview at the person's work site, so you can determine firsthand how it might feel to work there.
7. Keep to your agreed-upon time frame.
8. Thank your interviewee, and follow up with a thank-you note.

As we noted, it's tough making that first phone call. Here are some specific examples of telephone lead-ins to help you get started. Remember to identify yourself, state your purpose, and ask for an appointment with the appropriate person. This straightforward approach is generally effective.

Example:

Hello, Mr. Jones, I am Diane Smith from Moorpark College. I'm doing some research in the field of houseplant maintenance service, and I'd like to stop by at your convenience to ask you a few questions. I'd appreciate about 15 to 20 minutes of your time. When may I stop by? Is Thursday at 2 p.m. all right?

or:

Hello, Ms. Smith, this is George Brown. This morning I talked to Dr. Green about the opportunities in food supplement marketing, and he spoke very highly of you. I'm calling to find out when you might have a few minutes to talk to me. Would it be convenient to meet with you in the morning or afternoon?

Information Interviewing Outline

Once you have located your contacts and made definite appointments to interview them, you need to consider in specific detail the best questions to ask to gain the maximum useful information as quickly and pleasantly as possible. Remember, you will be talking to busy people with many demands on their time; they will expect you to be, and it's to your advantage to be, as businesslike as possible. Finally, having made the telephone contact and set the date to meet, you should send a note confirming the information interview appointment.

Here is a framework to help you design your interview for an information interview. You may think you already have answers to some of the questions, but personal interviews should help flesh out details and possibly fill in some gaps in your information that you don't realize are there. Try to choose your questions from the general categories of type of business, position classifications, position descriptions, work environment, benefits, and entrance requirements, as follows:

TYPE OF BUSINESS

What are the services, products, or functions of the organization?

Who utilizes the organization's services or products?

Who are the competitors in this field?

What sets the company apart or distinguishes it from others in the same industry?

What are the projections for future development or new directions?

POSITION CLASSIFICATIONS

In each major corporate division, what types of positions are available?

What are the qualifications for entry-level and experienced positions? (Consider education, skills, abilities, etc.)

POSITION DESCRIPTIONS

What duties and responsibilities are performed in the area in which you are interested?

What are some examples of projects currently under way and problems currently being solved?

What is a typical day like?

What contacts would there be (e.g., personal, telephone, e-mail) with other organizations?

WORK ENVIRONMENT

What type of physical localities are involved: outdoors, indoors, travel? Is there pressure? Routine? Variety? How much supervision is there? Do flexible work schedules exist? Is overtime typical or atypical?

BENEFITS

How does compensation compare to education and ability level?

What are the opportunities for advancement, promotions, or lateral mobility?

What opportunities are available for advanced training, on-the-job training, or academic course work? Is there a tuition reimbursement plan?

What other benefits are available? Possible benefits might include:

Medical/dental insurance	Profit sharing
Life, disability insurance	Retirement
Vacations, holidays	Preretirement planning
Expenses for moving, travel	Employee assistance programs
Outplacement	(counseling for work-related
Recreation, personal health	problems)
services	Job placement assistance (for
Child-care facilities	your spouse, when relocating)

ENTRANCE REQUIREMENTS

What suggestions do you have for an individual wishing to enter this field of employment?

What other companies might employ individuals to perform this type of work? Could you refer me to someone else for more information about opportunities in this field?

Be prepared with questions

Moving from a general categorical framework to more specific detail, here is a list of typical questions you might ask in your information interviews.

1. What do you like most about your job and why?
2. What do you like least about your job and why?
3. How did you decide to get into this field, and what steps did you take to enter the field? What alternative ways can one enter this field?
4. What training would you recommend for someone who wanted to enter this field now? What skills and background are needed to get into this field now?
5. What is the salary range for a person in this field? Entry-level to top salary?
6. What personal qualities do you feel are most important in your work and why?
7. What are the tasks you do in a typical workday? Would you describe them?
8. What types of stress do you experience on the job?
9. What types of people survive and do well in this field?
10. Are resumes important in getting a job here?
11. What are the opportunities for promotion?
12. Is this field expanding? Taking any new directions?
13. What related occupations might I investigate?
14. Can you give me the names of three other people who share your enthusiasm for this kind of work? How can I contact them?
15. Is there anything else about this field that would be helpful for me to know?

When you approach professionals in your field of interest from a research point of view and *not* as if you want a job, they will often be happy to talk with you. Even the busiest executives will often find time for you. If one person doesn't have time, ask to be referred to another professional in the field. It is the secretary's job to protect the boss from distractions. When a secretary asks, "What is this call regarding?" you might respond, "I was referred to Jane by her associate Don Reid." Be certain to sound confident and friendly. It's best to call on a Tuesday, Wednesday, or Thursday between 8 A.M. and 11 A.M. If the person isn't in and you must leave a message, leave just your name and phone number.

Interviewing people who work in a field that interests you will provide you invaluable information, either confirming or revising your views. But even better, you will make contacts who may be able to help you actually find a job in the future. These contacts can suggest groups or associations to join, colleges to attend, and classes to take, as well as the current status of employment activity in their field. If you use this information wisely, you too can become visible in these inner circles. It's never too early to start. If you would like to read some sample interviews on the Web, go to www.careerchase.net and click on Career Information Categories.

Arrange for informational interviews with people who work in a field that interests you. You may gain information as well as contacts for your job search later.

Practicing Information Interviews

Some people prefer to practice information interviews until they become confident in approaching people about their career. If you need to practice, you might try one of the following approaches. Either you can interview someone you already know about a hobby that sounds interesting or you can ask people about their hobbies and careers at any informal gathering you attend. These informal activities tend to build your self-confidence in asking questions. Once you get started, you might find you enjoy interviewing for leads through other people.

Two interesting success stories may help you get started. Thomas Shanks, a college assistant professor of communications, tells how one of his students moved from California to New York. For three months, the student sent his resume everywhere and knocked on the door of every friend, relative, and remote acquaintance that he could find. He even found out which after-hours spots the television crowd preferred, and he frequented those places. He eventually got offers from all three networks. Another student, a freshman, was a business major with an interest in art. In November, the vice president of industrial relations at an engineering firm gave a talk in her leadership class. After class she asked him about summer jobs with his firm (notice how early she did so). By January, he had arranged for her to interview in the graphic arts department of his firm.

Information interviewing leads to contacts and careers

She got the summer job, one many graduates of art programs would have coveted.

Last, if you are a student or have access to a college campus, teachers are valuable resources. Many faculty members have interesting summer jobs or worked in other positions prior to becoming a teacher. They have valuable contacts. In turn, if you are a teacher interested in a career change, you might find a lead through a student. Many times a teacher can design a lesson plan to find out the occupations of parents and then invite parents to speak in their class about their career. These parents can become future contacts for both students and teachers!

> *When people believe in themselves, it is truly amazing what they can accomplish.*
>
> SAM WALTON

Networking

Networking provides the edge

*N*etworking refers to the process of developing and maintaining contacts. While conducting information interviews, you will meet many people. Besides gathering information, you are making contacts. Contacts, if cultivated and used wisely, can lead to or become potential employers. As the job market becomes more competitive and economic conditions create uncertainty, more people will be seeking fewer available jobs. In this climate, networking becomes the key element for success in getting a job. Contacts often make the difference between your being selected or being passed by. This is true for several reasons. Often jobs need to be filled before there is time to advertise. Additionally, as has been mentioned, the majority of new jobs that are available each year are filled through business leads—they go to candidates who already have some connection, even if indirect, to the employer. Most people hear about jobs by word of mouth. You need to let people know that you are looking.

The best networking appointment is personal and never manipulative. The meeting is not a "hard sell" or a sales transaction. It is all about gaining trust, building visibility, and listening carefully to the contact's wisdom, experience, and insight. The respect and attention you communicate for the valuable time provided to you at the meeting are crucial to any further contact, referral, or consideration. Skilled networkers learn to put the contact person at ease. Always remember, the purpose of the meeting is not to request employment. It is to help you learn more about the field and company and about strategies or job search efforts that would be useful in increasing your chances of becoming successful in that field.

Information Interviewing Outline

Below is an outline/review of the points we have discussed about information interviewing. Use this form as a guide in preparing for each interview.

1. **Find someone with whom to start the interview process.** Make sure you get the person's name. Call the person directly, by name.

   What is the name of the person you're going to call?

   _____

2. **Make a specific appointment, for a specific length of time.**

   When is your appointment, and for how long?

   _____

3. **Make a list of specific questions, things you want to know about the job.**

   Your questions for this interview. (See list on pages 245–246.)

   _____

   _____

   _____

   _____

   _____

4. **Explain why you're calling for the interview.** Some explanations:

   a. You want to know more about this kind of work before you decide that you're interested, or before you decide you should choose it as a career.

   b. You are getting ready for a job interview and would like to get some advice from someone in the field before the interview.

   c. You are interested in the field but haven't found much information on it and would appreciate someone filling you in on it.

   d. You are doing some research for a career class and would like some specific information in this field.

   Which explanation will you give when you call? *(Create your own if you wish.)*

   _____

   _____

5. **Give the employer the name of the person who recommended that you call.** (A reference helps.)

   Who is your reference for this interview? _____

6. **After the interview, send a note thanking the person for their time and help.**

   Date sent: _____

The term *network* is both a noun and verb. As a noun, a *network* is defined as a group of individuals who are connected to and cooperate with each other. As a verb, *to network* is to develop contacts and exchange information with other people for purposes of developing business or expanding one's career opportunities. The verb form often becomes action-oriented and is changed to *networking*.

Your network can develop each day; anyone you know can be a good source. Each has friends and contacts and can make a difference in helping you secure an information interview. Think about it: The more people you get to know, the more information you gather. The more visible and proactive you are, the greater your chances will be of finding the right job. It may be a relative or neighbor who points you to a hidden job opening or provides you with valuable strategies.

You probably have many acquaintances willing to provide names and ideas to help you be successful in finding your preferred career. These friends and acquaintances may come from any of the following groups: clubs, organizations, health and sports team affiliations, teachers and professors (past and present), religious groups, coworkers, and previous employers. Exercise 9.1 will suggest people to contact.

Join professional associations

One form of networking is to meet professionals where they gather. For example, if you are interested in human resources management (HRM), you will find HRM personnel at association meetings such as American Society for Training and Development (ASTD); if you are interested in personal communications services, read the trade journal *Radio Communications Report* to find out about local meetings or national conventions.

Attend conferences

Check the local business section of the newspaper to keep up on what's happening in your community. Review the list of groups using your city's convention center, and plan on attending conventions related to your interests. For example, one trade show related to theme parks had 20,000 registrants and 800 exhibitors occupying 2,600 booths; it lasted four days. Students majoring in communications, radio–TV, theater arts, business, and computer science would all find experts related to their majors at such a conference. Such conventions usually offer reduced fees for attending only one day or entering the exhibit area only.

Use all available sources for contacts

Many professional associations have related student groups or student sections. You should already know whether there are groups active on campus related to the field you want to pursue. If you don't, make this your first networking step. Use the resources listed in Chapter 7 to obtain association names and addresses, or ask your adviser. For example, a very complete source is *The Encyclopedia of Associations,* but the *Occupational Outlook Handbook* also lists names and addresses after each occupation. Consider writing an association to inquire about local meetings and the possibility of becoming a student member. Explore the American Society of Association Executives' list of directories (www.asanet.org).

These are all ways of meeting professionals in your field of interest, a key factor in finding the job you want. A survey of 1,500 successful job applicants by *National Business Employment Weekly* found that 67 percent got their jobs through networking, 11 percent by answering an ad, and only 2 percent by sending out resumes and filling out applications.

While conducting information interviews or discussing people's careers at a conference, take advantage of these opportunities to find out what kinds of questions *they* were asked in interviews; ask what they considered to be the most difficult questions in their interviews. Another good question is to ask them what makes a candidate the best candidate. Their answers to questions like these will be helpful when you begin to practice for job interviews.

Moving Beyond the Fear of Networking

Many people are reluctant to develop contacts by networking. They may feel they are imposing on busy individuals whose time is precious. This hesitation can be overcome, however, by realizing that many people truly enjoy talking about themselves and their profession. Many remember their own difficulties in connecting to a new career and are, therefore, very receptive to others' requests.

Remember that as you meet people, you are finding out about the real work these new contacts do and finding out if you feel comfortable with their environment. You should also be finding out if your skills would be helpful in solving problems or meeting needs in each workplace you visit while networking. Let the contact know what you can do for them—you may be just the person they need! One graphic design student visited the company of a graphic designer who had spoken in her art class. When asked if she had used Adobe Photoshop (software for modifying photographs electronically), she was very enthusiastic in her answer about using the program in one of her classes. She was hired for a summer job on the spot!

Some job seekers find it difficult to network because they are introverts by nature. If this is the case for you, consider writing an introductory note to ask for a brief meeting. Then, stick to the agreed-upon time. Knowing general conversational techniques helps. For instance, discuss mutual professional interest as a conversation opener before starting to ask questions. This technique develops rapport and sets you both at ease.

Finally, be sure that every contact is made with courtesy and tact, and be prepared with specific questions. Thanking your contacts for their assistance pays huge dividends in the future. The best networking is not simply a one-time association, but a continuing connection. Networking can positively affect your job search and every aspect of your life.

Job Search While Unemployed

Although experts agree that it is best to look for a job while you are still employed, not everyone can be in that position. If you are unemployed and seeking employment, you will benefit by disciplining yourself to stick to a daily job search schedule. Otherwise, your best intentions may be thwarted by procrastination. Procrastination can then turn into the paralysis described in Chapter 8 related to poor decision-making strategies.

Create a disciplined job search to replace the work schedule missing from your life. You will be more productive if you begin the day as if you were going to work. Get dressed, have breakfast, and begin the day with a few hours of phone calls. Identify employers who can use your skills. Be aware that successful phone contacts rely on sheer numbers. The greater the number of calls you make, the greater are your chances of getting an interview.

Because many cold calls will result in responses such as "No one can speak to you today" or "Sorry, we have no openings," your daily routine must include predictably positive activities. For instance, plan to spend a portion of your day at the library or online researching job information, a portion looking for leads, and a portion filling out job applications. Another important part of the day should include being with supportive people, for example, attending networking and association meetings (local newspapers have business sections that announce weekly association meetings), joining friends for lunch, and enjoying recreation.

Keeping active will reenergize you and keep you visible to those who might be able to refer you to a job. Somewhere in your present circle of friends, coworkers, and acquaintances is someone who can link you with your next job. This process is further discussed under the topic of networking.

Reserve the final part of your day for returning phone calls and e-mails, redrafting letters, revising your resume and cover letter, and writing specific thank-you letters to people you have met. Planning and preparation can make the critical difference in turning telephone calls into interviews and interviews into job offers. (See Chapter 11 for interviewing techniques.)

Many unemployed people use the services of their state employment agency. (The unemployment office usually requires you to contact a minimum number of employers each week or month to remain eligible to collect unemployment insurance.) However, the state employment agency also offers workshops on job search strategy, assistance in writing a resume, and a computerized job bank. Some offices also conduct targeted group meetings for workers in designated fields, for example, aerospace, automotive, banking, executive, manufacturing, and the like. Support groups may meet on a regular basis to offer both encouragement and leads.

Your daily routine should include using the Internet

Planning for Action

Effective job search strategy requires that you master the skills of goal setting and action planning. This means that you set objectives such as those indicated in the following five suggestions and designate specific times to complete each one:

1. Schedule planning time.
2. Maintain a list of activities to get done; for example, write up a weekly calendar and enter each item per day or hour. A pocket calendar may be sufficient for one person whereas a notebook may work better for another.
3. Start a notebook with one section for contacts' names, addresses, and phone numbers and another section for notes about different companies.
4. Use Internet bookmarks for often-used addresses. (Bookmarks allow quick access to favorite sites.)
5. Review your progress by checking off completed activities.

An effective job search requires clerical and organizational skills. Every week you will need to update names, obtain more exact titles, and confirm addresses. This information can be kept in a file box or in your home computer. (Exhibit 9.1 provides a sample contact record.) Being able to retrieve at a moment's notice the information you have been collecting can make the difference between getting your resume to the potential employer today or tomorrow (which may be a day too late). The fastest way to update a resume is to have it stored in your own home computer or other digital storage device for use in a computer at school, at a local copy center, or at a friend's home.

Software packages can help you create a tracking system for all of your contacts and activities. One software program, for example, leads you through planning, analysis, targeted markets, and commitment to a schedule of tasks. After working through the program, you will have created a list of potential employers, a resume, and a cover letter, and you will have prepared for the interview.

If you do not already have Internet access, consider investing in a service such as America Online or Earthlink that provides access to computer bulletin boards. More and more companies are advertising job openings through these bulletin boards and even requiring electronic transmission of resumes (more about this in Chapter 10). Also, company insiders may provide information about job openings via these bulletin boards.

If you truly want to understand something, try to change it.

KURT LEWIN

It is advisable to have a designated area in your home for all of your career information. Keeping careful records of all contacts made, applications submitted, resumes sent, interviews held, and correspondence sent and received will make your job search more effective and easier to manage.

Implementing Your Job Search: A Lifelong Venture

The comprehensive approach to job hunting involves putting yourself in the right place at the right time again and again throughout your lifetime. It involves strategies that assist you in finding openings in your target area before the openings are publicly announced. In situations when you do not appear to be the ideal candidate, this approach will assist you in getting noticed and getting an interview.

Many times, this approach works best while you are still employed because potential employers tend to defer unemployed inquirers to the personnel office. Ideally, before starting a job search, you will have a specific field and job objective in mind. Let's say you have selected business administration and want to specialize in real estate finance. Your first decision is whether you want to work for a commercial bank, a private developer, the government (such as an appraisal office or bureau of land development), or a related association that employs people to interact with the government. The box titled "Meet Susan" offers an example.

Confirm your career objectives

High visibility helps

Networking opens up the hidden job market

EXHIBIT 9.1   Sample contact file format.

1. Company: Phone No.:   Contact Person & Title: Type of Contact & Date:
                                                                 Letter   _____
                   Referred By: E-mail: Phone   _____
   Address: Resume   _____
                                                                 Application _____
                   Job Target: Interview   _____

   Follow-up: Conclusions:

2. Company: Phone No.:   Contact Person & Title: Type of Contact & Date:
                                                                 Letter   _____
                   Referred By: E-mail: Phone   _____
   Address: Resume   _____
                                                                 Application _____
                   Job Target: Interview   _____

   Follow-up: Conclusions:

3. Company: Phone No.:   Contact Person & Title: Type of Contact & Date:
                                                                 Letter   _____
                   Referred By: E-mail: Phone   _____
   Address: Resume   _____
                                                                 Application _____
                   Job Target: Interview   _____

   Follow-up: Conclusions:

4. Company: Phone No.:   Contact Person & Title: Type of Contact & Date:
                                                                 Letter   _____
                   Referred By: E-mail: Phone   _____
   Address: Resume   _____
                                                                 Application _____
                   Job Target: Interview   _____

   Follow-up: Conclusions:

5. Company: Phone No.:   Contact Person & Title: Type of Contact & Date:
                                                                 Letter   _____
                   Referred By: E-mail: Phone   _____
   Address: Resume   _____
                                                                 Application _____
                   Job Target: Interview   _____

   Follow-up: Conclusions:

Meet Susan

As an assistant to a county supervisor, Susan finds many of her assignments relate to land development. While finishing work toward her bachelor's degree in business (attending college after work hours), she increasingly represents her supervisor when land developers appeal to the Board of Supervisors for zoning and code changes. When her supervisor decides not to run for reelection, Susan is hired as a director for the business-industry association to lobby the county for the industrialization of farmland. Within a few years, she becomes a consultant to land developers and interacts with her present boss, who hires her into his prospering real estate development firm as vice president of government relations.

Even while working in an entry-level job, Susan met people working in the field of her interest, real estate. As an assistant to the county supervisor, she met people in government, nonprofit associations, and private industry. She maintained high visibility by speaking at community events, representing her supervisor when necessary, and joining relevant organizations and community clubs. When Susan wanted to make a job change, she had already identified and made contact with the types of places and people with whom she wanted to work.

REAL STORIES

Susan had contacts who were insiders and could recommend her for jobs even before they were announced. But even more important, she had discovered the hidden job market. She knew the needs of the business-industry association and could tell its people how her skills and contacts could benefit them. She was able to sell herself. She knew she had skills and contacts with government that could enhance her present employer's expansive plans. She was hired because she was able to describe the job she wanted to do in the firm and because her ideal job meshed with the vision of the president of the company. She actually created her current position.

WHAT DO YOU THINK?

1. What job strategy did Susan use to great advantage?

2. How did Susan develop visibility while working on the job?

3. How did Susan use her knowledge and contacts to create the job of her dreams?

4. How can you develop your network through your job, internship, volunteer, or service learning experience?

To answer these questions online, go to the *Real Stories* module in Chapter 9 of the Companion Website.

Companion Website

Summary

This chapter has discussed the comprehensive job search. It is important that you confirm your impressions about your ideal job. You won't know the accuracy of your researched information until you volunteer in the field, do part-time work in the field, or find a job that will put you around the people doing the type of job you desire. Only then will you know how you feel about the real job environment. It also takes practice to remember to ask everyone you meet about his or her job. The more jobs you learn about, the more alternatives you will have.

A large but hidden job market exists out there, and the people you meet through the process of information interviewing can help you uncover it by informing you about potential jobs before they are advertised.

Selected Online Employment Databases

Searching online can be overwhelming. Thousands of Websites are available for job searching, but you may feel comfortable with only a few. Find a service suited to you and remember, the more you target your search, the more efficient it will be. Rather than typing "job search," use terms like "entry-level job" or "job in advertising." Here are a few sites to get you started.

The Monster Board (www.monster.com). The Monster Board has a database with more than one million job listings and includes a resume bank. There, you can develop your online resume and use it to apply for jobs. It will be matched to employers' needs at no charge. Students may find that their college lists jobs designed with the student in mind at a related site, www.monstertrak.com.

America's Job Bank (www.jobsearch.org). JobBank USA is one of the largest and most diverse databases, with almost 2 million jobs. This site provides resume writing, networking, and information services to job candidates, employers, and recruitment firms. This is a free service to job hunters. Also see www.careeronestop.org.

America's Job Line (www.nfb.org/jobline/ enter.htm). This is an audio version of America's Job Bank, partially sponsored by the National Federation of the Blind. To access by telephone, call 1-800-414-5748.

CareerBuilder (www.careerbuilder.com). The CareerBuilder site has its own database of job opportunities; it lists more than 500,000 jobs and directs the user to online job fairs, employer profiles, and special resources for students. Instructions and tips about electronic resumes are provided. You may search by job type, by industry, or by company.

Nation Job Network (www.nationjob.com). In addition to the standard search by job title

or company name, this site features Personal Job Scout, which keeps an eye on listing updates and notifies you via e-mail about related jobs. This service is free, but it also offers "for fee" services. This site is a good resource for government jobs and trade magazines.

Online Job Search Guide and Career Resource Center (JobHunt.org). Rated highly by *PC Magazine*, this site includes basics on job searching, good career articles, state-by-state job resources, and international job information. It also offers a comprehensive industry database and excellent links to employment supersites, job fairs, classified ads, and recruiting guides. Be sure to click on Online Job Search Guide.

Quintessential Careers (www.quintcareers.com). This site offers thousands of pages of career tools to help you with your search, including expert advice, career articles, and thousands of "best" job sites on the Web. This site is very user friendly.

The Riley Guide (www.rileyguide.com). *Riley's Job Guide* provides a wealth of information with many good links regarding job listings, resume postings, employer profiles, and current articles. It also contains articles from job searchers who have tried electronic job searches and can tell you how it really works. Very detailed information.

The Richard Bolles Parachute Site (www.Job HuntersBible.com). The author of *What Color Is Your Parachute?* has an abundance of career information and resources on his site, including job search information, resume writing tips, and company information. He also provides tips for using the Internet to conduct your search effectively.

Vault (www.vault.com). This is an excellent source for information on internships. Click on Career Topics.

Online Services with Good Career Sections.
America Online: www.aol.com
Microsoft Network: www.msn.com
Earthlink: www.earthlink.com
Yahoo! www.yahoo.com
Check with your local university or 800 directory for more online services.

Search Engines and Browsers. Below is a list of the most-used search engines as well as some unusual ones. Following the name is a description of how it catalogs various sites. Big search engines (such as AltaVista) are best for obscure searches because they cast a wider net, which increases your chances of finding what you want. Novices should start with Google, Yahoo!, or Lycos, all of which target mainstream users and are considered user-friendly. Consult the instructions for each search engine to learn how to search most effectively.

- **AltaVista (www.altavista.com)** is one of the most comprehensive indexes of documents on the Web. Unless you're very specific about your search criteria, it often turns up so many matches that you will have more than enough to meet your needs. This engine will locate the most obscure topics.

- **Excite (www.excite.com)** gives you reviews of all the sites it catalogs. You can also use Excite to search Vault career profiles and access classified ads.

- **Google (www.google.com)** rates sites by how many pages link to the site. This search engine is constantly expanding. If your search is too broad, try searching by "group."

- **Lycos (www.lycos.com)** also catalogs web-pages rather than entire sites and provides you with an outline and abstract for each page that matches your criteria. Lycos' "Career Section" links with Monster.com. Try typing "job search" into "search the web" to get a variety of sources.

- **Search (www.search.com)** is an excellent reference site.

- **Yahoo! (www.yahoo.com)** organizes sites by category. When Yahoo! finds a site that matches your request, it displays a summary of the site and a link to the site's category. Look for free information, as some links may be fee based.
    Similar to Yahoo! (searching by category) are the following: www.looksmart.com and ask.com.

Search Engine Watch (www.searchengine watch.com) provides a tutorial on using search engines and also rates them for a variety of subject areas.

For additional Websites, visit Chapter 7 and Chapter 9 in the Companion Website.

TARGETING YOUR JOB SEARCH

PURPOSE OF EXERCISES. The exercises that follow serve to increase your ability to network effectively. Exercise 9.1 asks you to identify specific people who are part of your network. Exercise 9.2 suggests that you conduct information interviews. Exercise 9.3 helps you expand information about your job target by using practice information gathering, expert information gathering, and interviewing for employment strategies.

To answer these questions online, go to the *Exercise* module in Chapter 9 of the Companion Website.

Companion Website

9.1 Support Network Checklist

Fill in the names of people who might help you in the list below. Specifically ask yourself: How can this person help (provide information, introduce me to someone, offer advice, write a reference, etc.)?

Former employers: _____

Former coworkers: _____

Present employer: _____

Friends: _____

Relatives: _____

Civic group members: _____

Professional association members: _____

Alumni group members: _____

Religious group members: _____

Clients: _____

Counselors: _____

Teachers: _____

Clergy: _____

Neighbors: _____

Classmates: _____

Bankers: _____

Accountants: _____

Financial planners: _____

Insurance agents: _____

Real estate agents: _____

Stockbrokers: _____

Salespeople: _____

Retail store owners: _____

Medical professionals: _____

Other: _____

_____

_____

_____

_____

Information Interviews 9.2

Select three individuals who work in fields that are interesting to you, and conduct brief information interviews using the list of sample information interview questions given in this chapter as your guide. Write a brief report of each.

Personal Contact Log 9.3

Prepare a log of personal contacts (at least five) that you make using the approaches described in this chapter under "Interviewing for Information." Focusing on your own job target, see how much information and how many new contacts you acquire. Use the appropriate format below for each type of contact you make.

Name: _____   Job Target: _____

PRACTICE INFORMATION GATHERING

Hobby or interest: _____

Contact: _____

Information gathered as a result of the interview: _____

_____

_____

_____

Other possible contacts: _____

_____

_____

EXPERT INFORMATION GATHERING

Occupational interest: _____

Contact (who, where employed, how you found this person): _____

_____

Information gathered: _____

_____

_____

New contacts: _____

_____

Any contradictions: _____

_____

Conclusions: _____

_____

_____

_____

INTERVIEWING FOR EMPLOYMENT, APPRENTICESHIP, OR VOLUNTEER EXPERIENCE

Choice of possible work site: _____

_____

What do you want (job, apprenticeship, volunteer experience)? _____

_____

Who is in a position to hire you? _____

Your approach (telephone, letter, in person): _____

Outcomes and follow-up: _____

_____

_____

_____

9.4 WWWebwise

For additional activities online, go to the WWWebwise module in Chapter 9 of the Companion Website.

Exercise Summary

9.5

Write a brief paragraph answering these questions.

What did you learn about yourself from these exercises? How does this knowledge relate to your career/life planning? Did you use the Internet? Was it helpful in locating job information? What was most useful?

_____

_____

_____

_____

_____

_____

_____

_____

_____

_____

_____

_____

_____

_____

_____

_____

_____

_____

_____

_____

10

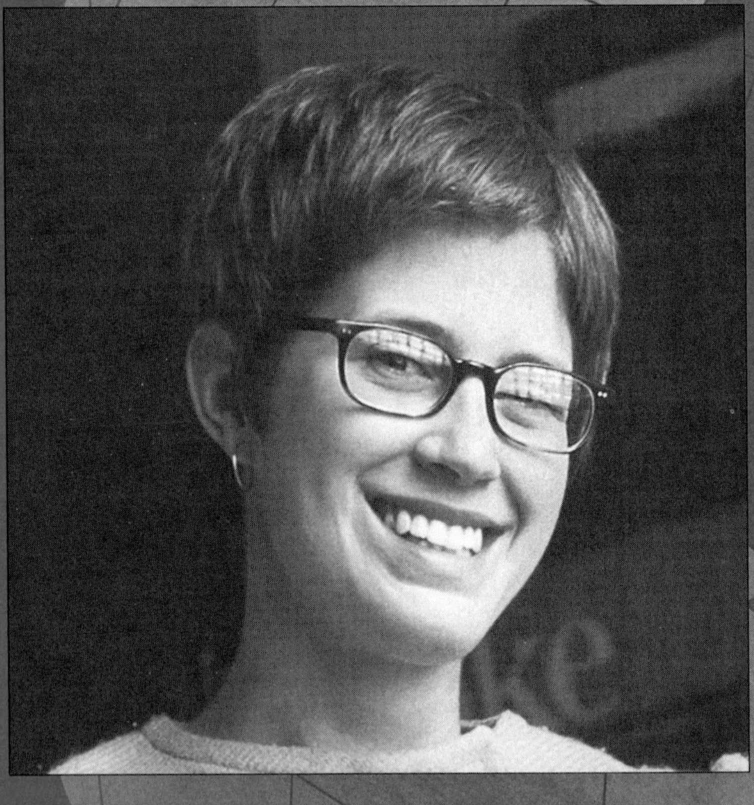

Preparing a Winning Resume

Learning Objectives

At the end of the chapter you will be able to . . .

- List the advantages of developing a resume

- Identify guidelines for resume preparation

- Write a resume and cover letter

Every good fitness program includes a chart that indicates visually where you started, where you are currently, and where you are going. In a career fitness program, this chart is called a *resume*. Eventually, in the course of job hunting, you will be asked to present a resume to a prospective employer. Some career counselors warn that the resume isn't going to get you an interview unless you already have a good contact inside the company; others suggest that a good resume can help you get your foot in the door. These days, a resume can

Life is 10 percent what you make of it, and 90 percent what you take from it.

IRVING BERLIN

be transmitted electronically via computer to reach thousands of potential employers at once. In any case, your resume will be an essential job search tool. A resume is:

1. A systematic assessment of your skills in terms of a specific job objective.

2. A memory jogger useful in an interview in responding to the following common requests/questions by interviewers: Tell me about yourself. Why should I hire you? What skills do you bring to this job?

3. An aid in filling out application forms.

4. A marketing device used to gain an interview.

This chapter offers guidelines for writing a resume and distributing it electronically. It presents three sample formats: functional, chronological, and a creative combination. Additionally, the importance of cover letters and application forms is addressed. Once you have completed this chapter, you will be prepared to compile your own winning resume.

The Resume

The purpose of the resume is to get an interview. Like an advertisement, the resume should attract attention, create interest, describe accomplishments, and provoke action. Brevity is essential; one page is best, and two are the limit. The resume tells the prospective employer what you can do and have done, who you are, and what you know. It also indicates the kind of job you seek. The resume must provide enough information for the employer to evaluate your qualifications, and it must interest the employer enough so that you will be invited for an interview.

Writing a well-constructed resume requires that you complete your research before compiling the resume. You need to keep in mind the type of employer and position as well as the general job requirements in order to tailor your resume to the specific requirements and personality of the employer. To be most effective, your resume should be designed to emphasize your background as it relates to the job you seek. It should look neat, clean, and organized. This means word-processed with no errors, and then laser-printed or photocopied on high-quality paper.

By now you should have completed all the necessary research. Use the information you gathered in Chapter 7, Information Integration, and

Chapter 9, Targeting Your Job Search. Integrate your answers with the categories listed in the box titled "Resume/Portfolio Review."

Portfolios

The portfolio is an expanded resume. It is usually a folder containing the basic resume and samples of your work related to the job objective. It is a good idea to begin storing work samples now. For instance, a marketing specialist might send a potential employer a resume along with fliers, brochures, and ads created in past jobs. For a marketing student with limited experience, the folder could include copies of term papers, proposals completed for classes, and homework assignments related to the job objective. Portfolios are useful to have during information interviews, when you are at association meetings and networking, or upon request in an interview.

Preparation for Composing Your Resume

A resume summarizes your particular background as it relates to a specific job. It summarizes your career objectives, education, work experience, special skills, and interests. Visualize a pyramid or triangle with the job objective at the top and everything beneath it supporting that objective. Although stating an objective is considered optional by some experts (because it can be

A resume customized for the job for which you are applying, accompanied by a well-written cover letter, will be much more effective than a general resume.

stated in your cover letter), it is to your advantage to include it on the resume. In actuality, one resume should be designed for each job objective. Remember, there are no jobs titled "anything."

The job objective is a concise and precise statement about the position you are seeking. This may include the type of firm in which you hope to work (e.g., a small, growing company). A clear objective gives focus to your job search and indicates to an employer that you've given serious thought to your career goals. When time does not allow you to develop a resume for each of several different jobs that interest you, the job objective may be emphasized in the cover letter (which will be discussed at the end of this chapter) and omitted from the resume.

A job objective is sometimes referred to as goal, professional objective, position desired, or simply objective. It can be as specific as "community worker," "personnel assistant," or "junior programmer"; it can be as general as "management position using administrative, communications, and research skills" or "to work as an administrative assistant in a creative atmosphere and have the opportunity to use my abilities." The more specific the objective statement, the better, because a clear objective enables you to focus your resume more directly on that objective. The effect is pointed, dramatic, and convincing.

In choosing information to include in your resume, avoid anything that may not be considered in a positive light or that has no relationship to your ability to do the job (e.g., marital status, number of children, political or religious affiliation, age, photos). When in doubt, leave it out. One clue: In the next chapter, you will be given information about illegal questions in an interview. If information is illegal for an employer to request in an interview, then it's unnecessary in a resume.

To write the rough draft of your resume, prepare a 5" × 8" index card for each job you've held (see Exhibit 10.1). The index card should contain the following information:

FRONT OF CARD

Put the most relevant information first

1. Name, address, phone number of employer, and immediate supervisor at work site
2. Dates employed (month/year to month/year)
3. Job title
4. Skills utilized (review the skills discussion in Chapter 5)

EXHIBIT 10.1   Front and back of resume index card (the format can easily be adapted for use in creating a computer file).

Elaine's House of Coffee
555 Stevens Circle   April 2005–Present
Roanoke, VA 23640
(540) 555-1211

Supervisor: Position:
Joe Smith   Bookkeeper & Shift Supervisor

Skills Utilized:

Related well with continuous flow of people. Attentive to detail; organized; energetic.

Bilingual—Spanish/English

Functions:

Management	—Coordinated service with customer needs, payroll, scheduled employees.
Communications	—Welcomed guests. Directed staff in performing courteous and rapid service. Responded to and resolved complaints.
Bookkeeping	—Maintained records of financial transactions. Balanced books. Compiled statistical reports.

Resume/Portfolio Review

A. Personal Data
  a. Name
  b. Address
  c. Phone

B. Current Job Objective

C. Education (This category may follow category D, Work Experience, on your actual resume, depending on which is more relevant to the position sought.)
  1. High school and college
     a. Favorite subjects
     b. Samples of best work in classes related to job objective
     c. Extracurricular interests
     d. Offices held
     e. Athletic achievements
     f. Other significant facts (e.g., honors, awards)
  2. Other (military service, volunteer work that provided training, correspondence courses, summer activities, languages, technical skills, licenses, and/or credentials)

D. Work Experience (This may precede category C, Education, on your actual resume. Refer to your experiography or your skills analysis for this information.)
  Employer
  Length of employment
  Position
  Skills and accomplishments (These may be featured in a bulleted list following Job Objective.)
  Samples of best work if relevant

E. Publications

F. Associations, Volunteer Work, and Community Involvement

G. Special Skills (e.g., language proficiency, computer skills)

BACK OF CARD

Duties divided into functional areas

Using Action Words

Remember that your writing style communicates the work activity in which you have been involved. Use phrases and document experiences that both involve the reader and make your resume outstanding and active. Following are basic guidelines for selecting your "power" words:

Select "Power" words

- Choose short, clear phrases.
- If you use complete sentences throughout, keep them concise and direct.
- Use the acceptable jargon of the work for which you are applying. Remember: You want your prospective employer to *read* your resume.
- Avoid general comments such as "My duties were . . . " or "I worked for . . . " Begin with action words that concisely describe what your tasks were; for example:

Implemented new filing system.

Developed more effective interviewing procedure.

Evaluated training program for new employees.

- List the results of your activities; for example:

    Reduced office filing by 25 percent.

    Developed interview evaluation summary form.

    Increased efficiency in delivering services.

- Don't dilute your action words with too many extraneous activities. Be *selective* and sell your *best* experiences.
- Target your words to the employer's needs.

Using the Right Key Phrases

In many large companies, human resources personnel now scan resumes into computer files and databases for storage and later retrieval. According to a poll by a management consulting firm, 31 percent of 435 human resource professionals indicated their firms use resume banks for recruiting. Many experts say the percentage of large and midsize companies using such programs is far higher, with employers such as Walt Disney World Company leading the way in their use of resume banks. A growing biotechnology firm, Amgen, Inc., receives more than 225 resumes a day, about 60 percent in conventional paper format and 40 percent by e-mail or fax. All end up in an automated tracking system. The manager of employment systems at Amgen says automated tracking allows the company to consider all applicants for all available jobs—which is especially important in a growing company. When an opening occurs, employers search their banks and databases for resumes using certain key phrases relevant to the position. For example, a company looking for "B.S., Information Systems, Cisco Certification" would first retrieve resumes containing these key words.

Depending on the field in which you hope to work and the type of companies you will apply to, this information may be vital to your writing a resume that gets retrieved during a key word search. In such cases, the appearance and style of your resume will be less significant than the manner in which you describe your specific skills: be certain to use concrete nouns to summarize past experience.

References

The expression "References available upon request" is usually not necessary on a resume. If references are requested, you will probably need to submit their names and contact information

---

SUCCESS STRATEGIES

Action words

Here are some examples of action words that could be used in your resume:

accomplished	evaluated	negotiated
achieved	expanded	organized
analyzed	facilitated	oriented
arranged	guided	planned
built	implemented	processed
controlled	improved	produced
created	increased	proved
demonstrated	initiated	raised profits
designed	inspired	reduced costs
developed	interpreted	researched
directed	invented	sold
effected	led	supervised
encouraged	managed	supported
established	motivated	wrote

For additional action verbs, see the section "Identifying Your Skills" in Chapter 5, including the Assessing Your Skills activity.

Meet Eduardo

It is almost one o'clock in the morning and Eduardo Garza is just finishing his shift at Elaine's House of Coffee. On Friday and Saturday nights, a small band plays at Elaine's until midnight. Eduardo has been working these weekend shifts ever since his mother's illness. Mrs. Garza is a single mother of five children, recently underwent surgery, and will not be able to work for approximately six months. Eduardo is the oldest child and he takes much of the responsibility for his family. Until his mother is well again, he must bring in as much of the income as possible.

Eduardo graduated from high school and attended community college for one year but he dropped out because of his family situation and because he was having trouble in some of his classes. He is a very quiet young man and likes to spend his spare time reading and listening to music. In high school, his favorite subject was math. Eduardo has a strong work ethic, and his supervisor at Elaine's promoted him to manager. He is not comfortable managing other employees, but he does enjoy his bookkeeping responsibilities.

Eduardo looks in the want ads daily for better-paying jobs with hours that will let him be home in the evenings, but many of the positions require a resume. Eduardo does not feel that he has enough skills to put on a resume, and he is very concerned about his ability to compete for a better job.

WHAT DO YOU THINK?

1. Based on the information you have about Eduardo, prepare a resume for him.

2. Where could Eduardo go for help in preparing a resume?

3. What other resources could Eduardo use to look for a job?

4. What might help Eduardo strengthen his self-esteem?

5. What resources might be available to help Eduardo's family?

To answer these questions online, go to the *Real Stories* module in Chapter 10 of the Companion Website.

Companion Website

---

on a separate form. Although you don't have to list specific names on the resume, you should have at least three people in mind who can talk about your work habits, your skills, and your accomplishments. When you are job hunting, ask these people in advance if you may use them as references, informing them of your job objective so that they will be prepared if a prospective employer calls.

Many college placement centers act as a clearinghouse for the collection of resumes and references. You establish a file, and the center sends out your resume and references when you make a request. The placement center often makes this service available for alumni, and it may have reciprocal agreements with other colleges across the country.

The Appearance of Your Resume

The appearance of this document is critical. Your resume must be clearly typed, well spaced, and visually attractive. Remember that many employers skim only the first page of a resume. Thus, it is crucial that your material be strategically placed so that what is most likely to be read is most relevant to the job desired. Employers may receive

FACTS & FIGURES

Resume problems

When scanning a resume, the HR manager looks for key "knockout" factors. On the other hand, survey results from human resources managers indicate that the following items help them to decide that the candidate has *not* matched their resume with the needs of the company:

- Job objective incompatible with current openings
- Inappropriate or insufficient educational credentials
- Incompatible salary requirements
- Geographic restrictions incompatible with current openings
- Lack of U.S. citizenship or permanent resident status
- Resume poorly organized, sloppy, or hard to read
- Too many employers in too short a period of time
- Too many pages
- Too many (or any!) errors in spelling

Source: www.FlipDog.com, July 2002.

THINK ABOUT IT

1. Have you ever created or submitted an electronic resume?

2. Do you know anyone who has gotten an interview by sending an electronic resume?

3. What do you think is the advantage of sending your resume by e-mail?

4. See Exhibit 10.4 for suggestions for composing your resume. Which points seem to be most relevant for you?

5. In addition to an electronic resume, what other steps or method of communication would you use to get a position?

Companion Website

To answer these questions online, go to the *Facts and Figures* module in Chapter 10 of the Companion Website.

---

hundreds of resumes each day, giving them only minutes to review each one. Therefore, even if you must use two pages, the first is more crucial.

Resume appearance counts

Experts advise against using a resume preparation service. An employer can usually spot a "canned" resume and might assume that the applicant lacks initiative or self-confidence. The time you spend writing your resume will be time well spent. It will give you the opportunity to summarize what you have to offer to an employer.

Personal computers and resume writing or word processing software can help turn an average-looking resume into a class act. If possible, store your resume in a digital format for easy retrieval and updating. Many print shops have personal computers available for an hourly fee.

Although offset printing was once the preferred method of producing resumes, quick copies made at professional copy centers are now acceptable if they are reproduced on high-quality equipment and are clean and free of smudges. Use an attractive bond paper for these copies of your resume; usually a neutral color such as ivory or white is best. Copy centers typically have a wide selection of stationery available. It is advisable to have a career counselor, potential employer, family member, or friend review a draft of your resume before you duplicate your final copy. Ask for a careful check of content, format, grammar, spelling, and appearance. Even if you plan to send your resume electronically via e-mail, make sure it is completely error-free.

Electronic Resumes

Whether you prepare your resume yourself or have it prepared professionally, once you have a document you can be proud to send to potential employers, you will need to make slight modifications to create the scannable version. Electronic resumes are entered into a resume bank, which means they are subject to electronic, as well as human, scanning. You may need to create two or more versions of your resume, emphasizing various skills and key words.

You will find this process easier if your resume is on computer disk. You are then free to copy it and make changes to the copy. This allows you to keep your hard work safe and protected in the original file. If your resume is prepared professionally, you will also want to have the service prepare an electronic version, or you may request a disk containing the file, so you may create the electronic version yourself if you feel competent to do so. The key is to work from a copy—not the original!

Another reason to have your resume on disk is that employers and online resume distribution services often have different requirements for file formats and design specifications. The Website for an online resume distribution service or potential employer will provide you with company-specific details; it may also offer assistance in preparing this very important promotional piece about you. The human resources department of a potential employer may also be able to provide you with electronic resume information.

Although it is highly recommended that your traditional resume be no more than one page, your electronic resume may be longer. The computer will easily scan more than one page. It uses all the information on your resume to determine if your skills match available positions. The computer searches for key words. Those key words can often be found in a general job description matching the position title for which you are applying. They also appear in classified ads and job postings. Or you may be able to glean some during information interviews. Be sure to write your resume to reflect the skill needs of the position—another reason why you may want to prepare multiple versions of your resume.

Please refer to the box titled "Guidelines for Preparing and Submitting Electronic Resumes" for detailed how-to information. You may wish to learn more about electronic resumes. Your college career center, many books on the subject, and job-search Internet sites (see Chapter 9) are excellent sources for additional information.

Types of Resumes

To reiterate, there are three general types of resume: functional, chronological, and combination. Comparing the two sample work experience entries in the box on page 274 (taken from

SUCCESS STRATEGIES

Guidelines for preparing and submitting electronic resumes

- Your resume will likely be viewed with 80-character lines and 24 lines to a screen page.

- Use an 8 ½" × 11" page format. (If you plan to fax it, print it on white paper.)

- Use an easy-to-read typeface (font), such as Times, Helvetica, or Courier, at a point size of 11 or 12.

- Avoid tabs (use the space key), underlining, boxes, columns, italics, and shading. Also avoid boldface, vertical or horizontal lines, columns, graphics, and bullets.

- Use capital letters for section headings. Use commonly recognized headings such as the ones shown in this book.

- Use key skill words from a job description or advertisement. Key words are normally nouns rather than action verbs. Key words indicate

qualifications and knowledge. For example, an administrative assistant might use key words such as *data entry*, *filing*, *database management*, *word processing*, and *Microsoft Office Professional*.

- Some resume banks offer fill-in-the-blank templates, complete with instructions.

- Be concise, but you may use more than one page if necessary. The computer can handle multiple-page resumes.

- E-mail a copy of your resume to yourself to see what it looks like. (You can do this from an Internet site that allows you to create your own resume using this format.) When including a resume in the body of an e-mail, use a 65-character line with a hard return at the end of every line.

Exhibits 10.5 and 10.11) will give you some idea of the basic difference between functional and chronological resumes. The next part of this chapter will discuss all three types in detail. The combination resume, as the name implies, is a combination of functional and chronological.

The Functional Resume

A functional resume presents your experience, skills, and job history in terms of the functions you have actually performed rather than as a simple chronological listing of the titles of jobs you have held. Like any resume, it should be tailored to fit the main tasks and competencies required by the job you are seeking. Essentially, you redefine your past experiences according to the functions in the job for which you are applying. You should select and emphasize those activities from previous employment that relate to the specific job sought and deemphasize or omit irrelevant background.

For example, an administrative assistant might perform some administration, communications, and clerical functions. A secretary for an elementary school rewrote his resume to highlight these categories. In order to better define the skills used in his secretarial job, he researched the job description of executive secretary and office manager in his school personnel manual and located the description of administrative assistant

Resume Template

Name
Address
Phone Number/E-mail Address

Job Objective

State and describe your objective as specifically as possible. Refer to O*NET or the *Dictionary of Occupational Titles* for appropriate descriptive vocabulary.

Education

Depending on your job objective and the amount of education you have had, you may want to place this category directly after Job Objective. (However, if your job experience is more relevant to the position or if your education is not recent, you will want to list job experience *prior* to education.) The most recent education should be listed first. Include relevant credentials and licenses.

As employers, educational institutions are usually more concerned with appropriate degrees than are other employers. Include special workshops, noncredit courses, and self-taught skills when they are appropriate to your job objective.

Experience

Describe *functionally* (by activities performed) your experience relevant to the particular job for which you are applying; start with the most relevant and go to the less relevant. Include without distinction actual job experience, volunteer experience, your work on class projects, and school and class offices held. Alternatively, show your experience *chronologically*, listing your most recent professional experience first.

There is no need to stress dates unless they indicate that you have been continuously advancing toward this job objective.

Use action verbs; do not use full sentences, unless you decide to write your resume as a narrative.

Use the *Dictionary of Occupational Titles* or O*NET to help you describe accurately what you have done, always keeping in mind how your experience relates to your job objective. Remember to use words and skills related to your job objective to describe yourself in the cover letter and during the interview. (See Chapter 5.)

Special Skills

Put this optional category directly after Job Objective if you feel that your professional experience does not adequately reflect the talents you have that best support this job objective.

Examples: Facility with numbers, manual dexterity, patience, workshops you have led, writing ability, self-taught skills, language fluency.

References

Include references only if you have space and if the names are well known to potential employers.

SAMPLE FUNCTIONAL ENTRY
UNDER PROFESSIONAL EXPERIENCE

Budgeting/Financial

Analyzed and coordinated payroll recordkeeping, budgeted expenditures, requisitioned supplies, prepared attendance accounting reports, and initiated budget system for $10,000 of instructional monies allocated to the school.

SAMPLE CHRONOLOGICAL ENTRY
UNDER PROFESSIONAL EXPERIENCE

Sales Associate

Builders Emporium, Wadsworth, Texas 76199, 2005–Present

Operated cash register and made change, worked well with public, motivated fellow employees, encouraged customers to buy products.

in the *Dictionary of Occupational Titles*. (See the section titled "Suggestions for Job Descriptions" that follows.) He then compiled his resume to show how his executive secretarial responsibilities relate to the administrative assistant position desired. (See the functional resume in Exhibit 10.5.) Review the organizational divisions described in Chapter 7 to assess how your past work or life experience can be described in such categories as marketing, human resources, finance, community services, or research and development.

Suggestions for Job Descriptions

Descriptions in the *Dictionary of Occupational Titles*, in O*NET, and in some personnel manuals provide helpful phrases and statements to use in describing your own job history and experience. The following two descriptions, for example, would be useful to you in composing a functional resume for a job in business. However, you would use only relevant sentences, adapting them to your personal background.

Office Manager

Coordinates activities of clerical personnel in the organization. Analyzes and organizes office operations and procedures such as word processing, bookkeeping, preparation of payrolls, flow of correspondence, filing, requisitioning of supplies, and other clerical services. Evaluates office production, revises procedures, or devises new forms to improve efficiency of work flow. Establishes uniform correspondence procedures and style practices. Formulates procedures for systematic retention, protection, retrieval, transfer, and disposal of records. Plans office layouts and initiates cost reduction programs. Reviews clerical and personnel records to ensure completeness, accuracy, and timeliness. Prepares activity reports for guidance of management. Prepares employee ratings and conducts employee benefits and insurance programs. Coordinates activities of various clerical departments or workers within department.

Administrative Assistant

Aids executive in staff capacity by coordinating office services such as personnel, budget preparation and control, housekeeping, records control, and special management studies. Studies management methods in order to improve work flow, simplify reporting procedures, and implement cost reductions. Analyzes unit operating practices, such as recordkeeping systems, forms control, office layout, suggestion systems, personnel and budgetary requirements, and performance standards, to create new systems or revise established procedures. Analyzes jobs to delineate position responsibilities for use in wage and salary adjustments, promotions, and evaluation of work flow. Studies methods of improving work measurements or performance standards.

If you are applying for a specific job, ask the human resources department for a copy of the job description; then tailor your resume to the skills listed in that description.

If you really want to succeed, double your failure rate.

THOMAS J. WATSON

Creative Functional Resume

Beginning or returning workers who have had no paid experience often find it particularly hard to make their activities sound transferable to the world of work. They dismiss their experience as academic work or homemaking, which they mistakenly think differs markedly from work in business. However, they usually have been performing business functions without realizing it. People without paid work experience and people returning to the job market after taking time out to be homemakers can persuade employers to recognize their ability and practical experience if they describe their life in categories such as these:

MANAGEMENT

- Coordinated the multiple activities of five people of different ages and varying interests, keeping within tight schedules and continuous deadlines.
- Established priorities for the allocation of available time, resources, and funds.

OFFICE PROCEDURES

- Maintained lists of daily appointments, reminders, items to be purchased, people to be called, tasks to be accomplished.
- Handled all business and personal correspondence—answered and issued invitations, wrote to stores about defective merchandise, made hotel reservations.

PERSONNEL

- Recruited, hired, trained, and supervised household staff; negotiated wages.
- Motivated children to assume responsibilities and helped them develop self-confidence.
- Resolved problems caused by low morale and lack of cooperation.

FINANCES

- Established annual household budget, and monitored costs to stay within budget.
- Balanced the checkbook and reconciled monthly bank statements.
- Calculated take-home pay of household staff, made quarterly reports to the government on Social Security taxes withheld.

PURCHASING

- Undertook comparison shopping for food, clothing, furniture, and equipment, and purchased at various stores at different times, depending on best value.

- Planned meals according to savings available at different food stores.
- Shopped for insurance and found lower premiums than current coverage, resulting in substantial savings.

Pros and Cons of the Functional Resume

The functional resume is especially useful if you have limited work experience or breaks in your employment record, or if you are changing fields. You need not include dates or distinguish paid activities from nonpaid volunteer activities. By omitting or deemphasizing previous employers' names, you downplay any stereotyped assumptions that a prospective employer may make about previous employers (McDonald's, the PTA, a school district). Similarly, highlighting skills and deemphasizing job titles help direct the future employer to the fact that you are someone with specific abilities that may be useful in the present job opening. This format also can emphasize your growth and development.

To use this format effectively, you must be able to identify and write about your achievements. This sometimes requires the assistance of an expert resume writer. Additionally, some employers may prefer resumes that include exact dates and job titles.

Exhibits 10.5, 10.6, 10.7, and 10.8 (at the end of this chapter) are examples of functional resumes for various positions.

The Chronological Resume

The chronological resume is the traditional and most frequently used resume style. It lists your work history in reverse chronological order, meaning the most recent position or occupation is listed first. The work history should include dates employed, job title, job duties, and employer's name, address, and telephone number.

Pros and Cons of the Chronological Resume

The chronological resume is most useful for people with no breaks in their employment record and for whom each new position indicates continuous advancement or growth. Recent high school and college graduates also find this approach simpler than creating a functional resume.

As dates tend to dominate the presentation, any breaks or undocumented years of work may stand out. If your present position is not related to the job you desire, you may be eliminated from the competition by employers who feel that current experience is the most important consideration in reviewing resumes. However, if you emphasize skills in your present job that will be important to the new position, this will be less of a problem.

Exhibits 10.9, 10.10, 10.11, and 10.12 (at the end of this chapter) are examples of chronological resumes tailored to various positions.

Obstacles are what a person sees when he takes his eyes off his goal.

E. JOSEPH CROSSMAN

The Combination Resume

If you have major skills important for success in your desired job in addition to an impressive record of continuous job experience with reputable employers, you can best highlight this double advantage with a *combination* of the functional and chronological styles of resume. This combination style usually lists functions followed by years employed with a list of employers. The combination style also satisfies the employer who wants to see the dates that you were actually employed. See Exhibits 10.13 and 10.14.

Cover Letter Guidelines

Want to turn off a prospective employer? Send a resume with no cover letter. Or send a form letter addressed to Personnel Manager. Or address your letter Dear Sir, only to have it received by a female manager.

A cover letter announces your availability and introduces the resume. It is probably one of the most important self-advertisements you will write.

The cover letter should indicate you have researched the organization and are clearly interested in a position there. Let the person to whom you are writing know what sources you used and what you know about the firm in the first paragraph—to get his or her attention and show your interest.

You may have heard people say, "It's not *what* you know, but *who* you know that counts." This is only partly true, but nonetheless important. You can often get to know someone with only a little effort.

An accurate, well-written, and personalized cover letter can help your resume stand out from the many others a manager will review.

Call or, better yet, visit the organization and talk to people who already hold the job you want. Be tactful and discreet, of course. You're not trying to take their position from them. See the section titled "Interviewing for Information" in Chapter 9. Ask about training, environment, salary, and other relevant issues. Then in your cover letter, mention that you talked with some of the firm's employees, and that these discussions increased your interest. You thereby show the reader you took the initiative to visit the company and that you know someone, if only casually. This is all part of networking, as discussed in Chapter 9.

Basic principles of letter and resume writing include being self-confident when listing your positive qualities and attributes, writing as one professional to another, and having your materials properly prepared. The next page offers a cover letter template.

First, address your letter to a specific person, with the name spelled correctly and the proper title. These details count. Your opening paragraph should contain the "hook." Arouse some work-related interest. Explain (very briefly) why you are writing. How did you become interested in that company? Summarize what you have to offer. Details of your background can show why you should be considered as a job candidate. The self-appraisal that went into preparation of your resume tells what you *can*

Resume Cover Letter Template

Address
City, State, ZIP
Phone/E-mail
Date

Name of Person
Company Name
Street Address or P.O. Box
City, State, ZIP

Salutation   (Dear M _____: or Greetings:)

The first paragraph should indicate the job you are interested in and how you heard about it. Use the names of contact persons here, if you have any.

Sample Entry   Your employment advertisement in Tuesday's *News Chronicle* indicating an opening for an administrative assistant is of special interest to me. Mary Smith, who is employed with your firm, suggested I write to you. I have heard that Rohn Electronics is a growing company and needs dynamic employees who want to learn and contribute to the firm.

The second paragraph should relate your experience, skills, and background to the particular position. Refer to your enclosed resume for details, and highlight the specific skills and competencies that could be useful to the company.

Sample Entry   During the last five years, I worked as office manager. In this position, I improved office efficiency by investigating and selecting word processing equipment. I understand that your opening includes responsibilities for supervising and coordinating word processing systems with your home office. I was able to reduce my firm's operating costs over 30 percent by selecting the best equipment for our purposes.

The third paragraph should indicate your plans for follow-up contact and that your resume is enclosed.

Sample Entry   I would appreciate the opportunity to apply my skills on behalf of your company. For your examination, I have enclosed a resume indicating my education and work experience. I will call your office early next week to determine a convenient time for an appointment to further discuss possible employment opportunities.

Sincerely,

NOTE: Don't forget
to sign the letter.

Your first and last name
Enclosure (or Attachment)

and *like* to do and where your strengths and interests lie. Your research on the prospective employer should have uncovered the qualifications needed. If your letter promises a good match—meaning your abilities match the company's needs—you've attracted attention.

Keep your letter short and to the point. Refer to your resume, highlighting relevant experiences and accomplishments that match the firm's stated needs. Ask for an interview. Indicate when you will be calling to confirm a convenient time for the interview. Let your letter express your individuality but within the context of the employment situation.

The cover letter should be individually typed for each job. Always review both the cover letter and resume for good margins, clarity, correct spelling, and accurate typing. Appearance does count! Review the sample cover letters in Exhibits 10.16 through 10.20, following the exercises.

Application Forms

A final type of form, accepted sometimes as a substitute for a resume, is an *application form*. The employment application is a form used by most companies to gain necessary information and to register applicants for work (see Exhibit 10.2). This information becomes a guide to determine a person's suitability for both the company and the job that needs filling. You should observe carefully the following guidelines when completing an application form.

You will probably be asked to fill out an employment application form before the interview takes place. Therefore, it is good practice to arrive at the employment office a little ahead of the time of your interview. Bring along a pen and your resume or a personal data sheet. You will be asked to provide your name, address, training or education, experience, special abilities, and possibly even your hobbies and interests. Practically all application forms request that you state the job you are seeking and the salary you have received in the past. Most firms require an applicant to complete an application form.

Many times the employer wants to make certain rapid comparisons and needs only to review the completed company employment application forms on file. For example, Ms. Ford needed a secretary who could type fast. She examined many application forms of people who had word processing skills. By referring to the same section each time, she quickly thumbed through dozens of applications, eliminating all candidates who had only average speed. Thus, there was no need for her to examine resumes or read dozens of letters to find out exactly how fast each candidate could type.

FACTS & FIGURES

Resumes for international jobs

Resume and curriculum vita (CV) guidelines vary from country to country. However, some rules apply in most cases. For example, letters that accompany a resume or CV, known as cover letters in the United States, are called letters of interest in some countries and motivation letters in others. The best advice is to find out what's appropriate according to the corporation, the country culture, and the culture of the person making the hiring decision. Ask employers or recruiters for examples of resumes or CVs that they think are particularly good. One good source for examples is *The College Journal: Global Careers Section*. Otherwise, your university career center should have some good resources to use to adjust your resume or CV. Additionally, whenever you happen to be traveling in a country in which you think you might like to work someday, drop into the local college career center and inquire and collect job search information before you really need it!

SUCCESS STRATEGIES

Filling out application forms

(See the next page for a sample form.)

1. Fill out the application form in ink or word process.

2. Answer every question that applies to you. If a question does not apply or is illegal (see Chapter 11), you may write *N/A*, meaning *not applicable*, or draw a line through the space to show that you did not overlook the question.

3. Give your complete address, including ZIP code.

4. Spell correctly. If you aren't sure how to spell a word, use the dictionary or try to use another word with the same meaning.

5. A question on job preference or "job for which you are applying" should be answered with a specific job title or type of work. Do not write "anything." Employers expect you to state clearly what kind of work you can do.

6. Have a prepared list of schools attended and previous employers. Include addresses and dates of employment.

7. Be prepared to provide several good references. It is advisable to ask permission of those you plan to list. Good references can include a recognized community leader, a former employer or teacher who knows you well, and friends who are established in business.

8. When you write or sign your name on the application, use your formal name—not a nickname. Your first name, middle initial, and last name are usually preferred.

9. Be as neat as possible. Employers expect that your application will be an example of your best work.

Neatness Counts

The way in which an application form has been filled out indicates the applicant's level of neatness, thoroughness, and accuracy. If two applicants seem to have equal qualifications but one's form is carelessly filled out, the application itself might tilt the balance in favor of the other applicant. Unless your handwriting is especially clear, print or type all answers. Look for "please print" instructions on the form.

Sometimes you may apply for a job by mail, and a form will be sent to you. Fill out the application form carefully, completely, and accurately. When you have completed the application, go over it again. Have you given the information asked? When an item asked for is not applicable, have you written in *N/A*? Return the completed application to the company. You may attach a copy of your resume, if you wish.

Date _____

PERSONAL INFORMATION:

Name _____

Last   First   Middle

Address_____

Street   City   State   Zip

Telephone Number (_____) _____   Are you over 17 years of age? ☐ Yes ☐ No

POSITION WANTED:

Job Title _____   Date Available _____   Salary Desired _____

Check any that apply: ☐ Full Time   ☐ Part Time   ☐ Day Shift   ☐ Night Shift

EDUCATION:

Begin with high school; include any military school you may have attended:

NAME OF SCHOOL   LOCATION OF SCHOOL   DEGREE OR COURSE OF STUDY

_____

_____

List any academic honors or professional associations:

_____

_____

WORK EXPERIENCE:

List last three employers. Start with the current or most recent.

Name and Address of Employer _____

Dates Worked _____   Pay _____   Reason for Leaving _____

Job Title _____   Job Description _____

Name and Address of Employer _____

Dates Worked _____   Pay _____   Reason for Leaving _____

Job Title _____   Job Description _____

Name and Address of Employer _____

Dates Worked _____   Pay _____   Reason for Leaving _____

Job Title _____   Job Description _____

Computer Skills (describe)   Typing Speed _____ *wpm*
   (if applicable)   (if applicable)

Do you have any physical condition or handicap that may limit your ability to perform the job applied for?   ☐ Yes ☐ No
If yes, what can be done to accommodate your limitation?

Have you ever been convicted of a felony? ☐ Yes   ☐ No   If yes, give kind and date.
A conviction will not necessarily disqualify you from employment.

Are you legally entitled to work in the U.S.? ☐ Yes ☐ No   Can you provide proof of citizenship after employment? ☐ Yes ☐ No

Are you a veteran? ☐ Yes ☐ No   If yes, give dates:

List the names of three references whom we may contact who have knowledge of your skills, talents, or technical knowledge:
(1)   *(2)*   *(3)*
Name and Relationship
(Supervisor, Teacher, etc.)
Address
Telephone & Area No.

I certify, by my signature below, that any false or omitted important facts in my answers on this application may be cause for dismissal.

_____   _____
Applicant's Signature   *Date*

Summary

This chapter has provided diverse examples of resumes and cover letters, as well as advice for filling out application forms. Putting the resume together is now your job. Use the exhibits and ideas in the following written exercises as well as the tips throughout the chapter to assist you in getting your resume into shape.

PREPARING A WINNING RESUME

PURPOSE OF EXERCISES. The exercises that follow will enable you to prepare a resume as well as critique it. Exercises 10.1 and 10.2 help you to organize pertinent information about yourself. Exercise 10.3 asks you to draft a resume. Exercise 10.4 reminds you to save copies of work for a portfolio. Exercises 10.5 and 10.6 provide guidelines for critiquing your own resume and obtaining valuable feedback from others. Exercise 10.7 reminds you to write a cover letter and get feedback before sending it.

Companion Website

To answer these questions online, go to the *Exercise* module in Chapter 10 of the Companion Website.

Resume Review Sheet   10.1

Fill in the review sheet on the following page. The answers will help you prepare a complete resume.

Create a Card File   10.2

Create a card file (or a computer file) describing your work experiences, using Exhibit 10.1 as a guide. This gives you a chance to write your job tasks in functional terms.

Write Your Resume   10.3

Choose the format desired and write your own resume, referring to Exercise 10.1 for data. Refer to the suggestions in the chapter and the samples that follow these exercises.

Save Sample Work for a Portfolio   10.4

Start now to keep a folder of the best work you have done in work-related classes and jobs, internships, and volunteer positions.

Resume/Portfolio Review

A. PERSONAL DATA

1. Name _____

2. Address _____

3. Phone _____

B. CURRENT JOB OBJECTIVE _____

C. EDUCATION

1. High school and college _____

   a. Favorite subjects _____

   b. Work samples _____

   c. Extracurricular interests _____

   d. Offices held _____

   e. Athletic achievements _____

   f. Other significant facts (e.g., honors, awards) _____

2. Other (military, volunteer, correspondence, summer work, languages, technical skills, licenses, and/or credentials)

D. WORK EXPERIENCE

Refer to your experiography or your skills analysis.

1. Employer _____

   Length of employment _____

   Position _____

   Skills/accomplishments/work samples _____

2. Employer _____

   Length of employment _____

   Position _____

   Skills/accomplishments/work samples _____

3. Employer _____

   Length of employment _____

   Position _____

   Skills/accomplishments/work samples _____

E. PUBLICATIONS _____

F. ASSOCIATIONS, SPECIAL SKILLS, AND COMMUNITY INVOLVEMENT

_____

G. REFERENCES (Do not include specific names on resume, but do homework regarding possible references *now*.)

_____

_____

Critique Your Resume   10.5

Use the resume checklist and critique form (Exhibit 10.3) to evaluate your resume.

Resume checklist and critique form.				EXHIBIT 10.3

	Strong	Average	Weak	Plans for Improvement
1. **Resume format.** Does it say "READ ME"?				
2. **Appearance.** Is it brief? Did you use a clear, engaging layout? Type clearly? Use a correct format?				
3. **Length.** Are the key points concise?				
4. **Significance.** Did you select your most relevant experiences?				
5. **Communication.** Do your words give the "visual" impression you want? Is the job objective clearly stated?				
6. **Conciseness.** Does your information focus on the experiences that qualify you for the position?				
7. **Completeness.** Did you include all important information? Have you made a connection between the job desired and your experience?				
8. **Accuracy.** Does the resume represent you well enough to get you an interview?				
9. **Skills.** Does your resume reflect the skills necessary for the job?				

10.6 *Ask Others to Critique Your Resume*

Ask other people (e.g., career counselors, those who have been receptive to you during informational interviews, teachers, friends) to give you feedback about your resume. Use the checklist of Dos and Don'ts in Exhibit 10.4 to help others give you feedback.

EXHIBIT 10.4   Resume DOs and DON'Ts.

DO

- Focus your job objective to illustrate specific skills and responsibilities.
- Interest your reader with significant employment, education, accomplishments, and skills.
- Present yourself positively, honestly, and assertively.
- Keep the resume to no more than two pages.
- Use an attractive and readable layout, including top-quality paper, for a professional appearance.
- Have your resume carefully proofread prior to its final printing.

DON'T

- Be too wordy or use buzzwords and unnecessary verbiage.
- Provide personal data on your age, race, marital status, religion, or other private matters.
- Suggest abilities or objectives beyond your reach or qualifications.
- Make reference to a desired salary or income.
- State a reason for leaving a previous job.
- Provide names of references in the resume.

10.7 *Write a Cover Letter*

Referring to Exhibits 10.16–10.20, write a cover letter to accompany your resume. Ask others to critique it, as you did in Exercise 10.6 with your resume.

WWWebwise **10.8**

For additional activities online, go to the WWWebwise module in Chapter 10 of the Companion Website.

Exercise Summary **10.9**

Write a brief paragraph answering these questions.

What did you learn about yourself from these exercises? How does this knowledge relate to your career/life planning? How do you feel?

_____

_____

_____

_____

_____

_____

_____

_____

_____

_____

_____

_____

_____

_____

_____

_____

_____

_____

_____

_____

_____

_____

_____

_____

_____

_____

EXHIBIT 10.5   Functional resume for an administrative assistant position.

SAMUEL GILDAR
P.O. Box 1111
Cincinnati, OH 14528

Day Phone: (513) 555-1212
E-mail: sgildar@aol.com

GOALS

To work as an administrative assistant in a creative
atmosphere and have the opportunity to use my abilities.

SUMMARY OF EXPERIENCE

Ten years of increasing responsibility in the area of office management involving organization, problem solving, finances, and public relations.

MANAGEMENT

Initiated and organized procedures used in the office, coordinated activities of clerical personnel, and formulated procedures for systematic retention, protection, transfer, and disposal of records. Coordinated preparation of operating reports, such as time and attendance records, of performance data. Reviewed, composed, and answered correspondence. Directed services, such as maintenance, repair, supplies, mail, and files. Aided executive by coordinating office services, such as personnel, budget preparation and control, housekeeping, records control, and special management studies.

PUBLIC RELATIONS

Coordinated communications with state, county, and district officials as well as district and local employees, student body, staff members, and parents in our community. Planned and coordinated social functions for school, staff, and two social clubs. Promoted sales of jewelry, gourmet foods, and liquors in sales-related jobs.

PROBLEM SOLVING

Made decisions according to district policy in the absence of the principal. Worked under constant pressure and interruption while attending to student problems regarding their health and welfare. Served as liaison between school and community, resolving as many problems as possible before referring them to superior.

BUDGETING/FINANCIAL

Analyzed and coordinated payroll recordkeeping, budgeted expenditures, requisitioned supplies, prepared attendance accounting reports, and initiated budget system for $10,000 of instructional monies allocated to the school.

CREATIVE

Created news copy and layouts using PageMaker and QuarkXPress. Designed fliers, posters, calendars, and bulletins sent home from school to parents. Personal hobbies include ceramics, oil painting, sculpting, and interior design.

EMPLOYERS

Cincinnati Unified School District
1115 Old School Road
Cincinnati, OH 14528
(513) 555-2345

Cincinnati Blue Cross
5900 Erwin Road
Cincinnati, OH 14526
(513) 555-3698

OLIVIA MARTINEZ
2406 Adams Avenue
Los Angeles, CA 90025
213-555-0862
e-mail: om@msn.com

PROFESSIONAL OBJECTIVE:

Management position utilizing administrative, communications, and research skills.

SUMMARY OF SKILLS:

Administrative

Designed and implemented evaluation program for compensatory education project.

Coauthored grant proposal.

Served as liaison between volunteers and university administration.

Directed registration program and coordinated staff at registration desk, Western Psychological Association Annual Convention, 2004.

As student senator, initiated Earth Day activities and helped establish faculty evaluation program.

Communications

Planned discussion sections, provided guidance to students, cowrote and graded examinations for undergraduate courses in developmental psychology and statistics.

Prepared tutorials in science and study methods and offered educational guidance to economically disadvantaged high school students.

Participated in human growth seminar led by clinical psychologist, trained in therapy methods, and helped devise therapy program for young people.

Research

Designed and conducted study investigating memory in four-year-olds.

Studied mathematical structure underlying Piagetian developmental theory.

Implemented computer simulation model of certain cognitive behaviors of children. Analyzed and categorized data for cognitive anthropologist and psychologist.

EDUCATION:

M.A., August 2006 Developmental Psychology, University of California, Los Angeles, California. California State Graduate Fellow, National Science Foundation Honorable Mention.

B.A., 2004 Psychology, University of California, Irvine. *Summa Cum Laude*, Outstanding Scholar, Honor Scholar.

EXPERIENCE:

Teaching Assistant and Reader. Psychology Department, University of California, Los Angeles, August 2003–June 2004.

Administrative Assistant. Psychology Department, California State University, Fullerton, February–June 2003.

Business Manager, Education Motivation. Community Projects Office, University of California, Irvine, August 2002–January 2003.

Research Assistant. Departments of German and Russian, University of California, Irvine, October 2000–June 2001.

EXHIBIT 10.7 Functional resume for a teacher changing careers.

STACY L. MOLLARD

1001 Gainsborough Street
Chicago, IL 60664

stacymollard@cox.net

312-555-3581 (home)
312-555-4343 (work)

POSITION OBJECTIVE:

Employee Training Specialist

QUALIFICATIONS IN BRIEF:

B.A. in English, Mundelein College, Chicago.

Six years' elementary teaching with experience in communications, human relations, instruction, and supervision.

Bilingual (English, Spanish).

EXPERIENCE SUMMARY:

COMMUNICATIONS:

Conducted staff development workshops; presented new curriculum plans to parent groups, sent periodic progress reports to parents, and developed class newsletter; presented workshops in parent effectiveness training at state and local conferences.

HUMAN RELATIONS:

Directed effective problem solving/conflict resolution between individual students and student groups; initiated program of student self-governance; acted as liaison between families of diverse cultural, ethnic, and economic backgrounds and school personnel/services; conducted individual and group conferences to establish rapport with parents and discuss student progress.

INSTRUCTION:

Developed instructional modules to solve specific learning problems; developed instructional audiovisual materials; used audiovisual equipment such as overhead, opaque, and movie projectors and audio- and videocassettes; did extensive research in various curricula; served as a member of curriculum development committee; introduced new motivational techniques for students.

CURRENTLY EMPLOYED:

Austin Elementary School, Chicago, Illinois

COMMUNITY INVOLVEMENT:

Board member, Chicago Community Services Center

Allocations Committee, Chicago United Way

ABDUL MUHAMMED

66 Cheyenne Dr.
Billings, MT 46060
(712) 555-1212
abdulm@earthlink.net

Professional Objective

Administrative assistant position utilizing administrative, bookkeeping, and communications skills.

Summary of Skills

Administrative

Answered phones, scheduled appointments, sorted mail, filed
Implemented new filing and retrieval system
Software programs used include Windows XP and Office Professional XP
Maintained appearance of office

Bookkeeping

Handled cash register
Closed cash register at the end of the evening
Recorded cash transactions

Communications

Served as peer counselor for 2 years
Assisted in dental office
Demonstrated proper dental hygiene to children
Fed, clothed, and entertained children

Education

Billings Community College, Transfer Program, 2005 to present, Dean's List
Billings High School, graduated 2004

Experience

Lombard Medical Group, Billings, MT, October 2005–present
Sandy Murphree, Billings, MT, February 2004–present
Oakbrook Dental, Billings, MT, June 2003–October 2003
Fantastic Sam's, Billings, MT, June 2001–August 2002

JOHN JONES
(480) 555-1221

1050 Baez Street
Mesa, AZ 85201
jj123@aol.com

OBJECTIVE:	An entry-level position as a salesperson that affords opportunities to learn and progress.
SUMMARY:	Three years of part-time and summer employment related to sales, public contact, and accounting while attending high school.
EDUCATION:	2006 Red Mountain High School, Mesa, Arizona

Graduated with emphasis in mathematics and business.

Courses included:

Word processing	Trigonometry
Excel	Geometry
English	Business math
Journalism	Accounting principles
Algebra	

EXPERIENCE: 2004–2006 Mesa General Store, Mesa, Arizona

Salesperson. Sold apparel in men's and children's departments.

2003–2004 Tower Records & Video, Mesa, Arizona

Counterperson. Assisted customer selections. Handled monetary transactions.

2001–2002 Miscellaneous employment: babysat for four families with one to four children. Stayed with children weekends and while parents were on vacation, and assumed full responsibility for normal household routines.

HONORS: Vice president, Future Business Managers Association, 2005–2006

ACTIVITIES: Future Business Managers Association, Journalism Club, Student Tutoring Association, Young Republicans Club

THUY NGUYEN

532 Castilian Court   (206) 799-1212 (Home)
Seattle, WA 98102   (206) 555-1212 (Work)
                                                      thuynguyen@netstar.net

---

OCCUPATIONAL OBJECTIVE:

A position as office manager leading to increased responsibilities for business operations.

SUMMARY OF QUALIFICATIONS:

Three years of increasingly responsible experience in different positions.

BOOKKEEPER   *Hungry Hunter and El Torito Restaurants*
                                                  Seattle, WA 2005 to present

Kept records of financial transactions, entering them in computer. Balanced books and compiled reports to show statistics, such as cash receipts and expenditures, accounts payable and receivable, and other items pertinent to operation of business. Calculated employee wages from time cards and updated computerized records.

RESTAURANT GREETER   *Hungry Hunter Restaurant*
                                              Thousand Oaks, CA 2003–2005

Welcomed guests, seated them in dining area, maintained quality of facilities. Directed others in performing courteous and rapid service; also assisted in settling complaints. Related well with the continuous flow of people, coordinating the service with customers' needs.

SPECIAL ACCOMPLISHMENTS:

National Forensic League, vice president (third place, statewide oratory competition); Athletic Association (gymnastic team); Honor Roll and Dean's List; Alpha Gamma Sigma; *Who's Who Among American High School Students,* 2002–2003.

EDUCATION:

Seattle Pacific University, Seattle, WA

Majoring in Business Administration

GPA: 3.5 on a 4.0 scale

EXHIBIT 10.11 Chronological resume for a bank teller position.

ELEANOR RUTLEDGE
3388 North Dallas
Wadsworth, TX 77065
909-555-0026
eprutledge@theriver.net

JOB OBJECTIVE:	A position as a bank teller that offers opportunities to learn and progress.

EDUCATION:

2005 to present—Glencoe College, Dallas, Texas
Courses included:

Accounting	Sociology 1
Business Computers	English 1A
Excel	

2005—Wadsworth High School, Wadsworth, Texas
Graduated with Honors; Treasurer for Honor Society
Courses included:

Windows 2000	Algebra
English	Geometry
Public Speaking	

SPECIAL SKILLS:

Facility with numbers, manual dexterity, patience, excellence in telephone communications, organized fund-raisers for church group.

EXPERIENCE:

2004 to present—Cashier, Builders Emporium, Wadsworth, Texas. Operated cash register and made change, worked well with public, motivated fellow employees, encouraged customers to buy products.

2002–2003—Miscellaneous employment: babysat for local families; assumed full responsibility while parents were away; helped children with their homework.

SARITA SANDHA
980 Victory Blvd.
Brooklyn, NY 11321
(405) 555-4150
ssandha@aol.com

JOB OBJECTIVE:	**Public Representative or Community Service Worker**
SUMMARY OF QUALIFICATIONS:	Six years' experience in public relations, media work, and writing press releases and newsletters. Organized concerts, rallies, walk-a-thons, and volunteer-a-thons. Basic qualifications in office procedures: phone networking, word processing, mailing, leafletting, outreach, and public speaking.
EDUCATION:	**Brooklyn College, currently attending, 2005–present** Sociology major. Additional specialized institute training at Loyola Marymount University in social organizing. Two years as teacher's aide in New York City school system. Interrelated with a variety of cultural groups. **Alemany High School, graduated**
EXPERIENCE:	**2004 to present Community service organizations in New York** Organized, educated, persuaded, created social change, raised over $25,000 and performed security work. **2002–2004 Self-employed** Managed and maintained family residence. **2000–2002 Receptionist and secretary** Interviewed applicants for positions in sales, maintained records, answered phones, and performed light clerical work.
SPECIAL SKILLS:	Interact easily with diverse people while under pressure. Knowledge of fund-raising practices. Self-motivated. Experienced in analyzing and working with issues and strategies underlying a particular campaign. Computer literate.

EXHIBIT 10.13   Combination resume for a sales executive position.

JOHN BENNETT   (803) 555-3692 (w)
304 Amen Street   (803) 555-1126 (h)
Columbia, SC 29260   E-mail: jben@msn.com

OBJECTIVE

MARKETING DIRECTOR

SALES PROMOTION

Designed and supervised sales promotion projects for large business firms and manufacturers, mostly in the electronics field. Originated newspaper, radio, and television advertising. Coordinated sales promotion with public relations and sales management. Analyzed market potentials, and developed new techniques to increase sales effectiveness and reduce sales costs. Created sales training manuals.

As sales executive and promotion consultant, handled a great variety of accounts. Sales potentials in these firms varied from $100,000 to $5 million per annum. Raised the volume of sales in many of these firms 25 percent within the first year.

SALES MANAGEMENT

Hired and supervised sales staff on local, area, and national bases. Established branch offices throughout the United States. Developed uniform systems of processing orders and maintaining sales records. Promoted new products, as well as improved sales of old ones. Developed sales training program. Devised a catalog system involving inventory control to facilitate movement of scarce stock between branches.

MARKET RESEARCH

Originated and supervised market research projects to determine sales potential, as well as need for advertising. Wrote detailed reports and recommendations describing each step in distribution, areas for development, and plans for sales improvement.

SALES

Retail and wholesale. Direct sales to consumer, jobber, and manufacturer. Hard goods, small metals, and electrical appliances.

EMPLOYERS

2004–Present	B. B. Bowen Sales Development Co., Columbia, South Carolina	Sales Executive
2001–2004	James Bresher Commercial and Industrial Sales Research Corp., Oakland, California	Senior Sales Promotion Manager
1998–2001	Dunnock Brothers Electronics Co., San Francisco, California	Order Clerk, Salesworker, Sales Manager

EDUCATION

University of California, Berkeley, B.S.; Major: Business Administration

ALBERT CHAN
111 East Maple
Minneapolis, MN
(508) 866-1592 • albertchan34@aol.com

JOB OBJECTIVE	Programmer Trainee or Junior Programmer
QUALIFICATIONS BY EXPERIENCE	Flowcharted, coded, tested, and debugged interactive programs for the HP3000. Created a system of five programs from a system problem statement and flowchart. Built a KSAM file for use by the system. Designed system flowcharts and wrote other documentation for improved payroll system for previous employer, as Systems Analysis course project.
	Tutored students in Visual BASIC, C+ and C++, working with Hispanics, Vietnamese, and reentering adults, as well as other students.
	Currently creating a bibliographic database as a volunteer at Minneapolis Public Library and designed library's Web page.
EDUCATION	2006 Associate in Science Degree in Computer Science, Minneapolis Central College. Courses included UNIX and C++.
	3.6 GPA in computer science classes.
	2002 B.A. in English, Florida Southern College.
	Graduate work in research methods.
	Supported self through college by security work at various firms. Gained secret clearance while at IBM Federal System Division.
SPECIAL SKILLS	Attentive to detail, organized, work well with little supervision, enterprising, enjoy problem-solving and interacting with others to plan projects, work well under pressure, able to see relationships between abstract ideas, good at communication, concise.
COMMUNITY SERVICE EXPERIENCE	Organized CROP Walks (fund-raisers for Church World Service), which resulted in raising $6,000 in 2005 and $10,000 in 2006.
	Chaired the planning committee, recruited members, mapped walk route.
	Obtained parade permits and business tax exemptions.
	Wrote press releases and walkers' instruction sheets.

EXHIBIT 10.15   A poorly constructed resume. (see corrected version on the following page).

Omit entirely

1 PROFESSIONAL EXPERIENCE AND TRAINING OF SARA CRANE:
SOCIAL CASE WORKER

Place name, address, phone on
top of page in correct format;
include e-mail address

2 4234 S. Platt Avenue, Salt Lake City, Utah 84100 (801) 765-4321

List as job objective, with
specific summary

3 Social case worker with RN degree wants a responsible position
with a large medical firm that could benefit from my experience in
both nursing and social work.

EXPERIENCE

Edit and highlight key
responsibilities

4 2004–present . . . Family caseworker. Working through Parker General
Hospital Services in Salt Lake. Worked directly with families at
their homesites. Met with family and formulated a plan after con-
sultation and comprehensive investigation of needs. Developed
assistance and support as appropriate with follow-up services.

Same as #4

5 2000–2004 . . . RN and convalescent services. Grandjunction, Utah.
Treated patients with disabilities. Reviewed financial aspects
and fee payments, all inpatient and outpatient services, and full
family participation in health program to ensure cooperation
and support.

EDUCATION

1994–2000 . . . Bachelor of Science. Social Work. Brigham Young
School of Social Work. Training in all areas of social work including internships in pediatrics, psychiatric, rehabilitation, and
gerontology sections.

Omit years (if over 10) and
reduce excess words

6 1990–1994 . . . Registered Nurse. Baker College, Salt Lake City, Utah.
General nursing curriculum including family health concerns. Took
additional courses in specialized nursing for retired patients and
also advanced psychiatric techniques. I realized that my experience and interests were becoming directed into social work.

PROFESSIONAL AFFILIATIONS

The National Association of Case and Social Workers

INTERESTS

Too wordy and unrelated to
job objective. Edit to highlight language ability.

7 Travel and reading. Conversational abilities in Spanish and French,
including reading knowledge. Good cook and enjoy theater productions. Any references regarding my education or work experience

Separate and edit

8 may be requested at any time.

SARA CRANE
4234 S. Platt Avenue
Salt Lake City, UT 84100
(801) 765-4321
scrane@earthlink.net

JOB OBJECTIVE

Social Worker utilizing skills developed as a Registered Nurse and Financial Planner

EXPERIENCE

Family Caseworker. Parker General Hospital, Salt Lake City, Utah, 2005

Report to Social Services Director of largest family assistance program in Salt Lake City, attached to hospital intake services. Duties include:

- Interviewing family members at the hospital and in their homes to determine needs.
- Investigating claims and proposing plans for assistance.
- Counseling and guiding families in special circumstances, including personal and health issues.
- Providing follow-up treatment and reports.

Convalescent Service as an RN. Grandjunction Hospital, Grandjunction, Utah, 2000–2004.

Reported to Health Services Center with following responsibilities:

- Interviewed patients' families to determine financial capabilities.
- Arranged fee structures.
- Planned outpatient plan and referral services.
- Counseled families for inpatient and/or convalescent needs.

EDUCATION

Bachelor of Science, Social Work, Brigham Young University, School of Social Work, Provo, Utah.

Internships in pediatric, psychiatric, rehabilitation, and gerontology sections.
Additional courses in Financial Planning.

Registered Nurse, Baker College, Salt Lake City, Utah.

Full training in general nursing with specialization in psychiatric nursing. Workshops in family health led to social work career path.

SPECIAL SKILLS/AFFILIATIONS

Fluency in Spanish and French. Membership in the National Association of Case and Social Workers.

EXHIBIT 10.16   Cover letter for a community health worker position.

March 4, 2006

Mr. Harvey J. Finder
Executive Director
Lung Association of Alma County
1717 Opportunity Way
Santa Ana, CA 92706

Dear Mr. Finder:

I am interested in the position of community health education program coordinator with the Lung Association of Alma County. I feel that my education, skills, and desire to work in this area make me a strong candidate for this position.

My education has helped me develop sound analytical abilities and has exposed me to the health-care field. My involvement with health-care and community organizations has provided me with a working knowledge of various public and private health institutions, which has increased my ability to communicate effectively with health-care professionals, patients, and the community at large. This combination of education and exposure has stimulated my interest in seeking a career in the health-care field.

Please review the enclosed resume and contact me at your convenience regarding a personal interview. If I do not hear from you in the next week, I will contact you. I look forward to talking with you.

Sincerely yours,

Denise M. Hunter
18411 Anticipation Drive
Northridge, CA 91330
(213) 555-0217
DMH@hotmail.com

Enclosures

532 Glendora Avenue
Anytown, IN 45420
April 1, 2006

Ms. Joan Addeman
Director of Personnel
ABC Corporation
Anytown, MO 90000

Dear Ms. Addeman:

I am applying for the administrative assistant position currently available at your firm. I have been impressed for some time with the outstanding reputation that ABC Corporation holds in our community.

As you read my resume, please note that my twelve years of business experience directly relate to the needs of your company. One of my greatest assets is seven years in motivational psychology related to personnel management and public school teaching. I am aware that strength in business and management is considered important in your firm, and I would like the opportunity to discuss with you, at your earliest convenience, how we might work together for our mutual benefit.

Enclosed is my resume for your review. I will telephone your secretary next week to see when we might set up an appointment to further discuss the administrative assistant position and any other ways that I could serve your corporation.

Sincerely,

Fatima Nasser

Enclosure: Resume

EXHIBIT 10.18   Cover letter for an electronics technician position.

412 Melbrook Avenue
Omaha, NE 77050
June 17, 2006

Mr. Lloyd Johnson
Sonat Technical Supervisor
Lear Electronic Company
1229 Van Owen
Knoxville, TN 37917

Dear Mr. Johnson:

I am interested in working for your company as an electronics technician in the field of systems installation and calibration.

During my tour of duty in the service, I became acquainted with many of your electronic systems aboard ship and was extremely impressed with their design and documentation. I have since pursued a course of studies at Hastings College to increase my competence in the field of electronics. For these reasons, I feel I would be an asset to your company.

I have enclosed a copy of my resume for your consideration. I will contact you by telephone next week to set up a meeting to discuss employment opportunities with your company.

Sincerely yours,

Emilio Reyna

Enclosure

1234 Evanston Avenue
Cambridge, IL 61238
May 16, 2006

Mr. Harrison MacBuren
Director of Personnel
North Hills Mall
Cambridge, IL 61238

Dear Mr. MacBuren:

I am very interested in the position currently available in your public relations department for an assistant to the director of public relations.

As you can see by my resume, my previous administrative experience would be a definite asset to your company. I feel that a vital part of any public relations job is the ability to deal with people. This is a skill I have acquired through many years of volunteer work.

I would like to meet with you to discuss how we might work together for our mutual benefit. I will be contacting you within the week to arrange a convenient meeting time.

Sincerely,

George Herounian

Enclosure

EXHIBIT 10.20   Cover letter for a marketing manager position.

1736 D Street NW
Washington, DC 20006
(202) 555-8192
May 3, 2006

Ms. Emma Major, President
Vendo Corporation
1742 Surf Drive
Fort Lauderdale, FL 33301

Dear Ms. Major:

I was intrigued by the write-up about your new portable vending centers in *Sales Management* magazine. I think it is an extremely good idea.

As you will note from the enclosed resume, my marketing, planning, and sales management experience could be of great assistance to you at this early stage in your project. Enclosed are some specific marketing ideas you might like to review. I would like to make arrangements to meet with you in Florida during the week of May 17 to discuss some of these ideas.

Because of my familiarity with the types of locations and clients you are seeking, I am sure that if we were able to work together in this new venture, the results would reflect my contribution.

I am looking forward to meeting with you and will call next week to arrange for an appointment.

Very truly yours,

Janet Perrill

Enclosure

EXHIBIT 10.21

TO WHOM IT MAY CONCERN:

This will introduce Mary Smith, a trusted and valued member of my staff for the past two and a half years.

During this time she has held a key position, performing a variety of secretarial tasks, as well as having full charge of the ordering procedures, maintenance work, and updating in our career resources library. She is keen at spotting deficiencies and was instrumental in developing a more efficient system of updating our materials.

She has been recognized by other members of the staff, including the counselors and our program director, the dean of student personnel, as being outstanding in poise, appearance, and reliability. Additionally, and probably most important, she has been exceptionally effective in working with the students, faculty, and professionals who use the resources of our center.

Mary is a good organizer, capable of dealing with concepts and goals and devising systems approaches to problem solving. She is loyal and discreet in dealing with unusual situations and those calling for confidentiality.

If there is anything more you feel you would like to discuss regarding Mary's qualifications, please feel free to contact me.

Very truly yours,

W. T. Jones
Philo Corp.

11

Interviewing Successfully

Learning Objectives

At the end of the chapter you will be able to . . .

- Describe the art of interviewing

- Summarize how to prepare for an interview

- Use guidelines and techniques for good interviewing

Once you begin to feel comfortable with the notion of networking and practice interviewing, you are ready to begin preparing for the "Olympic Finals"—the interview.

The trouble is, if you do not risk anything,

you risk even more.

ERICA JONG

Before the Interview

Be prepared

Here are the three most important tips to consider as you approach your first interview or refine your current interviewing style: *prepare, prepare, prepare.*

Some of the best preparation for the interview occurs when you research the prospective employer. Your goal is to show the employer why you will be the best person for the job, relating your personal strengths and past accomplishments to this particular enterprise. Specifically, you want to tell the employer how you can help with current problems or function as a valuable member of the organization. To find out more about a prospective employer and the job you're interviewing for, call or write the organization to request a current publication that describes the organization, such as an annual report, along with the job description. You may find recent newspaper or magazine articles about the company in your library's computerized retrieval system or through such computer networks as America Online or msn.com. Also refer to Internet sources listed in Chapter 9 for company information locations on the Web. If the firm does business with the government, you may also find relevant information in the library's government section.

Before the interview, or at least early into it, try to find out what the essential responsibilities of the job are. Make a mental note of them, and throughout the interview, feed back the kind of information from your background that shows you can handle these responsibilities.

Don't let a formal job description disqualify you for a job. Remember that job descriptions are only guidelines; once in a job, you are allowed to imprint your own style. Additionally, it is expected that over 50 percent of the work in any job is learned on the job.

If you are turned down for the position, consider calling to get information to improve subsequent interviews: "I realize that this is a bit unusual and I am aware that you've chosen someone else for the job, but could you spend a few moments giving me some ideas as I continue my job search?" You could end up with some valuable leads; it's worth a try!

Interviewing becomes easier as you gain practice. Don't be overly discouraged if you don't get the first job for which you interview. Interviews and even rejections are actually invaluable opportunities to reassess and reaffirm your qualifications, strengths, weaknesses, and needs.

In the competitive job market of today, you can maximize your chance of successful interviewing by doing practice interviews and being prepared to answer an employer's typical questions. Always be prepared to support your general answers with specific examples from your experience. Your interviewers will remember your examples! Consider using a video camera to sharpen your interviewing skills. Ask a friend or classmate to be the interviewer. Using the questions below and those found in the section on practice questions, practice your responses. Then play the tape, and use the Interview Critique Form in Exhibit 11.2 to evaluate your performance and improve your answers for the next interview.

Ask for feedback

The sample questions below are representative of the types of questions commonly asked in an employment interview. Review these, and be prepared beforehand to answer such questions.

SUCCESS STRATEGIES

Job search tips

- Your ability to express what your skills are, how you can contribute to the company, and your willingness to learn new skills is as important as being able to do each task listed in the job description. In fact, if you can already do each task described, you might be labeled as overqualified and not get the job!

- Your resume and cover letter become the written and mental outline upon which you elaborate to translate your skills into potential benefits to the employer. Use your resume as a point of reference; write on index cards the key points you want to remember and convey during the interview. It's fine to bring these cards with you to your interview.

- In applying for jobs, a male increases his chances by trying to enter a field that has previously been primarily a female domain (e.g., nursing). Similarly, a female increases her chances if she applies for a position that has previously been primarily a male domain (e.g., electronics).

- Don't be afraid to reapply and reinterview at the same company. Your interview skills will probably have improved in the meantime, and different areas of the company may be interested in you for different positions.

- Be creative if you are applying for a creative job (advertising, design, sales, art), but be conservative if you are applying for a conservative job (banking, insurance, accounting).

- Before the interview, verify the particulars. Write down the interviewer's name, the location, and the time and date of your appointment. Last-minute nervousness can block such details from your memory. Plan on arriving 15 minutes early.

- Apprehension, tension, and anxiety are a normal part of the preinterview jitters. Relaxation techniques, deep breathing, and chatting with the receptionist may help.

- The successful job candidate demonstrates how he or she is the best person for the job.

1. Tell me about yourself.

Refer mentally to your resume; do not assume that the interviewer has even read it! Briefly recap your skills and experiences as they relate to this particular job. Include a clear demonstration of the ways your education, training, skills, and experiences match the needs of the company.

2. Why do you want this job? Why did you apply here?

Refer to information about *this job* and *this company* or institution that makes it particularly appealing to you. Do not give the impression that you're here just because the firm has a job opening. Refer to the company's history, products, and services. Let your interviewer know that you have researched the organization.

3. Why should I hire you?

"Because, with my skills, experience, positive attitude, and enthusiasm, I am obviously the best person for the job. I agree with your philosophy and feel that I will fit in. I will be an asset to your enterprise." (Reemphasize your strengths.) Also emphasize how you can contribute to the company.

4. What are your career plans? Where do you see yourself five years from now?

Employers generally like to think you will be with them forever; you can't make any promises, but you can indicate you would like to be with a company that allows you to grow, asks you to assume more responsibility, and challenges you continuously.

FACTS & FIGURES

Company knowledge

A recent survey reveals that a lack of company knowledge is—by far—the most frequent interview mistake. The chances are great in any given interview that you will be asked some variation of the question, "What do you know about our company?" The questions could be "What attracted you to our company?" or "Why do you want to work for our company?" or one of a number of other variations. Employers want to see that you've done your homework; in fact, 44 percent of executives recently surveyed by Accountemps said the most common interview pitfall for today's candidates is insufficient company research.

THINK ABOUT IT

1. What are you doing now to make sure that you know about the company for which you are interviewing?

2. Name the sources that you will use when you have to find out information about a company or industry.

To answer these questions online, go to the *Facts and Figures* module in Chapter 11 of the Companion Website.

Companion Website

5. What salary do you expect?

If you have done your homework, you should have an idea of the general range for the position. Find out whether this company has a fixed salary schedule. You may want to defer the matter until you know more about what the job entails. If the interviewer does not mention salary, it is best not to bring up the subject at a first interview.

6. Why did you leave your last job?

If asked why you left your last position, avoid mentioning a personality conflict. Rather say, "I felt I had gone as far in that company as possible, and I was ready for more responsibility, challenge, hours (etc.)." If your work history reflects many job changes, explain how you have transferred existing skills and learned new skills that can now benefit this employer.

7. Do you have any questions?

You might ask just what kind of person the interviewer is really looking for, then show how you fit the bill. Or you might clarify expected follow-up, or add some information. "When can I expect to hear about the position?" "Oh, yes, I forgot to mention earlier that ..." "I would like to reiterate that ..." (See the box titled "Sample Questions to Ask at the Interview.")

Leave the interviewer convinced that you are ready and able to do the job. Never answer a question "No" without qualifying it positively. "Are you familiar with Excel?" "No, but I have mastered other software, and I'm certain I won't have any problems learning."

"Can you 10-key?" "No, I didn't realize it was part of the job description. If it's necessary, I can learn. Just how much numerical data entry will be involved?"

Interview Guidelines

The interview—and ultimately, a job—is the goal of your job search strategy. Generally, people who are interviewed are assumed qualified to do the job; the question becomes one of an appropriate meshing of personalities. Both the interviewer and interviewee are relying on their communications skills, judgment, intuition, and insight. It is a two-way process. While you are being evaluated, you should be evaluating the position and the people offering it. Remember that a good interview is a dialogue, an exchange of information.

Dressing for Success

The moment we see someone, we form powerful first impressions that are hard to change. Much of a first impression comes from the visual impact of an individual, and much of the visual impact comes from what we choose to wear. Our clothes and accessories speak and sometimes shout volumes about us. What we want to communicate to prospective employers is that we fit in and that we can be trusted to interact appropriately with other employees and customers.

An interview is a two-way process

Many workplaces have become increasingly more casual in dress norms, and in many instances, "casual Friday" has now been extended to every workday. You may be looking forward to this more casual, comfortable norm, but it is generally a good rule to dress a bit more formally for the interview. More people are passed over for jobs because they were too casually dressed than because they were too formally dressed. In this instance, when in doubt, you should err on the side of formality. This also communicates a sense of respect for the potential interviewers who are evaluating you and comparing you with other candidates. You are communicating that this is not just another casual encounter but a meeting that has importance to you.

It's always best to check out the scene firsthand before the day of your interview to get a general sense for the "look" of employees. Of course, having done your informational interviewing, you will know how employees in your field of interest generally dress. For the interview, it is generally accepted that you should dress one or two levels up from the job you are applying for, while remaining consistent with the occupational norms of your field.

With these general guidelines in mind, it is best to have an interview outfit or two selected and ready to wear. Except for certain fields such as fashion, the arts, entertainment, and advertising, it is always best to err on the conservative and understated side for an interview so that your outfit or accessories don't compete with you for the interviewer's attention. It is also wise to get feedback on your outfit from trusted friends and advisers before the day of the interview.

Tomorrow is often the busiest time of the year.

SPANISH PROVERB

Take a good look at yourself and ask others you trust for their opinions. If you are serious about getting a job, then you had better look and dress the part. No interviewer will tell you what you are supposed to wear, but the person will measure your maturity and judgment partially by your appearance. Remember that the first impression is often a lasting one. It's often not the best qualified person who gets the job, but the one who makes the best impression. *You never get a second chance to make a good first impression!*

Practical Preparation

If possible, drive by the interview site a day or two before so you'll know where it is, where to park, and how long it takes to get there. Plan to arrive for your interview at least 15 minutes early. Establish a friendly relationship with the secretary or receptionist. Develop a firm handshake (practice), and use it when being introduced. Practice good eye contact. Above all, try to relax. Remember, you will be talking about someone you know very well—you!

You may have to handle some trick or stress questions; be prepared beforehand with responses that feel comfortable to you (see the sample questions later in this chapter). If a question seems inappropriate, you may ask, "How does this information relate to or affect my employment here?" This may prompt an employer to express the real concerns, such as your record of stability on the job, age, child-care needs, or commitment to the job and company. You may even consider bringing up these relevant issues. Often seemingly unimportant conversation is an attempt to put you and the interviewer at ease or to assess your ability to socialize.

Body language can speak louder than words

Remember that many interviewers are just as nervous about the process as you. Feel free to make the first attempts to break the ice; when you try to relieve another's anxiety, yours becomes secondary. Say something about the office decor, the cordial welcome, whatever makes sense. If you are nervous, you will find that focusing on the question "What would it be like to work here?" rather than "How am I being perceived by them?" will relax you. Relax in the chair; a rigid posture reinforces your tenseness. Actually, a slightly forward position with head erect indicates interest and intimacy. Maintain eye contact.

In answering questions, use your knowledge of yourself to transmit the idea that you are the best person for the job; allow strengths such as goodwill, flexibility, enthusiasm, and a professional approach to surface. Bring samples of your work if they are related. On an index card, note your strengths or key selling points in addition to the questions you may have and some cue words like "smile, speak up, relax"; review them from time to time, especially just before you go into the interview. Forthright statements about what you do well, with examples of accomplishments, are of key importance. Talk with pride, honesty, and confidence about your accomplishments and your potential, your interest and commitment, and your readiness to learn on the job.

Express yourself *positively.* You are selling yourself; allow your personal *energy* and *enthusiasm* to surface.

Segments of an Interview

Although every interview is different, most follow a general pattern. A typical half-hour session can be roughly divided into four segments:

1. The first five or 10 minutes are usually devoted to establishing rapport and opening the lines of communication. Instead of wondering why the interviewer is taking valuable time chatting about the weather, your parking problems, etc., relax and enjoy the conversation. He or she will get to deeper subjects soon enough. The interview begins the moment you introduce yourselves and shake hands. Don't discount the initial period. Your ability to converse, expressing yourself intelligently, is being measured.

Establish initial rapport

2. The adept interviewer will move subtly from a casual exchange to a more specific level of conversation. The second part of the interview gives you a chance to answer some "where, when, and why" questions about your background—to supply information that does not appear on your resume.

Now is the time to describe some extracurricular activities or work experience that may explain your less-than-perfect GPA. Or to talk of changes you effected as president of a campus organization or community group. This is your chance to elaborate on your strong points and emphasize whatever you have to offer. Don't monopolize the conversation; let the interviewer lead. But don't confine your statements to yes-or-no answers. Ask some questions to let the interviewer know you have researched the firm thoroughly and have a keen interest in the position.

The interviewer will be interested not only in what you say but also how you say it. Equally as important as the information you communicate will be the evidence of logical organization and presentation of thoughts. The interviewer will be mentally grading your intelligence, leadership potential, and motivation.

3. Part three begins when the interviewer feels your skills and interests have been identified and can see how they might fit the organization. If a good match seems possible, the interviewer will discuss the company and the openings available.

4. At the end of an interview, try to find out where you stand. "How do you feel I relate to this job?" "Do you need any additional information?" "When can I expect to hear from you?"

Ask questions

After you leave, take 10 or 15 minutes to analyze how you did. What questions did you find difficult? What did you forget to say? How can you improve on the next interview? You might even keep a diary or log with written notes on each of these concerns as well as a list of the specific interview questions asked and a note about how you responded. Also list any specific things that you can do in following up with an employer to increase your chances of getting the offer you want. If you feel you forgot to mention something or there was a misunderstanding,

Although a job interview can be stressful, careful preparation on your part will allow you to relax, respond to questions more naturally, and make a good impression.

correct or elaborate on these points in a letter or telephone call.

Send a thank-you letter to the interviewer, recalling a significant fact or idea of the interview that will set you apart from the other applicants. Write the letter while the interview is still fresh in your mind. One paragraph is usually sufficient. See the sample thank-you letters on the following page.

Practice Questions

The following are questions that may be asked during interviews, intended to create a *stress* response. Often they are asked out of pattern, intended to throw you. The interviewer sometimes is more interested in *how* you respond than in what you say, to observe how you react and how you think on your feet. Decide which of the following questions are likely to be asked of you in your situation. PRACTICE!

1. What kind of job do you expect to hold five years from now? Ten years? Twenty years?
2. Why do you want to work for this company?
3. Why did you choose this company over our competitors?
4. Why did you choose your particular field of work?
5. What do you know about this company?
6. Describe your perfect job.
7. What qualifications do you have that make you feel you will be successful in your field?
8. What are your salary expectations?
9. What determines a person's progress in a good company?
10. Do you prefer working with others or by yourself?
11. Describe how you handle stress.
12. How do you react to criticism?
13. What interests you about our product/service?
14. What is your major weakness? (What are three of your strong points? Three of your weak points?)
15. Are you willing to go where the company sends you? Travel? Relocate?

Sample Thank-You Letters

Use these sample thank-you letters as a guide and write your own to an imaginary or real interviewer.

19574 Delaware
Detroit, MI 48223
February 8, 2006

Ms. Dorothy Smith
Michels' Manufacturing Corporation
1928 North Berry Street
Livonia, MI 48150

Dear Ms. Smith:

Thank you for your time this morning. I was certainly impressed with the efficiency, friendliness, and overall climate of Michels' Manufacturing Corporation.

Now that you've told me more about Michels' recent contract with the U.S. Tank Command, I feel my degree in industrial engineering and two years of part-time work in task force analysis should be of value to you.

I hope you will consider me favorably for the position of junior project engineer.

Sincerely,

Steven B. Boyd

1010 Yourstreet Avenue
Elizabeth, NJ 07208
July 12, 2006

Mr. John Jones
Widget Manufacturing Company
345 Widget Avenue
Newark, NJ 07210

Dear Mr. Jones,

Thank you for an interesting and informative interview on July 12, 2006. The position of manufacturing representative is of considerable interest to me, as I am most impressed with Widget's excellent growth record.

One point was not brought out in our interview that may be of interest to you. In my previous position with Ferrals Manufacturing, I took ten weeks of intensive training in billing and credit, skills that would directly relate to the position as you described it.*

Again, thank you for the time you spent interviewing me.

Yours truly,

Rosario Ortega

*Note: This is your chance to mention anything helpful to your campaign that you forgot to tell the employer in the interview. However, the point should be brief and precise.

16. What kind of supervision gets the best results from you?

17. What are your own special abilities?

18. Do you object to working overtime?

19. What is your philosophy of life?

20. Do you have any objections to a psychological test or interview?

21. What are the main elements needed to develop a team spirit?

22. What are your career goals?

23. What are the things that motivate you?

24. In what ways will this company benefit from your services?

25. If you were me, why would you hire you?

26. How would you describe yourself as an employee?

How to Handle Illegal Questions

Certain hiring practices, employment application form questions, and specific interviewing procedures are illegal under the Fair Employment Practices Act, the Americans with Disabilities Act, and other governmental regulations. Review Exhibit 11.1 to familiarize yourself with the subject matter and specifics of the illegal issues.

If the question is on an application, you always have the option to put N/A in the blank. If you are asked illegal questions in an interview, try to anticipate the concerns a potential employer might have about hiring you and bring them up in a manner that is comfortable for you.

Example:

Interviewer: "Do you have any children?"

Interviewee: "I guess you are wondering about the care of my school-aged children. I'd like you to know I have an excellent attendance record. You are welcome to check with my past employer, and, besides, I have a live-in sitter. Additionally, I have researched the needs of this position and can assure you that I have no family responsibilities that will interfere with my ability to do this job."

Anticipate concerns and address them

Not only will employers appreciate your sensitivity to their concerns, but your statement provides you with an additional opportunity to sell yourself and to evaluate whether this position is one that you want to consider. It is often advisable for you, the interviewee, to bring up any issue that may be on the employer's mind but that, because of legal concerns, will not be addressed unless you mention it. Such issues as age, children, spouse's feelings about this position, gender, disabilities, and qualifications can all be addressed by you in such a way as to enhance your chances of getting the job. Basically, you want to show how your age, qualifications, gender, or disability will be an advantage to your employer. This requires some thinking on your part before the interview. The payoff—getting the job you want—is well worth the effort.

SUBJECT	ACCEPTABLE PREEMPLOYMENT INQUIRIES	UNACCEPTABLE PREEMPLOYMENT INQUIRIES
Photograph	Statement that a photograph may be required after employment.	Requirement that applicant affix a photograph to application form. Request that applicant submit photograph at applicant's option. Requirement of photograph after interview but before hiring.
Race or Color		Complexion, color of skin, or other questions directly or indirectly indicating race or color, such as color of applicant's eyes and hair.
Citizenship	Request that applicant state whether residency status is: (a) U.S. citizen. (b) Legal right to remain permanently in the United States. Statement that, if hired, applicant may be required to submit proof of citizenship.	What is your country of citizenship? Inquiry whether an applicant or applicant's parents or spouse are naturalized or native-born U.S. citizens; date when applicant or parents or spouse acquired citizenship. Requirement that applicant produce naturalization papers or first papers.
National Origin	Inquiry into applicant's proficiency in foreign language must be job-related.	Applicant's nationality, lineage, national origin, descent, or parentage. Date of arrival in United States or port of entry; how long a resident of the United States. Nationality of applicant's parents or spouse; maiden name of applicant's wife or mother. Language commonly used by applicant; "What is your mother tongue?" How applicant acquired ability to read, write, or speak a foreign language.
Education	Inquiry into academic, vocational, or professional education of an applicant and schools attended.	Any inquiry asking specifically the nationality, race, or religious affiliation of a school.
Name	Inquiry about having worked for the company under a different name. Maiden name of married female applicant, assumed name, or change of name, if necessary to check education or employment records.	Former name of applicant whose name has been changed by court order or otherwise.
Address or Duration of Residence	Inquiry into place and length of residence at current and previous addresses.	Specific inquiry into foreign addresses that would indicate national origin.

(continued)

EXHIBIT 11.1   Preemployment inquiries: lawful and unlawful (continued)

SUBJECT	ACCEPTABLE PREEMPLOYMENT INQUIRIES	UNACCEPTABLE PREEMPLOYMENT INQUIRIES
Gender		If not based on a bona fide occupational qualification, it is extremely unlikely that gender would be considered a lawful subject for preemployment inquiry.
Birthplace	Requirement that applicant submit, after employment, a birth certificate or other proof of legal residence.	Birthplace of applicant, applicant's parents, spouse, or other relatives.
Age	Requirement that applicant submit, after employment, a birth certificate or other document as proof of age.	Requirement that applicant produce proof of age in the form of a birth certificate, baptismal record, employment certificate, or certificate of age issued by school authorities.
Religion		Inquiry into applicant's religious denomination, affiliation, church, parish, or pastor, or which religious holidays observed. Applicant may not be told, "This is a Catholic/ Protestant/Jewish/atheist, etc., organization."
Workday and Shifts	Request that applicant state days, hours, or shift(s) available to work.	It is unlawful to request applicants to state days, hours, or shift(s) that they can work if it is used to discriminate on the basis of religion.

The Behavioral/Situational Interview

Employers use this type of interview to gain information from an interviewee about possible job performance and to ascertain your ability to problem-solve in stressful job situations. It includes a series of questions that challenge the candidate about how job stress was managed in the past to determine the probability of success in the future. Some of the behavioral characteristics that interviewers have deemed to be most important include:

- **Listening skills.** Active and caring responses showing empathy and concern for others.
- **Writing skills.** Clear and concise communication to resolve issues utilizing shared action plans with suitable outcomes.
- **Organizational/teamwork skills.** Assuming responsibility for self and others; developing mutual agreements, monitoring progress and evaluating results.

Meet Jose

"I can't believe how poorly I did on my interview," Jose said to his friend Debra. "My hands were so sweaty and I know the committee members tried not to notice when I shook their hands, but I could see it in their eyes."

Jose had just finished his first interview after graduating with his bachelor's degree in applied science. He had asked a friend to help him rehearse his answers to a list of general questions he found in a career planning pamphlet, and he felt confident going into the interview. But everything went downhill from the moment he sat down. He lost his concentration a couple of times and had to ask for the question to be repeated, and he completely forgot the questions he had prepared to ask the committee. He did feel that he connected with the committee on a couple of questions, and they seemed pleased that he did. After the interview, he was given a tour of the facilities and he was still so upset that he missed several opportunities to redeem his previous behavior.

At home that night, Jose thought about his preparation for the interview and how he could have prepared differently. He was so upset and sure that he would not be called for a second interview that he didn't bother to write thank-you notes. Two days later, Jose received a call inviting him back for a second interview.

WHAT DO YOU THINK?

1. Describe how Jose was feeling after his interview.

2. What led Jose to believe he didn't perform well in the interview?

3. What suggestions would you give Jose regarding interview preparation?

4. Why do you think Jose was given a second interview?

5. Would it be appropriate for Jose to bring thank-you notes to his second interview? Would it be too late to mail them, knowing they will arrive after the second interview is over?

6. Do you think Jose was too confident before his interview?

7. What advice would you give Jose to reduce his stress level for the next interviewing opportunity?

Companion Website

To answer these questions online, go to the *Real Stories* module in Chapter 11 of the Companion Website.

For each of these behaviors, the interviewer challenges the candidate to provide examples of real situations where concerns were addressed and resolved. A sample question related to working effectively with others might be: *"Can you give me an example that would show you have been able to develop and maintain productive relations with others, even though they may have differing points of view?"*

Since these types of questions cannot always be clearly anticipated, you can best prepare by analyzing the requirements of the job before the interview and thinking of situations that occurred in previous job settings. By preparing in advance, you will be better able to provide clear and concise examples that will impress the interviewer.

Body Language

Your body language speaks just as loudly as your words. Eye contact is crucial. Remember that at a distance of five or six feet from another person, you can be looking at the person's nose or forehead or mouth and still maintain the sense of eye contact. Try it with friends.

Present yourself assertively

Voice tone, volume, and inflection are important. A soft, wispy voice will seldom convince another that you mean business; a loud or harsh voice tends to be blocked out. Listen to yourself on a tape recorder or, preferably, watch yourself on videotape. How do you sound to yourself? Remember, however, that our own recorded voice always sounds odd to us, so ask others for their comments. Lessons in voice and diction are available in most schools. Try varying your voice pitch and volume while reading something into a tape recorder. You may find a range that sounds better.

Don't chew gum!

Try accenting your words with appropriate hand gestures to gain emphasis. Before the interview, analyze your practice interviews. Consider the option of being videotaped during a practice interview. The instant feedback is very helpful, particularly if you use the form set out in Exhibit 11.2 to critique your performance. If you are in a class, practice with one or more classmates, evaluating your own and your classmates' interview techniques according to the critique form.

Video Interviewing

Some companies are beginning to use video as a prescreening and screening tool. Video interviewing occurs most often in the fields of education, government, and private manufacturing. According to *EEO BiMonthly (Equal Employment Opportunity Magazine)*, six factors are important to consider:

1. Are you articulate? How do you come across on videotape?
2. Be prepared; practice what you will say before you are taped.
3. If you are a person who usually plays off another's body language in an interview, you will need to practice to make your answers and conversation flow as if you were actually talking to someone.
4. Dress professionally and conservatively; pay attention to the colors and patterns you wear. Solid colors work best on video.
5. Communicate with enthusiasm and confidence through facial expressions and voice tone.
6. Do not exaggerate your movements. Overdone gestures can be distracting and may even cause "waves" in the air.

Learning from the Interview

As much as they are interviewing you, you are in turn interviewing the representatives of a company. Ideally, you will do only about 40 percent of the talking. In the remaining time, you can listen and assess whether or not you want to work for that company. Although an interview tends to be rather formal, you can still gain a feeling about the climate of the organization. Entering its offices, you can observe the receptionist, support staff, people talking or not talking in the hallways. The colors and decor of the furnishings should generate a positive or negative impression.

Interview critique form.

EXHIBIT 11.2

Name _____
(individual being interviewed)

	Very good	Satisfactory	Fair—could be better	Needs improvement	Comments
1. Initial, or opening, presentation (impression).					
2. Eye contact.					
3. Sitting position.					
4. General appearance: grooming (hair, makeup, shave, beard, mustache, etc.), clothing.					
5. Ability to describe past work experiences, education, and training.					
6. Ability to explain equipment, tools, and other mechanical aids used.					
7. Ability to explain skills, techniques, processes, and procedures. Ability to emphasize how skills are related to job.					
8. Ability to explain personal goals, interests, and desires.					
9. Ability to explain questionable factors in personal life (functional limitations, frequent job changes, many years since last job).					
10. Ability to answer questions or make statements about company or job being applied for.					
11. Ability to listen attentively to interviewer's questions and to notice and respond to interviewer's body language.					
12. Manner of speech or conversation (voice, tone, pitch, volume, speed).					
13. Physical mannerisms (facial expressions, gestures).					
14. Enthusiasm, interest in this job.					
15. Attitude (positive?), confidence.					
16. Overall impression. Would you hire this applicant?					

SUCCESS STRATEGIES

Sample questions to ask at the interview

Going one step further than just *answering* the interviewer's questions involves being prepared to take the initiative in *asking* several questions.

- Where does this position fit into the organization?
- Please describe your ideal candidate for this job.
- Is this position new?
- What experience is ideally suited for this job?
- Was the last person promoted?
- To whom would I be reporting? Can you tell me a little about these people?
- What have been some of the best results you have received from people in this position?
- Who are the primary people I would be working with?

- What seem to be the strengths and weaknesses of the people with whom I would work?
- What are your expectations for me?
- May I talk with present and previous employees about this job?
- What are some of the problems I might expect to encounter on this job (e.g., efficiency, quality control, declining profits, evaluation)?
- What has been done recently regarding . . . ?
- How is this program going? Is it growing?
- What kind of on-the-job training is allocated for this position?
- What is the normal pay range for this job?
- When will I hear from you about the outcome of this interview?
- If you don't mind, can I let you know by (*date*)?

*When you have completed 95%
of your journey, you are
halfway there.*

JAPANESE PROVERB

Take note of whether the interview begins punctually, the arrangement of the seating in the interview room, and the dress of the interviewers. The entrance and handshake are important first impressions. Some companies deliberately set up awkward or uncomfortable situations to observe your response. They may ask tough questions just to see how well you think on your feet. If you can maintain your composure and enthusiasm in the interview, they will probably conclude that you are able to work equally as well under stress.

In selecting your own questions, you might ask who the last person in the position was and what happened to him or her; if the person resigned, you may ask why. Another related question would be, "Given the current economy, how have careers at my level been affected?" You may also ask about the background of your potential supervisor and professional mobility within the company. Although you want to emphasize your interest and commitment to the position for which you are interviewing, these questions can illustrate your interest in a future with the company.

A final bit of information that you should gather or confirm about the company relates to its *corporate culture*. Corporate culture refers to the personality of the organization. Primarily you want to seek employment with a firm that is likely to meet your personality needs. Do you need a competitive environment in order to thrive? Most likely a job in a high school or a government position won't satisfy those needs. Do you need security? The aerospace field may be a bit too unsteady for you. The prime question that is related to corporate culture and that you may ask during an interview is, "Can you explain the management style or philosophy of your company?" If you want to have the opportunity for input into management, you might also ask about the use of quality circles or the use of total quality management in the organization. If you are hoping to enter the field of business but have little relevant background, it might help to take a college class or read a book on the world of business so that you can ask intelligent questions about business practices.

Factors Influencing Hiring

We have seen that many things must be considered in preparing for an interview. Some of these factors we can control; other considerations are beyond our control. Look over the box on the following page to distinguish between the two.

A national survey of employers (NACE, 2002) found 10 top qualities that employers seek in new employees. To make an outstanding and lasting impression, emphasize the traits listed below during any contact with a company (e.g., informational or formal interview). As you review the list, check each item you feel comfortable discussing in an interview:

_____   1. Communication skills (verbal and written)

_____   2. Honesty/integrity

_____   3. Teamwork skills

_____   4. Interpersonal skills

_____   5. Strong work ethic

_____   6. Motivation/initiative

_____   7. Flexibility/adaptability

_____   8. Analytical skills

_____   9. Computer skills

_____   10. Organizational skills

Realize that interpersonal skills may consist of many of the "emotional IQ skills" discussed in Chapter 2. It is interesting to note that some traits listed 10 years ago as important are not as important today, such as competitive spirit and self-knowledge. Employers now want to know that you are a team player who has the ability to learn and make decisions (motivational skills and analytical skills).

Each of the traits you checked can strengthen your chances for a successful interview. Those you did not check are areas for additional homework prior to preparing the final version of your resume and going to the interview.

SUCCESS STRATEGIES

Factors that influence your success

OUT OF YOUR CONTROL

- Too many applicants.
- Cannot pay you what you are making.
- Indecisiveness on part of business owner.
- Only trying to fill a temporary position.
- A current employee changed plans and decided not to leave.
- Introduction of new personnel policies.
- Death of a company management employee.
- Looking for a certain type of person.
- Lack of experience on part of interviewer.
- Accepting applications only for future need.
- Looking for more experience.
- Looking for less experience.
- Your skills are more than are needed for the position.
- Company management decided that morning on a temporary freeze on hiring—for many business reasons.
- Illness of interviewer.
- Change in management.
- Further consideration of all applicants.
- A more important post must be filled first.
- Company stock went down 65 percent since you applied.
- Company went bankrupt.

FACTORS YOU CAN CONTROL OR GUARD AGAINST

- A poor personal appearance.
- An overbearing, overaggressive, conceited attitude; a superiority complex; being a know-it-all.
- An inability to express yourself clearly; poor voice, diction, or grammar.
- A lack of career planning; no purpose or goals.
- A lack of interest and enthusiasm; appearing passive, indifferent.
- A lack of confidence and poise; nervousness, being ill at ease.
- An overemphasis on money; interest only in best dollar offer.
- A poor scholastic record; just squeaking by.
- An unwillingness to start at the bottom; expecting too much too soon.
- Making excuses; evasiveness, hedging on unfavorable factors in record.
- Lack of courtesy; being ill-mannered.
- Talking negatively about past employers or coworkers.
- Failure to look interviewer in the eye.
- A limp, fishlike handshake.
- A sloppy application form.
- Insincerity; merely "shopping around."
- Wanting job only for short time.
- Lack of interest in company or in industry.
- Emphasizing whom you know over what you can do.
- An unwillingness to be transferred.
- Intolerance; strong prejudices.
- Having narrow interests.
- Arriving late for interview without good reason.
- Never having heard of company.
- Failure to express appreciation for interviewer's time.
- Failure to ask questions about the job.
- Directing a high-pressure style at interviewer.
- Providing vague responses to questions.

A greater range of jobs now require a college degree. Often a degree will be required primarily because so many applicants have degrees. Even your liberal arts degree can compete with a specialist degree in business if the following factors apply:

1. You have an excellent grade point average.

2. You have a record of extracurricular activities (club or community involvement). It's especially good to have had leadership positions.

3. You worked your way through college (it helps even more if the work was at the company with which you seek full-time employment or at least in the same field).

4. You've made some contacts within the firm who can serve as positive references.

5. You either minored in business or, at least, selected business courses as electives (e.g., accounting, economics, marketing, information systems).

6. You have defined goals, exude enthusiasm and confidence, and can verbalize these characteristics in an interview.

For example, Walt Disney World Company employs thousands of new college graduates each year; more than one-third are liberal arts graduates.

Generally attributed to all college graduates, but especially to liberal arts graduates, are intellectual ability (verbal and quantitative) and skills in planning, organizing, decision making, interpersonal relations, leadership, and oral communication. The less your major is related to the job desired, the more effectively you must be able to discuss your transferable skills.

If you are offered and you accept a job, be prepared to begin work with a great attitude, determined to do your best.

If You Are Offered the Job

Congratulations! Your career fitness efforts have paid off. Before deciding to accept a job offer, it's important to determine how well the position meets your needs. Consider the following questions before making a decision:

- How does this job fit into your long-range career goals?
- If it doesn't fit well, are there factors that may influence your decision to accept the position anyway?
- Have you considered the scope of the job, the reputation of the company, the possibility for growth and advancement, the geographic location, the salary and benefits package?

SUCCESS STRATEGIES

Summary: reviewing the interview process

PREPARATION

✓ Have resume, contacts, and letters of reference.

✓ Make interview log for contacts; write initial contact letters.

✓ Mail letters out; make appointments with contacts.

✓ Make 3″ × 5″ cards on each interview.

✓ Maintain "I can do it" attitude. Visualize that you have the job.

✓ Dress the part.

✓ Know your resume. Bring extra copies to the interview.

✓ Know something about the company (use *Dun and Bradstreet, Moody's, Standard & Poor's, Fortune 500*, annual report, magazine articles).

✓ Have five or six good questions. Know when to ask them.

✓ Keep a computer log or journal.

✓ Keep control.

✓ Be on time!

THE INTRODUCTION

✓ Maintain good posture, shake hands, breathe.

✓ Use good eye contact and posture.

✓ The first four minutes are key—establish rapport and generate the proper chemistry.

✓ Tell what you can do for the company, your major strengths, your background.

✓ Be positive—convert negatives to pluses.

THE INTERVIEW

✓ Smile.

✓ Supply information, referring to your resume.

✓ Seek the next interview (or the job).

✓ Overcome any objections—try to anticipate objections.

✓ Keep answers brief.

✓ Ask questions about the field.

✓ Know the rules, including when a decision will be made.

✓ Ask for the job if it exists.

✓ Be positive.

✓ Ask "When will you make a decision?"

AFTER THE INTERVIEW

✓ Debrief yourself—make notes (name, address, phone, impressions; if a panel of interviewers, write down names and positions of all panel members). Add to computer journal.

✓ Formally thank the employer or panel chairperson by letter.

✓ Plan a follow-up strategy—if you don't hear from them, call and ask if a decision has been made.

✓ Don't be defeated—keep interviewing!

ALTERNATIVES

✓ Continue learning and searching.

✓ Consider volunteer work to gain more experience.

✓ Join or create a job support group.

✓ Keep current and updated.

Negotiating for Salary and Benefits

Although you may be excited and eager to accept a job offer, it's important to realize that your prospective employer is trying to hire the most talented individual at the lowest possible salary. If you are offered a position, your aim should be to start at the highest possible salary. In order to achieve your goal, it is important for you to determine what the salary range is for comparable positions. There are numerous sites on the Internet that will assist you in this research. Check out the Web exercises at the end of each chapter for specific sites.

It is always wisest to wait for the employer to bring up the topic of compensation, which includes salary and benefits. In some instances, the salary is fixed, as with government jobs, but in most cases there is a range. You will usually be offered a salary at the bottom of the range, and it is up to you to move it up. The most effective way to do that is to hold off accepting the first offer by saying, "I'll think about it," or "Is that the very best you can offer me?" Don't worry about offending your employer. This is an expected negotiation and will only confirm in your employer's mind that you know your value in the job market.

Even if the initial salary cannot be raised, you can ask for an earlier performance review date, which normally has a raise attached for good performers. In addition to or instead of a higher salary, you may be able to negotiate a fringe benefit package that is uniquely tailored to your needs and preferences. Such fringe benefits as flexible working hours or reimbursement for continued education may be equal to or far more valuable than a pay increase! Remember that the best time to negotiate is before you accept the job offer. Summon up your courage and assertiveness, and ask for what you want and deserve.

If You Do Not Get the Job

Should you find that, despite your solid efforts, you do not get the desired job, remember that all your dedicated preparation will pay off in time. The next interview will be easier; you will benefit from your experience. The key is to keep a positive attitude and not to give up. Keep your goals in mind, and remember that persistent people achieve their objectives by focusing on the target and believing in the future.

Unfortunately, continuing unemployment can undermine a person's confidence. You will be better prepared to handle temporary setbacks and rejection if you remember that your situation is far from unique; everyone with a job was once a job searcher. As you persist in your job search, remind yourself that you *will* find a job and build a career.

How well you cope with stress and rejection will depend on your attitude and actions. Put any anger or frustration you feel to positive use. Concentrate on your strengths; review them each day. A healthy diet, physical exercise, and adequate rest are time-tested prescriptions for overcoming worry and anxiety.

One of the best antidotes for feeling depressed is doing something to help someone else. You have time, talents, and skills that will mean a great deal to others. And remember, each time you volunteer, you gain valuable experience and contacts.

Finally, try to accomplish something every day. Accomplishments are activities that make you feel good about yourself. Even minor tasks such as cleaning out a closet or refining your resume can invigorate you and give you new direction.

When you take care of yourself and strive to maintain a positive attitude, your self-image is enhanced, and you improve your chances of success.

PURPOSE OF EXERCISES. The written exercises that follow serve to prepare you for a job interview. Exercise 11.1 asks you to review and be ready to answer sample questions. Exercise 11.2 asks you to practice and critique an interview.

To answer these questions online, go to the *Exercise* module in Chapter 11 of the Companion Website.

Question Review   11.1

Review the interview questions listed under "Practice Questions," beginning on page 314, and be prepared to answer all of them.

Practice Interview   11.2

Arrange a practice interview with a friend, colleague, career counselor, or potential employer (someone you've met during your information interviewing). If possible, have the practice interview videotaped so you can review your performance. Use the Interview Critique Form (see Exhibit 11.2) to evaluate your practice session.

WWWebwise   11.3

For additional activities online, go to the WWWebwise module in Chapter 11 of the Companion Website.

Exercise Summary   11.4

Write a brief paragraph answering these questions:

What did you learn about yourself from these exercises? How does this knowledge relate to your career/life planning? How do you feel?

_____

_____

_____

_____

_____

_____

12

Future Focus

Learning Objectives

At the end of the chapter you will be able to . . .

- Understand the concept of lifelong career management and career fitness

- Recognize the role of the future in your current career-planning efforts

- Explain the philosophy of personal empowerment and career flexibility

By the time you reach this chapter in your career fitness workout, you may find that your career is in shape and you are exercising your options in a career of your choice. Alternatively, if you are not yet in the career of your choice, you now have the skills to find and enter your most desired field.

This book has provided tools to help you identify who you are; define what you want to do; research, identify, and develop your skills; and create a context in which you are able to find meaningful work. Following the book's guidelines puts you in full control, for you are creating your own possibilities instead of spending time preparing for the "predicted future" only to find that it does not

I am always doing that which I cannot do, in order that
I may learn to do that which I cannot do.

PABLO PICASSO

exist. The only predictable future is the one that you create for yourself. During positive economic times there are plenty of opportunities for you to find your ideal position; during down economic times, you are guaranteed nothing but your own persevering attitude. With the right attitude, you can stay focused on the need for constant self-renewal, continuous lifelong learning, and deliberate lifelong networking.

Although congratulations are in order for completing this book, you haven't completed your career fitness program—you've just started it! The job of managing your career has just begun.

Managing Your Career

Every job or work activity, whether it's your dream job or not, is a step in your career. You have the choice on a daily basis merely to get by or to put your all (your values, interests, skills, and unique personality) into your work. Employers are eager to acknowledge and reward individuals who have a strong work ethic. These individuals routinely arrive on time, display an optimistic, can-do attitude, and are not only willing to do their job but eager to take on additional assignments. They are savvy enough to know that they are responsible for their own career development. They recognize that in these uncertain times, a promotion may not be around the corner, but there are always opportunities to grow on the job. This willingness to take on new challenges not only results in job enrichment for the employee, but it also sets that individual apart from those individuals who may not be as willing to jump in when needed. This attitude is what often determines whom an employer chooses for a promotion, above and beyond the required skill sets.

It is, in fact, the personality factors as reviewed in Chapter 2 that make the difference when a promotion, another opportunity, or a raise is available. Not only are these qualities essential to getting the right job, they are also critical in successfully managing your career. It is in your best interest to cultivate a developmental outlook on your current job. Every opportunity you take to learn, grow, stretch, and further develop your skills is an opportunity that no one can take away from you. The experience becomes part of your portfolio. You are enriched and your marketability is enhanced. Yes, there are cynics who might think that you are being taken advantage of; after all, it's not really your job. You may even be putting in some of your own time to learn and demonstrate your newly acquired skill sets. But the successful career decision maker knows that as you build mental muscle and develop your skill sets, you have a better chance of sustaining a lead in the competitive job market. Even more important, you become more deeply connected to your profession and you demonstrate the courage to be the person (in your work) who you really want and need to be. We are using the word *courage* because it is derived from the old French *cuer*, which means heart. To be courageous means to be heartfelt. It is only when your heart connects with your work that you become the best person that you can be—and others will respond.

Developing Your Relationship Savvy

It's often been said that it's not what you know but who you know. In today's world, it's both. As you move up and around the career ladder, individuals often move away from technical tasks to jobs where people skills and communication skills are essential to success. Take every opportunity to participate in meetings and special projects that will put you in contact with people outside your everyday work team. According to the manager of accountancy at Sony, quoted in Chapter 5, 80 percent of her job was dealing with people. Her subordinates also have to deal with these people.

People skills and communication skills are vital to success in any job. Build a support network, developing and nuturing your professional relationships.

Consider taking a leadership position when appropriate. Develop and nurture your relationships at work. Refer back to the information on personality types in Chapter 4 to remind you of the natural differences among individuals that must be acknowledged and appreciated. If an individual is puzzling or perplexing, take the extra effort to try to understand this person and to cultivate a relationship. This exercise will develop your relationship skills and provide you with a rich network of associates and colleagues. You will cultivate mutual respect and appreciation for each other's uniqueness, and you will develop a strong support network in the process.

Although on one hand employers want you to think and act as if you owned the company so that you will feel empowered to make wise decisions on behalf of the company, even more so, you will also be expected to be part of a team. As a team player you will be expected to act as a part of something bigger than yourself. There is a unique energy that a team experiences when its members are working well together. It's called *synergy*, and it means that something bigger and better can come from combining the forces of several people working together.

Can you think of a time when being part of a group or team was a definite advantage in accomplishing a goal? There are endless examples from the sports world and the performing arts. Think about your favorite singer. Could he or she be a success without the many people that make up the team? Being a team player means being willing to listen to and learn from others, even when their ideas or approaches to solving a problem seem very different. It also means being willing to contribute your ideas and thoughts genuinely, even when you know they will probably be modified or perhaps discounted as part of the process.

Developing Career Stamina

Even if you are following your passion, doing what you love, there will be some times in the course of your work when you may feel stuck, frustrated, unmotivated, burned out, stressed out, or bored. It's similar to what happens when we are on a physical fitness path. There are times when we've peaked and may be in a slump or a plateau. According to George Leonard in his book *Mastery,* the cycle of learning, growth, and mastery has ups and downs. Since plateaus are part of the process of regrouping, reflecting, and getting ready for another leap, accept them as part of the cycle, and use them to reflect and recoup your physical and mental resources. Again, think about some of your favorite sports and entertainment figures. They have all experienced painfully public moments of stall before going to ever greater heights.

Embracing Career Fitness as a Way of Life

You are responsible for your own development. Learning to learn will be the most essential survival skill of this new millennium. If you are constantly on the lookout for new ways to use your current skills and new skills, you will remain in demand in the job market. Even if you feel content and secure in your current position, you must constantly be aware of emerging trends, opportunities, and danger signals that may affect your situation. In essence, make the world your classroom; learn something new from everything you do!

Your future is determined by the choices you make in the present. For that reason, this book has emphasized the development of your decision-making skills. This takes the focus away from *predicting* your future and puts the emphasis on *creating* your future. As we experience the 21st century, the world is in flux and you are continually changing, so why shouldn't your career evolve as well? No longer are people staying in one job until retirement.

Unfortunately, however, it is human nature to resist change. Thus, many people do not turn to career counselors or books about career change until they are terminated from what they had assumed was a secure job. If you are wise enough to prepare for change before it is forced on you, you have a head start. The time to seek the career of your choice is while you are still employed or still in school!

Life transitions and unemployment can lead to feelings of desperation and a closed or confused mind. The anxiety and confusion generated by a life crisis make career planning difficult, if not impossible. If you are unemployed or underemployed, you are likely to feel depressed, lethargic, and hopeless about the future. It is precisely during this time that you need to immerse yourself in the career-planning process. During times of personal transition and uncertainty, this process will give you a structure to cope with anxiety and depression and to reconnect with your dreams and passions.

Each time you begin a job search, review the accomplishments and skills you recorded in this book. This may help relieve your apprehension about another job search. You will be reminded of the skills you have and the many alternatives that can be equally satisfying career goals. Your emotional intelligence will enable you to recognize that the uncertainty of transition provides you with fertile ground on which to learn and grow. In fact, a change of direction *now* may become the best opportunity of your lifetime.

In the course of reevaluating your personal strengths and skills, your self-confidence will blossom. You will regain a sense of purpose and direction by setting meaningful and achievable goals. Through networking, information interviewing, and volunteering, your interaction with people will enable you to choose, confirm, or change current goals and be energized and inspired by people who are doing the kind of work you find challenging and rewarding.

Exercising your options may take more effort than crystal-ball gazing, but the results are worth it. Finding a career is a full-time effort. We hope you have pulled, stretched, and grown in the process.

SUCCESS STRATEGIES

Risking

To laugh is to risk appearing the fool.

To weep is to risk appearing sentimental.

To reach out for another is to risk involvement.

To expose feelings is to risk exposing your true self.

To place your ideas, your dreams before the crowd is to risk their loss.

To love is to risk not being loved in return.

To live is to risk dying.

To hope is to risk despair.

To try is to risk failure.

But risks must be taken because the greatest hazard in life is to risk nothing.

The person who risks nothing does nothing, has nothing, is nothing.

One may avoid suffering and sorrow, but one simply cannot learn, feel, change, grow, live, or love.

Chained by certitude and safety, one becomes enslaved.

Only the person who risks is free.

—*Unknown*

References

Basta, Nicholas. 1991. *Major Options*. New York: HarperCollins.

Beatty, Richard H. 2006. *The Resume Kit*, 6th edition. New York: John Wiley & Sons.

Bolles, Richard Nelson. 2006. *Quick Job Hunting Map*. Berkeley, CA: Ten Speed Press.

Bolles, Richard N. 2006. *Job Hunting on the Internet*. Berkeley, CA: Ten Speed Press.

Bolles, Richard N. 2006. *What Color Is Your Parachute? A Practical Manual for Job Hunters and Career Changers*. Revised edition. Berkeley, CA: Ten Speed Press.

Bridges, William. 2003. *Managing Transitions*. Cambridge, MA: Perseus Publishing.

Brown, Lola. 2007. *Resume Writing Made Easy*, 8th edition. Upper Saddle River, NJ: Prentice Hall.

Bureau of Labor Statistics. 2003. *Tomorrow's Jobs* found at www.bls.gov/oco/oco2003.

Burg, Bob. 2005. *Job Interview*. Indianapolis, IN: JIST Works.

Bureau of Labor Statistics. 2004. "20 Facts on Women Workers." *Statistical Abstracts of the United States*. Washington, DC: Bureau of Labor Statistics, U.S. Department of Labor, Women's Bureau.

Business Week Online. 2006. *Hiring Outlook 2006*.

Career Opportunities News. 2004. Garrett Park, MD: Garrett Park Press. (Six issues annually.)

Career Planning and Adult Development Newsletter. San Jose, CA: CPAD Network. (Six newsletters and four journals annually.)

Career Planning Program Handbook. 2003. American College Testing Program.

Crispin, Gerry, and Mark Mehler. 2002. *Career X Roads*. New York: MMC Group.

Cubbage, Sue A., and Marcia P. Williams. *National Job Hotline Directory: The Job Finder's Hot List 2004*. Planning Communications.

Curtis, Rosa, and Warren Simons. 2004. *The Resume.com Guide to Writing Unbeatable Resumes*. New York: McGraw Hill.

Dictionary of Occupational Titles. 2006. Washington, DC: U.S. Department of Labor, Employment and Training.

Dyer, Wayne. 1992. *Real Magic*. New York: HarperCollins.

Edwards, Paul, and Sara Edwards. 2001. *Changing Directions Without Losing Your Way*. Los Angeles: J. P. Tarcher.

Eikleberry, Carol. 2006. *The Career Guide for Creative and Unconventional People*, 3rd edition. Berkeley, CA: Ten Speed Press.

Elliott, Myrna. 1982. *Transferable Skills for Teachers*. Moorpark, CA: Statewide Career Counselor Training Project.

Enelow, Wendy, and Louise Kursmark. 2005. *Expert Resumes for Career Changers*. Indianapolis, IN: JIST Works.

Eyler, David R. 2005. *Resumes That Mean Business*. New York: Random House.

Farr, Michael. 2005. *Next Day Job Interview*. Indianapolis, IN: JIST Works.

Farr, Michael. 2006. *Best Jobs for the 21st Century*. Indianapolis, IN: JIST Works.

Farrell, Warren. 2005. *Why Men Earn More: The Startling Truth Behind the Pay Gap and What Women Can Do About It*. New York: AMACOM.

Fein, Richard. 2005. *Cover Letters! Cover Letters! Cover Letters!* Franklin Lakes, NJ: Career Press.

Fortune Magazine. 2006. "100 Best Companies to Work For."

Fournier, Myra, and Jeffrey Spin. 2005. *Encyclopedia of Job Winning Resumes*, 3rd edition. Ridgefield, CT: Round Lake Publishing.

Friedman, Thomas. 2005. *The World Is Flat: A Brief History of the Twenty-First Century*. New York: Farrar, Straus and Giroux.

Gardner, Howard. 1993. *Frames of Mind: The Theory of Multiple Intelligences*. New York: Basic Books.

Gardner, Howard. 2000. *Intelligence Reframed: Multiple Intelligences for the Twenty-First Century*. New York: Basic Books.

Gawain, Shakti. 2000. *Creative Visualization*. Novato, CA: New World Library.

Gelatt, H. B. 1991. *Creative Decision Making: Using Positive Uncertainty*. Menlo Park, CA: Crisp.

Goleman, Daniel. 1995. *Emotional Intelligence*. New York: Bantam Press.

Goleman, Daniel. 2002. *Working with Emotional Intelligence*. New York: Audio Renaissance.

Graber, Steven (ed.). 2005. *Adams Job Almanac 2005*. Holbrook, MA: Adams Media Corporation.

Guide for Occupational Exploration. Supplement to the *Dictionary of Occupational Titles*, Volume 2. Washington, DC: U.S. Government Printing Office.

Half, Robert, and Max Messmer. 2005. *Job Hunting for Dummies*. Chicago: IDG Books Worldwide.

Hammer, Allen L. (Ed.) *MBTI Applications: A Decade of Research on the Myers-Briggs Type Indicator*. Palo Alto, CA: Consulting Psychologists Press.

Handy, Charles. 2002. *The Future of Work*. Malden, MA: Blackwell Publishing.

Harvard Business Review. March 2005. "Off-Ramps and On-Ramps: Keeping Talented Women on the Road to Success."

Hayes, Cassandra. 2002. *Black Enterprise: Guide to Building Your Career*. New York: John Wiley & Sons.

Herzberg, Frederick. 1966. *Work and the Nature of Man*. New York: World.

Hewlett, Sylvia A., and Carolyn B. Luce. March 2005. "Off-Ramps and On-Ramps: Keeping Talented Women on the Road to Success," *Harvard Business Review*, vol. 83, no. 3.

Hirsch, Arlene. 2005. *Interviewing*. New York: John Wiley & Sons.

Holland, John. 1985. *Making Vocational Choices: A Theory of Vocational Personalities and Work Environments*, 2nd edition. Englewood Cliffs, NJ: Prentice Hall.

Job Choices. Bethlehem, PA: National Association of Colleges and Employers 2006. (Annual publication.)

Journal of Career Development. New York: Human Sciences Press.

Jung, Carl. 1923. *Psychological Types*. New York: Harcourt Brace.

Kauffman, Draper L., Jr. 1976. *Teaching the Future: A Guide to Future Oriented Education*. Palm Springs, CA: ETC.

Kaye, Beverly L., and Sharon Jordan-Evans. 2005. *Love 'Em or Lose 'Em: Getting Good People to Stay*. San Francisco: Berrett Koehler.

Keirsey, David, and Marilyn Bates. 1984. *Please Understand Me: Character and Temperament Types*. Del Mar, CA: Prometheus Nemesis.

Kleiman, Carol. 2006. *Winning the Job Game*. New York: John Wiley & Sons.

Krannich, Ronald, and Caryl Krannich. 2004. *The Best Jobs for the 21st Century*. Manasses, VA: Impact Publications.

Kreigel, Robert, and Marilyn Kreigel. 1985. *The C Zone*. Garden City, NY: Fawcett.

Leonard, George. 1991. *Mastery*. New York: Dutton.

Levinson, D. J. 1978. *The Seasons of a Man's Life*. New York: Knopf.

Martin, Carole. 2005. *Boost Your Interview IQ*. New York: McGraw Hill.

Martin, Carole. 2005. *Perfect Phrases for the Perfect Interview*. New York: McGraw Hill.

Maslow, Abraham. 1987. *Motivation and Personality*, 3rd edition. Upper Saddle River, NJ: Pearson Education.

Moreira, Paula, and Robyn Thorpe. 2002. *Ace the IT Resume*. New York: McGraw-Hill.

Myers, Isabel. 1962. *Manual: The Myers–Briggs Type Indicator*. Palo Alto, CA: Consulting Psychologists.

National Business Employment Weekly. P.O. Box 300. Princeton, NJ 08543. (Published quarterly.)

Occupational Outlook Quarterly. 2005–2006. Washington, DC: U.S. Department of Labor, Bureau of Labor Statistics.

Parker, Yana. 2006. *The Damn Good Resume Guide.* Berkeley, CA: Ten Speed Press.

Peterson's Internships 2006. 2006. Princeton, NJ: Peterson's Guide Publisher.

Phelps, Stanlee, and Nancy Austin. 1997. *The Assertive Woman, A New Look.* San Luis Obispo, CA: Impact.

Radcliffe Public Policy Center. July 2000. "Life's Work," Harris Interactive Poll.

Reich, Robert B. 2002. *The Future of Success: Working and Living in the New Economy.* New York: Vintage Books.

Rocks, Celia. 2001. *Organizing the Good Life: A Path to Joyful Simplicity—Home to Work and Back.* New York: Demand Press.

Roehm, Frances E., and Margaret Riley Dikel. 2006. *The Guide to Internet Job Searching.* Chicago: Contemporary Books.

SCANS (Secretary's Commission on Achieving Necessary Skills): What Work Requires of Schools: A SCANS Report for America 2000. June 1991. Washington, DC: U.S. Department of Labor.

Sheehy, Gail. 1996. In Joelle Delbourgo (ed.), *New Passages: Your Life Across Time.* New York: Ballantine.

Simon, Sidney B., Leland W. Howe, and Howard Kirschenbaum. 1995. *Values Clarification.* New York: Warner Books.

Snodgrass, Jon. 1996. *Follow Your Career Star: A Career Quest Based on Inner Values.* New York: Kensington.

Stein, Marky. 2004. *Fearless Interviewing.* New York: McGraw Hill.

Super, Donald E. 1957. *The Psychology of Careers.* New York: Harper.

Tieger, Paul, and Barbara Barron-Tieger. 2001. *Do What You Are.* New York: Little, Brown & Company.

Tischler, Linda. Jan. 2005. "Bridging the (Gender Wage) Gap," *Fast Company*, vol. 90, p. 85.

Tischler, Linda. March 2004. "Where are the Women?," *Fast Company*, vol. 79, p. 52.

Tracy, Diane. 2006. *Take This Job and Love It.* Naperville, IL: Sourcebooks.

Tulgan, Bruce, and Carolyn Martin. 2001. *Managing Generation Y.* Amherst, MA: Human Resource Development Press.

Tullier, L. Michelle. 2005. *The Unofficial Guide to Landing a Job.* New York: Wiley.

Vicusi, Stephen. 2001. *On the Job: How to Make It in the Real World of Work.* New York: Three Rivers Press.

Working Mother. 2006. "Annual Survey of Best Companies." www.workingmother.com/list/shtml.

Yaeger, Neil M., and J. Hough. 2006. *Power Interviews.* New York: John Wiley & Sons.

Yate, Martin. 2005. *Knock 'Em Dead: The Ultimate Job Seeker's Handbook.* Holbrook, MA: Adams.

Index

About.com, 183
Accomplishments, 102–103
  (see also Skills)
  listing exercise, 118
Action:
  initiating, 33–34
  planning for, 252–253
    (see also Job search)
  words, 267–268
ADA, see American with
    Disabilities Act
Adaptive skills, 100, 113
Administration, as organizational
    division, 168
Adolescence, 6
Ads, classified, 96, 234
Adulthood, 6
Affirmations, 23–40
  and self-esteem, 29–30
  change and, 197
  creating, 44–45
Affirmative action, 128, 132, 134
Age, questions concerning, 318
Ageism, 128, 131–132
Agencies, employment, 236
America's Job Bank, 172, 182, 256
American College Testing
    Program (ACT), 81, 91–93
American Society for Training and
    Development (ASTD), 238
Americans with Disabilities Act
    (ADA), 128, 134, 316
Appearance:
  interviews and, 311–312
  of resume, 269–271, 285
Application forms, 279–281
Armstrong, Lance, 39
Artistic, personality type, 18,
    82, 84
Assertiveness, 26–27
Assessment:
  experiography and, 117
  instruments, 74–78
  interest, 81–93 (see also
    Interests)
  of interview technique,
    320–321

of resume, 284–285
of values, 60–69 (see also
    Values)
personal, 4–6, 13
personality, 72–80
skills, 99–121
Assessment tools:
  American College Testing
    (ACT) program, 81
  Guide for Occupational
    Exploration, 81
  Holland Interest
    Environments, 81, 82–86
Association for Multimedia
    Communications, 239
Associations, professional, 250
Assumptions:
  decision making and, 194
  testing, 215–216
Attitude, 14, 24
  assertive, 26–27
  positive outlook and, 25–26

Baby boomers, 145
Balance, life, 57–58
  vs. wages, 130
  workaholics and, 57
Barriers, 128
  to decision making, 192–193
Behavioral interviews, 318–319
Belief system, self-esteem and, 25
Benefits, 245, 327
Birthplace, questions
    concerning, 318
Black Voices, 183
Blogs, 182
Body language, 312, 319–320
Bolles, Richard, 104, 256
Bridges, William, 8
Briggs, Katherine, 73
Browsers, 257
Budgeting, 203–204
Bush, George, 39
Business:
  entrepreneurs and, 145
  franchises, 241, 242
  home, 239–240

starting your own, 239–241
organizational divisions,
    168–169, 170
small, 143–145
woman-owned, 144, 241

Career:
  age and, 131–132
  changers, 11–14
  changing, 132
  choosing, 11–14 (see also
    Career planning; Job
    search)
  clusters, 91–93
  counseling, 237, 241–242
  defined, 232
  equality in the workforce and,
    127–135
  family and, 127–128
  fantasy, 41–42
  fitness, embracing, 334–335
  gender roles and, 127–131
  identifying ideal, 119
  identifying interests, 89
    (see also Interests)
  identifying personality and
    interests, 71–96
  interests, 95
  managing your, 332–333
    (see also Career planning)
  objective, 12, 253
  resilience, 37
  self-employment, 106
  societal influences on,
    126–127
  stamina, 334
  success, self-knowledge and, 73
  technology and, 137–141
  transferable skills and,
    109–112
  using planning services,
    241–242
  values related to, 66
  values in choosing, 51–52
  vs. job, 8–11
CareerBuilder, 256
Career clusters, map of, 93

Career Information Service
(CIS), 180
Career planning (see also
Job search):
application forms and,
279–281
as continuous loop, 11
entrepreneurship and, 239–241
identify personality and
interests, 71–96
information interviews and,
242–249
job search, 231–260
management of career and,
332–333
networking and, 248–251
resumes and, 263–305
(see also Resumes)
Career satisfaction, 9–11
self-knowledge and, 73
Career sites, Internet, 182–184
Careers:
brainstorming options,
166–167
creative, 149
decision making and,
191–217
fastest-growing, 152–157
for artistic types, 85
for conventional types, 86
for creators, 85
for doers, 85
for enterprising types, 86
for helpers, 86
for investigative types, 85
for organizers, 86
for persuaders, 86
for realistic types, 85
for social types, 86
for thinkers, 85
goal setting and, 192,
200–201, 202
government, 172–174
growth in next decade, 151
Holland Interest Environments
and, 82–86
in media-related fields, 149
in-demand, 145–146
information technology, 140
liberal arts major and, 146
lifelong learning and, 136–137,
148–149
multiple, 8

nontraditional for
women, 129
paths, 168–169, 170
research, 169–184
researching requirements, 169,
171–172
SCANS skills and, 146
training, 206
women in, 127–131, 133
Carrey, Jim, 39
Catalog, college, 96
Center for Women's Business
Research, 241
Change:
conditions for, 196–197
deciding on, 206
Checklists:
emotional intelligence, 43
values grid, 60–61
Chronological resumes, 276
sample, 292–295
CIS (Career Information Service),
116, 180
Citizenship, questions
concerning, 317
Classified ads, 96, 234
Clothing, interviews and,
311–312
College catalog, 96
Combination resumes, 276–277
sample, 296–297
Community work, 33 (see also
Volunteer work)
Companies:
internal job postings, 180
knowledge of, 310
new economy adjustments,
141–142
organizational divisions,
168–169, 170
web organization, 169
Compensation, 245, 310, 317
Competencies, in SCANS
report, 114
Computerized information
sources, 180–181
Conferences, attending, 250
Contacts:
cultivating, 243 (see also
Information interviews;
Networking)
file format, 254
personal log for, 259–260

Continuing education,
see Lifelong learning
Contract, employee, 8
Conventional, personality type,
19, 83, 84
Cooperative education, 239
Cooperative Education
Association, 239
Corporate culture, 322–323
Corporate relations, as
organizational division, 168
Counseling, career, 237,
241–242
Cover letters, 277–279
exercise, 286
samples, 300–304
template for, 278
Creativity, leisure and, 58
Creators, 82, 84, 85 (see also
Holland Interest
Environments)
Credit rating, 202–203
Cross-functional skills, 169
Culture:
considerations in workplace,
134–135
corporate, 322–323
influence on career, 126–127
perception of needs and, 56
Curriculum vitae, 279

Databases, employment,
256–257
Debts, paying off, 203
Decision making, 191–217
assumptions about, 194
avoiding ultimatums, 194
change and, 196–197, 206
choosing a major, 205
examining behavior, 194–195
exercises for, 208–216
feelings about, 194
goal setting review, 208–209
intuitive, 199
model for, 197–198
overcoming barriers to,
192–193
personality and, 199
ranking yourself, 208
rational/linear, 197, 199
risks and, 196
strategies, 193–196
stress and, 204–205

styles, 199
training and, 206
Decisions, factors affecting, 213–214
Decisive types, 79
Degree, earnings and, 138, 140
Department of Labor, interest inventory, 81
Dictionary of Occupational Titles (DOT), 104–105, 175, 180, 273, 274
Directories, employer, 176
Disabilities, and workplace accommodations, 134
Discipline, 34, 36
DISCOVER, 180
Discrimination, 128, 134–135
  age, 131–132
Disengagement, in Super's self-concept theory, 5
Distance learning, 148
Distribution, as organizational division, 169
Diversity, 134–135 (*see also* Gender)
Doers, 82, 84, 85 (*see also* Holland Interest Environments)
DOT, 104–105, 175, 180, 273, 274

E-commerce, 142–143
Economy:
  global, 141–143
  knowledge-based, 136–137
  NAFTA and, 141
  new vs. old, 139
  service-based, 135
Education:
  continuing, 136–137, 148–149
  cooperative, 239
  distance learning, 148
  on resumes, 273
  questions concerning, 317
  salary and, 138, 140
  trends, 148–149
Efficiency, corporate, 141
Electronic resumes, 271, 272
E-mail, promoting yourself via, 234–235
Emotional intelligence, 36
  checklist, 43
Employee portfolio, 106

Employer directories, 176
Employment (*see also* Jobs, Careers):
  ads, 234
  agencies, 236
Encyclopedia of Associations, 250
Engineering, as organizational division, 169
Enterprising, personality type, 19, 83, 84
Enthusiasm, 47
  for job search, 233
  self-esteem and, 28
  showing in interview, 312
Entrance requirements, 246
Entrepreneurship, 145, 239–241
EQ (emotional intelligence quotient), 36, 43
Equal Employment Opportunity BiMonthly, 320
Equality, in workforce, 127–135
Equity, definitions of, 128
Establishment, in Super's self-concept theory, 5
Ethics, values related to, 67
EUREKA, 116, 180
Experience:
  listed on resumes, 273
  rated by employers, 239
Experiography, 117
Exploration, in Super's self-concept theory, 5
External motivators, 56–57
Extraverted type, 74–75

Fair Employment Practices Act, 316
Family, influence on career, 121
Fantasy careers, 45–46
Fantasy, making it real, 46
Federal Careers Opportunities, 174
Federal Jobs Digest, 172
Feeling type, 76
Feelings, decision making and, 194
Fieldwork, 238
Finance, as organizational division, 169
Financial resources, managing, 201–204
First impressions, 15, 158–159
Flexibility:
  corporate, 142
  self-esteem and, 37–38

Franchising, 241, 242
Free Agent Nation, 106
Freelance career, 106
Functional resumes, 272–276
  sample, 288–291
Functional skills, 100
Future:
  vision, 42–43
  focus on, 331–335
  views of, 25–26
Future of Work, The, 106

Gallop Poll, 11
Gardner, Howard, 31–32
Gates, Bill, 39
Gen Xers, life balance vs salary, 56
Gender:
  and career, 127–131
  bias, 128
  fair, 128
  questions concerning, 318
  roles, 128, 159
  stereotyping, 128
Generalist, 169
Generation X, 145
GIS (Guidance Information System), 180
Global economy, 141–143
Globalization, 135, 141–143
Goals:
  as completed accomplishments, 104
  financial, 202
  long-term, 13
  realistic, 192
  rewards for reaching, 201
  self-esteem and, 36–37
  short- and long-term, 13, 200–201
  specific, 192
  statement of, 209–210
  timelines for, 201
Goal setting, 200–201, 202
  review exercise, 208–209
GOE, *see Guide for Occupational Exploration*
Golden years, 7
Golden, Bonnie, 74
Goleman, Daniel, 36
Government jobs, 172–175
GPA, 313
Graduate school, 145

Growth, in Super's self-concept theory, 4–5
Guide for Occupational Exploration (GOE), 81, 89, 176

Habits:
    changing negative, 42
    in decision making, 194
Handy, Charles, 106
Health needs, 203
Helpers, 82, 84, 85 (*see also* Holland Interest Environments)
Help-wanted ads, 234
Herzberg, Frederick, 56
Herzberg's theory of motivation, 56–57
Hierarchy of needs, 55–57
High-order need, 56–57
Hiring, factors influencing, 323–325
Hobbies, 28
Holland Interest Environments, 81, 82–86, 94–95
    abilities related to, 85
    artistic type, 82, 84
    careers related to, 85
    conventional type, 83, 84
    creators, 82, 84, 85
    doers, 82, 84, 85
    enterprising type, 82, 84
    helpers, 82, 84, 85
    hobbies related to, 85
    investigative type, 82, 84
    majors related to, 77–84
    organizers, 83, 84, 85
    persuaders, 83, 84, 85
    realistic type, 82, 84
    social type, 82, 84
    thinkers, 82, 84, 85
Holland types, *see* Holland Interest Environments
Home businesses, 239–240
Hotlines, job, 243
Human resources management, 250
Humor, self-esteem and, 27

Imagery, 24
Inborn tendencies, identifying, 74–78
Industries, creative, 149

Influences, past, 41–42
Information, integrating, 165–188
    exercises, 185–188
Information interviews, 242–249
    activity, 259
    practicing, 247–248
    sample questions, 245–246
Information technology, wages in, 140
In-house bulletins, job search in, 179
Initiative, self-esteem and, 33–34
Innovation, 40
Inquiries, preemployment, 316–318
Insurance, 203
Intelligence:
    emotional, 36
    Gardner's theory of, 31–32
    quotient, 36
Intelligences, multiple, 31–32
Interest clusters, 81
Interest inventories, *see* Assessment tools
Interests:
    Holland Interest Environments and, 81, 82–86
    identifying your, 18, 81–93
    inventory, 81
    personality and, 71–96
Internal motivators, 56–57
International Franchise Association, 242
Internet:
    browsers/search engines, 257
    distance learning and, 148
    employment databases on, 256–257
    job research and, 171
    job research and, 181–184, 253
    O*NET, 175
    resumes and, 271, 272
    Yellow Pages, 176
Internships, 33, 103, 237–239
Internships 2005, 237
Interpersonal intelligence, 32
Interviews, 307–329
    behavioral/situational, 318–319
    body language and, 312, 319–320
    critique form, 321
    factors influencing hiring, 323–325

guidelines for, 311–314
    illegal questions and, 316–318
    information, 242–249 (*see also* Information interviews)
    learning from, 320–322
    sample questions, 309–310, 314, 316, 322
    segments of, 313–314
    summary of process, 326
    thank you letters and, 314, 315
    video, 320
Intrapersonal intelligence, 32
Introduction, letter of, 305
Introverted type, 74–75
Intuition:
    decision making and, 199
    following, 8
Intuitive type, 75–76
Inventories, interest, *see* Assessment tools
Investigative type, 82, 84
Investigative, personality type, 18
IQ, 36

Job:
    and survival needs, 55–57
    banks, 256–257
    classifications, 245
    descriptions, 62–64, 245, 274
    experiography and, 117
    growth trends, 151
    hotlines, 243
    identifying your ideal, 233
    interviews, *see* Interviews
    knowledge sector growth and, 136–137
    objective, 265, 273
    offer, 325–327
    research, 169–184 (*see also* Job search)
    researching requirements, 169, 171–172 (*see also* Research)
    sample descriptions from *DOT*, 104–105
    seeking entry-level, 233
    technology and, 137–141
    training, 206
    transferable skills and, 109–112
    trends, 145–150
    vs. career, 8–11
    women in, 127–131, 133

Job clusters, 95 (*see also* Career clusters)
Job performance, leisure and, 58
Jobs:
brainstorming options, 166–167
fastest-growing, 152–157
government, 172–174
growth in next decade, 151
identifying ideal, 119
international, 279
lifelong learning and, 148–149
Job satisfaction, 9–11
internal vs. external motivators and, 56–57
Job search, 231–260
application forms and, 279–281
as lifelong venture, 253
classified ads and, 234
designing a comprehensive, 232–234
e-mail and, 234–235
enthusiasm for, 233
experience and, 239
getting started, 234–239
Internet, *see* Internet
interning and, 237–239
interviewing and, 307–329 (*see also* Interviews)
networking and, 248–251
newspapers and, 177
online employment databases, 256–257
resume writing and, 263–305 (*see also* Resumes)
starting your own business and, 239–241
stress and, 204–205
tips, 309
trade journals and, 177
using career planning services, 241–242
volunteering and, 236–237
while unemployed, 251–252
Judging type, 77
Jung, Carl, 72–73

Key phrases, 268
Kinesthetic intelligence, 32
King, Martin Luther, 39
Knowledge workers, 136–137

Labor costs, 141
Lawrence, Gordon, 74
Leasing companies, 144–145
Leisure, 58
Lesh, Kay, 74
Letters:
cover, *see* Cover letters
of introduction, 305
thank-you, 314, 315
Library resource centers, 181
Life balance, 57–58
vs. wages, 130
Life stages, 6–8
Life transitions, 335
Lifeline, preparing your, 16–18
Lifelong learning, 136–137, 148–149
Limitations, habits as, 194
Linguistic intelligence, 32
Listening skills, 318
Logical/mathematical intelligence, 31–32
Low-order need, 55
Luck, 34
decision making and, 199

Magazines, job search and, 171, 177–179
Mail, promotion through, 234–235
Maintenance, in Super's self-concept theory, 5
Major, deciding on, 205
Majors:
exploring, 79
liberal arts, 109, 112, 146
personality type and, 79
related to Holland Interest Environments, 84
Managing Transitions: Making the Most of Change, 8
Maslow, Abraham, 55, 57
Maslow's hierarchy of needs, 55–57
Mathematical intelligence, 32
MBTI, *see* Myers-Briggs Type Indicator
Media careers, 149
Mega-corporations, 142
Mental imagery, 30–31
Mental rehearsal, 30–31
Minorities, affirmative action and, 132, 134

Model, decision-making, 197–198
Money management, 201–204
Monster Board, 183, 256
Moody's Corporate Profiles, 181
Motivation:
Herzberg's theory of, 56–57
internal and external, 56–57
needs and, 55–57
Motivators, compared to needs, 56–57
Multimedia revolution, 149
Multiple intelligences, 31–32
Musical/rhythmic intelligence, 31
Myers-Briggs Type Indicator, 73, 74, 78
Myers, Isabel Briggs, 73

NAFTA, 141
Nation Job Network, 256
National Business Employment Weekly, 250
National origin, questions concerning, 317
Natural abilities, 112–113
Neatness, applications and, 280
Needs, 55–57
Negotiating benefits, 327
Network, 232
Networking, 248–251
checklist for, 258–259
contact file format, 254
during job, 311
New economy, 139, 141
Newspapers, job search in, 171, 177
Nontraditional jobs, 128, 129
North American Free Trade Agreement (NAFTA), 141

O*NET (Occupational Information Network), 106, 175, 1880, 273, 274
Objectives:
goals and, 200
job, 265, 273
specific vs. nonspecific, 200, 215
Occupational interests, 95
Occupational Outlook Handbook (OOH), 175–176, 180, 250
Occupational Outlook Quarterly, 176
Occupational status, 19–20

Occupations (*see also* Careers; Jobs)
    new/emerging, 153
    nontraditional for women, 129
Old economy, salaries and, 139–141
One Stop Career Centers, 172
OOH, *see Occupational Outlook Handbook*
Optimism vs. pessimism, 30
Organizational divisions, 168–169, 170
Organizational skills, 318
Organizers, 83, 84, 85 (*see also* Holland Interest Environments)
Origin, national, questions concerning, 317
Outlook, positive, 25–26
Outsourcing, 142

Passion, having, 38
Peace Corps, 236
People skills, 112
Perceiving type, 77
Persistence, self-esteem and, 34
Personal assessment, 4–6, 13
Personal growth, leisure and, 58
Personal philosophy, self-esteem and, 25
Personal preferences:
    exercise for identifying, 74–78
    extraversion vs. introversion, 74–75
    four-letter indicator, 78
    four-part framework for, 74–78
    judging vs. perceiving, 77
    sensing vs. intuition, 75–76
    thinking vs. feeling, 76
Personality (*see also* Personality types):
    career and, 8
    decision making and, 199
    decisive, 79
    environments, 81
    exploring, 72–80
    interests and, 71–96
    traits, as assets, 112–113
Personality types, 18–19, 94
    artistic, 82, 84
    choosing majors and, 79
    conventional, 83, 84

    enterprising, 82, 84
    extraverted, 74–75
    feeling, 76
    interests and, 81
    introverted, 74–75
    intuitive, 75–76
    investigative, 82, 84
    judging, 77
    perceiving, 77
    realistic, 82, 84
    sensing, 75–76
    social, 82, 84
    thinking, 76
Persuaders, 83, 84, 85 (*see also* Holland Interest Environments)
Photograph, request for prior to employment, 317
Pink, Daniel, 106
Portfolio employee, 106–107
Portfolios, 265, 284
Position descriptions, 245
Positive outlook, self-esteem and, 25–26
Positive self-talk, 29–30 (*see also* Affirmations)
Preemployment inquiries, 316–318
Princeton Review Online, 238, 239
Productivity, role of leisure in, 58
Professional associations, 171, 250
Purpose, having, 38

Quality of life, 9
QUEST, 180
Questions:
    illegal interview, 316–318
    information interviewing, 245–246
    preemployment, 316–318
    sample interview, 309–310, 314, 316, 322
Quick Job Hunting Map, 104

Race or color, questions concerning, 317
Rapport, establishing in interview, 313
Realistic, personality type, 18, 82, 84
Recareering, 11–14
References, 268–269
Relationships, developing, 333–334

Religion, questions concerning, 318
Renewal, 7
Research:
    computerized information sources, 180–181
    Dept. of Labor publications, 175–176
    exercises, 185–188
    Internet, 181–184 (*see also* Internet)
    of career options, 169–184
    software for, 180–181
Responsibility, 39
Restabilization, 7
Resume/portfolio review, 267
Resumes, 263–305
    action words on, 267–268
    appearance of, 269–271
    chronological, 276
    combination, 276–277
    common problems with, 270
    cover letters for, 258–260
    critiquing, 285
    do's and don'ts, 286
    electronic, 271, 272
    for international jobs, 279
    formatting electronic, 272
    functional, 272–276
    index cards for tracking info, 266
    job objective and, 265
    key phrases on, 268
    portfolios and, 265
    references on, 268–269
    review, 284
    sample, 288–299
    template for, 273
    types of, 271–277
Retirement, 7, 132
Rewards, for reaching goals, 201
Rhythmic intelligence, 32
RIASEC, 19, 82–83 (*see also* Holland Interest Environments)
    artistic type, 82, 84
    conventional type, 83, 84
    enterprising type, 83, 84
    in world-of-work map, 93
    investigative type, 82, 84
    realistic type, 82, 84
    social type, 82, 84
Richard Bolles Parachute Site, 256

Riley Guide, 256
Risk, 196, 335
Role models, 32–33
Rooting, life stage, 6–7

Salary, 245, 310, 327
    in *OOH*, 175
    vs. life issues, 130
Sales, as organizational
        division, 169
Savings, 202–204
SCANS skills/report, 109,
        110–111, 114–115,146
    review exercise, 119
    worksheet for identifying, 120
SCORE, 240
Search engines, 257
*Secretary's Commission on
        Achieving Necessary Skills,*
        see SCANS
Self-concept, Super's theory of, 4–6
Self-confidence, 27–28
Self-control, 34, 36
Self-Directed Search, 81
Self-discipline, 34, 36
Self-esteem, 23, 24–25
    affirmations and, 29–30
    assertiveness and, 26–27
    building blocks of, 23–40
    emotional intelligence and, 36
    enthusiasm and, 28
    flexibility and, 37–38
    goals and, 36–37
    humor and, 27
    initiative and, 33–34
    innovation and, 40
    passion and, 38
    persistence and, 34
    positive outlook and, 25–26
    responsibility and, 39
    role models, and, 32–33
    self-confidence and, 27–28
    self-discipline and, 34, 36
    self-reliance and, 37
    sense of purpose and, 38
    sources of, 24
    visualization and, 30–31
Self-expression, leisure and, 58
Self-image, positive, 31 (*see also*
        Self-esteem)
Self-knowledge, 14
Self-management skills, 100
Self-motivators, 52, 100

Self-reliance, self-esteem and, 37
Self-talk, 40, 29–30, 44–45
Sensing type, 75–76
Service Corps of Retired
        Executives (SCORE), 240
Sexism, 128
Shapiro, Stephen M., 40
Sheehy, Gail, 8
SIGI Plus (System of Interactive
        Guidance and Information),
        116, 180
Single-parent households, 7, 129
Situational interviews, 318–319
Skills, 101, 116, 118, 121
    adaptive, 100, 113
    analysis software, 116
    analyzing accomplishments
        and, 102–103
    as self-motivators, 100
    as source of satisfaction, 116
    assessment of, 99–122
    communication, 112
    critical thinking, 112, 114
    defined, 100–101
    functional, 100
    homemakers and, 101–102
    human relations, 112
    identifying, 101–112
    interpersonal, 110, 114
    lifelong learning and, 136–137
    listening, 318
    natural abilities as, 112–113
    of liberal arts majors, 146
    organizational, 112, 318
    people, 112
    portfolio of, 106
    problem solving, 112
    ranking favorite, 118
    research, 112 (*see also* Research)
    SCANS, 109, 110–111,
        114–115
    talking about, 101–102
    teamwork, 318
    technology, 114
    that influence hiring, 323
    thinking, 111, 114
    transferable, 109–112, 113, 169
    used in writing research
        report, 104
    work-content, 100
    worksheet for identifying, 120
    writing, 318
    writing stories to identify, 104

Small businesses, 143–145
Small Business Development
        Centers, 240
Social Readjustment Rating
        Scale, 204
Social, personality type, 19, 82, 84
Society, influence on career,
        126–127
Software:
    for skills analysis, 116
    job search, 180–181
SOHO, 138
Spatial intelligence, 32
Specialist, 169
Stamina, career, 334
Stereotypes, exploring, 159
Strategies:
    decision-making, 193–196
    job search, 232 (*see also*
        Job search)
    stress management, 205
    time management, 201
Stress, leisure and, 58
Stress management, 204–205
Strong Interest Inventory, 81
Success, 25, 34–38
    clearly defined goals and, 36–37
    factors that influence, 324
    profile, 46–47
    programming yourself for,
        23–49 (*see also* Self-esteem)
    visualizing, 30–31
Super, Donald, 4
Survival needs, 55, 57
Synergy, 333

Teamwork skills, 318
Technology, in workplace,
        137–141
    SOHOs and, 138
Telecommuting, 137–139
Temporary agencies, 144–145
Temps, 142, 144–145
Thank-you letters, 314, 315
Thinkers, 82, 84, 85 (*see also*
        Holland Interest
        Environments)
Thinking type, 76
Time management, strategies
        for, 201
Timelines, setting, 201
Trade associations, for job
        search, 171

Trade journals, 177, 184
Training, 206 (*see also* Education; Lifelong learning)
Transferable skills, 109–112, 113, 169
  liberal arts majors and, 146
  of teacher, 113
Transitions, life, 335
Trends:
  distance learning, 148
  job growth, 145–150
  lifelong learning, 148–149
Truman, Harry, 39
Turning-point years, 7
24/7 Innovation, 40

Ultimatums, decision making and, 194
UN Volunteers, 236
Underemployment, 335
Unemployment, 335
  job search during, 251–252
U.S. Department of Labor, publications, 175–176

Values:
  as part of a pattern, 55
  clarification, 51–69
  consequence and, 53
  defined, 51–52
  ethics and, 66–67
  exercises for clarifying, 60–69
  exploring, 62–64
  finding balance and, 56–57

grid checklist, 60–61
job descriptions exercise, 62–64
public affirmation and, 53
relating to careers, 64–65
vs. needs, 55
Verbal/linguistic intelligence, 31
Videotape, interviewing and, 320
Virtual corporation, 141–142
Visibility, maintaining, 253
  (*see also* Networking)
Vision, having, 39–40
VISTA, 236
Visual/spatial intelligence, 32
Visualization, 30–31
Volunteer work, 28, 33, 35, 236–237

Wages, vs. life issues, 58, 130
Want ads, 177
Web-based instruction, 148–149
Weblogs, 182
Web organization, 169
Wetfeet, 183
Whole New Mind, A, 106
Women (*see also* Gender):
  in the workplace, 133
  nontraditional occupations for, 129
  owned businesses, 144, 241
Woods, Tiger, 39
Words, action, 267–268
Work (*see also* Job):
  environment, 245
  experiography and, 117

identifying ideal, 119
relevant experience, 239
technology and, 137–141
Workaholics, finding balance and, 57
Work-content skills, 100
Worker Trait Groups, 81, 87–88
Workers:
  knowledge, 136–137
  new economy and, 139–141
  temporary, 142, 144–145
Workforce, equality in, 127–135
Workplace, changing, 135–150
  diversity in, 134–135
  importance of lifelong learning, 136–137
  know-how identified in SCANS report, 114–115
  new technology and, 137–141
  non-traditional schedules and, 135
  women in, 133
  workers with disabilities and, 134
World Wide Web, job research and, 171 (*see also* Internet)
World-of-work map, 93
Worldwide Franchise Directory, 242
Writing skills, 318

Yellow Pages, research and, 176